TALES FROM THE DEEP That Are Completely FABRICATED

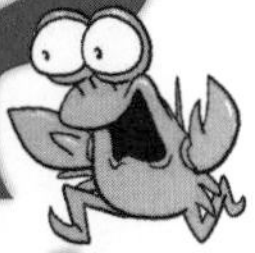

Other Books by Jim Toomey

Sherman's Lagoon: Ate That, What's Next?

Poodle: The Other White Meat

An Illustrated Guide to Shark Etiquette

Another Day in Paradise

Greetings from Sherman's Lagoon

Surf's Up!

The Shark Diaries

Catch of the Day

A Day at the Beach

Surfer Safari

Planet of the Hairless Beach Apes

Yarns & Shanties (and Other Nautical Baloney)

Sharks Just Wanna Have Fun

Confessions of a Swinging Single Sea Turtle

Discover Your Inner Hermit Crab

Never Bite Anything That Bites Back

Think Like a Shark

Here We Go Again

Lunch Wore a Speedo

Treasuries

Sherman's Lagoon 1991 to 2001: Greatest Hits and Near Misses

In Shark Years I'm Dead: Sherman's Lagoon Turns Fifteen

TALES FROM THE DEEP
That Are Completely
FABRICATED

The Twentieth *Sherman's Lagoon* Collection
Jim Toomey

Andrews McMeel
Publishing®
a division of Andrews McMeel Universal

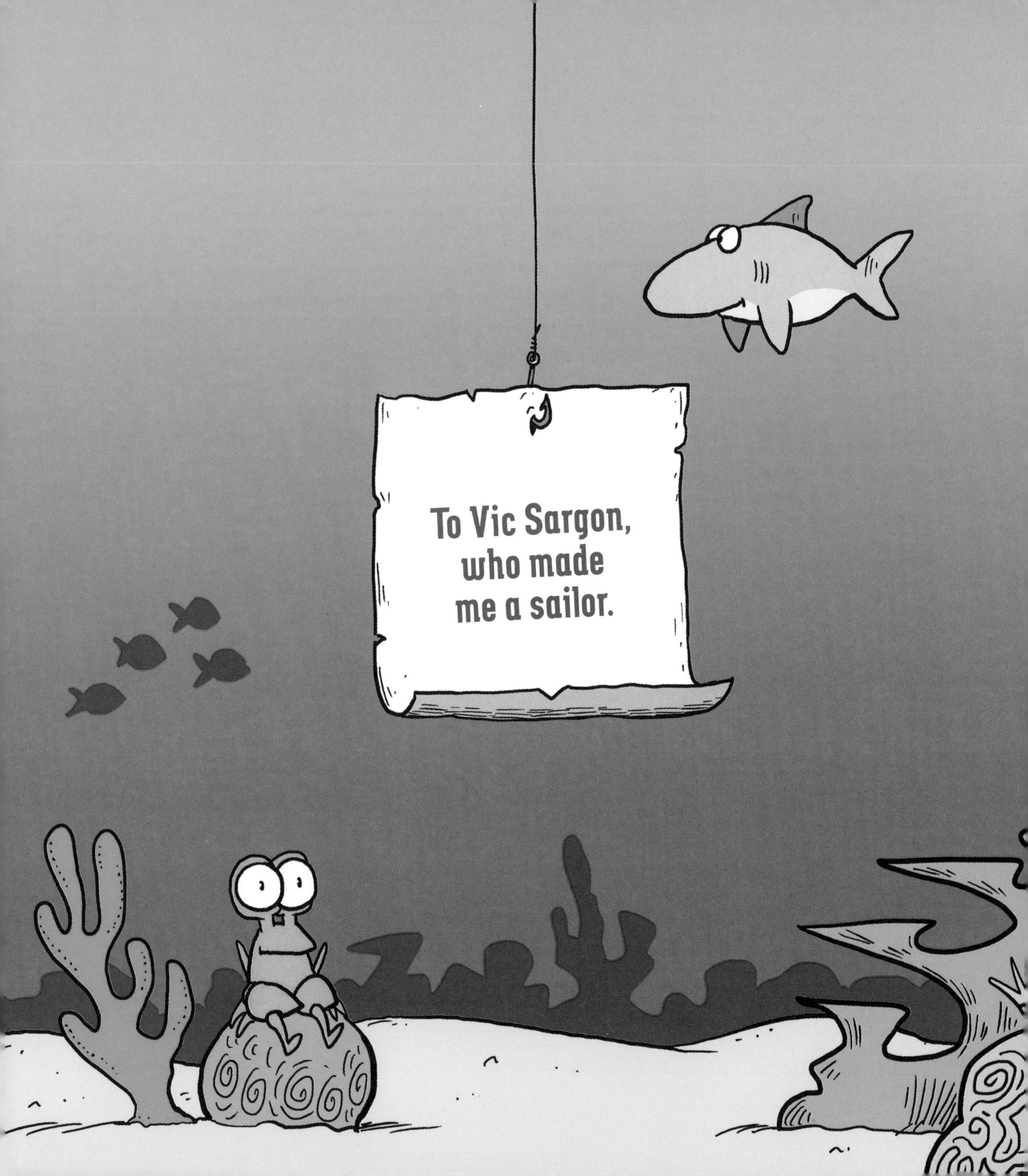
To Vic Sargon,
who made
me a sailor.

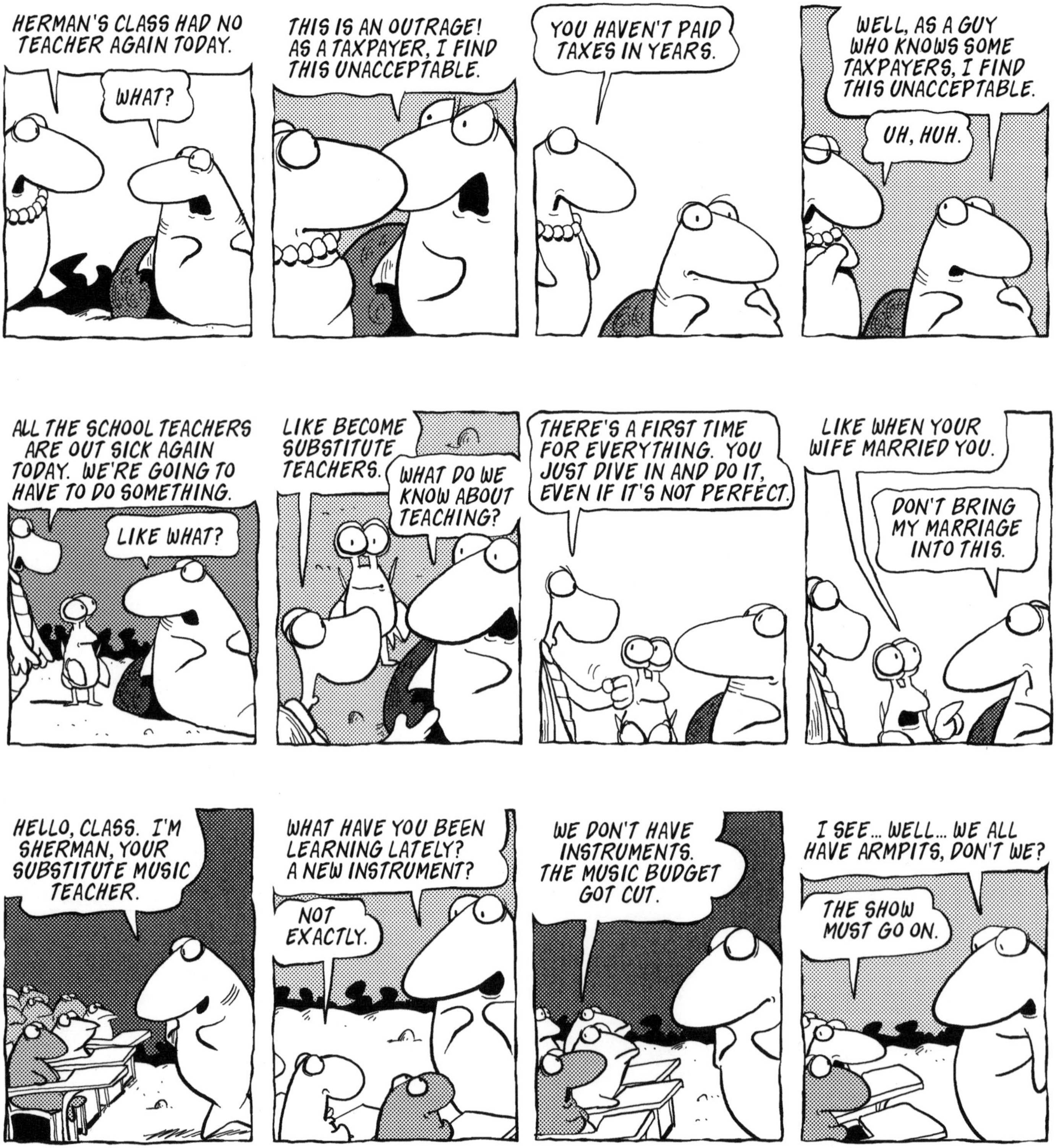
HERMAN'S CLASS HAD NO TEACHER AGAIN TODAY.
WHAT?
THIS IS AN OUTRAGE! AS A TAXPAYER, I FIND THIS UNACCEPTABLE.
YOU HAVEN'T PAID TAXES IN YEARS.
WELL, AS A GUY WHO KNOWS SOME TAXPAYERS, I FIND THIS UNACCEPTABLE.
UH, HUH.
ALL THE SCHOOL TEACHERS ARE OUT SICK AGAIN TODAY. WE'RE GOING TO HAVE TO DO SOMETHING.
LIKE WHAT?
LIKE BECOME SUBSTITUTE TEACHERS.
WHAT DO WE KNOW ABOUT TEACHING?
THERE'S A FIRST TIME FOR EVERYTHING. YOU JUST DIVE IN AND DO IT, EVEN IF IT'S NOT PERFECT.
LIKE WHEN YOUR WIFE MARRIED YOU.
DON'T BRING MY MARRIAGE INTO THIS.
HELLO, CLASS. I'M SHERMAN, YOUR SUBSTITUTE MUSIC TEACHER.
WHAT HAVE YOU BEEN LEARNING LATELY? A NEW INSTRUMENT?
NOT EXACTLY.
WE DON'T HAVE INSTRUMENTS. THE MUSIC BUDGET GOT CUT.
I SEE... WELL... WE ALL HAVE ARMPITS, DON'T WE?
THE SHOW MUST GO ON.

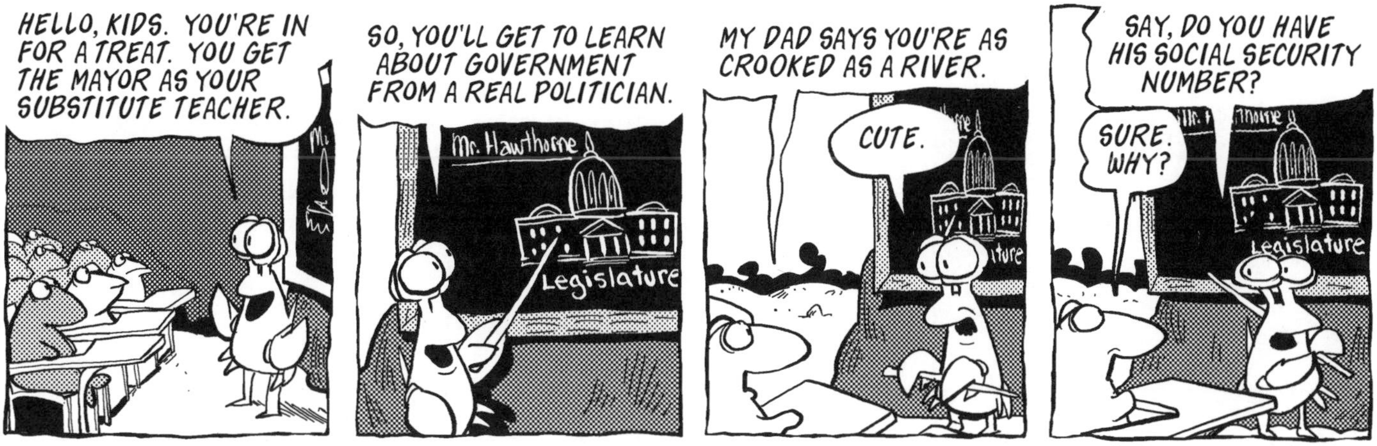
HELLO, KIDS. YOU'RE IN FOR A TREAT. YOU GET THE MAYOR AS YOUR SUBSTITUTE TEACHER.
SO, YOU'LL GET TO LEARN ABOUT GOVERNMENT FROM A REAL POLITICIAN.
Mr. Hawthorne
Legislature
MY DAD SAYS YOU'RE AS CROOKED AS A RIVER.
CUTE.
SAY, DO YOU HAVE HIS SOCIAL SECURITY NUMBER?
SURE. WHY?
Legislature

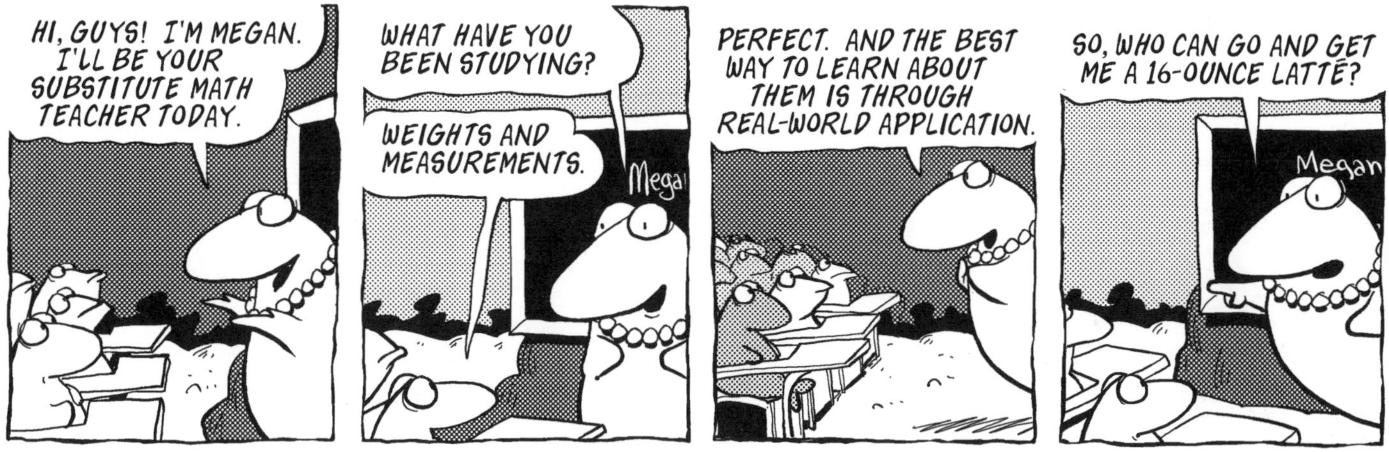
HI, GUYS! I'M MEGAN. I'LL BE YOUR SUBSTITUTE MATH TEACHER TODAY.
WHAT HAVE YOU BEEN STUDYING?
WEIGHTS AND MEASUREMENTS.
PERFECT. AND THE BEST WAY TO LEARN ABOUT THEM IS THROUGH REAL-WORLD APPLICATION.
SO, WHO CAN GO AND GET ME A 16-OUNCE LATTÉ?
Megan

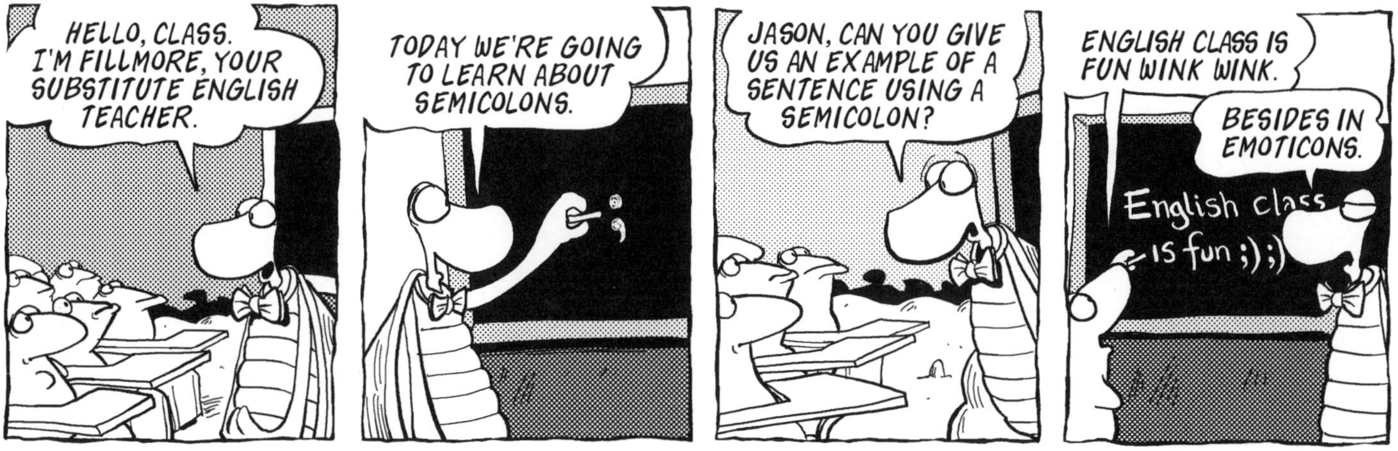
HELLO, CLASS. I'M FILLMORE, YOUR SUBSTITUTE ENGLISH TEACHER.
TODAY WE'RE GOING TO LEARN ABOUT SEMICOLONS.
JASON, CAN YOU GIVE US AN EXAMPLE OF A SENTENCE USING A SEMICOLON?
ENGLISH CLASS IS FUN WINK WINK.
BESIDES IN EMOTICONS.
English class is fun ;) ;)

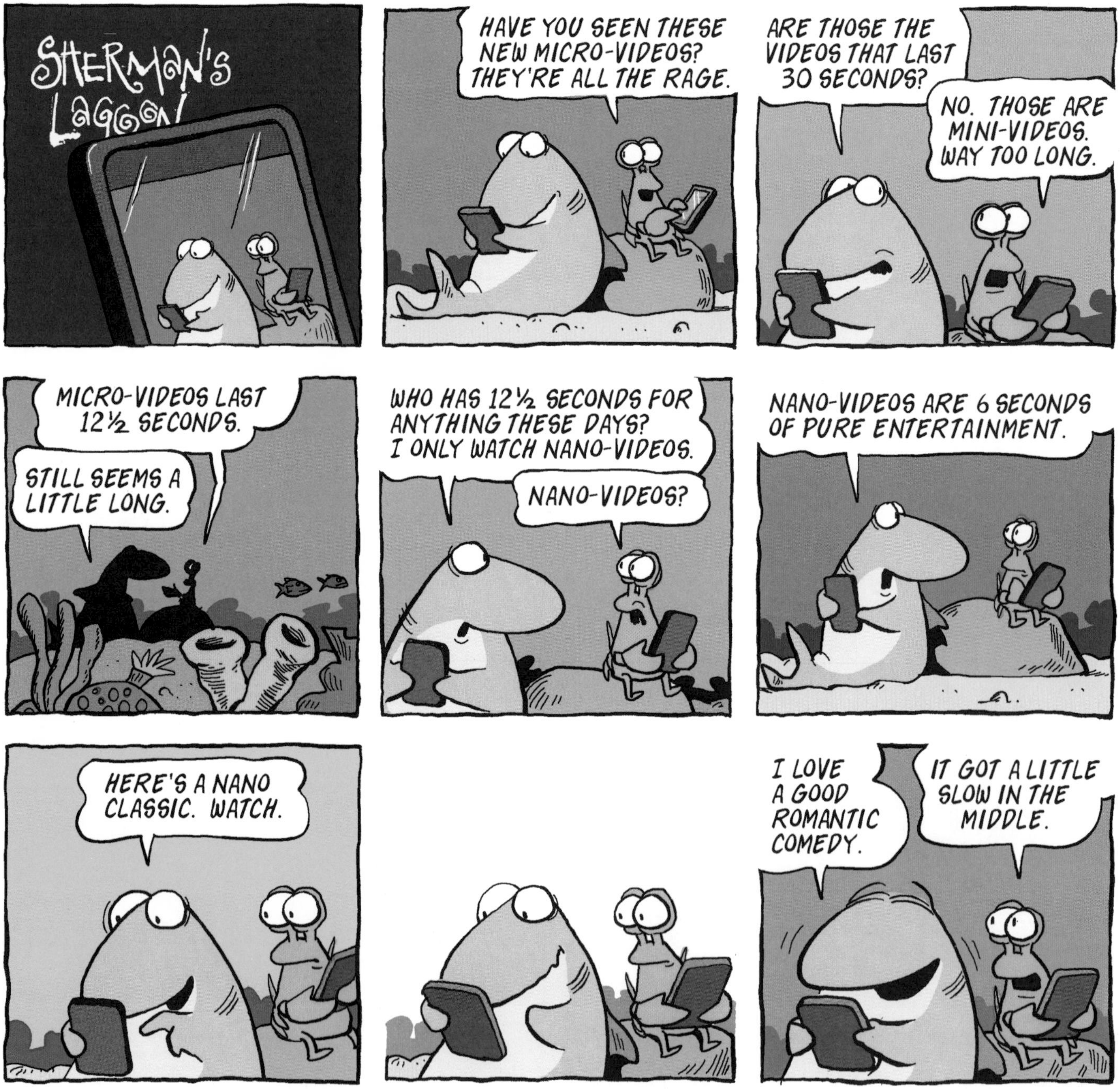
SHERMAN'S LAGOON
HAVE YOU SEEN THESE NEW MICRO-VIDEOS? THEY'RE ALL THE RAGE.
ARE THOSE THE VIDEOS THAT LAST 30 SECONDS?
NO. THOSE ARE MINI-VIDEOS. WAY TOO LONG.
MICRO-VIDEOS LAST 12½ SECONDS.
STILL SEEMS A LITTLE LONG.
WHO HAS 12½ SECONDS FOR ANYTHING THESE DAYS? I ONLY WATCH NANO-VIDEOS.
NANO-VIDEOS?
NANO-VIDEOS ARE 6 SECONDS OF PURE ENTERTAINMENT.
HERE'S A NANO CLASSIC. WATCH.
I LOVE A GOOD ROMANTIC COMEDY.
IT GOT A LITTLE SLOW IN THE MIDDLE.

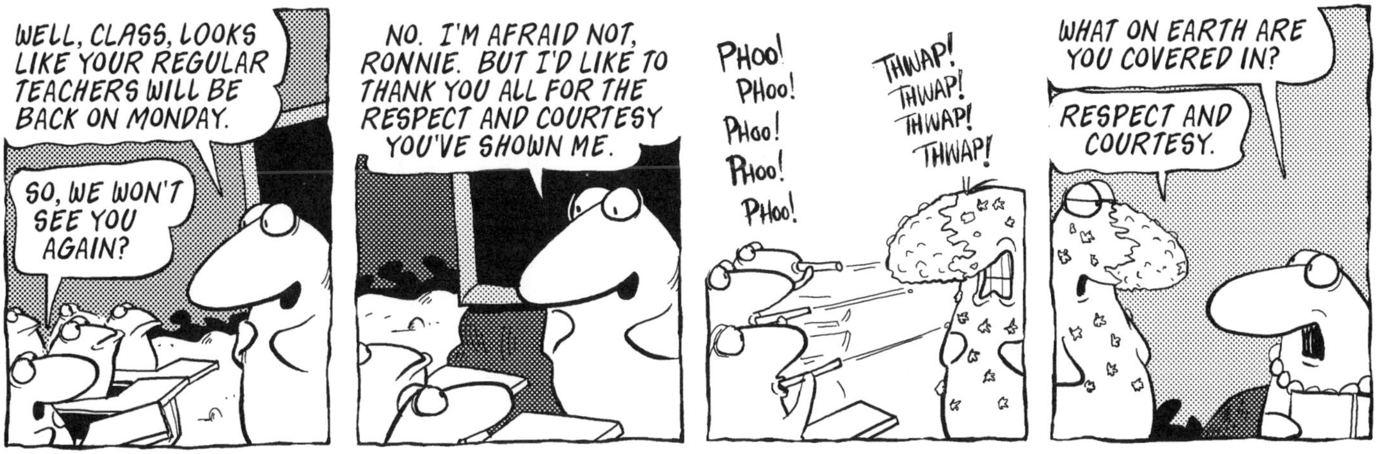
WELL, CLASS, LOOKS LIKE YOUR REGULAR TEACHERS WILL BE BACK ON MONDAY.
SO, WE WON'T SEE YOU AGAIN?
NO. I'M AFRAID NOT, RONNIE. BUT I'D LIKE TO THANK YOU ALL FOR THE RESPECT AND COURTESY YOU'VE SHOWN ME.
PHOO! PHOO! PHOO! PHOO! PHOO!
THWAP! THWAP! THWAP! THWAP!
WHAT ON EARTH ARE YOU COVERED IN?
RESPECT AND COURTESY.

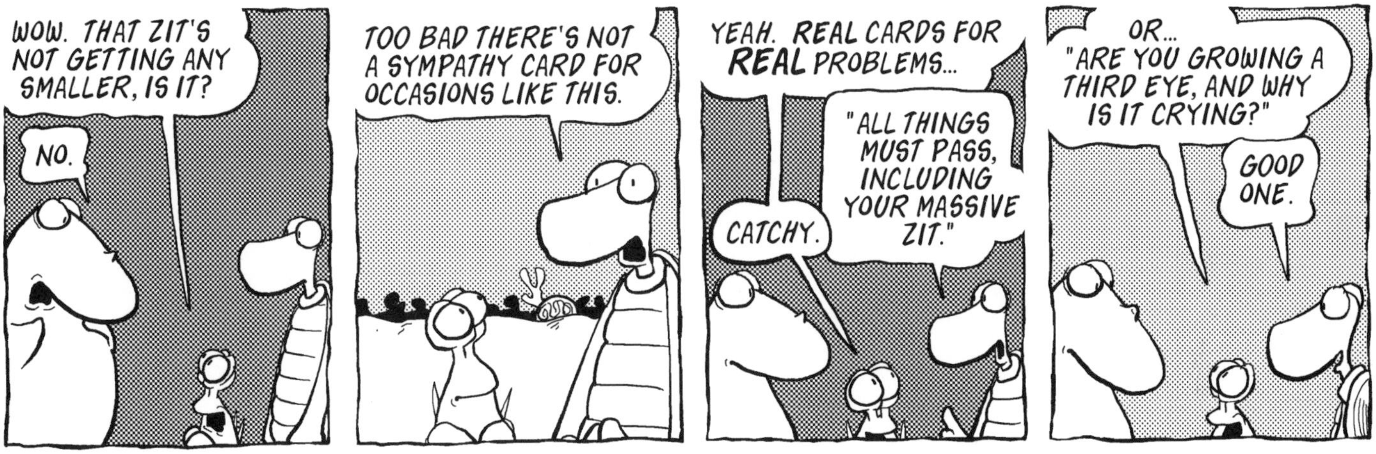
WOW. THAT ZIT'S NOT GETTING ANY SMALLER, IS IT?
NO.
TOO BAD THERE'S NOT A SYMPATHY CARD FOR OCCASIONS LIKE THIS.
YEAH. REAL CARDS FOR REAL PROBLEMS...
"ALL THINGS MUST PASS, INCLUDING YOUR MASSIVE ZIT."
CATCHY.
OR... "ARE YOU GROWING A THIRD EYE, AND WHY IS IT CRYING?"
GOOD ONE.

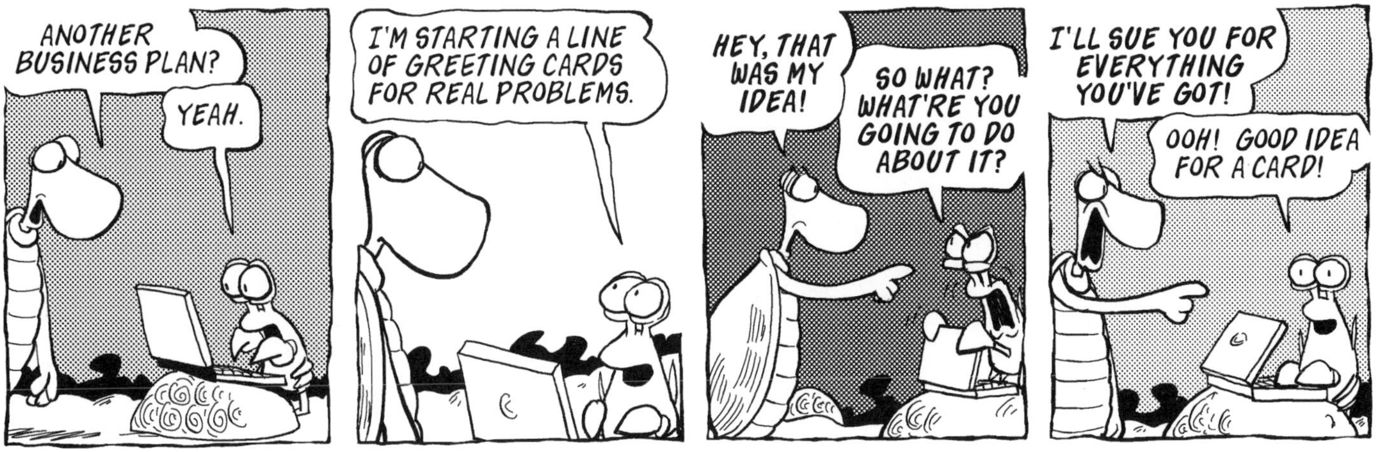
ANOTHER BUSINESS PLAN?
YEAH.
I'M STARTING A LINE OF GREETING CARDS FOR REAL PROBLEMS.
HEY, THAT WAS MY IDEA!
SO WHAT? WHAT'RE YOU GOING TO DO ABOUT IT?
I'LL SUE YOU FOR EVERYTHING YOU'VE GOT!
OOH! GOOD IDEA FOR A CARD!

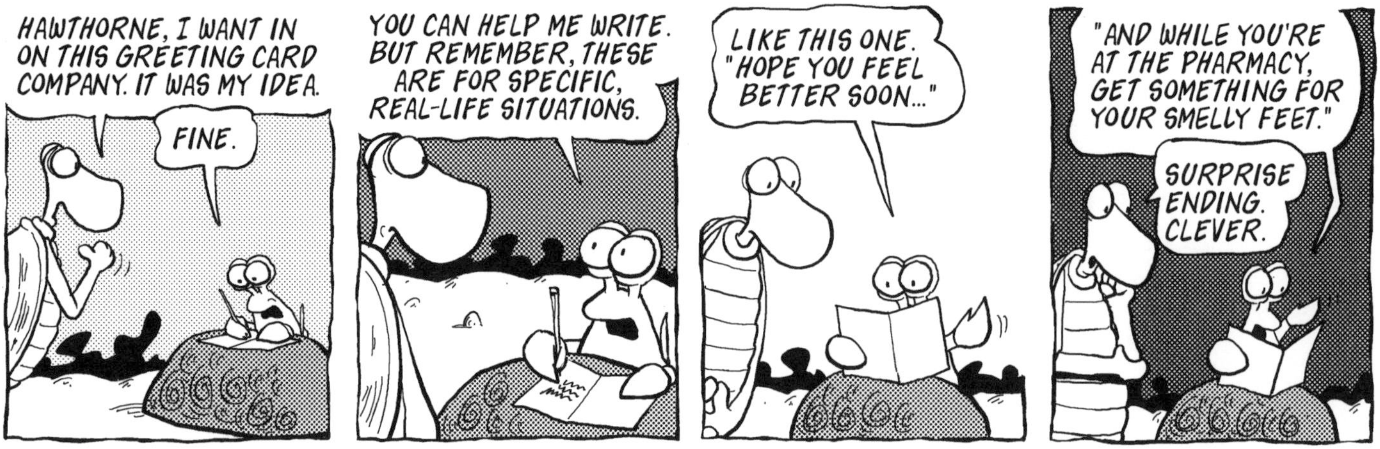
HAWTHORNE, I WANT IN ON THIS GREETING CARD COMPANY. IT WAS MY IDEA.
FINE.
YOU CAN HELP ME WRITE. BUT REMEMBER, THESE ARE FOR SPECIFIC, REAL-LIFE SITUATIONS.
LIKE THIS ONE. "HOPE YOU FEEL BETTER SOON..."
"AND WHILE YOU'RE AT THE PHARMACY, GET SOMETHING FOR YOUR SMELLY FEET."
SURPRISE ENDING. CLEVER.

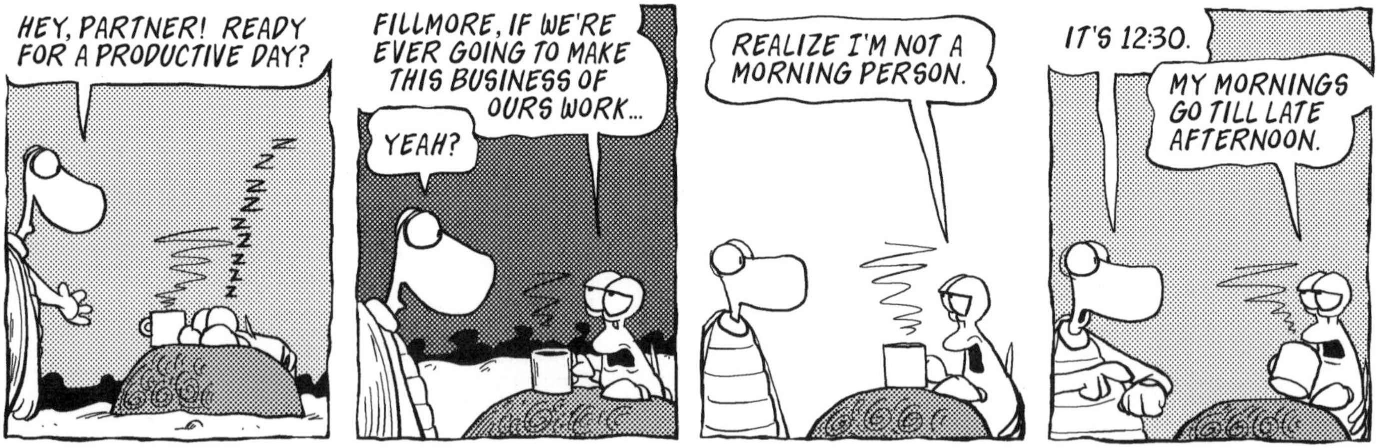
HEY, PARTNER! READY FOR A PRODUCTIVE DAY?
Z Z Z Z Z Z Z Z
FILLMORE, IF WE'RE EVER GOING TO MAKE THIS BUSINESS OF OURS WORK...
YEAH?
REALIZE I'M NOT A MORNING PERSON.
IT'S 12:30.
MY MORNINGS GO TILL LATE AFTERNOON.

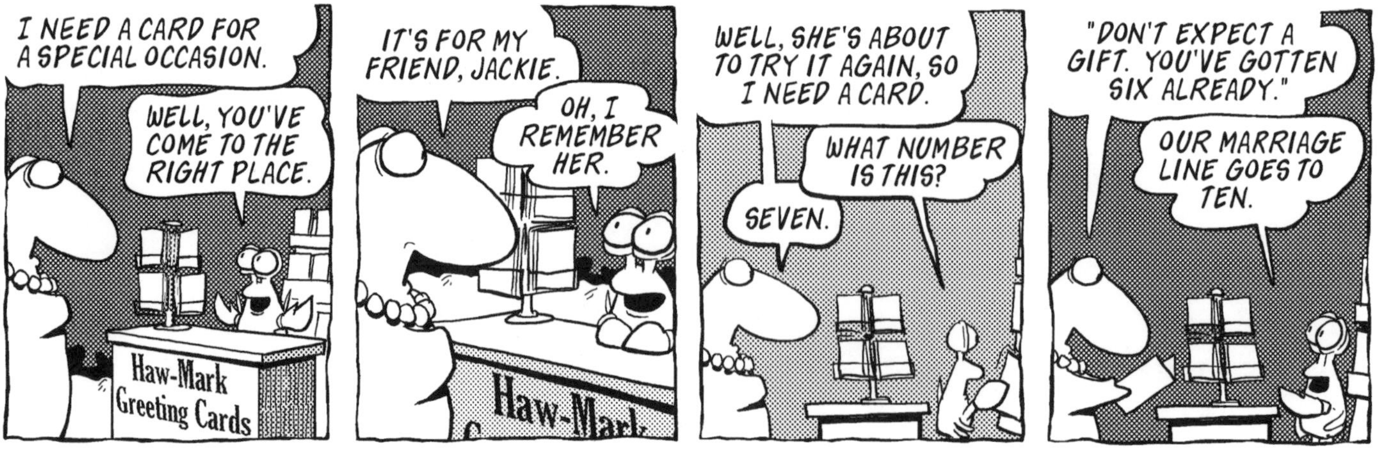
I NEED A CARD FOR A SPECIAL OCCASION.
WELL, YOU'VE COME TO THE RIGHT PLACE.
Haw-Mark Greeting Cards
IT'S FOR MY FRIEND, JACKIE.
OH, I REMEMBER HER.
Haw-Mark
WELL, SHE'S ABOUT TO TRY IT AGAIN, SO I NEED A CARD.
WHAT NUMBER IS THIS?
SEVEN.
"DON'T EXPECT A GIFT. YOU'VE GOTTEN SIX ALREADY."
OUR MARRIAGE LINE GOES TO TEN.

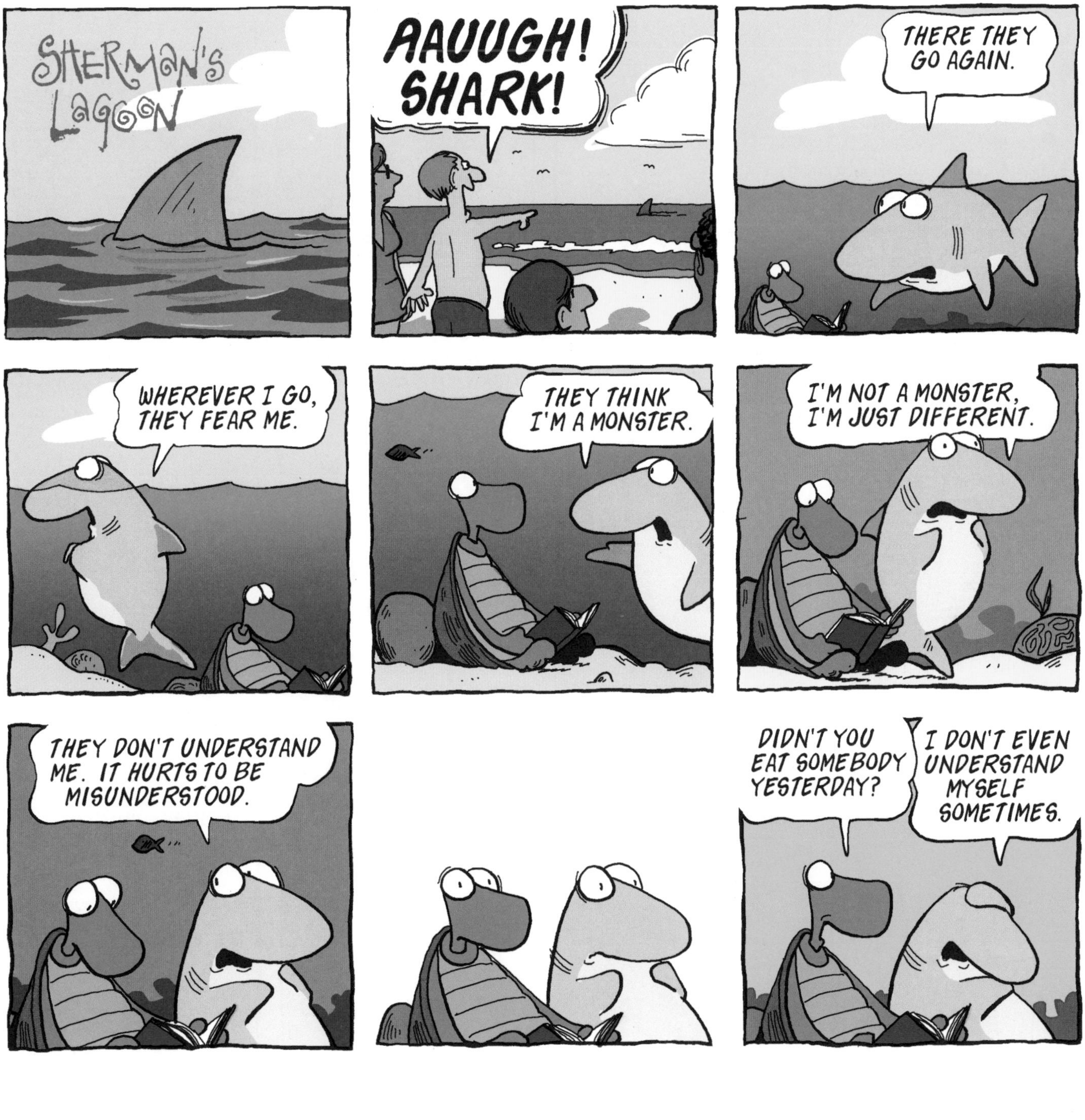
SHERMAN'S LAGOON
AAUUGH! SHARK!
THERE THEY GO AGAIN.
WHEREVER I GO, THEY FEAR ME.
THEY THINK I'M A MONSTER.
I'M NOT A MONSTER, I'M JUST DIFFERENT.
THEY DON'T UNDERSTAND ME. IT HURTS TO BE MISUNDERSTOOD.
DIDN'T YOU EAT SOMEBODY YESTERDAY?
I DON'T EVEN UNDERSTAND MYSELF SOMETIMES.

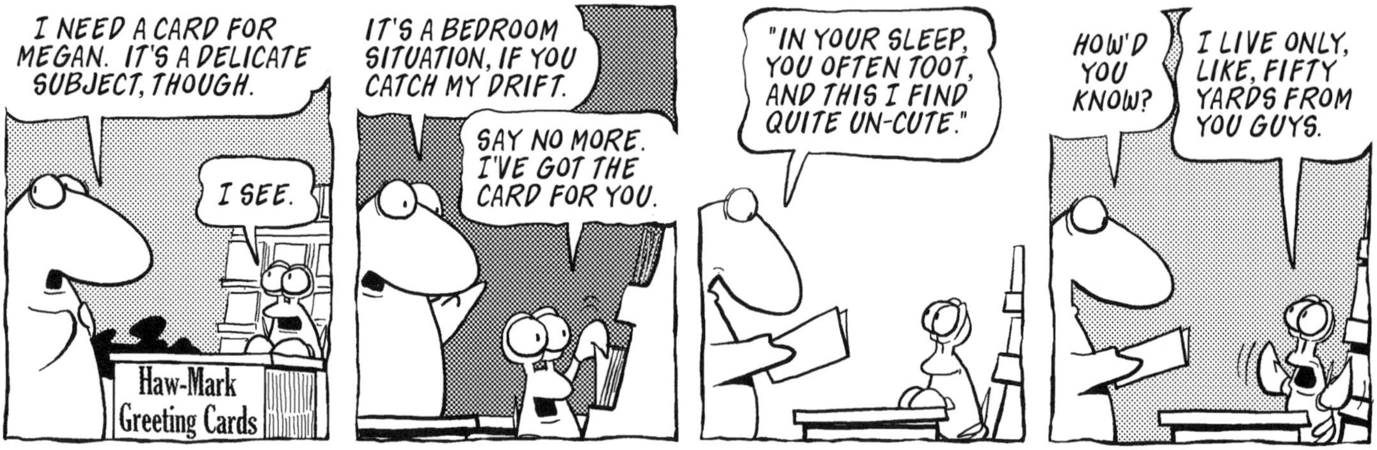
I NEED A CARD FOR MEGAN. IT'S A DELICATE SUBJECT, THOUGH.
I SEE.
Haw-Mark Greeting Cards
IT'S A BEDROOM SITUATION, IF YOU CATCH MY DRIFT.
SAY NO MORE. I'VE GOT THE CARD FOR YOU.
"IN YOUR SLEEP, YOU OFTEN TOOT, AND THIS I FIND QUITE UN-CUTE."
HOW'D YOU KNOW?
I LIVE ONLY, LIKE, FIFTY YARDS FROM YOU GUYS.

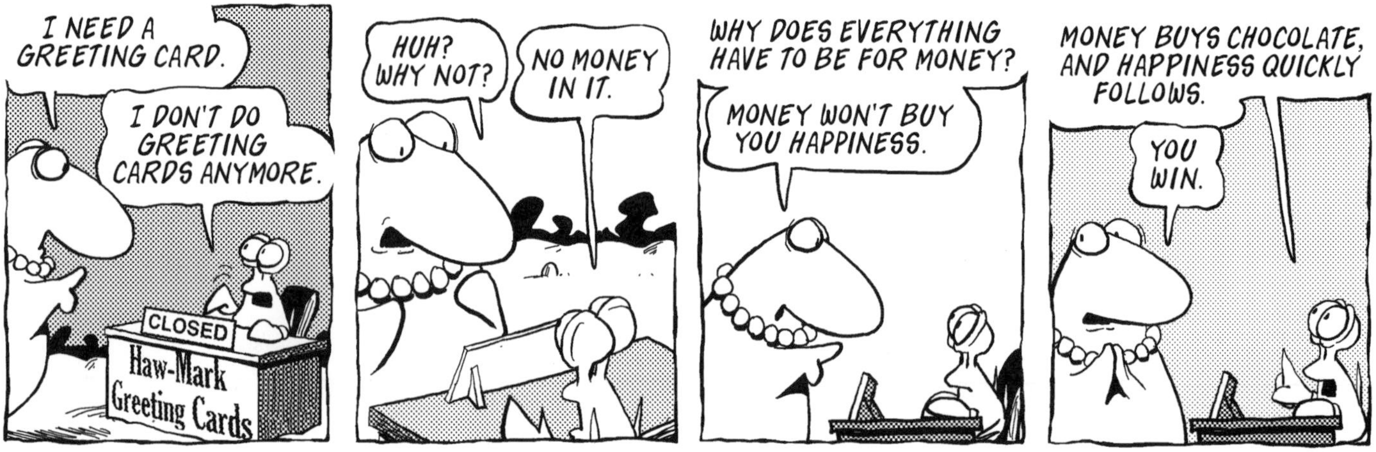
I NEED A GREETING CARD.
I DON'T DO GREETING CARDS ANYMORE.
CLOSED
Haw-Mark Greeting Cards
HUH? WHY NOT?
NO MONEY IN IT.
WHY DOES EVERYTHING HAVE TO BE FOR MONEY?
MONEY WON'T BUY YOU HAPPINESS.
MONEY BUYS CHOCOLATE, AND HAPPINESS QUICKLY FOLLOWS.
YOU WIN.

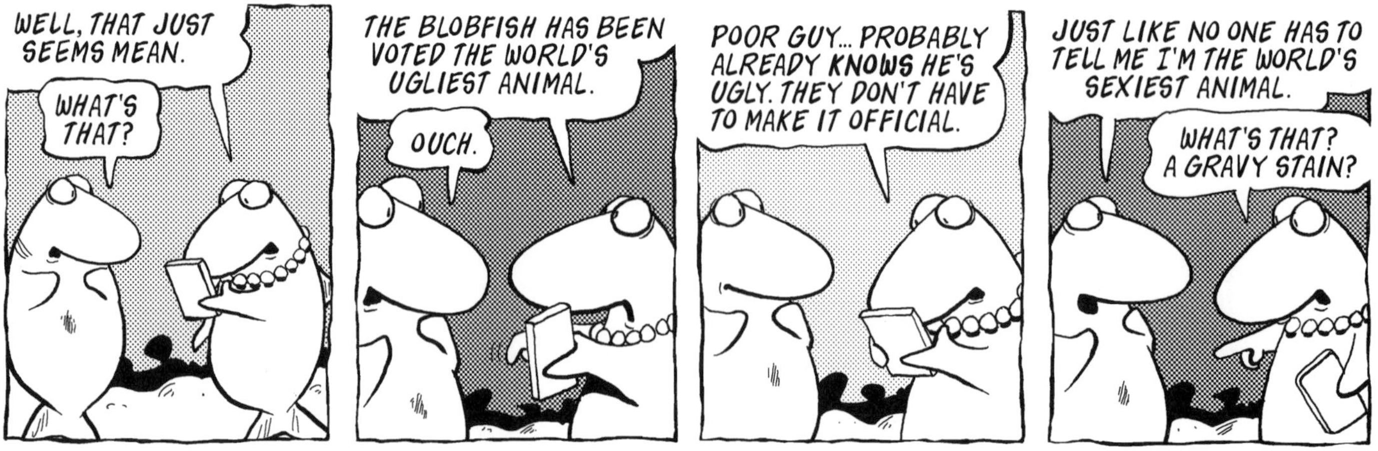
WELL, THAT JUST SEEMS MEAN.
WHAT'S THAT?
THE BLOBFISH HAS BEEN VOTED THE WORLD'S UGLIEST ANIMAL.
OUCH.
POOR GUY... PROBABLY ALREADY **KNOWS** HE'S UGLY. THEY DON'T HAVE TO MAKE IT OFFICIAL.
JUST LIKE NO ONE HAS TO TELL ME I'M THE WORLD'S SEXIEST ANIMAL.
WHAT'S THAT? A GRAVY STAIN?

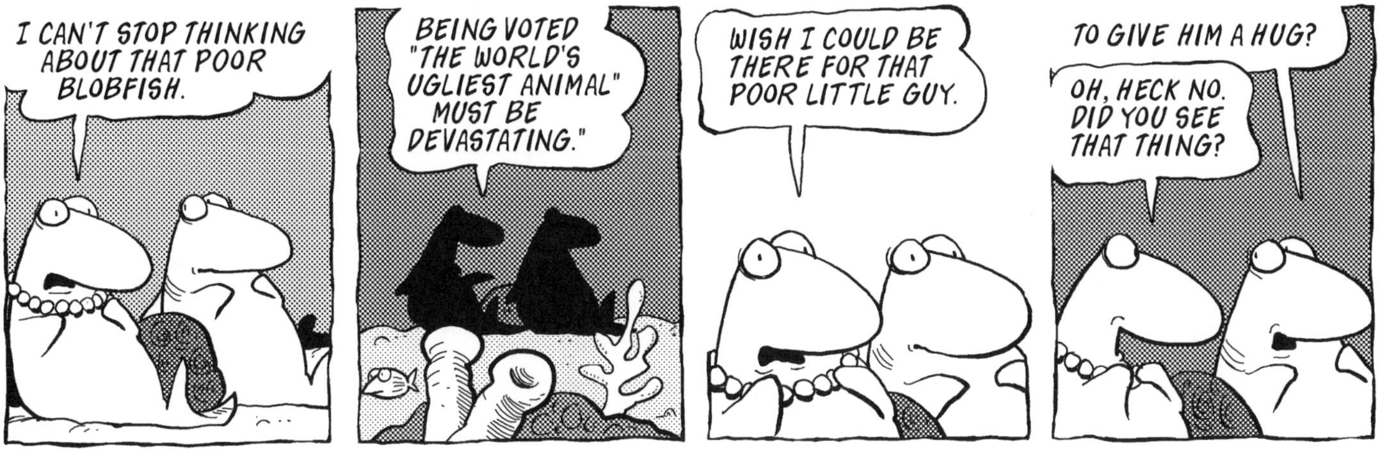
I CAN'T STOP THINKING ABOUT THAT POOR BLOBFISH.
BEING VOTED "THE WORLD'S UGLIEST ANIMAL" MUST BE DEVASTATING."
WISH I COULD BE THERE FOR THAT POOR LITTLE GUY.
TO GIVE HIM A HUG?
OH, HECK NO. DID YOU SEE THAT THING?

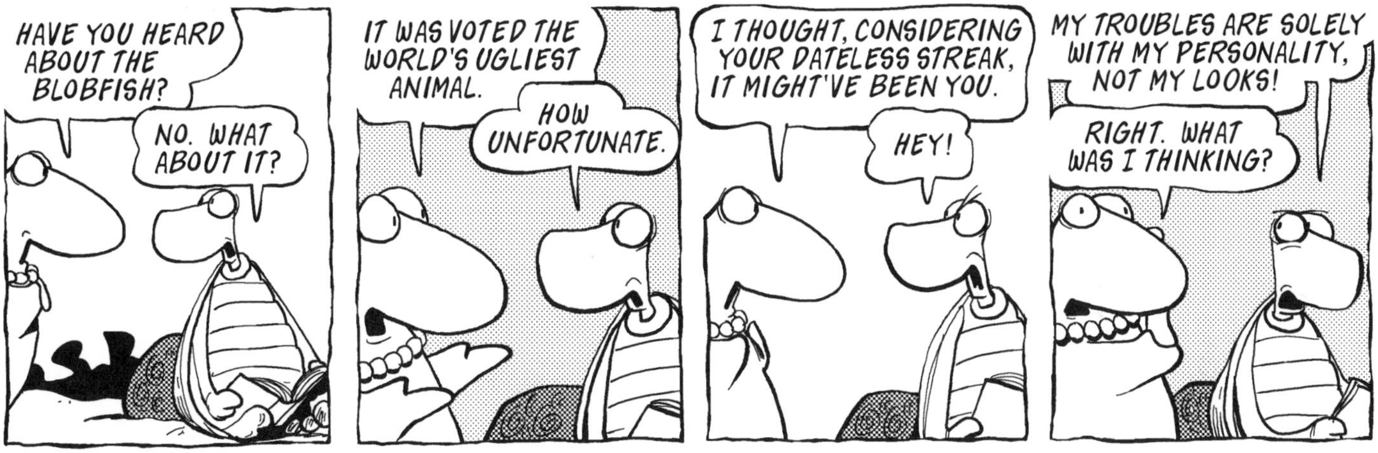
HAVE YOU HEARD ABOUT THE BLOBFISH?
NO. WHAT ABOUT IT?
IT WAS VOTED THE WORLD'S UGLIEST ANIMAL.
HOW UNFORTUNATE.
I THOUGHT, CONSIDERING YOUR DATELESS STREAK, IT MIGHT'VE BEEN YOU.
HEY!
MY TROUBLES ARE SOLELY WITH MY PERSONALITY, NOT MY LOOKS!
RIGHT. WHAT WAS I THINKING?

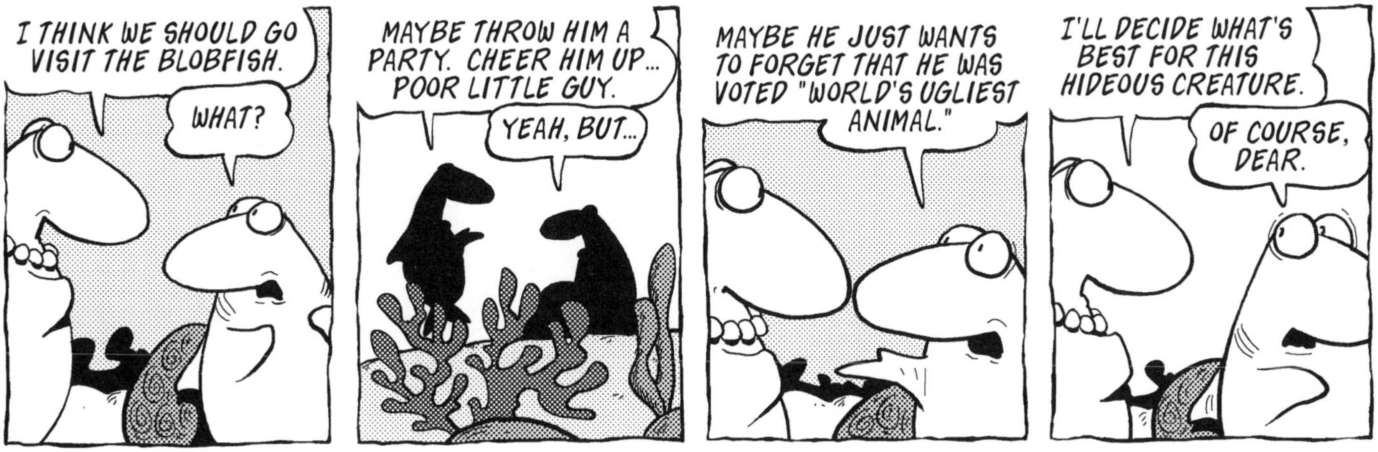
I THINK WE SHOULD GO VISIT THE BLOBFISH.
WHAT?
MAYBE THROW HIM A PARTY. CHEER HIM UP... POOR LITTLE GUY.
YEAH, BUT...
MAYBE HE JUST WANTS TO FORGET THAT HE WAS VOTED "WORLD'S UGLIEST ANIMAL."
I'LL DECIDE WHAT'S BEST FOR THIS HIDEOUS CREATURE.
OF COURSE, DEAR.

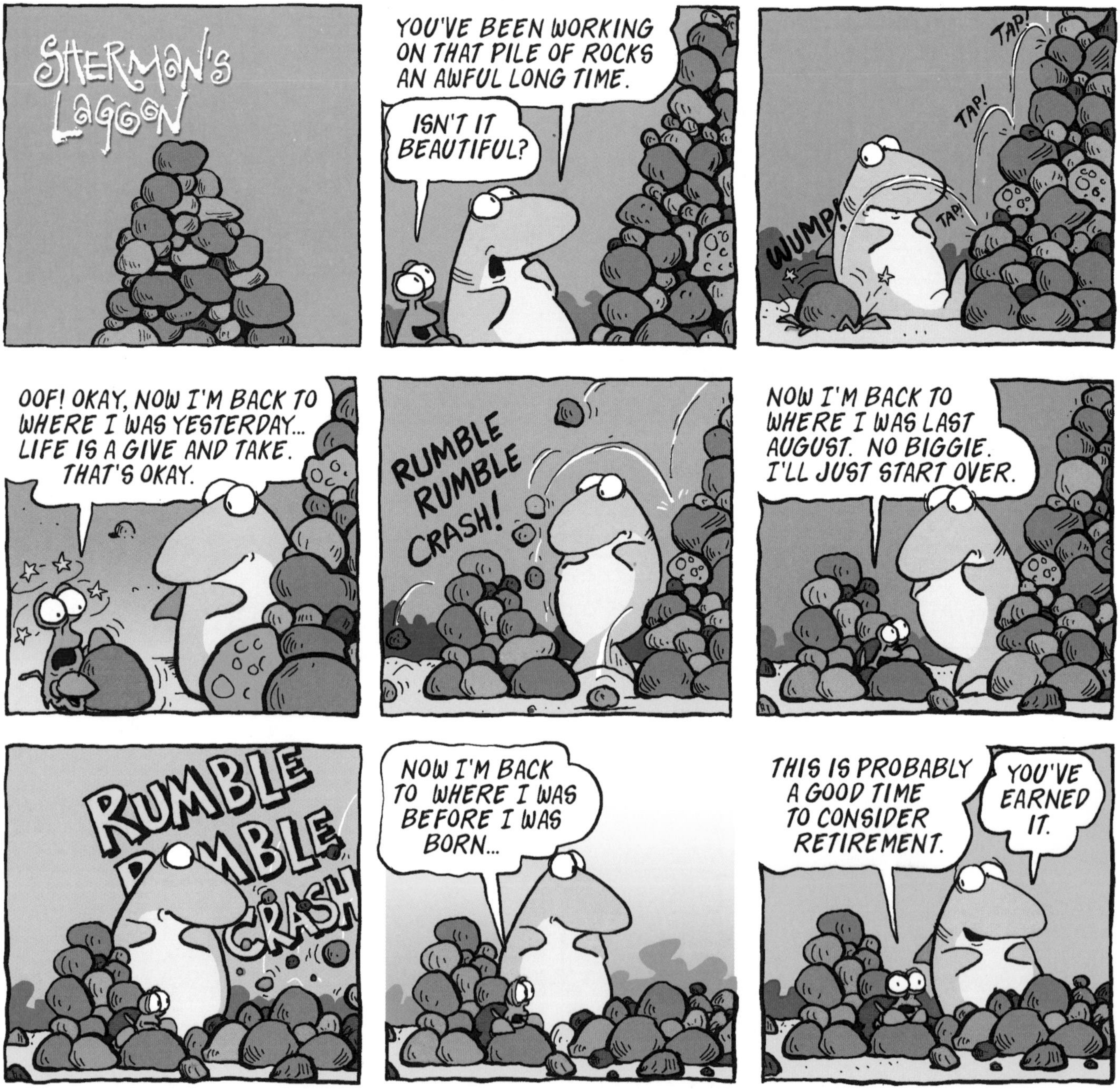
SHERMAN'S LAGOON
YOU'VE BEEN WORKING ON THAT PILE OF ROCKS AN AWFUL LONG TIME.
ISN'T IT BEAUTIFUL?
TAP!
TAP!
TAP!
WUMP!
OOF! OKAY, NOW I'M BACK TO WHERE I WAS YESTERDAY... LIFE IS A GIVE AND TAKE. THAT'S OKAY.
RUMBLE RUMBLE CRASH!
NOW I'M BACK TO WHERE I WAS LAST AUGUST. NO BIGGIE. I'LL JUST START OVER.
CRASH
NOW I'M BACK TO WHERE I WAS BEFORE I WAS BORN...
THIS IS PROBABLY A GOOD TIME TO CONSIDER RETIREMENT.
YOU'VE EARNED IT.

WHAT ARE WE DOING IN AUSTRALIA AGAIN?

IT'S A GOODWILL MISSION.

THE BLOBFISH WAS VOTED THE WORLD'S UGLIEST ANIMAL. WE'RE HERE TO CHEER HIM UP.

GOTCHA.

THERE'S ONE NOW. I'LL GO OVER AND BREAK THE ICE.

AAUUGH!! IT'S EVEN UGLIER IN REAL LIFE!

ICE, AND SELF-ESTEEM BROKEN.

HI THERE, MISTER BLOBFISH... I'M MEGAN.

MY FRIENDS AND I CAME ALL THE WAY FROM KAPUPU LAGOON TO THROW YOU A PARTY.

BY THE WAY, I DON'T THINK YOU DESERVE THE TITLE "WORLD'S UGLIEST ANIMAL." I THINK YOU'RE ONE HANDSOME DUDE.

I'M A GIRL.

OH, SWEET MERCY.

SO, WHAT'S YOUR NAME?

CAROLINE.

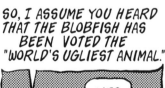

SO, I ASSUME YOU HEARD THAT THE BLOBFISH HAS BEEN VOTED THE "WORLD'S UGLIEST ANIMAL."

YES.

WE BEAT OUT THE FLIGHTLESS DUNG BEETLE FOR THE TITLE.

I SEE.

HERE'S MY TIARA.

WOW. I'VE NEVER SEEN A TIARA NOT IMPROVE A SITUATION.

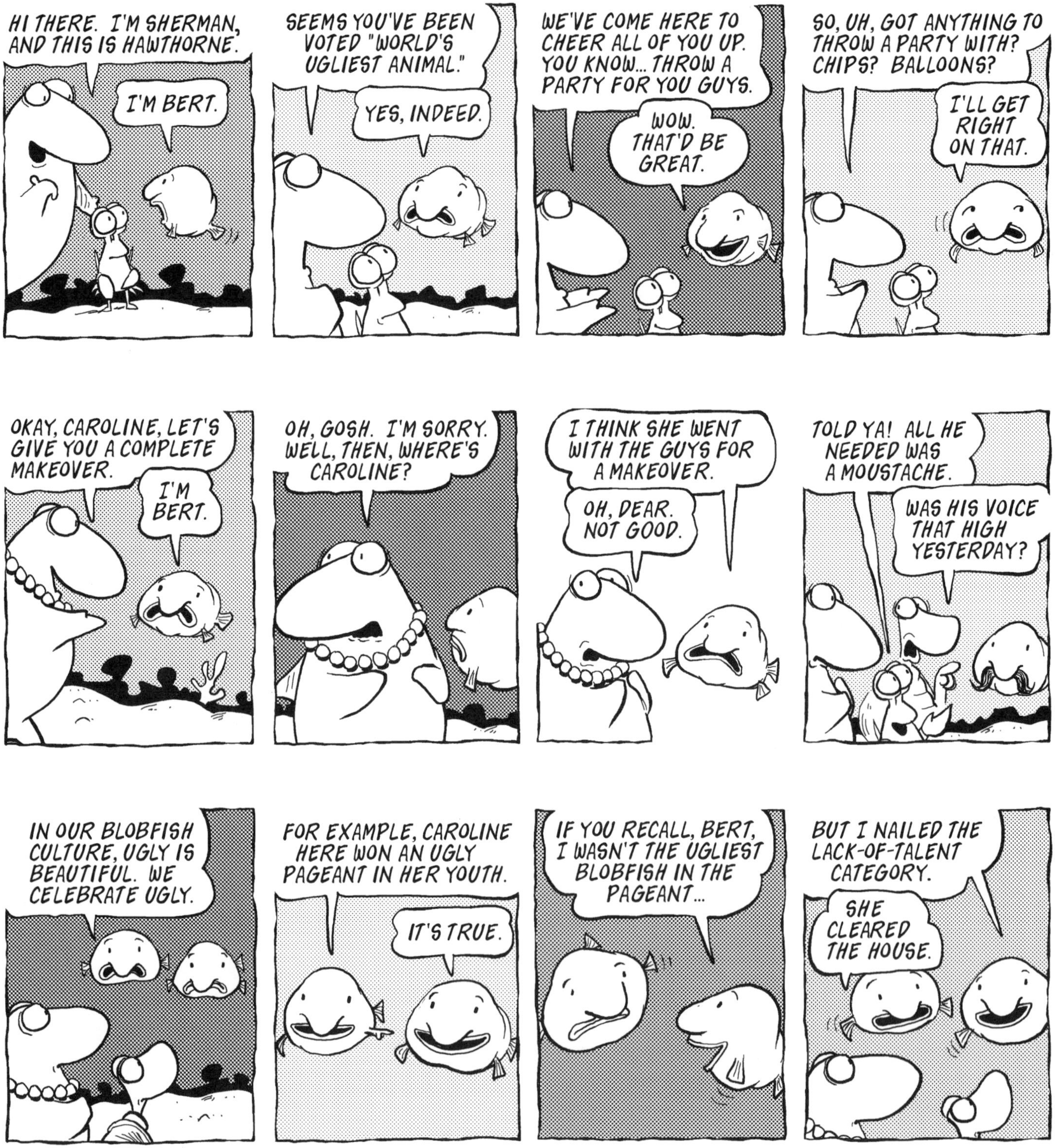
HI THERE. I'M SHERMAN, AND THIS IS HAWTHORNE.
I'M BERT.
SEEMS YOU'VE BEEN VOTED "WORLD'S UGLIEST ANIMAL."
YES, INDEED.
WE'VE COME HERE TO CHEER ALL OF YOU UP. YOU KNOW... THROW A PARTY FOR YOU GUYS.
WOW. THAT'D BE GREAT.
SO, UH, GOT ANYTHING TO THROW A PARTY WITH? CHIPS? BALLOONS?
I'LL GET RIGHT ON THAT.
OKAY, CAROLINE, LET'S GIVE YOU A COMPLETE MAKEOVER.
I'M BERT.
OH, GOSH. I'M SORRY. WELL, THEN, WHERE'S CAROLINE?
I THINK SHE WENT WITH THE GUYS FOR A MAKEOVER.
OH, DEAR. NOT GOOD.
TOLD YA! ALL HE NEEDED WAS A MOUSTACHE.
WAS HIS VOICE THAT HIGH YESTERDAY?
IN OUR BLOBFISH CULTURE, UGLY IS BEAUTIFUL. WE CELEBRATE UGLY.
FOR EXAMPLE, CAROLINE HERE WON AN UGLY PAGEANT IN HER YOUTH.
IT'S TRUE.
IF YOU RECALL, BERT, I WASN'T THE UGLIEST BLOBFISH IN THE PAGEANT...
BUT I NAILED THE LACK-OF-TALENT CATEGORY.
SHE CLEARED THE HOUSE.

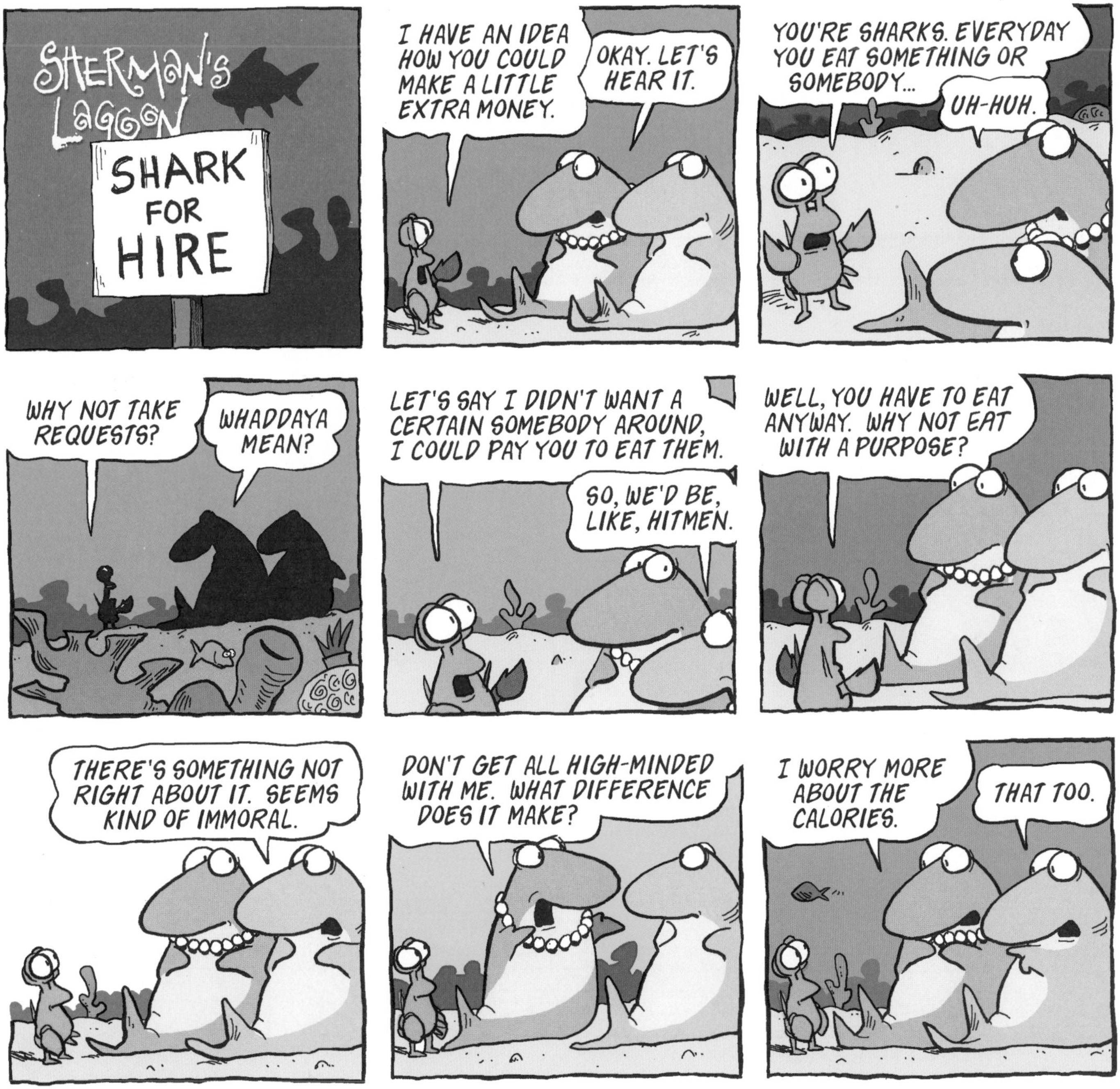
SHERMAN'S LAGOON
SHARK FOR HIRE
I HAVE AN IDEA HOW YOU COULD MAKE A LITTLE EXTRA MONEY.
OKAY. LET'S HEAR IT.
YOU'RE SHARKS. EVERYDAY YOU EAT SOMETHING OR SOMEBODY...
UH-HUH.
WHY NOT TAKE REQUESTS?
WHADDAYA MEAN?
LET'S SAY I DIDN'T WANT A CERTAIN SOMEBODY AROUND, I COULD PAY YOU TO EAT THEM.
SO, WE'D BE, LIKE, HITMEN.
WELL, YOU HAVE TO EAT ANYWAY. WHY NOT EAT WITH A PURPOSE?
THERE'S SOMETHING NOT RIGHT ABOUT IT. SEEMS KIND OF IMMORAL.
DON'T GET ALL HIGH-MINDED WITH ME. WHAT DIFFERENCE DOES IT MAKE?
I WORRY MORE ABOUT THE CALORIES.
THAT TOO.

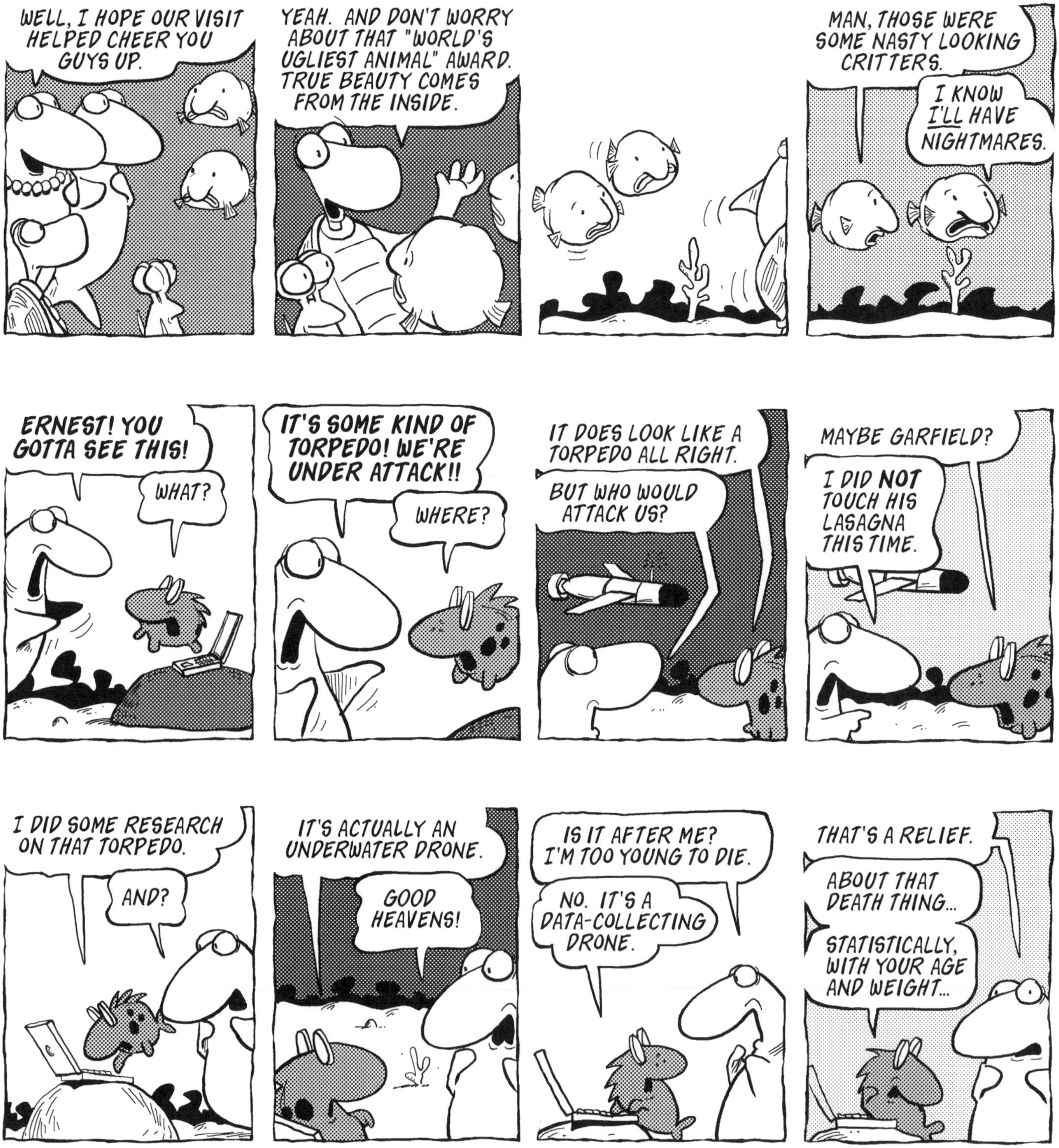
WELL, I HOPE OUR VISIT HELPED CHEER YOU GUYS UP.
YEAH. AND DON'T WORRY ABOUT THAT "WORLD'S UGLIEST ANIMAL" AWARD. TRUE BEAUTY COMES FROM THE INSIDE.
MAN, THOSE WERE SOME NASTY LOOKING CRITTERS.
I KNOW I'LL HAVE NIGHTMARES.
ERNEST! YOU GOTTA SEE THIS!
WHAT?
IT'S SOME KIND OF TORPEDO! WE'RE UNDER ATTACK!!
WHERE?
IT DOES LOOK LIKE A TORPEDO ALL RIGHT.
BUT WHO WOULD ATTACK US?
MAYBE GARFIELD?
I DID NOT TOUCH HIS LASAGNA THIS TIME.
I DID SOME RESEARCH ON THAT TORPEDO.
AND?
IT'S ACTUALLY AN UNDERWATER DRONE.
GOOD HEAVENS!
IS IT AFTER ME? I'M TOO YOUNG TO DIE.
NO. IT'S A DATA-COLLECTING DRONE.
THAT'S A RELIEF.
ABOUT THAT DEATH THING...
STATISTICALLY, WITH YOUR AGE AND WEIGHT...

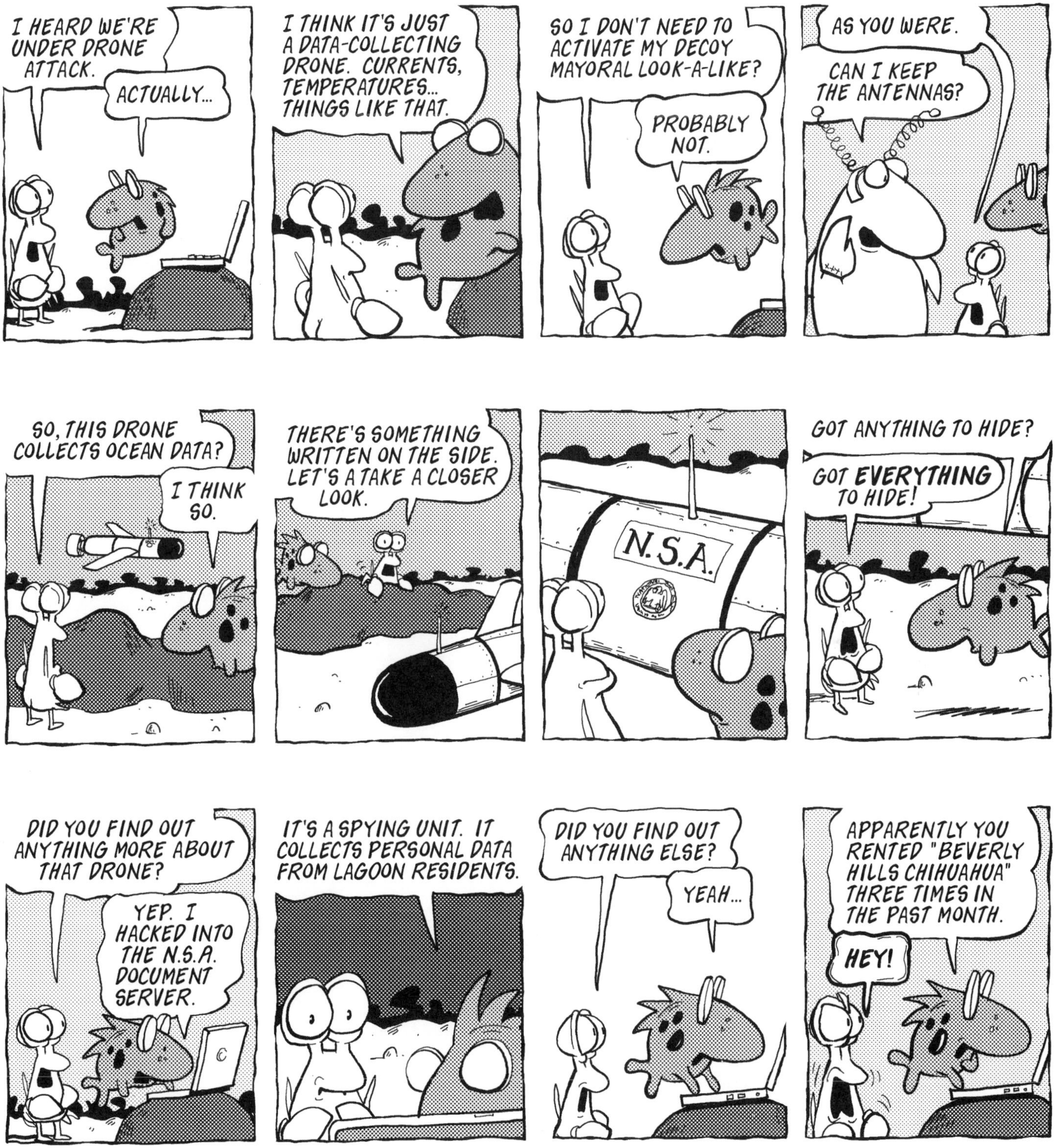
I HEARD WE'RE UNDER DRONE ATTACK.
ACTUALLY...
I THINK IT'S JUST A DATA-COLLECTING DRONE. CURRENTS, TEMPERATURES... THINGS LIKE THAT.
SO I DON'T NEED TO ACTIVATE MY DECOY MAYORAL LOOK-A-LIKE?
PROBABLY NOT.
AS YOU WERE.
CAN I KEEP THE ANTENNAS?
SO, THIS DRONE COLLECTS OCEAN DATA?
I THINK SO.
THERE'S SOMETHING WRITTEN ON THE SIDE. LET'S A TAKE A CLOSER LOOK.
N.S.A.
GOT ANYTHING TO HIDE?
GOT EVERYTHING TO HIDE!
DID YOU FIND OUT ANYTHING MORE ABOUT THAT DRONE?
YEP. I HACKED INTO THE N.S.A. DOCUMENT SERVER.
IT'S A SPYING UNIT. IT COLLECTS PERSONAL DATA FROM LAGOON RESIDENTS.
DID YOU FIND OUT ANYTHING ELSE?
YEAH...
APPARENTLY YOU RENTED "BEVERLY HILLS CHIHUAHUA" THREE TIMES IN THE PAST MONTH.
HEY!

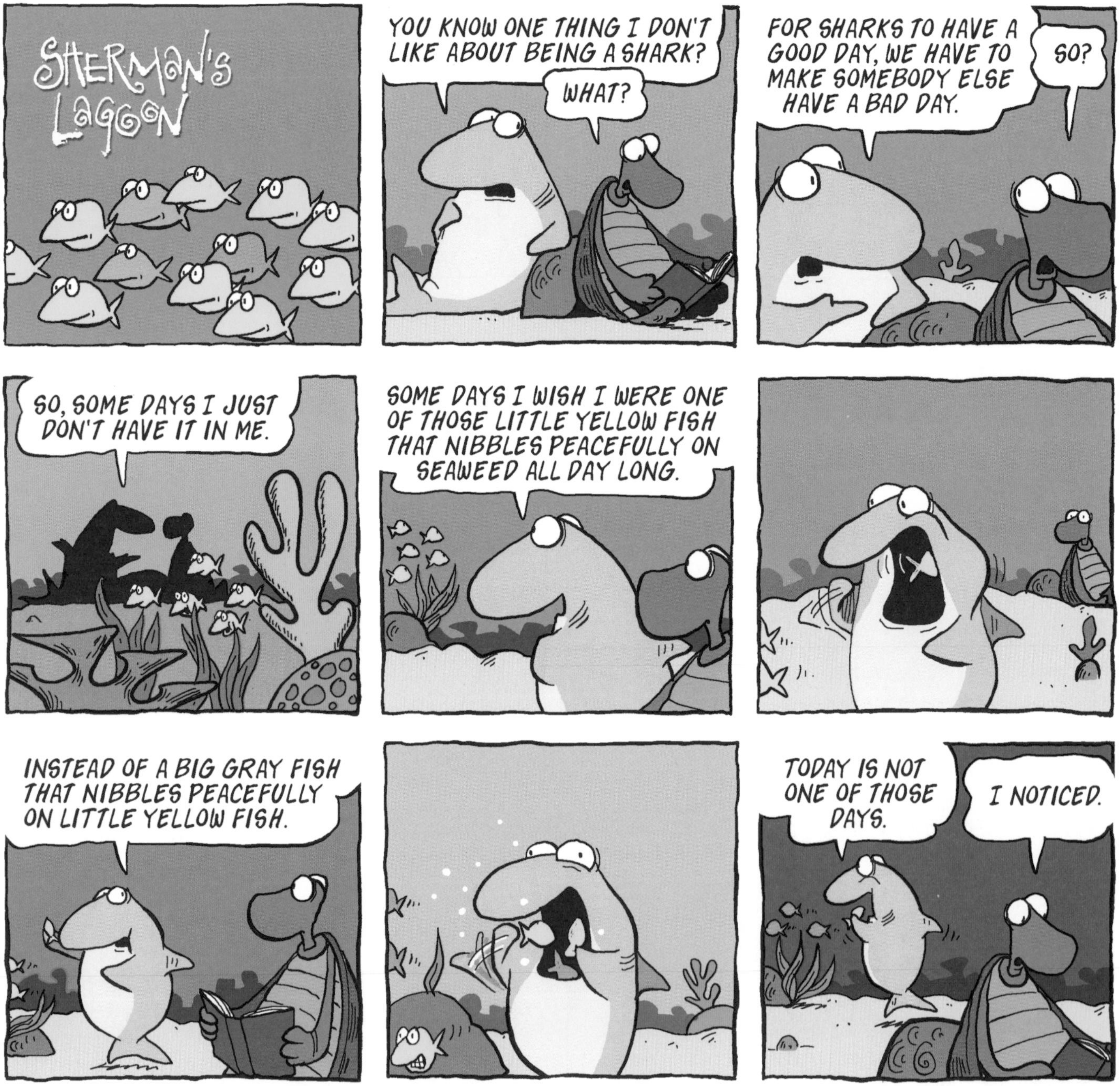
SHERMAN'S LAGOON
YOU KNOW ONE THING I DON'T LIKE ABOUT BEING A SHARK?
WHAT?
FOR SHARKS TO HAVE A GOOD DAY, WE HAVE TO MAKE SOMEBODY ELSE HAVE A BAD DAY.
SO?
SO, SOME DAYS I JUST DON'T HAVE IT IN ME.
SOME DAYS I WISH I WERE ONE OF THOSE LITTLE YELLOW FISH THAT NIBBLES PEACEFULLY ON SEAWEED ALL DAY LONG.
INSTEAD OF A BIG GRAY FISH THAT NIBBLES PEACEFULLY ON LITTLE YELLOW FISH.
TODAY IS NOT ONE OF THOSE DAYS.
I NOTICED.

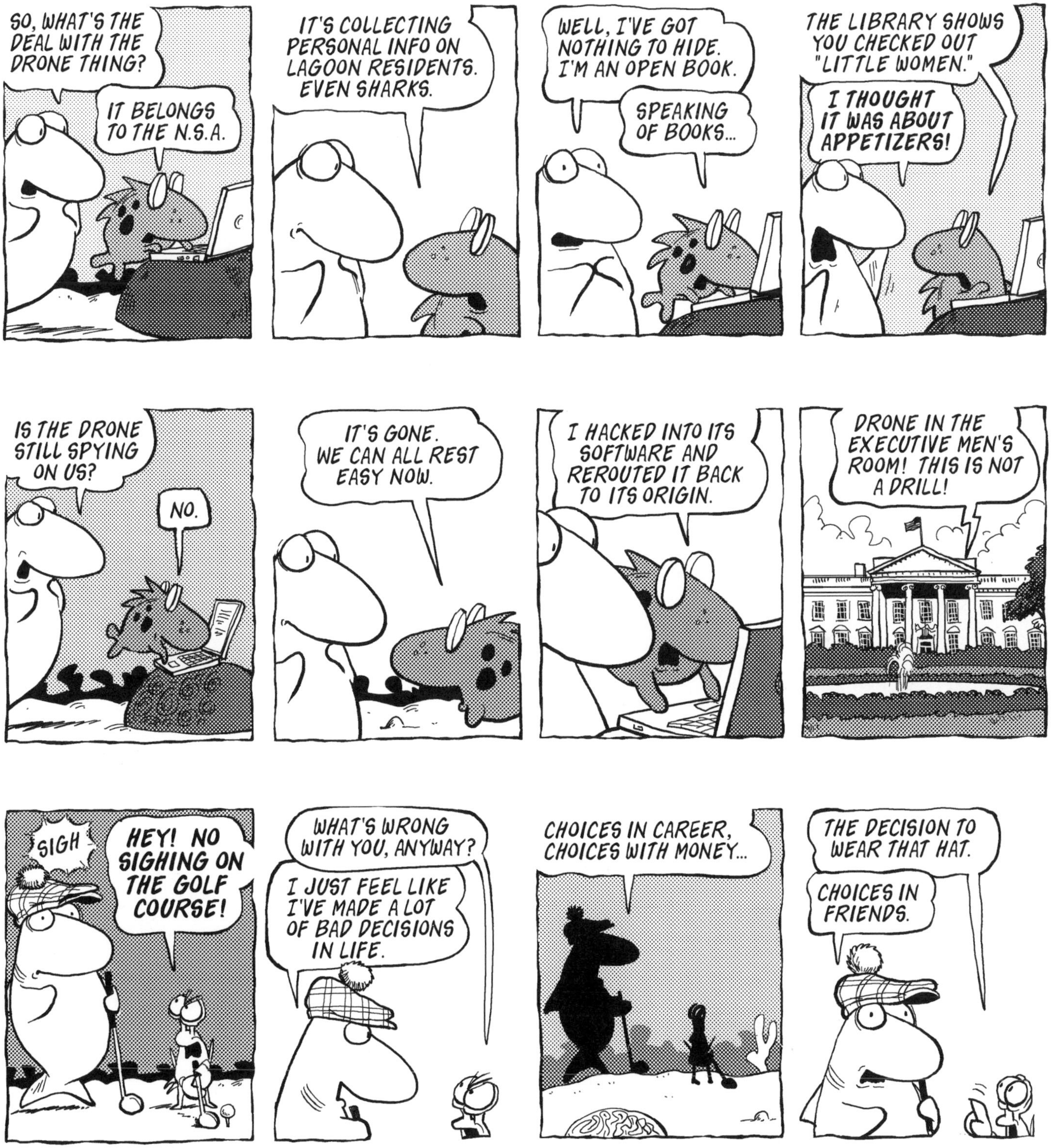
SO, WHAT'S THE DEAL WITH THE DRONE THING?
IT BELONGS TO THE N.S.A.
IT'S COLLECTING PERSONAL INFO ON LAGOON RESIDENTS. EVEN SHARKS.
WELL, I'VE GOT NOTHING TO HIDE. I'M AN OPEN BOOK.
SPEAKING OF BOOKS...
THE LIBRARY SHOWS YOU CHECKED OUT "LITTLE WOMEN."
I THOUGHT IT WAS ABOUT APPETIZERS!
IS THE DRONE STILL SPYING ON US?
NO.
IT'S GONE. WE CAN ALL REST EASY NOW.
I HACKED INTO ITS SOFTWARE AND REROUTED IT BACK TO ITS ORIGIN.
DRONE IN THE EXECUTIVE MEN'S ROOM! THIS IS NOT A DRILL!
SIGH
HEY! NO SIGHING ON THE GOLF COURSE!
WHAT'S WRONG WITH YOU, ANYWAY?
I JUST FEEL LIKE I'VE MADE A LOT OF BAD DECISIONS IN LIFE.
CHOICES IN CAREER, CHOICES WITH MONEY...
THE DECISION TO WEAR THAT HAT.
CHOICES IN FRIENDS.

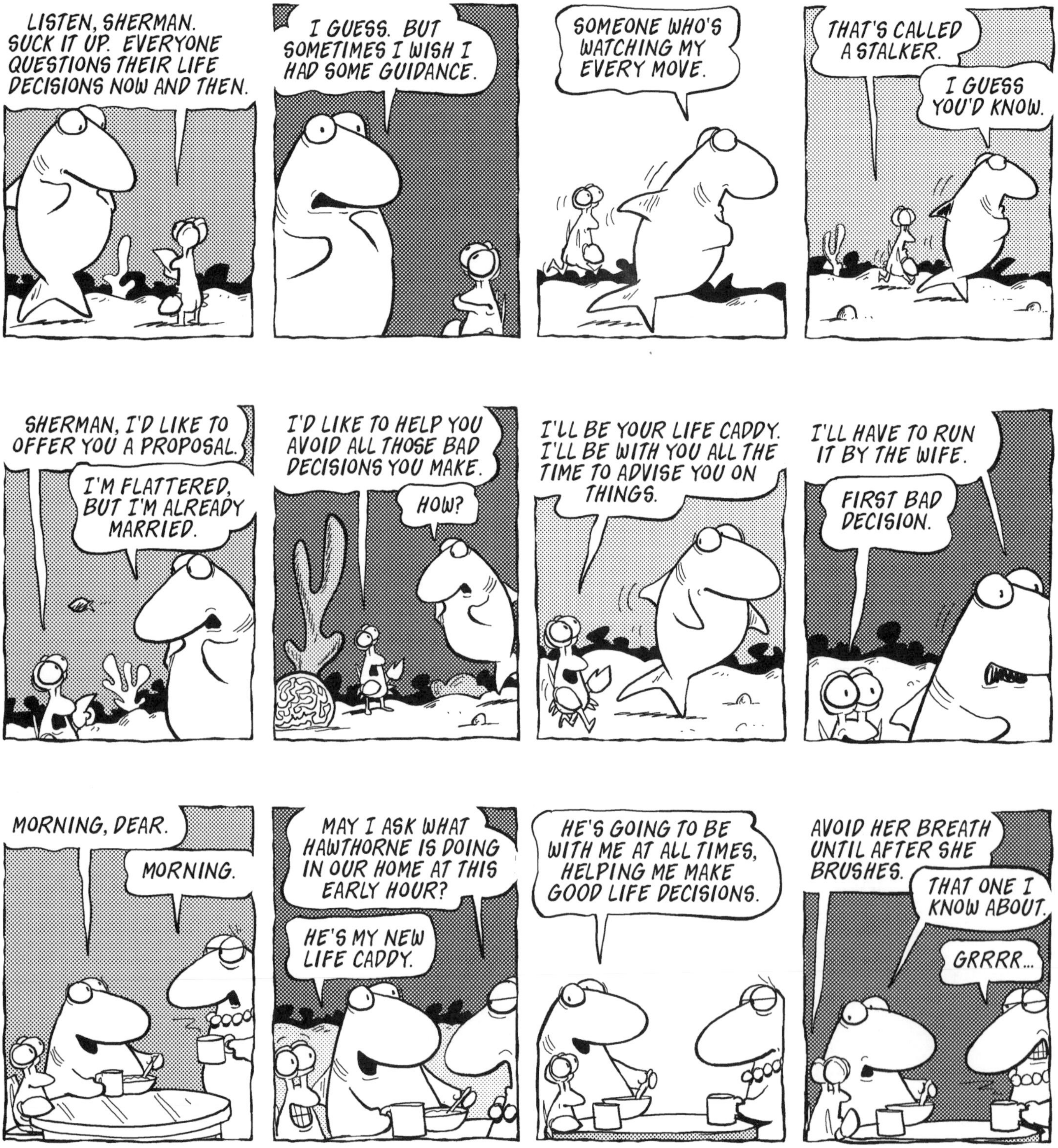
LISTEN, SHERMAN. SUCK IT UP. EVERYONE QUESTIONS THEIR LIFE DECISIONS NOW AND THEN.
I GUESS. BUT SOMETIMES I WISH I HAD SOME GUIDANCE.
SOMEONE WHO'S WATCHING MY EVERY MOVE.
THAT'S CALLED A STALKER.
I GUESS YOU'D KNOW.
SHERMAN, I'D LIKE TO OFFER YOU A PROPOSAL.
I'M FLATTERED, BUT I'M ALREADY MARRIED.
I'D LIKE TO HELP YOU AVOID ALL THOSE BAD DECISIONS YOU MAKE.
HOW?
I'LL BE YOUR LIFE CADDY. I'LL BE WITH YOU ALL THE TIME TO ADVISE YOU ON THINGS.
I'LL HAVE TO RUN IT BY THE WIFE.
FIRST BAD DECISION.
MORNING, DEAR.
MORNING.
MAY I ASK WHAT HAWTHORNE IS DOING IN OUR HOME AT THIS EARLY HOUR?
HE'S MY NEW LIFE CADDY.
HE'S GOING TO BE WITH ME AT ALL TIMES, HELPING ME MAKE GOOD LIFE DECISIONS.
AVOID HER BREATH UNTIL AFTER SHE BRUSHES.
THAT ONE I KNOW ABOUT.
GRRRR...

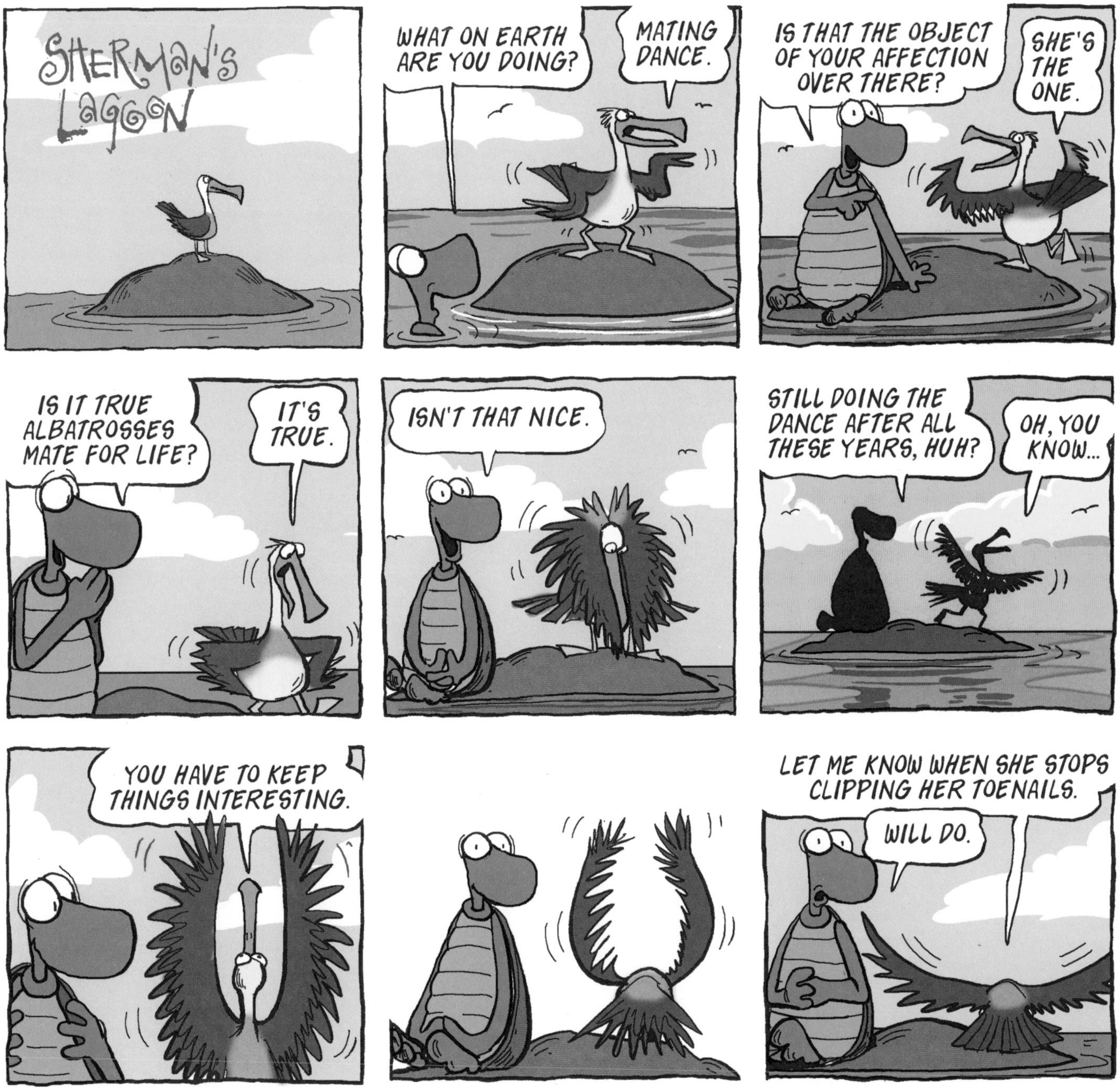
SHERMAN'S LAGOON
WHAT ON EARTH ARE YOU DOING?
MATING DANCE.
IS THAT THE OBJECT OF YOUR AFFECTION OVER THERE?
SHE'S THE ONE.
IS IT TRUE ALBATROSSES MATE FOR LIFE?
IT'S TRUE.
ISN'T THAT NICE.
STILL DOING THE DANCE AFTER ALL THESE YEARS, HUH?
OH, YOU KNOW...
YOU HAVE TO KEEP THINGS INTERESTING.
LET ME KNOW WHEN SHE STOPS CLIPPING HER TOENAILS.
WILL DO.

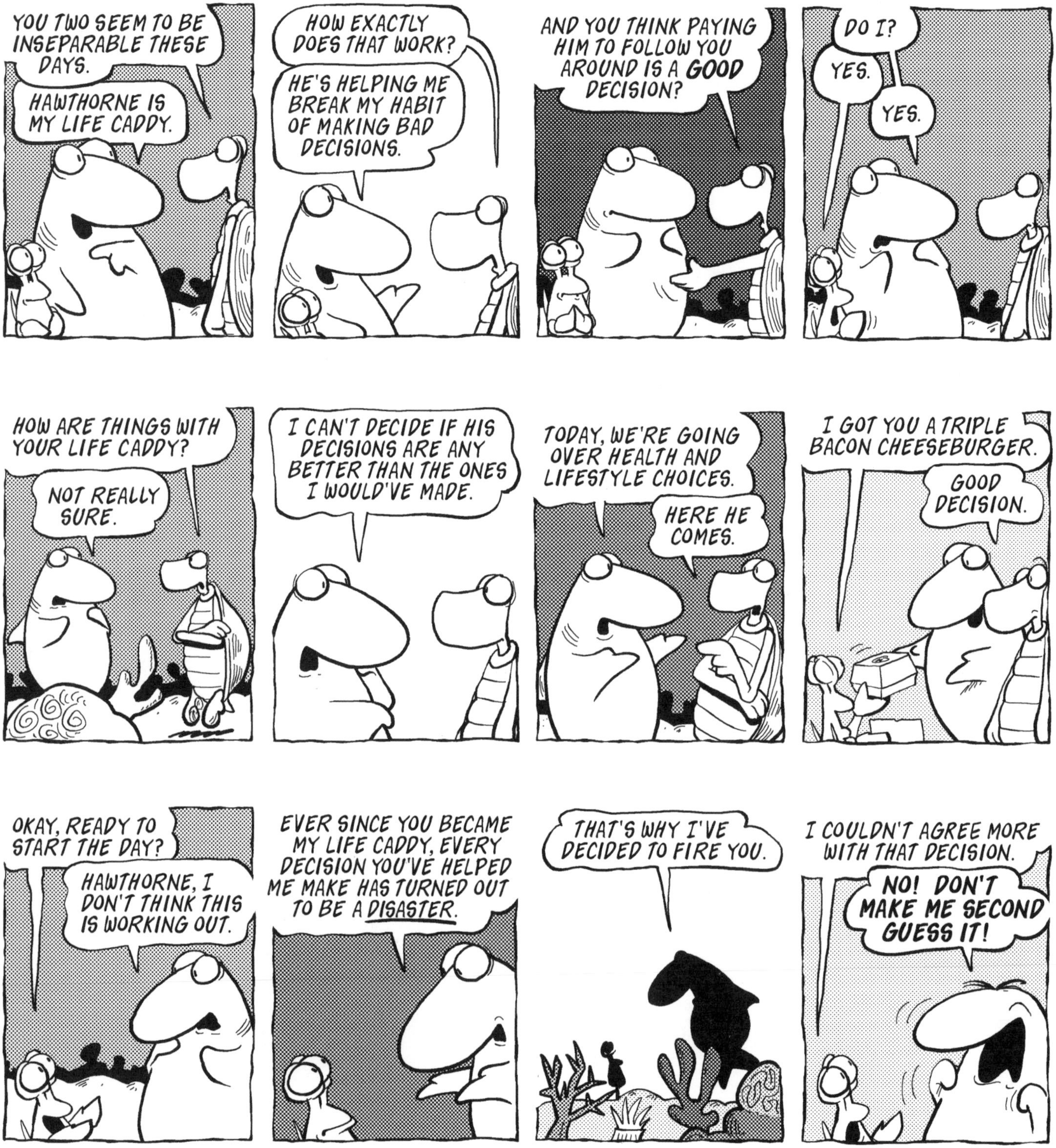
YOU TWO SEEM TO BE INSEPARABLE THESE DAYS.
HAWTHORNE IS MY LIFE CADDY.
HOW EXACTLY DOES THAT WORK?
HE'S HELPING ME BREAK MY HABIT OF MAKING BAD DECISIONS.
AND YOU THINK PAYING HIM TO FOLLOW YOU AROUND IS A GOOD DECISION?
DO I?
YES.
YES.
HOW ARE THINGS WITH YOUR LIFE CADDY?
NOT REALLY SURE.
I CAN'T DECIDE IF HIS DECISIONS ARE ANY BETTER THAN THE ONES I WOULD'VE MADE.
TODAY, WE'RE GOING OVER HEALTH AND LIFESTYLE CHOICES.
HERE HE COMES.
I GOT YOU A TRIPLE BACON CHEESEBURGER.
GOOD DECISION.
OKAY, READY TO START THE DAY?
HAWTHORNE, I DON'T THINK THIS IS WORKING OUT.
EVER SINCE YOU BECAME MY LIFE CADDY, EVERY DECISION YOU'VE HELPED ME MAKE HAS TURNED OUT TO BE A DISASTER.
THAT'S WHY I'VE DECIDED TO FIRE YOU.
I COULDN'T AGREE MORE WITH THAT DECISION.
NO! DON'T MAKE ME SECOND GUESS IT!

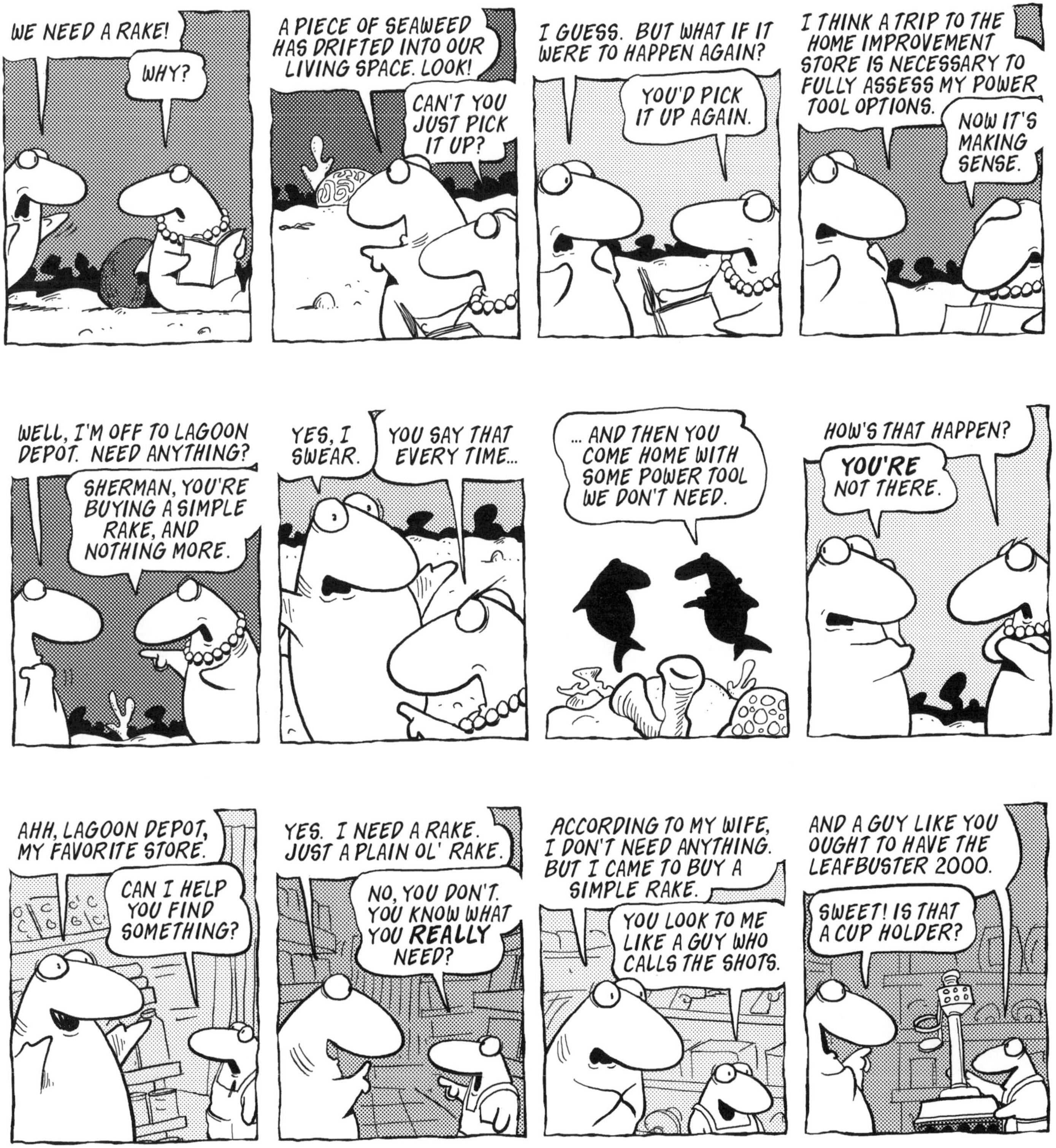
WE NEED A RAKE!
WHY?
A PIECE OF SEAWEED HAS DRIFTED INTO OUR LIVING SPACE. LOOK!
CAN'T YOU JUST PICK IT UP?
I GUESS. BUT WHAT IF IT WERE TO HAPPEN AGAIN?
YOU'D PICK IT UP AGAIN.
I THINK A TRIP TO THE HOME IMPROVEMENT STORE IS NECESSARY TO FULLY ASSESS MY POWER TOOL OPTIONS.
NOW IT'S MAKING SENSE.
WELL, I'M OFF TO LAGOON DEPOT. NEED ANYTHING?
SHERMAN, YOU'RE BUYING A SIMPLE RAKE, AND NOTHING MORE.
YES, I SWEAR.
YOU SAY THAT EVERY TIME...
... AND THEN YOU COME HOME WITH SOME POWER TOOL WE DON'T NEED.
HOW'S THAT HAPPEN?
YOU'RE NOT THERE.
AHH, LAGOON DEPOT, MY FAVORITE STORE.
CAN I HELP YOU FIND SOMETHING?
YES. I NEED A RAKE. JUST A PLAIN OL' RAKE.
NO, YOU DON'T. YOU KNOW WHAT YOU **REALLY** NEED?
ACCORDING TO MY WIFE, I DON'T NEED ANYTHING. BUT I CAME TO BUY A SIMPLE RAKE.
YOU LOOK TO ME LIKE A GUY WHO CALLS THE SHOTS.
AND A GUY LIKE YOU OUGHT TO HAVE THE LEAFBUSTER 2000.
SWEET! IS THAT A CUP HOLDER?

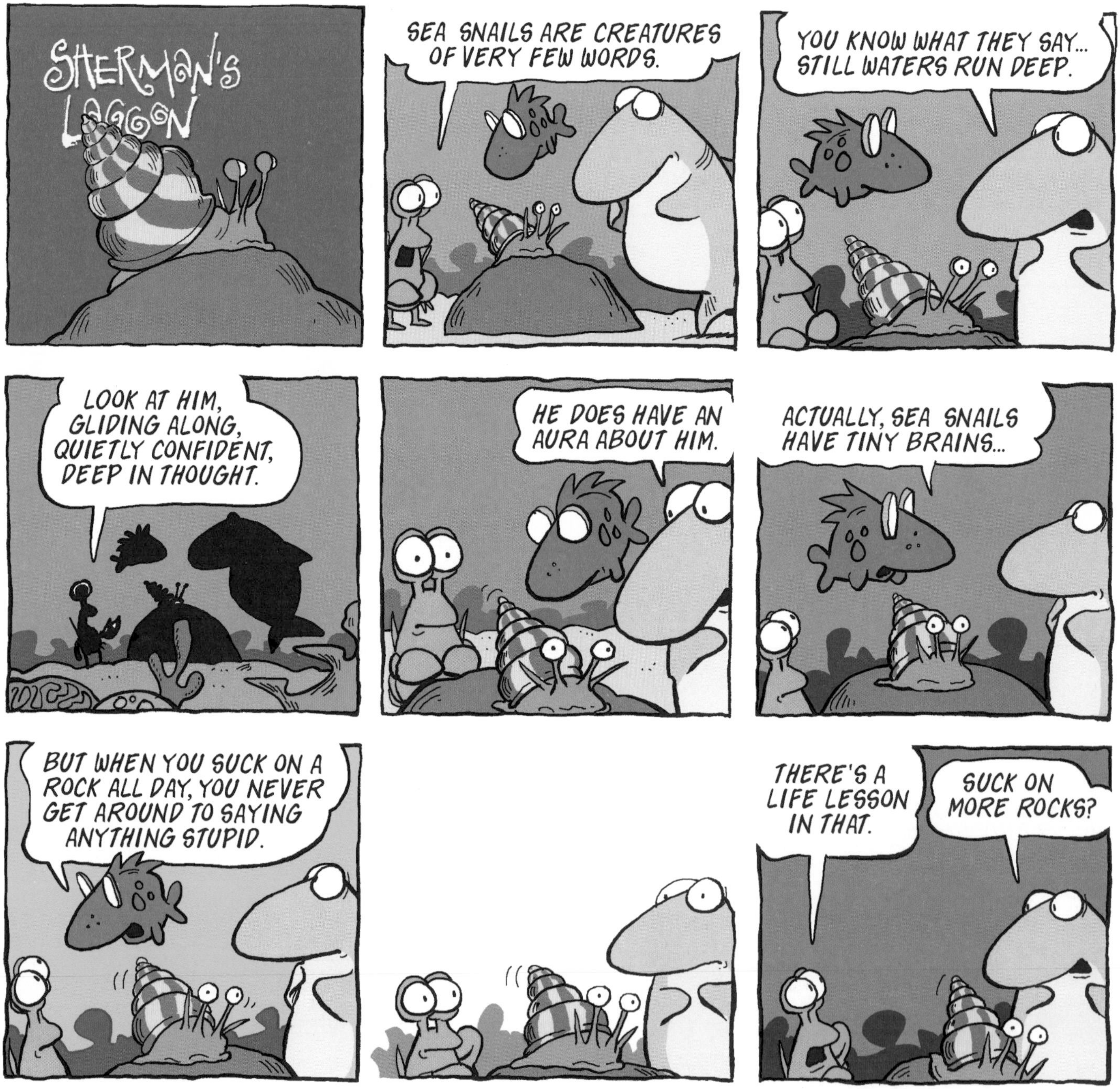
SHERMAN'S LAGOON
SEA SNAILS ARE CREATURES OF VERY FEW WORDS.
YOU KNOW WHAT THEY SAY... STILL WATERS RUN DEEP.
LOOK AT HIM, GLIDING ALONG, QUIETLY CONFIDENT, DEEP IN THOUGHT.
HE DOES HAVE AN AURA ABOUT HIM.
ACTUALLY, SEA SNAILS HAVE TINY BRAINS...
BUT WHEN YOU SUCK ON A ROCK ALL DAY, YOU NEVER GET AROUND TO SAYING ANYTHING STUPID.
THERE'S A LIFE LESSON IN THAT.
SUCK ON MORE ROCKS?

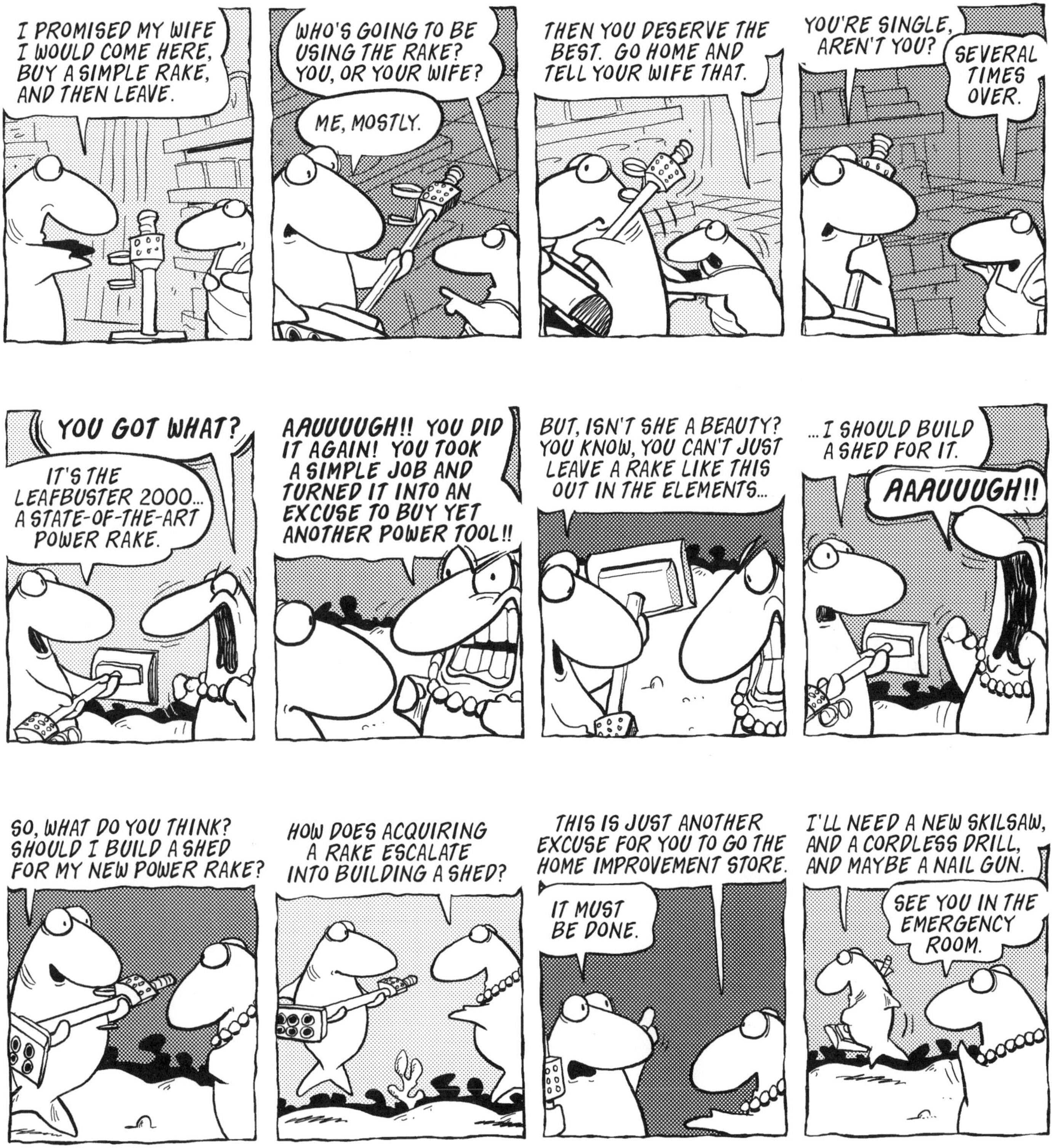
I PROMISED MY WIFE I WOULD COME HERE, BUY A SIMPLE RAKE, AND THEN LEAVE.
WHO'S GOING TO BE USING THE RAKE? YOU, OR YOUR WIFE?
ME, MOSTLY.
THEN YOU DESERVE THE BEST. GO HOME AND TELL YOUR WIFE THAT.
YOU'RE SINGLE, AREN'T YOU?
SEVERAL TIMES OVER.
YOU GOT WHAT?
IT'S THE LEAFBUSTER 2000... A STATE-OF-THE-ART POWER RAKE.
AAUUUUGH!! YOU DID IT AGAIN! YOU TOOK A SIMPLE JOB AND TURNED IT INTO AN EXCUSE TO BUY YET ANOTHER POWER TOOL!!
BUT, ISN'T SHE A BEAUTY? YOU KNOW, YOU CAN'T JUST LEAVE A RAKE LIKE THIS OUT IN THE ELEMENTS...
...I SHOULD BUILD A SHED FOR IT.
AAAUUUGH!!
SO, WHAT DO YOU THINK? SHOULD I BUILD A SHED FOR MY NEW POWER RAKE?
HOW DOES ACQUIRING A RAKE ESCALATE INTO BUILDING A SHED?
THIS IS JUST ANOTHER EXCUSE FOR YOU TO GO THE HOME IMPROVEMENT STORE.
IT MUST BE DONE.
I'LL NEED A NEW SKILSAW, AND A CORDLESS DRILL, AND MAYBE A NAIL GUN.
SEE YOU IN THE EMERGENCY ROOM.

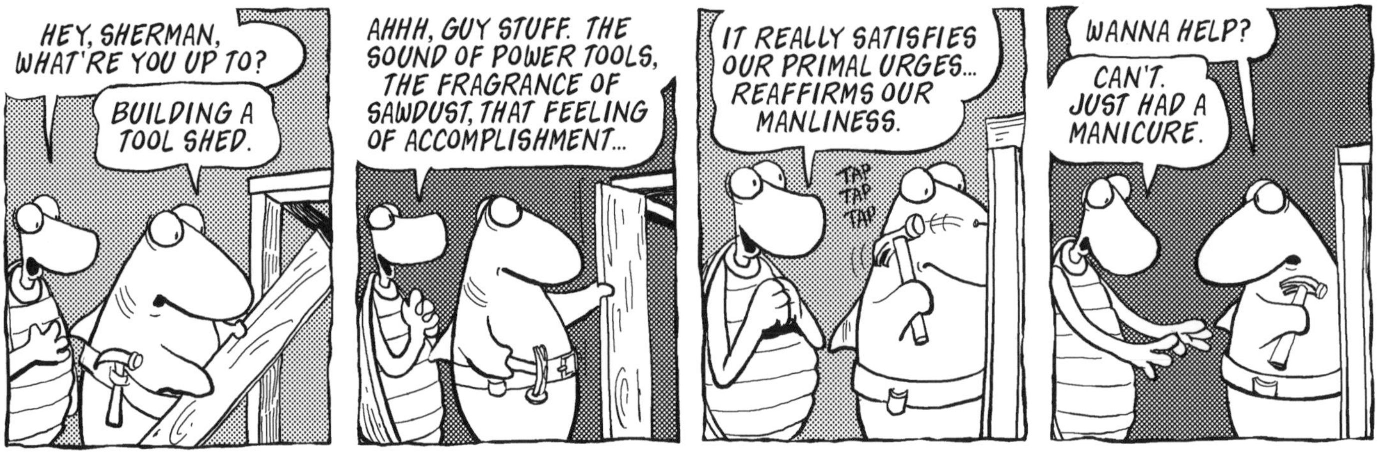
HEY, SHERMAN, WHAT'RE YOU UP TO?
BUILDING A TOOL SHED.
AHHH, GUY STUFF. THE SOUND OF POWER TOOLS, THE FRAGRANCE OF SAWDUST, THAT FEELING OF ACCOMPLISHMENT...
IT REALLY SATISFIES OUR PRIMAL URGES... REAFFIRMS OUR MANLINESS.
TAP TAP TAP
WANNA HELP?
CAN'T. JUST HAD A MANICURE.

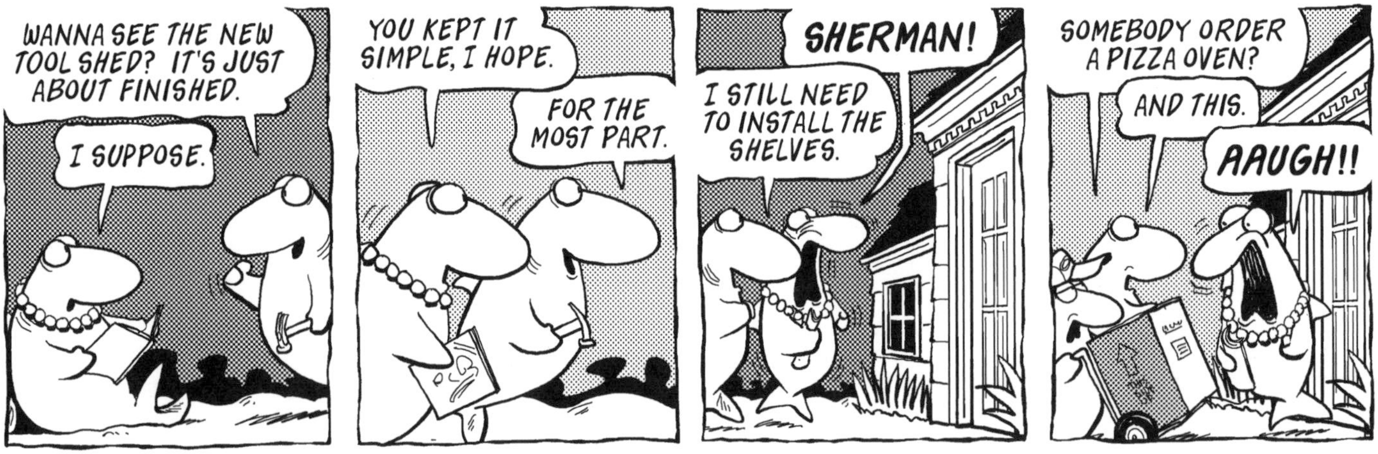
WANNA SEE THE NEW TOOL SHED? IT'S JUST ABOUT FINISHED.
I SUPPOSE.
YOU KEPT IT SIMPLE, I HOPE.
FOR THE MOST PART.
SHERMAN!
I STILL NEED TO INSTALL THE SHELVES.
SOMEBODY ORDER A PIZZA OVEN?
AND THIS.
AAUGH!!

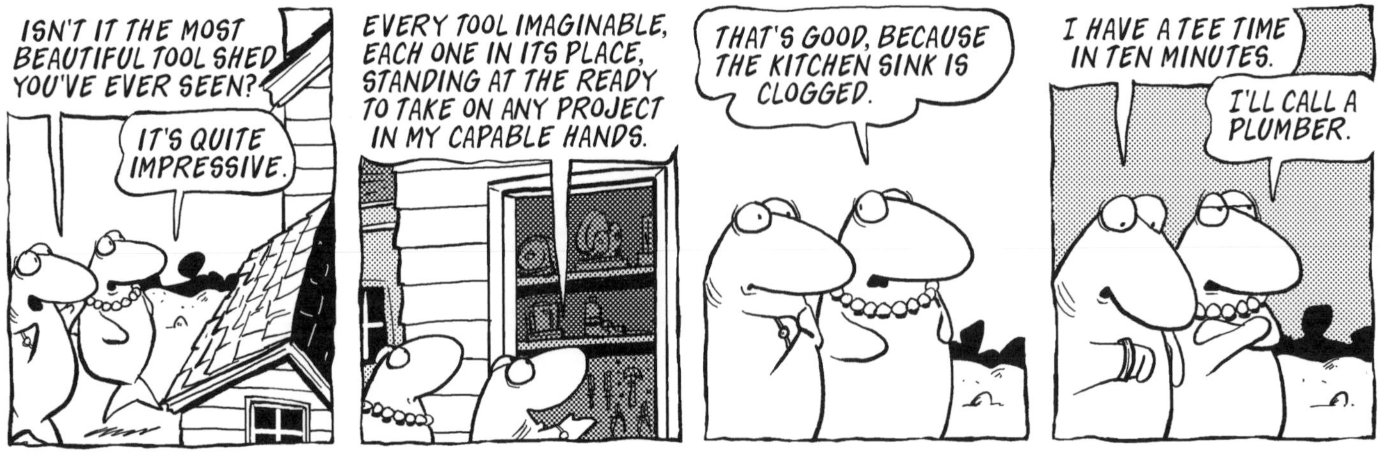
ISN'T IT THE MOST BEAUTIFUL TOOL SHED YOU'VE EVER SEEN?
IT'S QUITE IMPRESSIVE.
EVERY TOOL IMAGINABLE, EACH ONE IN ITS PLACE, STANDING AT THE READY TO TAKE ON ANY PROJECT IN MY CAPABLE HANDS.
THAT'S GOOD, BECAUSE THE KITCHEN SINK IS CLOGGED.
I HAVE A TEE TIME IN TEN MINUTES.
I'LL CALL A PLUMBER.

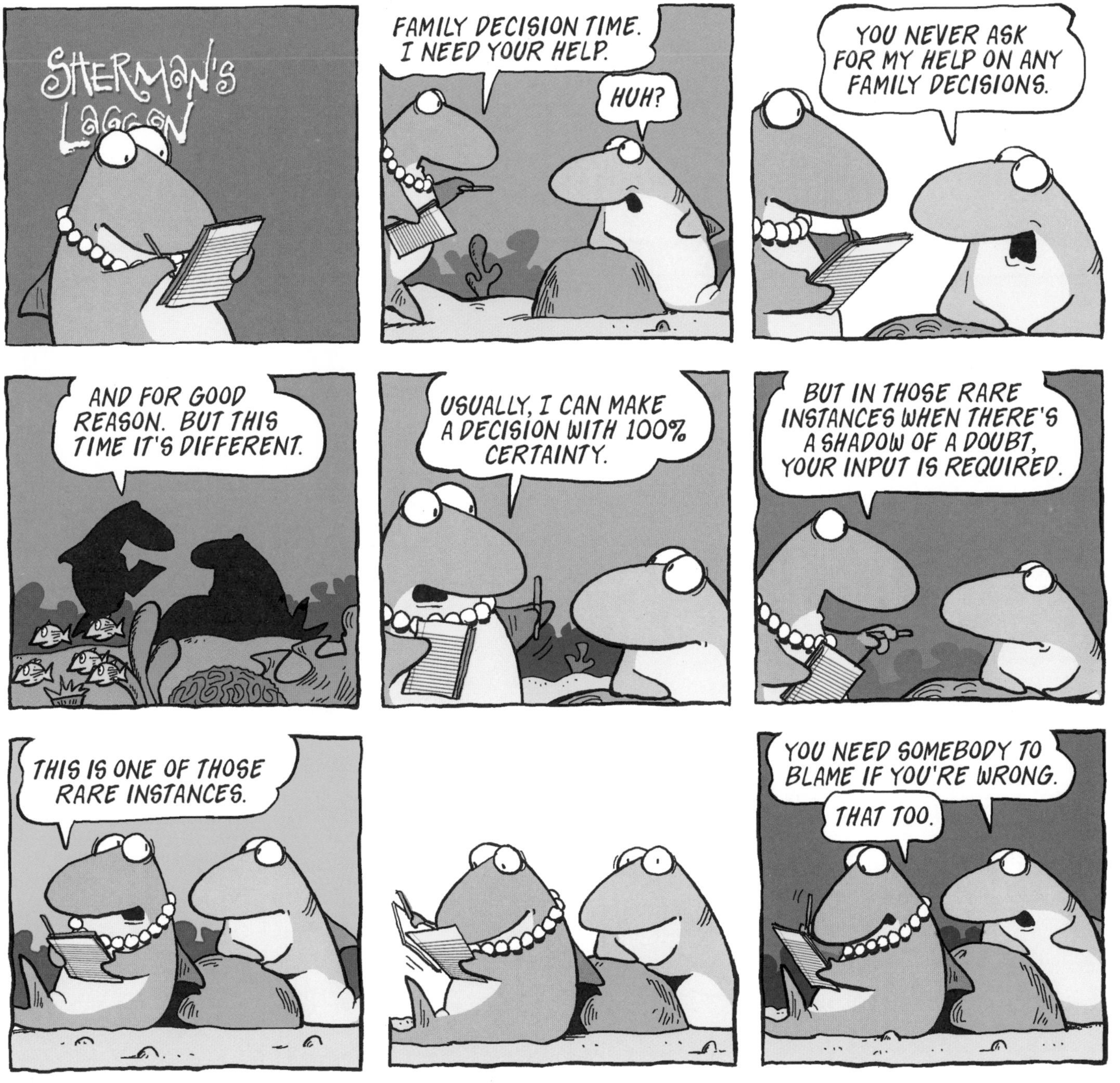
SHERMAN'S LAGOON
FAMILY DECISION TIME. I NEED YOUR HELP.
HUH?
YOU NEVER ASK FOR MY HELP ON ANY FAMILY DECISIONS.
AND FOR GOOD REASON. BUT THIS TIME IT'S DIFFERENT.
USUALLY, I CAN MAKE A DECISION WITH 100% CERTAINTY.
BUT IN THOSE RARE INSTANCES WHEN THERE'S A SHADOW OF A DOUBT, YOUR INPUT IS REQUIRED.
THIS IS ONE OF THOSE RARE INSTANCES.
YOU NEED SOMEBODY TO BLAME IF YOU'RE WRONG.
THAT TOO.

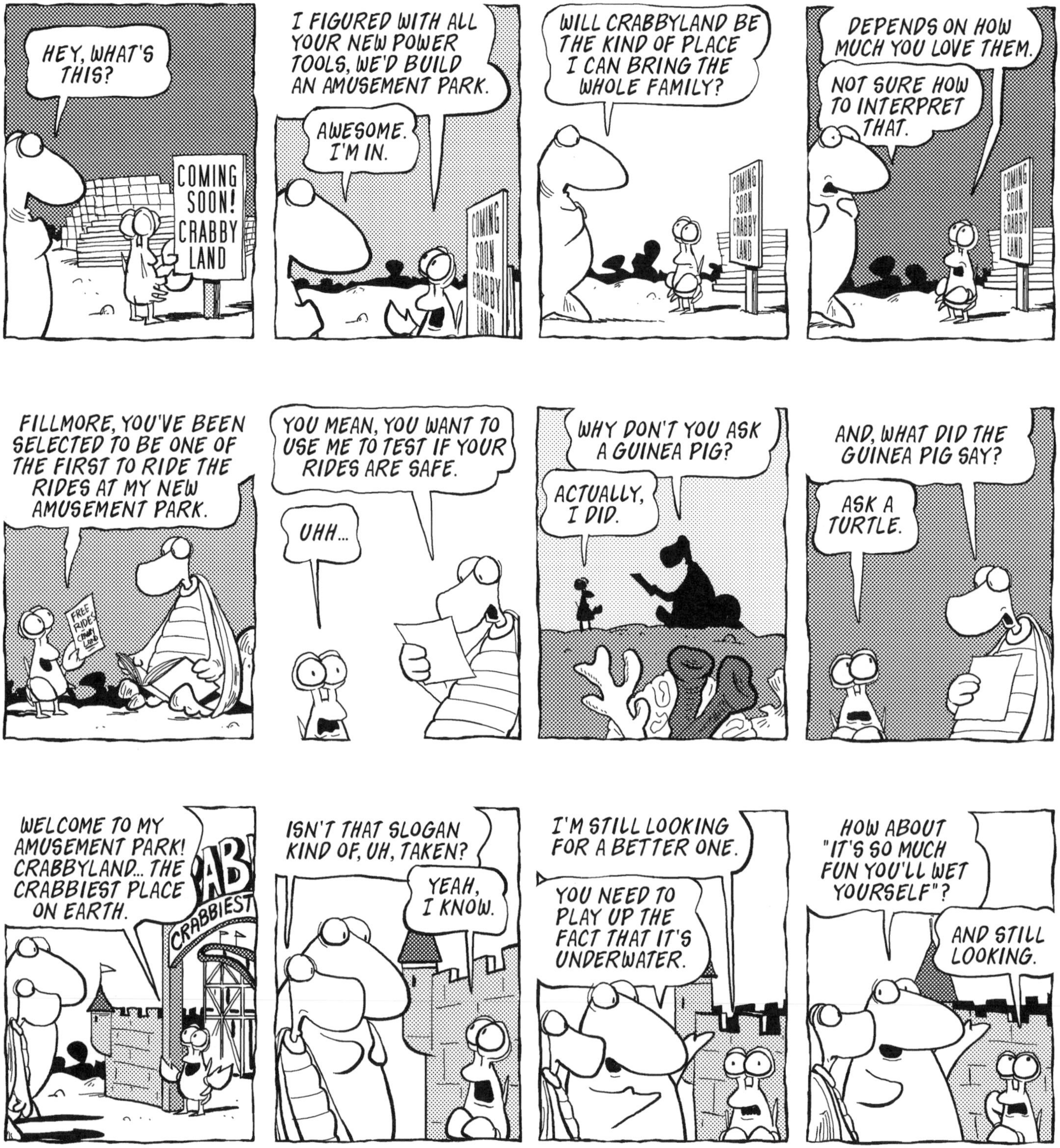
HEY, WHAT'S THIS?
COMING SOON! CRABBY LAND
I FIGURED WITH ALL YOUR NEW POWER TOOLS, WE'D BUILD AN AMUSEMENT PARK.
AWESOME. I'M IN.
COMING SOON CRABBY LAND
WILL CRABBYLAND BE THE KIND OF PLACE I CAN BRING THE WHOLE FAMILY?
COMING SOON CRABBY LAND
DEPENDS ON HOW MUCH YOU LOVE THEM.
NOT SURE HOW TO INTERPRET THAT.
COMING SOON CRABBY LAND
FILLMORE, YOU'VE BEEN SELECTED TO BE ONE OF THE FIRST TO RIDE THE RIDES AT MY NEW AMUSEMENT PARK.
FREE RIDES
YOU MEAN, YOU WANT TO USE ME TO TEST IF YOUR RIDES ARE SAFE.
UHH...
WHY DON'T YOU ASK A GUINEA PIG?
ACTUALLY, I DID.
AND, WHAT DID THE GUINEA PIG SAY?
ASK A TURTLE.
WELCOME TO MY AMUSEMENT PARK! CRABBYLAND... THE CRABBIEST PLACE ON EARTH.
CRABBIEST
ISN'T THAT SLOGAN KIND OF, UH, TAKEN?
YEAH, I KNOW.
I'M STILL LOOKING FOR A BETTER ONE.
YOU NEED TO PLAY UP THE FACT THAT IT'S UNDERWATER.
HOW ABOUT "IT'S SO MUCH FUN YOU'LL WET YOURSELF"?
AND STILL LOOKING.

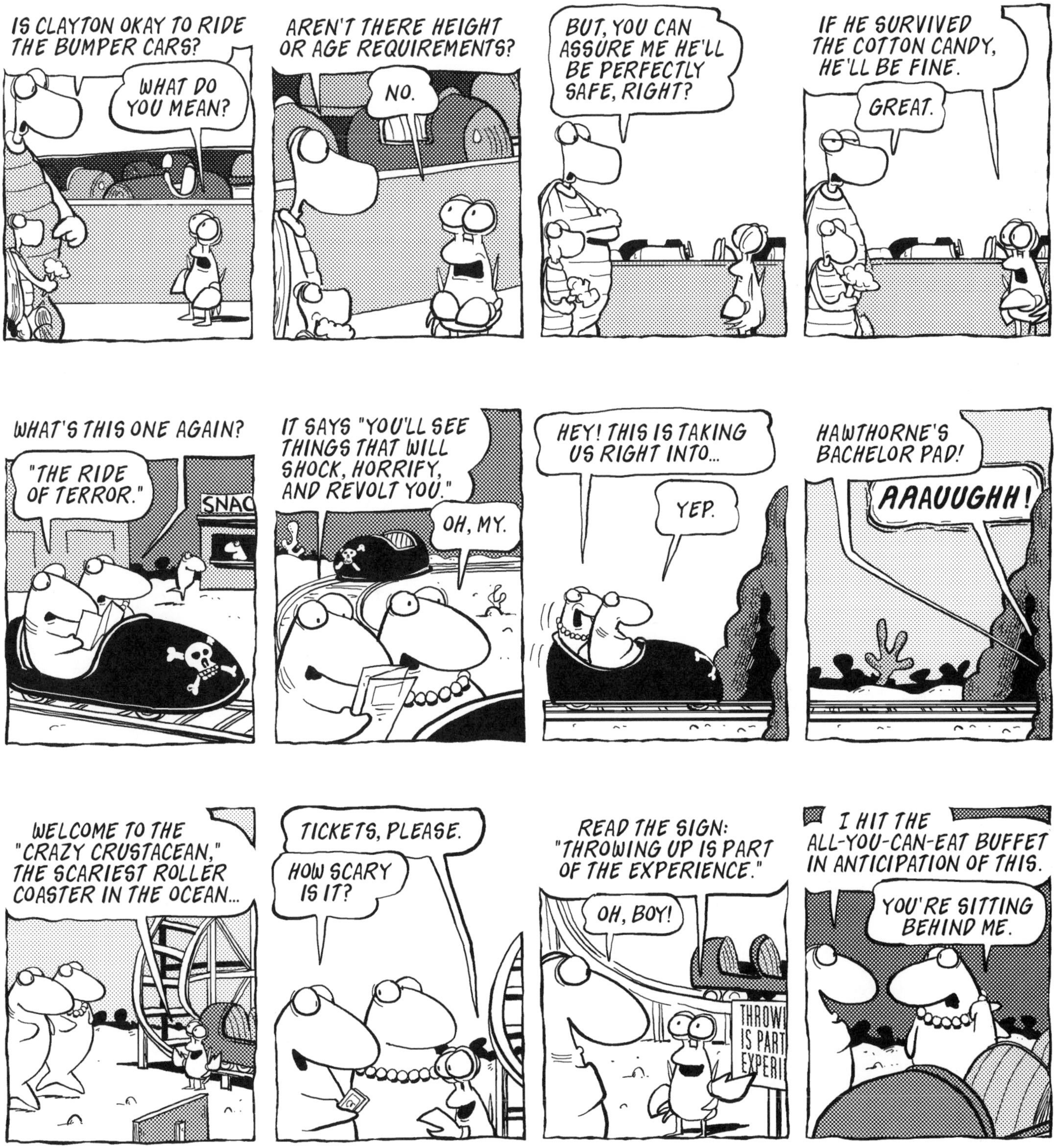
IS CLAYTON OKAY TO RIDE THE BUMPER CARS?
WHAT DO YOU MEAN?
AREN'T THERE HEIGHT OR AGE REQUIREMENTS?
NO.
BUT, YOU CAN ASSURE ME HE'LL BE PERFECTLY SAFE, RIGHT?
IF HE SURVIVED THE COTTON CANDY, HE'LL BE FINE.
GREAT.
WHAT'S THIS ONE AGAIN?
"THE RIDE OF TERROR."
SNAC
IT SAYS "YOU'LL SEE THINGS THAT WILL SHOCK, HORRIFY, AND REVOLT YOU."
OH, MY.
HEY! THIS IS TAKING US RIGHT INTO...
YEP.
HAWTHORNE'S BACHELOR PAD!
AAAUUGHH!
WELCOME TO THE "CRAZY CRUSTACEAN," THE SCARIEST ROLLER COASTER IN THE OCEAN...
TICKETS, PLEASE.
HOW SCARY IS IT?
READ THE SIGN: "THROWING UP IS PART OF THE EXPERIENCE."
OH, BOY!
THROWI IS PART EXPERI
I HIT THE ALL-YOU-CAN-EAT BUFFET IN ANTICIPATION OF THIS.
YOU'RE SITTING BEHIND ME.

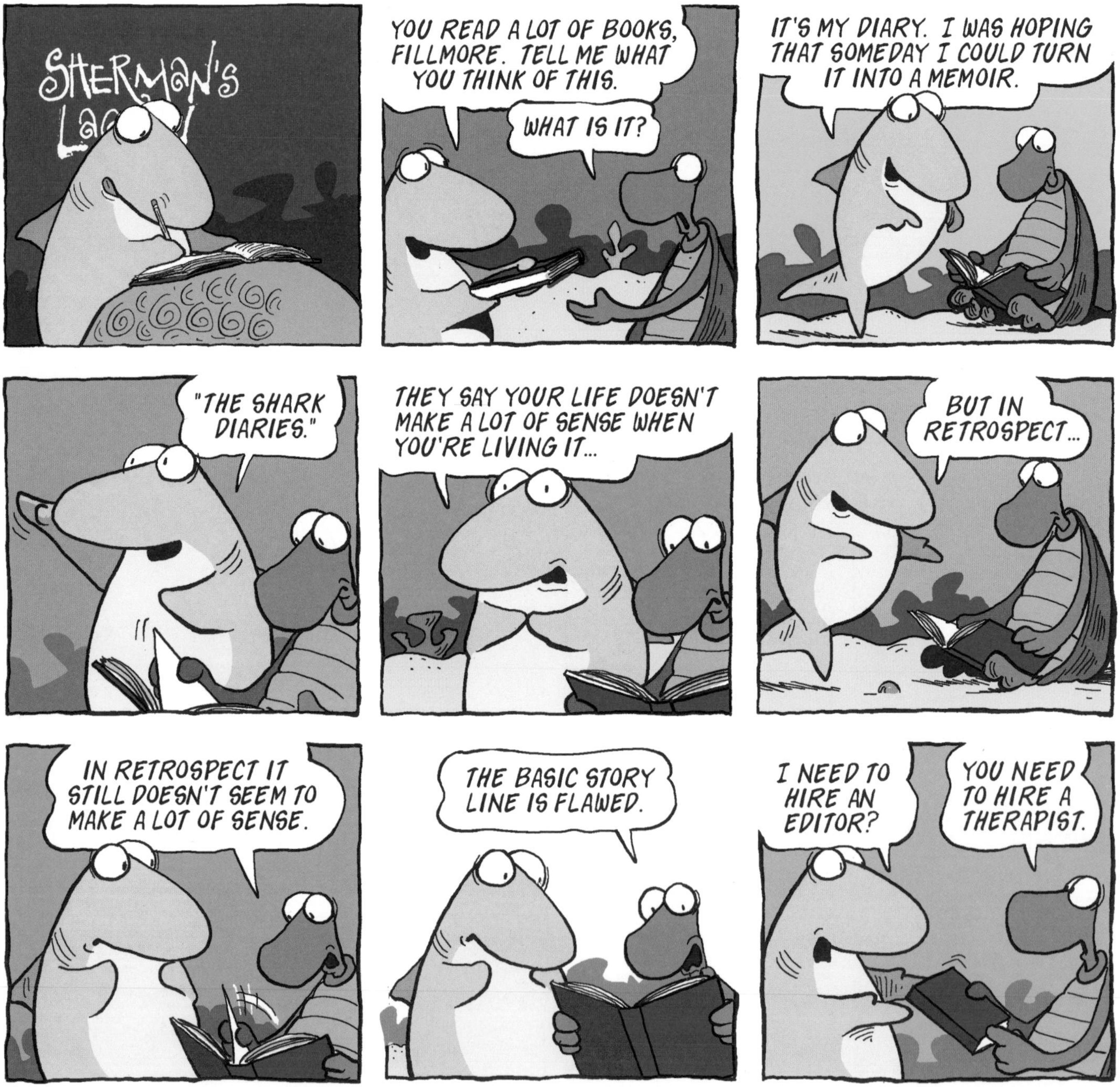
SHERMAN'S LAGOON
YOU READ A LOT OF BOOKS, FILLMORE. TELL ME WHAT YOU THINK OF THIS.
WHAT IS IT?
IT'S MY DIARY. I WAS HOPING THAT SOMEDAY I COULD TURN IT INTO A MEMOIR.
"THE SHARK DIARIES."
THEY SAY YOUR LIFE DOESN'T MAKE A LOT OF SENSE WHEN YOU'RE LIVING IT...
BUT IN RETROSPECT...
IN RETROSPECT IT STILL DOESN'T SEEM TO MAKE A LOT OF SENSE.
THE BASIC STORY LINE IS FLAWED.
I NEED TO HIRE AN EDITOR?
YOU NEED TO HIRE A THERAPIST.

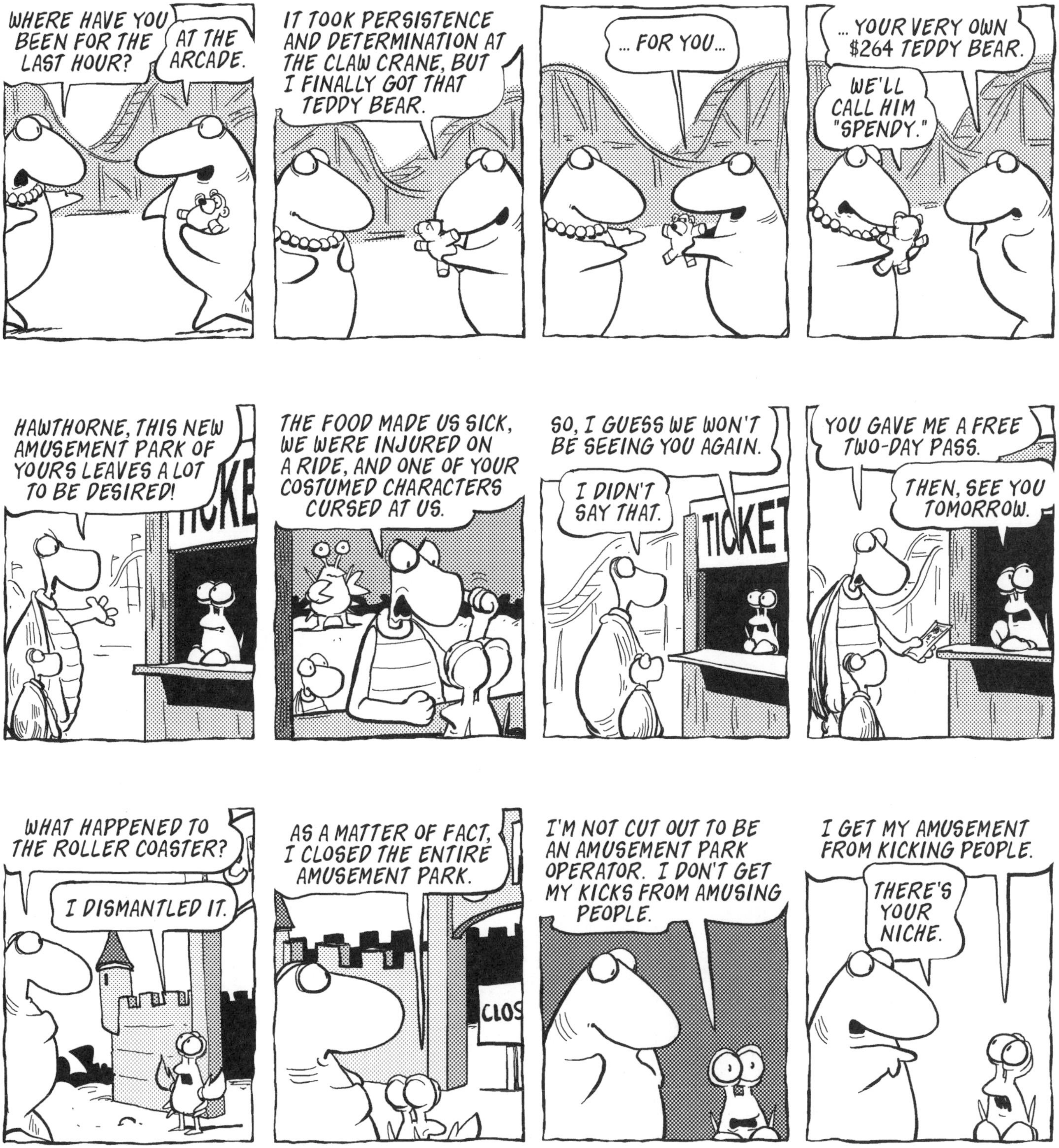
WHERE HAVE YOU BEEN FOR THE LAST HOUR?
AT THE ARCADE.
IT TOOK PERSISTENCE AND DETERMINATION AT THE CLAW CRANE, BUT I FINALLY GOT THAT TEDDY BEAR.
... FOR YOU...
... YOUR VERY OWN $264 TEDDY BEAR.
WE'LL CALL HIM "SPENDY."
HAWTHORNE, THIS NEW AMUSEMENT PARK OF YOURS LEAVES A LOT TO BE DESIRED!
TICKE
THE FOOD MADE US SICK, WE WERE INJURED ON A RIDE, AND ONE OF YOUR COSTUMED CHARACTERS CURSED AT US.
SO, I GUESS WE WON'T BE SEEING YOU AGAIN.
I DIDN'T SAY THAT.
TICKET
YOU GAVE ME A FREE TWO-DAY PASS.
THEN, SEE YOU TOMORROW.
WHAT HAPPENED TO THE ROLLER COASTER?
I DISMANTLED IT.
AS A MATTER OF FACT, I CLOSED THE ENTIRE AMUSEMENT PARK.
CLOS
I'M NOT CUT OUT TO BE AN AMUSEMENT PARK OPERATOR. I DON'T GET MY KICKS FROM AMUSING PEOPLE.
I GET MY AMUSEMENT FROM KICKING PEOPLE.
THERE'S YOUR NICHE.

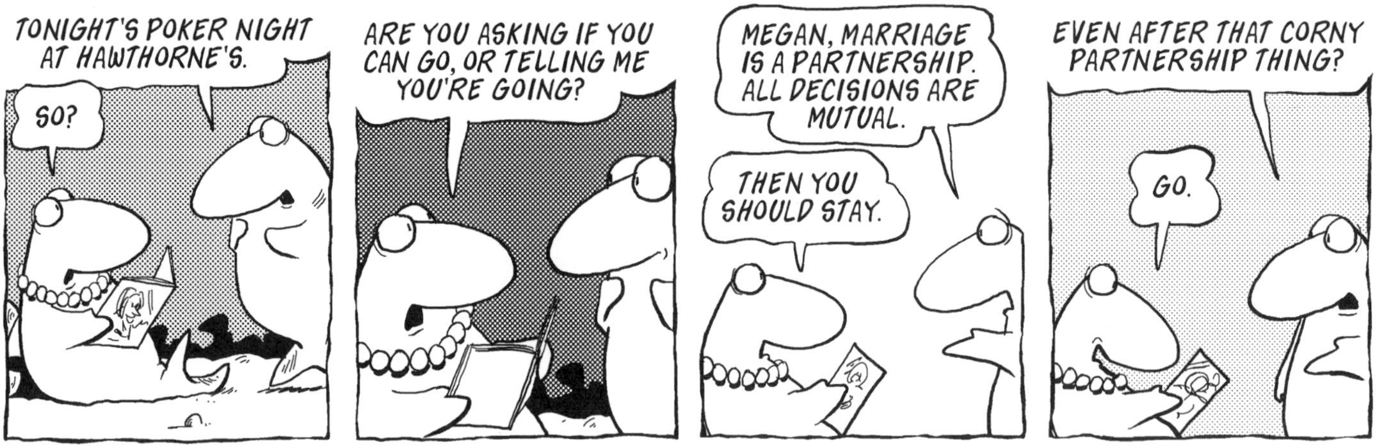
TONIGHT'S POKER NIGHT AT HAWTHORNE'S.
SO?
ARE YOU ASKING IF YOU CAN GO, OR TELLING ME YOU'RE GOING?
MEGAN, MARRIAGE IS A PARTNERSHIP. ALL DECISIONS ARE MUTUAL.
THEN YOU SHOULD STAY.
EVEN AFTER THAT CORNY PARTNERSHIP THING?
GO.

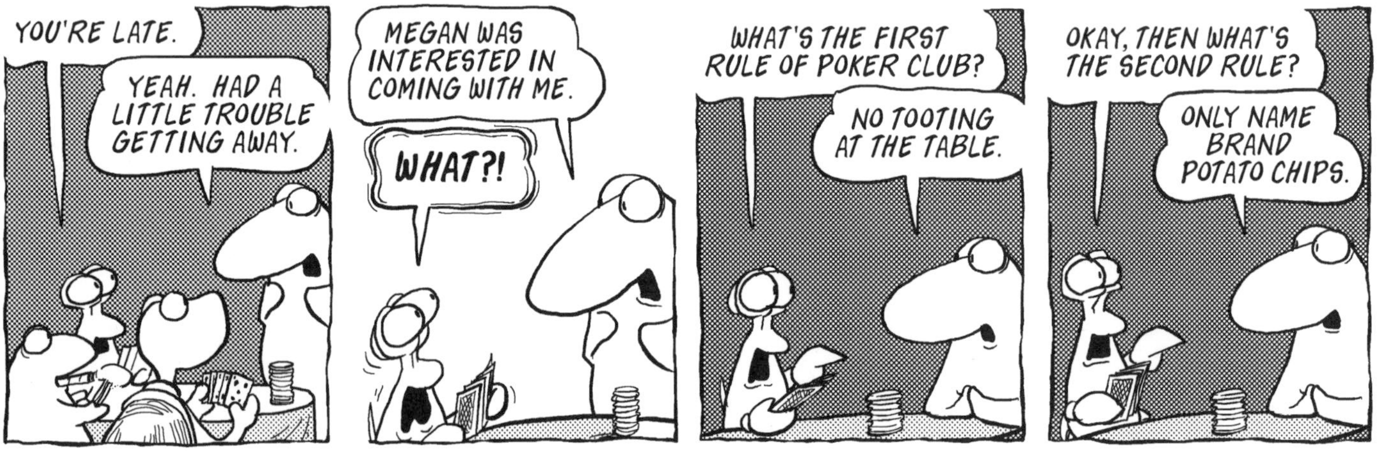
YOU'RE LATE.
YEAH. HAD A LITTLE TROUBLE GETTING AWAY.
MEGAN WAS INTERESTED IN COMING WITH ME.
WHAT?!
WHAT'S THE FIRST RULE OF POKER CLUB?
NO TOOTING AT THE TABLE.
OKAY, THEN WHAT'S THE SECOND RULE?
ONLY NAME BRAND POTATO CHIPS.

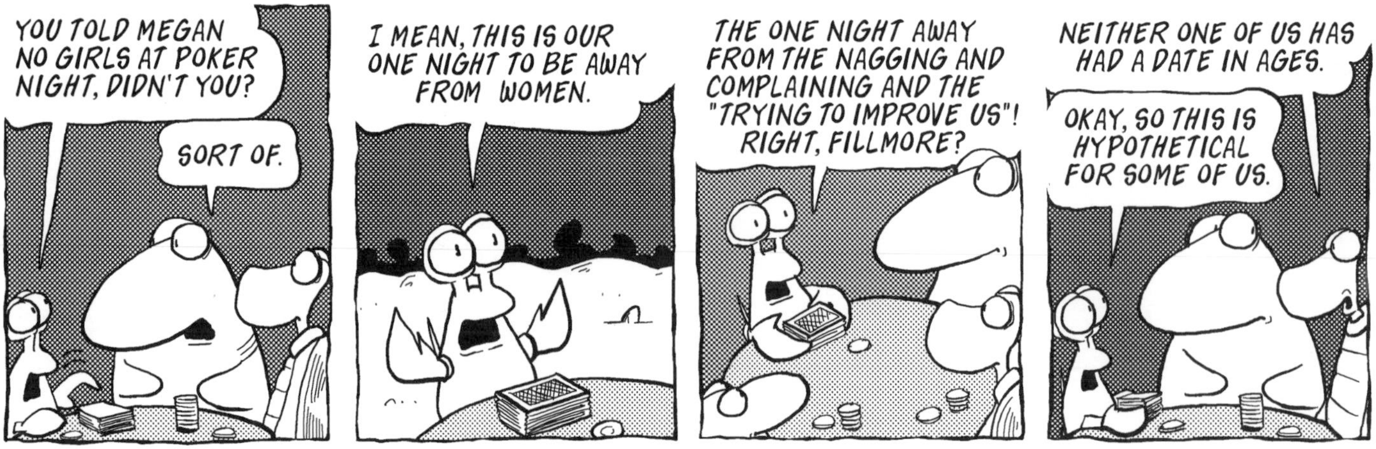
YOU TOLD MEGAN NO GIRLS AT POKER NIGHT, DIDN'T YOU?
SORT OF.
I MEAN, THIS IS OUR ONE NIGHT TO BE AWAY FROM WOMEN.
THE ONE NIGHT AWAY FROM THE NAGGING AND COMPLAINING AND THE "TRYING TO IMPROVE US"! RIGHT, FILLMORE?
NEITHER ONE OF US HAS HAD A DATE IN AGES.
OKAY, SO THIS IS HYPOTHETICAL FOR SOME OF US.

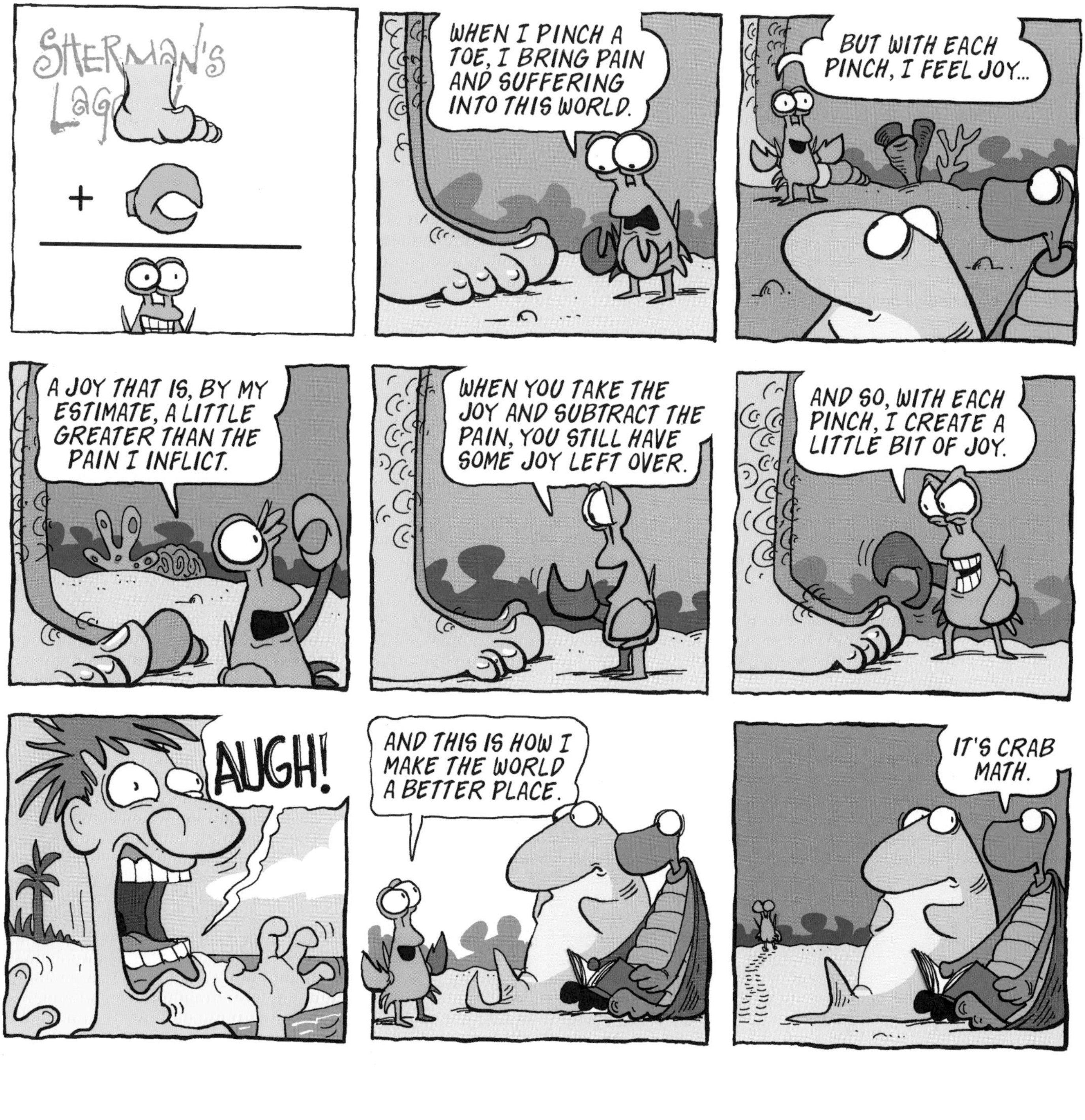
SHERMAN'S LAGOON
WHEN I PINCH A TOE, I BRING PAIN AND SUFFERING INTO THIS WORLD.
BUT WITH EACH PINCH, I FEEL JOY...
A JOY THAT IS, BY MY ESTIMATE, A LITTLE GREATER THAN THE PAIN I INFLICT.
WHEN YOU TAKE THE JOY AND SUBTRACT THE PAIN, YOU STILL HAVE SOME JOY LEFT OVER.
AND SO, WITH EACH PINCH, I CREATE A LITTLE BIT OF JOY.
AUGH!
AND THIS IS HOW I MAKE THE WORLD A BETTER PLACE.
IT'S CRAB MATH.

YOU KNOW, MY WIFE MENTIONED WANTING TO COME TO POKER NIGHT, ALSO.

NATHAN, YOU TOO?

'FRAID SO.

WELL, MAYBE WE SHOULD CONSIDER IT.

LET THEM GET A TASTE OF WHAT IT'S LIKE TO PLAY A ROUGH-AND-TUMBLE, CUT-THROAT POKER GAME WITH THE BOYS.

QUICHE SQUARE?

LOVELY.

HEY, WHAT'S THIS?

I'M ORGANIZING A POKER TOURNAMENT.

Lagoon Hold 'Em Tournament
SIGN UP HERE

THIS WAY, THE WIVES AND GIRLFRIENDS CAN PLAY, AND SEE JUST HOW DIFFICULT POKER IS.

oon Hold 'E

"LAGOON HOLD 'EM"? DON'T WE USUALLY PLAY "TEXAS HOLD 'EM."

Lagoon Hold 'Em Tournament

THIS CAN'T BE GOOGLED. GIVES ME MORE WIGGLE ROOM ON THE RULES.

GOTCHA.

Lagoon Hold 'Er Tournament

WELCOME TO THE FIRST LAGOON POKER TOURNAMENT.

I KNOW SOME OF YOU LADIES MIGHT BE UNFAMILIAR WITH ALL THE INTRICACIES OF THE GAME...

SO, LET ME START WITH A BASIC OVERVIEW OF THE 52-CARD DECK...

THIS IS A JACK. I DON'T KNOW HIS LAST NAME - DON'T ASK.

OH, BOY.

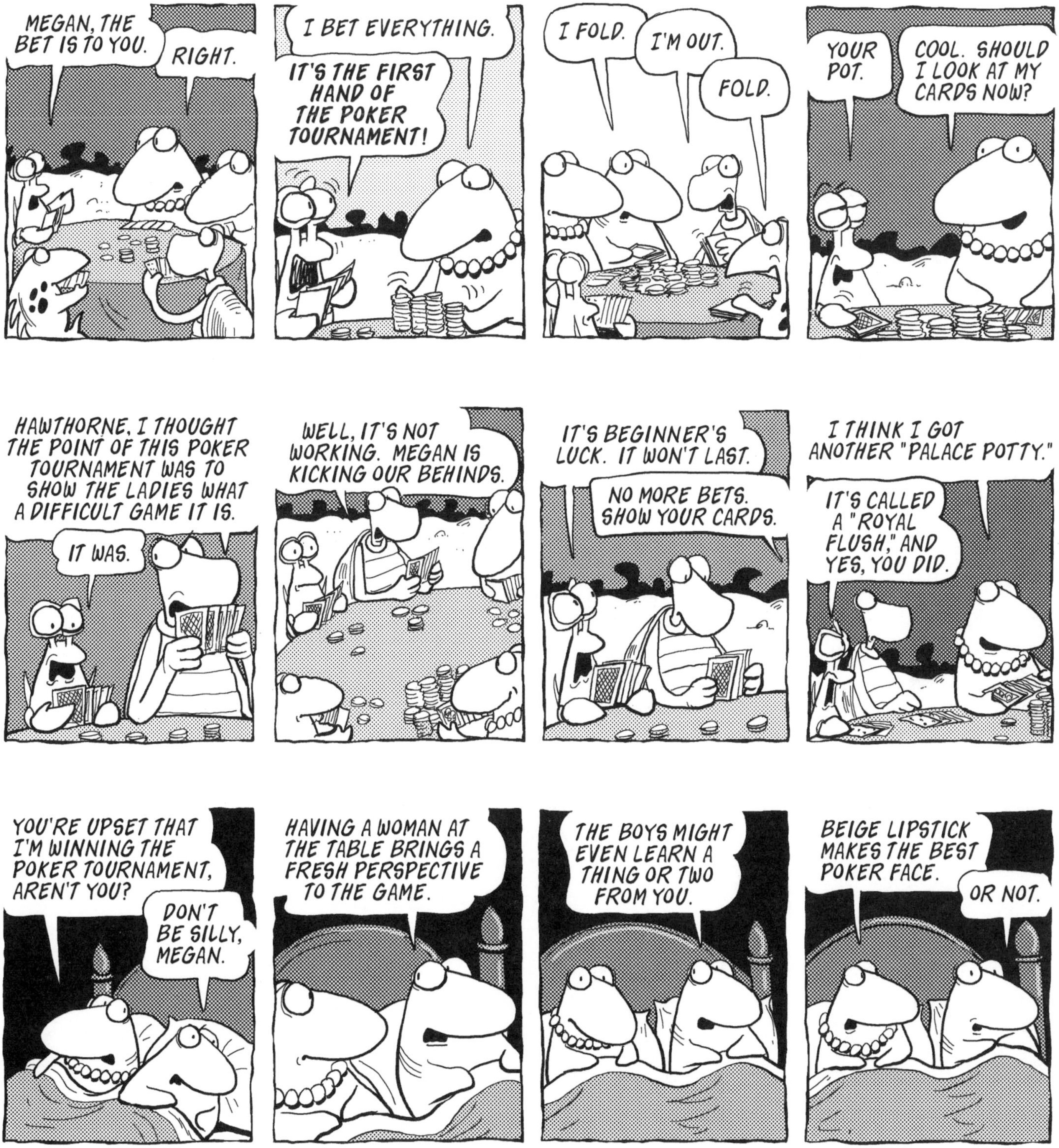
MEGAN, THE BET IS TO YOU.
RIGHT.
I BET EVERYTHING.
IT'S THE FIRST HAND OF THE POKER TOURNAMENT!
I FOLD.
I'M OUT.
FOLD.
YOUR POT.
COOL. SHOULD I LOOK AT MY CARDS NOW?
HAWTHORNE, I THOUGHT THE POINT OF THIS POKER TOURNAMENT WAS TO SHOW THE LADIES WHAT A DIFFICULT GAME IT IS.
IT WAS.
WELL, IT'S NOT WORKING. MEGAN IS KICKING OUR BEHINDS.
IT'S BEGINNER'S LUCK. IT WON'T LAST.
NO MORE BETS. SHOW YOUR CARDS.
I THINK I GOT ANOTHER "PALACE POTTY."
IT'S CALLED A "ROYAL FLUSH," AND YES, YOU DID.
YOU'RE UPSET THAT I'M WINNING THE POKER TOURNAMENT, AREN'T YOU?
DON'T BE SILLY, MEGAN.
HAVING A WOMAN AT THE TABLE BRINGS A FRESH PERSPECTIVE TO THE GAME.
THE BOYS MIGHT EVEN LEARN A THING OR TWO FROM YOU.
BEIGE LIPSTICK MAKES THE BEST POKER FACE.
OR NOT.

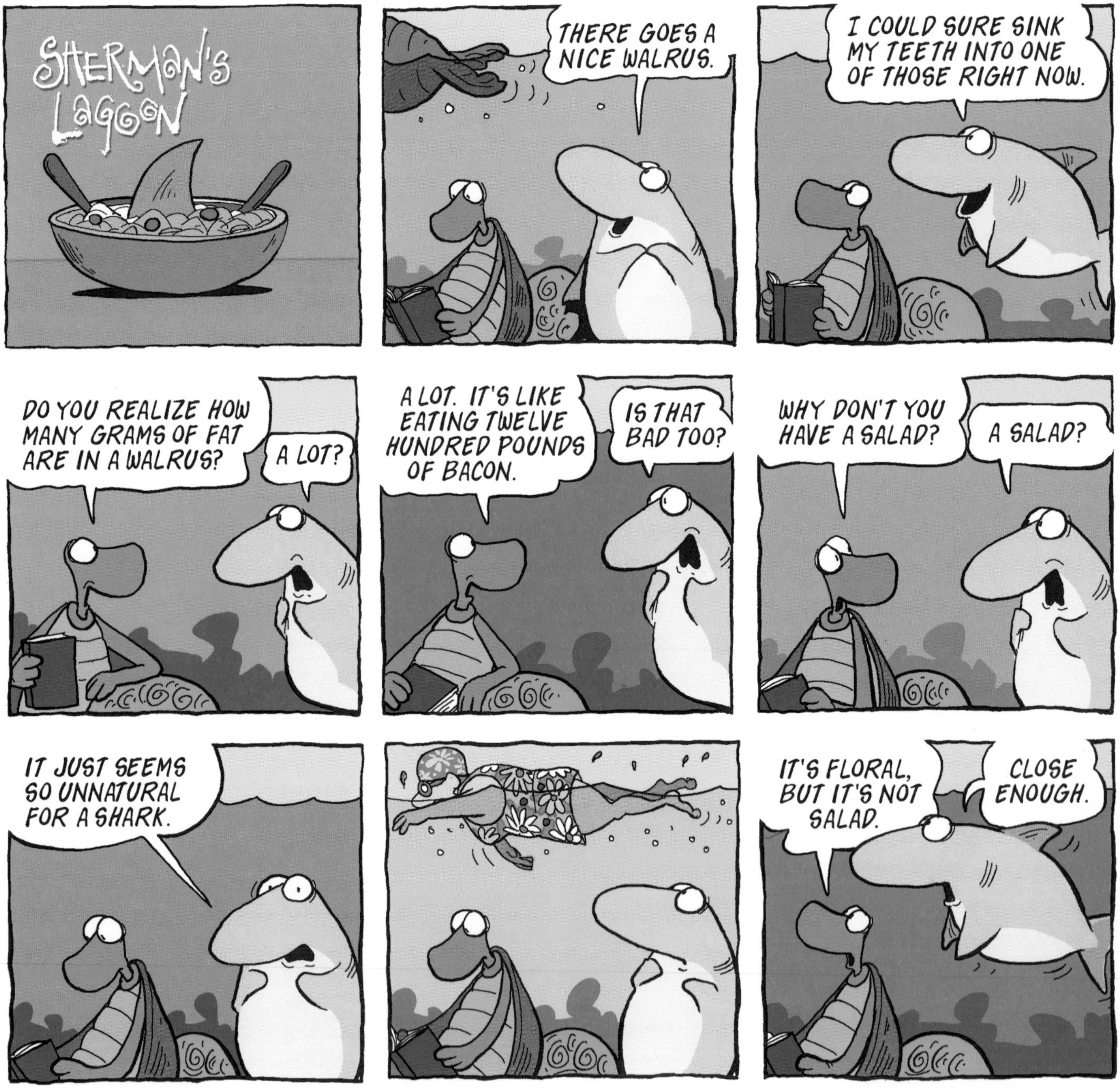
SHERMAN'S LAGOON
THERE GOES A NICE WALRUS.
I COULD SURE SINK MY TEETH INTO ONE OF THOSE RIGHT NOW.
DO YOU REALIZE HOW MANY GRAMS OF FAT ARE IN A WALRUS?
A LOT?
A LOT. IT'S LIKE EATING TWELVE HUNDRED POUNDS OF BACON.
IS THAT BAD TOO?
WHY DON'T YOU HAVE A SALAD?
A SALAD?
IT JUST SEEMS SO UNNATURAL FOR A SHARK.
IT'S FLORAL, BUT IT'S NOT SALAD.
CLOSE ENOUGH.

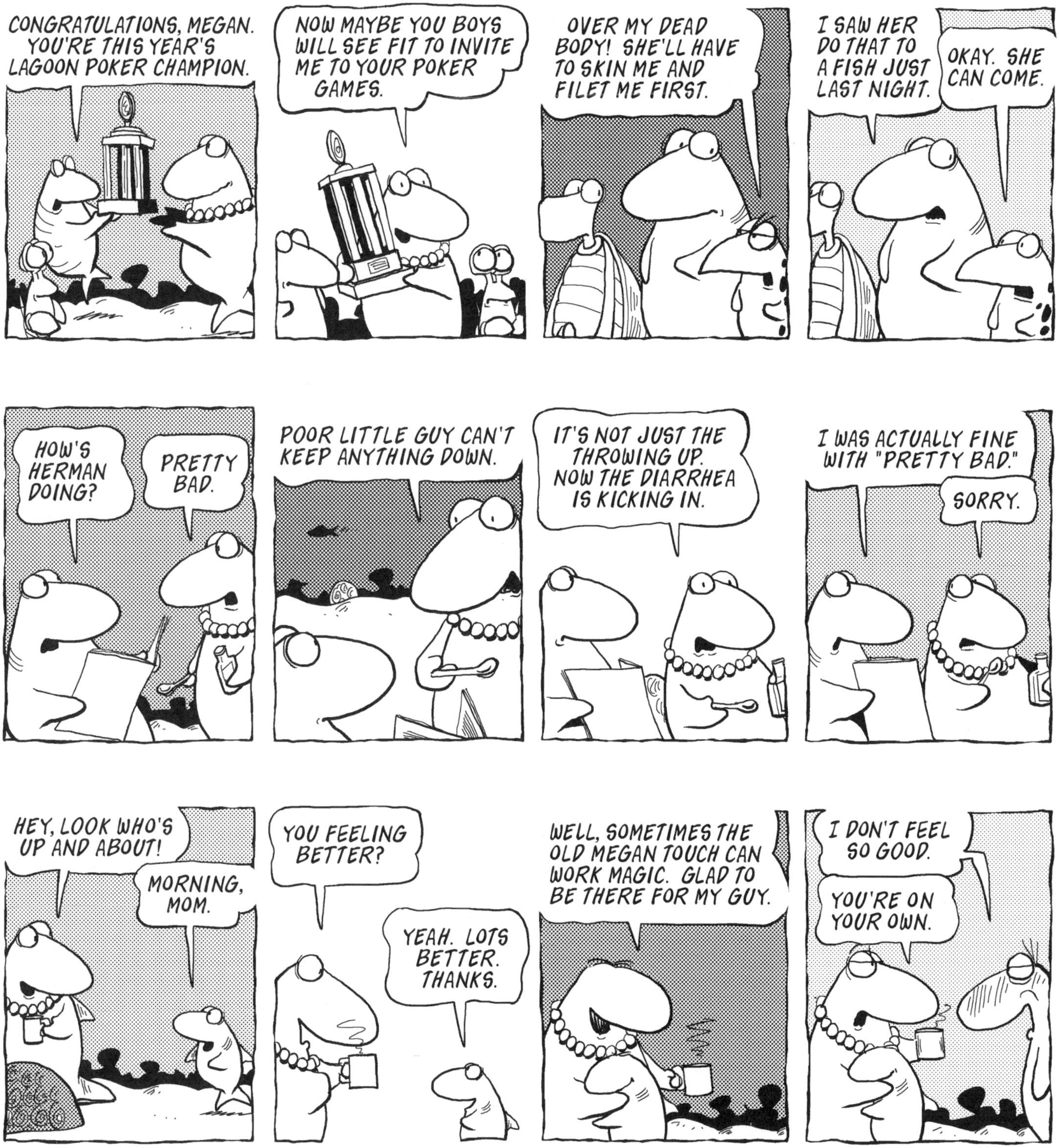
CONGRATULATIONS, MEGAN. YOU'RE THIS YEAR'S LAGOON POKER CHAMPION.
NOW MAYBE YOU BOYS WILL SEE FIT TO INVITE ME TO YOUR POKER GAMES.
OVER MY DEAD BODY! SHE'LL HAVE TO SKIN ME AND FILET ME FIRST.
I SAW HER DO THAT TO A FISH JUST LAST NIGHT.
OKAY. SHE CAN COME.
HOW'S HERMAN DOING?
PRETTY BAD.
POOR LITTLE GUY CAN'T KEEP ANYTHING DOWN.
IT'S NOT JUST THE THROWING UP. NOW THE DIARRHEA IS KICKING IN.
I WAS ACTUALLY FINE WITH "PRETTY BAD."
SORRY.
HEY, LOOK WHO'S UP AND ABOUT!
MORNING, MOM.
YOU FEELING BETTER?
YEAH. LOTS BETTER. THANKS.
WELL, SOMETIMES THE OLD MEGAN TOUCH CAN WORK MAGIC. GLAD TO BE THERE FOR MY GUY.
I DON'T FEEL SO GOOD.
YOU'RE ON YOUR OWN.

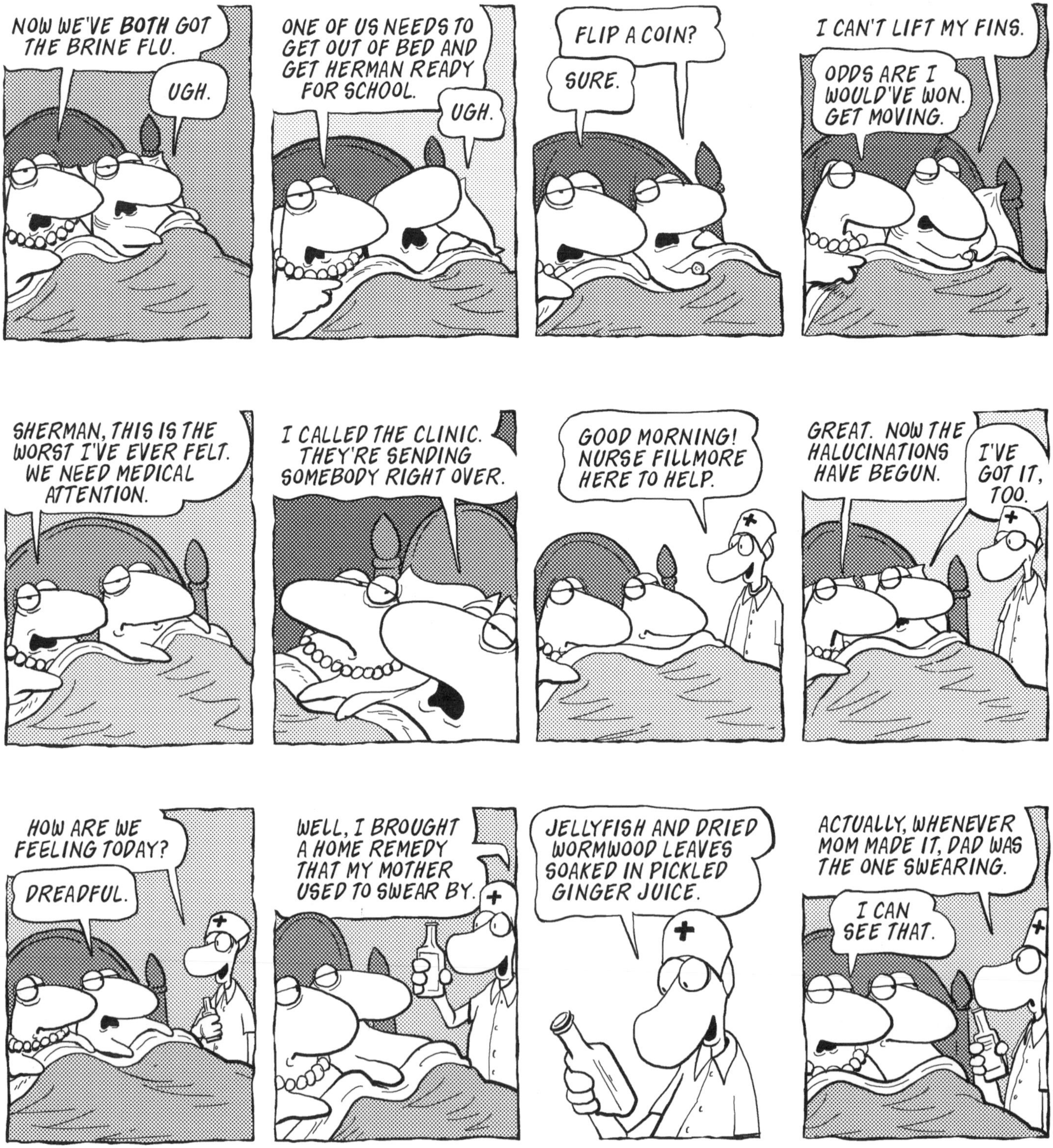
NOW WE'VE BOTH GOT THE BRINE FLU.
UGH.
ONE OF US NEEDS TO GET OUT OF BED AND GET HERMAN READY FOR SCHOOL.
UGH.
FLIP A COIN?
SURE.
I CAN'T LIFT MY FINS.
ODDS ARE I WOULD'VE WON. GET MOVING.
SHERMAN, THIS IS THE WORST I'VE EVER FELT. WE NEED MEDICAL ATTENTION.
I CALLED THE CLINIC. THEY'RE SENDING SOMEBODY RIGHT OVER.
GOOD MORNING! NURSE FILLMORE HERE TO HELP.
GREAT. NOW THE HALUCINATIONS HAVE BEGUN.
I'VE GOT IT, TOO.
HOW ARE WE FEELING TODAY?
DREADFUL.
WELL, I BROUGHT A HOME REMEDY THAT MY MOTHER USED TO SWEAR BY.
JELLYFISH AND DRIED WORMWOOD LEAVES SOAKED IN PICKLED GINGER JUICE.
ACTUALLY, WHENEVER MOM MADE IT, DAD WAS THE ONE SWEARING.
I CAN SEE THAT.

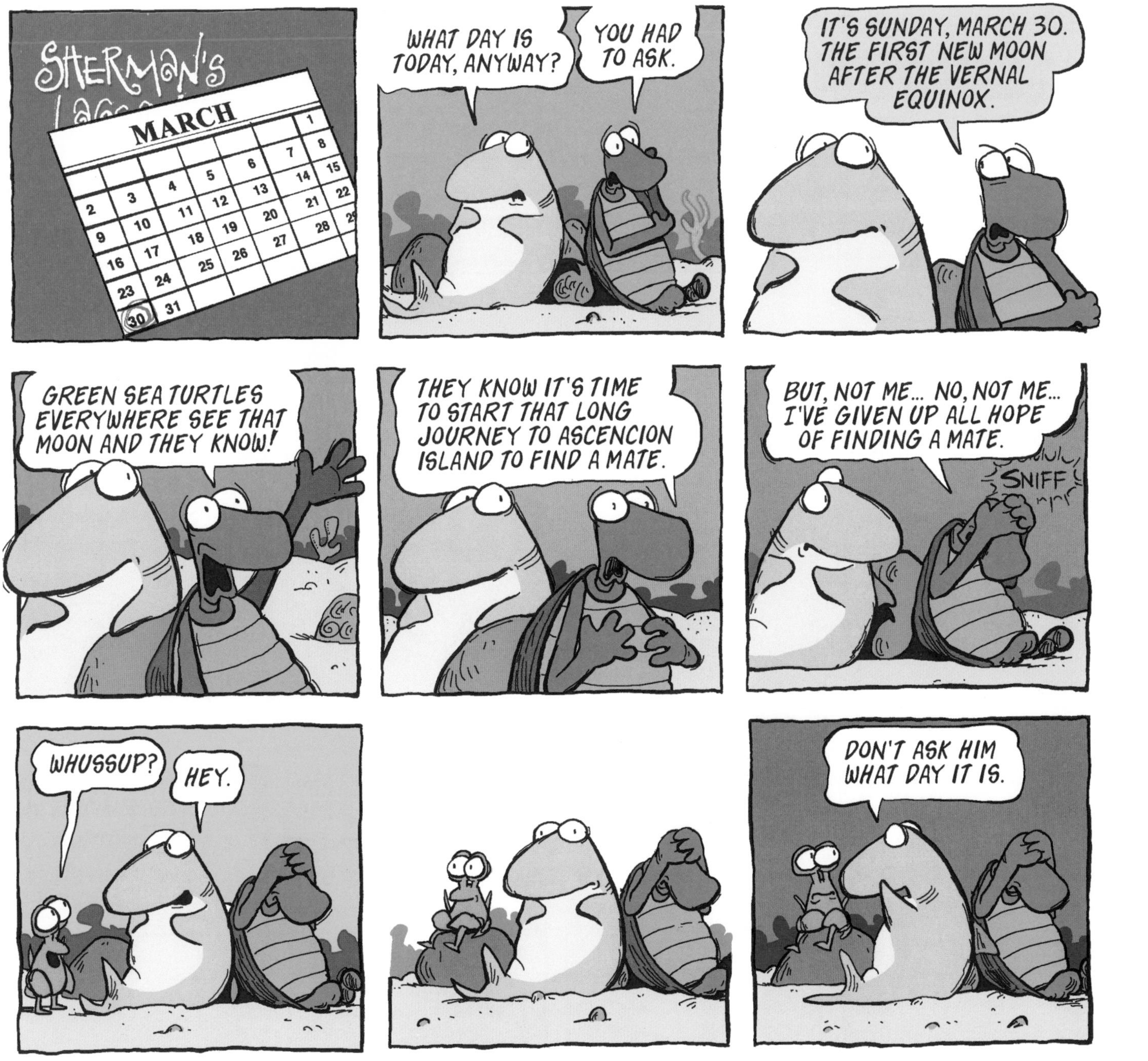
SHERMAN'S
MARCH
WHAT DAY IS TODAY, ANYWAY?
YOU HAD TO ASK.
IT'S SUNDAY, MARCH 30. THE FIRST NEW MOON AFTER THE VERNAL EQUINOX.
GREEN SEA TURTLES EVERYWHERE SEE THAT MOON AND THEY KNOW!
THEY KNOW IT'S TIME TO START THAT LONG JOURNEY TO ASCENCION ISLAND TO FIND A MATE.
BUT, NOT ME... NO, NOT ME... I'VE GIVEN UP ALL HOPE OF FINDING A MATE.
SNIFF
WHUSSUP?
HEY.
DON'T ASK HIM WHAT DAY IT IS.

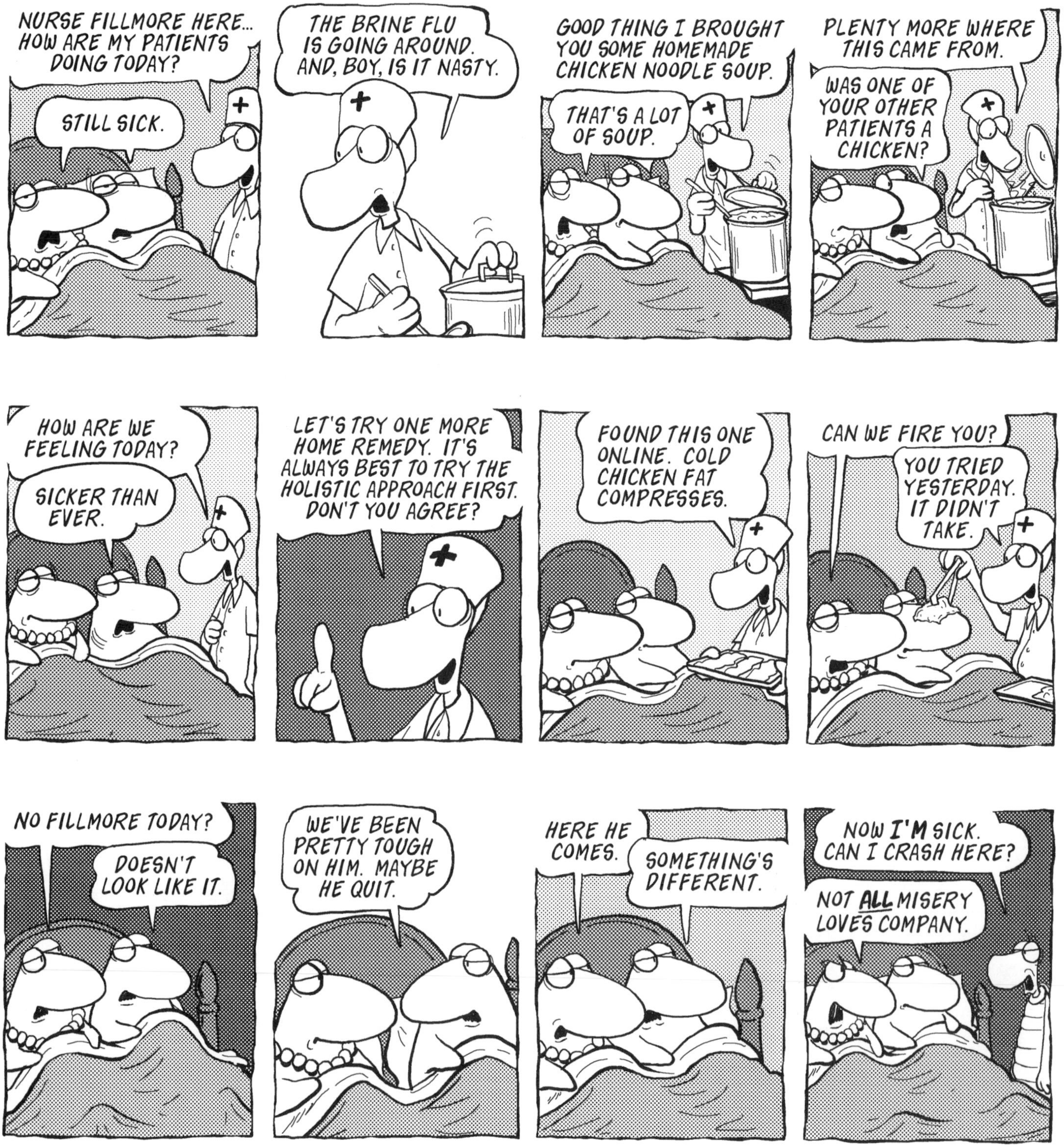
NURSE FILLMORE HERE... HOW ARE MY PATIENTS DOING TODAY?
STILL SICK.
THE BRINE FLU IS GOING AROUND. AND, BOY, IS IT NASTY.
GOOD THING I BROUGHT YOU SOME HOMEMADE CHICKEN NOODLE SOUP.
THAT'S A LOT OF SOUP.
PLENTY MORE WHERE THIS CAME FROM.
WAS ONE OF YOUR OTHER PATIENTS A CHICKEN?
HOW ARE WE FEELING TODAY?
SICKER THAN EVER.
LET'S TRY ONE MORE HOME REMEDY. IT'S ALWAYS BEST TO TRY THE HOLISTIC APPROACH FIRST. DON'T YOU AGREE?
FOUND THIS ONE ONLINE. COLD CHICKEN FAT COMPRESSES.
CAN WE FIRE YOU?
YOU TRIED YESTERDAY. IT DIDN'T TAKE.
NO FILLMORE TODAY?
DOESN'T LOOK LIKE IT.
WE'VE BEEN PRETTY TOUGH ON HIM. MAYBE HE QUIT.
HERE HE COMES.
SOMETHING'S DIFFERENT.
NOW I'M SICK. CAN I CRASH HERE?
NOT ALL MISERY LOVES COMPANY.

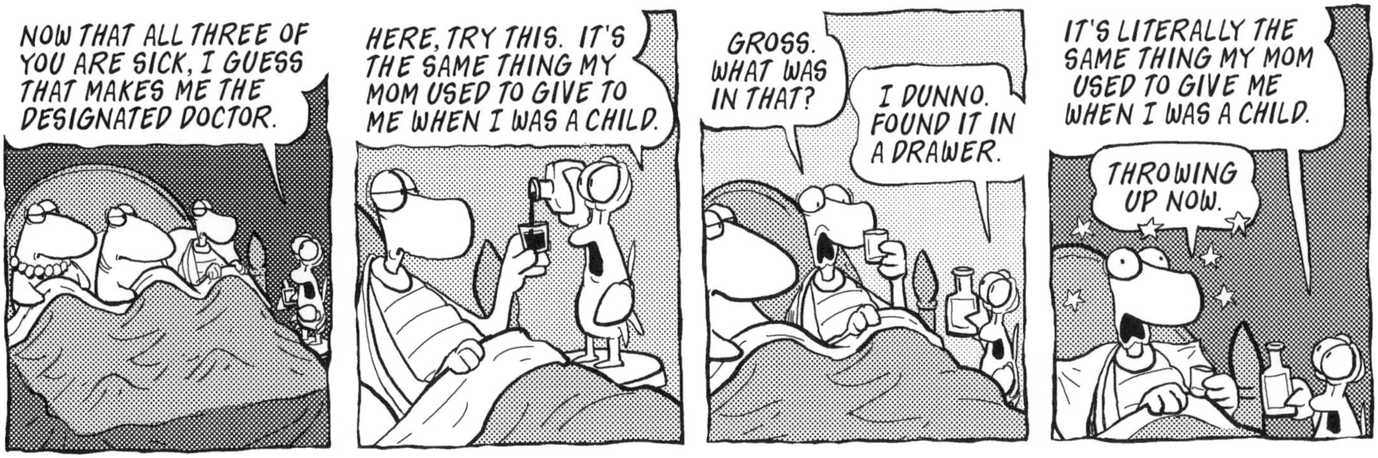

NOW THAT ALL THREE OF YOU ARE SICK, I GUESS THAT MAKES ME THE DESIGNATED DOCTOR.
HERE, TRY THIS. IT'S THE SAME THING MY MOM USED TO GIVE TO ME WHEN I WAS A CHILD.
GROSS. WHAT WAS IN THAT?
I DUNNO. FOUND IT IN A DRAWER.
IT'S LITERALLY THE SAME THING MY MOM USED TO GIVE ME WHEN I WAS A CHILD.
THROWING UP NOW.

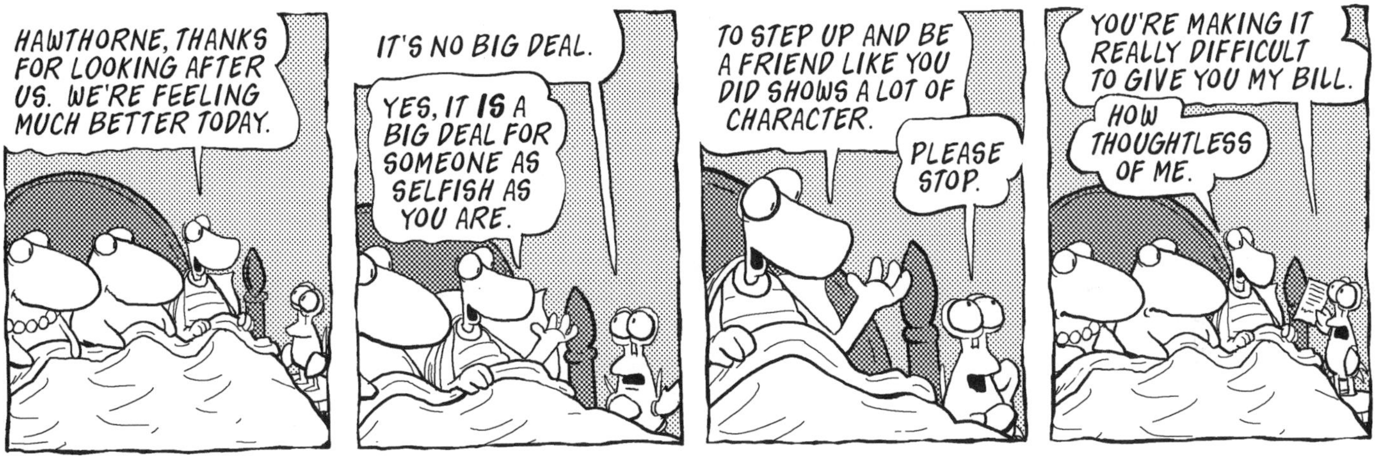

HAWTHORNE, THANKS FOR LOOKING AFTER US. WE'RE FEELING MUCH BETTER TODAY.
IT'S NO BIG DEAL.
YES, IT **IS** A BIG DEAL FOR SOMEONE AS SELFISH AS YOU ARE.
TO STEP UP AND BE A FRIEND LIKE YOU DID SHOWS A LOT OF CHARACTER.
PLEASE STOP.
YOU'RE MAKING IT REALLY DIFFICULT TO GIVE YOU MY BILL.
HOW THOUGHTLESS OF ME.

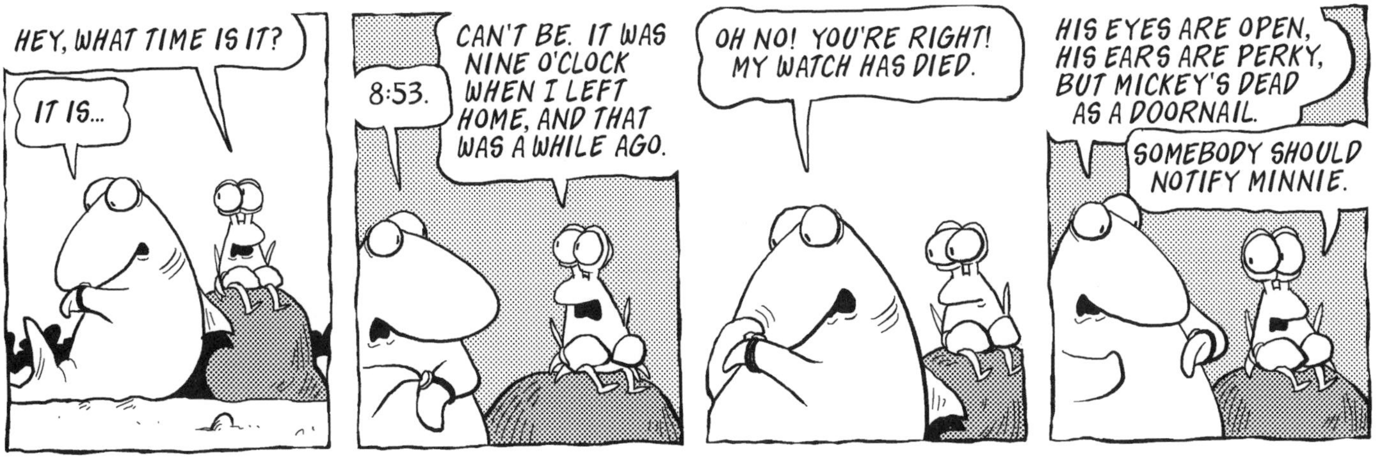

HEY, WHAT TIME IS IT?
IT IS...
8:53.
CAN'T BE. IT WAS NINE O'CLOCK WHEN I LEFT HOME, AND THAT WAS A WHILE AGO.
OH NO! YOU'RE RIGHT! MY WATCH HAS DIED.
HIS EYES ARE OPEN, HIS EARS ARE PERKY, BUT MICKEY'S DEAD AS A DOORNAIL.
SOMEBODY SHOULD NOTIFY MINNIE.

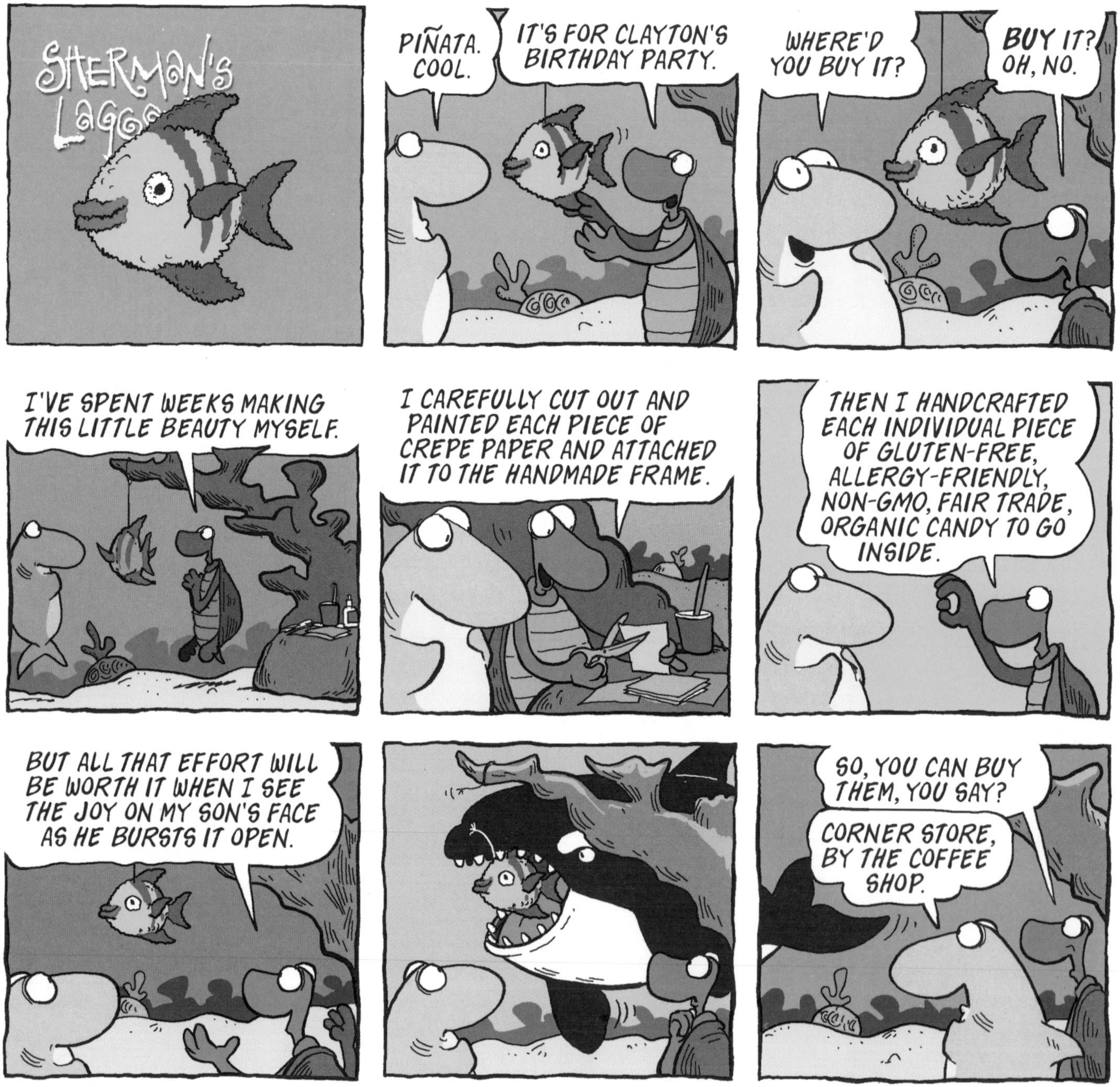
SHERMAN'S LAGOON
PIÑATA. COOL.
IT'S FOR CLAYTON'S BIRTHDAY PARTY.
WHERE'D YOU BUY IT?
BUY IT? OH, NO.
I'VE SPENT WEEKS MAKING THIS LITTLE BEAUTY MYSELF.
I CAREFULLY CUT OUT AND PAINTED EACH PIECE OF CREPE PAPER AND ATTACHED IT TO THE HANDMADE FRAME.
THEN I HANDCRAFTED EACH INDIVIDUAL PIECE OF GLUTEN-FREE, ALLERGY-FRIENDLY, NON-GMO, FAIR TRADE, ORGANIC CANDY TO GO INSIDE.
BUT ALL THAT EFFORT WILL BE WORTH IT WHEN I SEE THE JOY ON MY SON'S FACE AS HE BURSTS IT OPEN.
SO, YOU CAN BUY THEM, YOU SAY?
CORNER STORE, BY THE COFFEE SHOP.

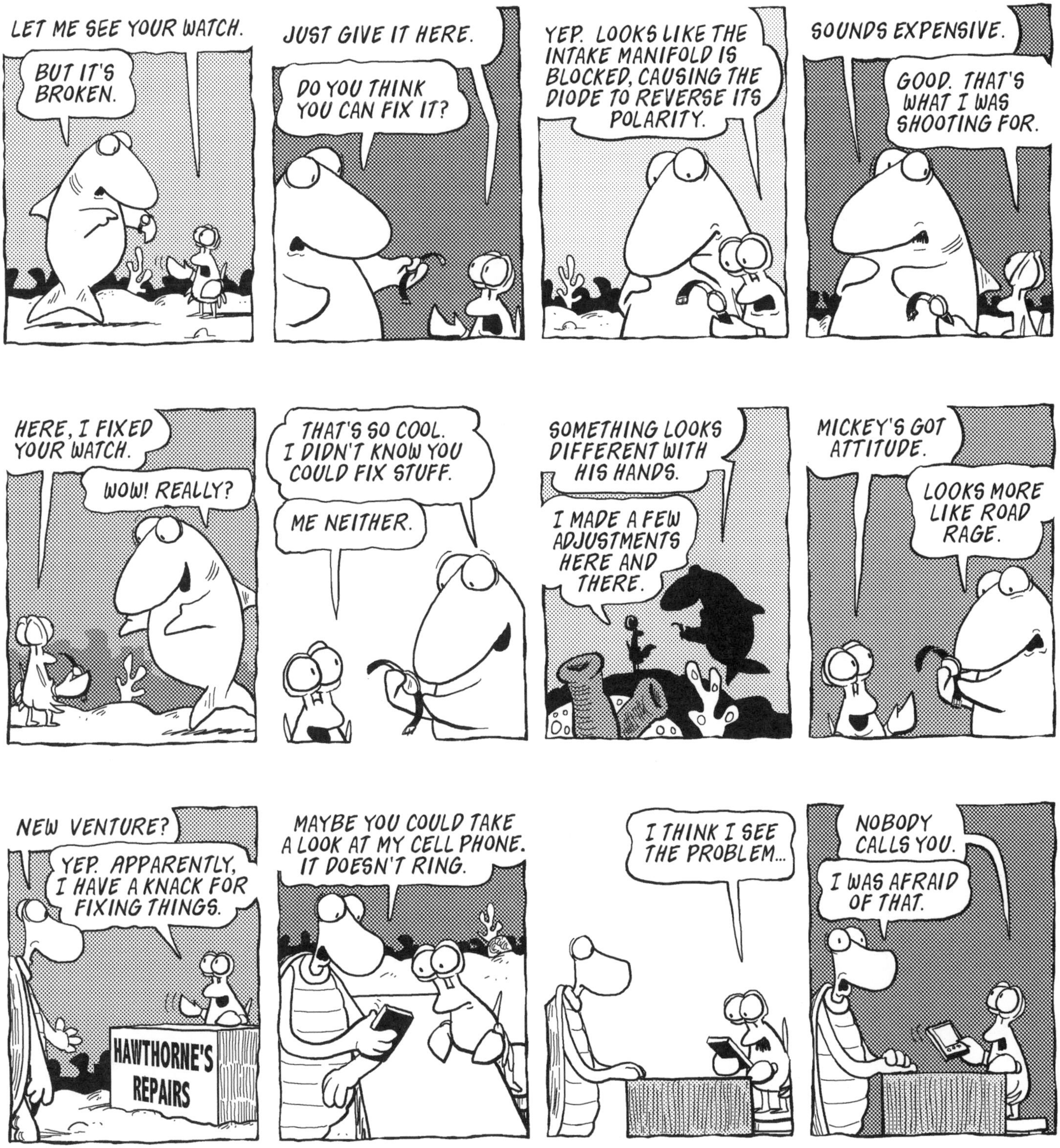
LET ME SEE YOUR WATCH.
BUT IT'S BROKEN.
JUST GIVE IT HERE.
DO YOU THINK YOU CAN FIX IT?
YEP. LOOKS LIKE THE INTAKE MANIFOLD IS BLOCKED, CAUSING THE DIODE TO REVERSE ITS POLARITY.
SOUNDS EXPENSIVE.
GOOD. THAT'S WHAT I WAS SHOOTING FOR.
HERE, I FIXED YOUR WATCH.
WOW! REALLY?
THAT'S SO COOL. I DIDN'T KNOW YOU COULD FIX STUFF.
ME NEITHER.
SOMETHING LOOKS DIFFERENT WITH HIS HANDS.
I MADE A FEW ADJUSTMENTS HERE AND THERE.
MICKEY'S GOT ATTITUDE.
LOOKS MORE LIKE ROAD RAGE.
NEW VENTURE?
YEP. APPARENTLY, I HAVE A KNACK FOR FIXING THINGS.
HAWTHORNE'S REPAIRS
MAYBE YOU COULD TAKE A LOOK AT MY CELL PHONE. IT DOESN'T RING.
I THINK I SEE THE PROBLEM...
NOBODY CALLS YOU.
I WAS AFRAID OF THAT.

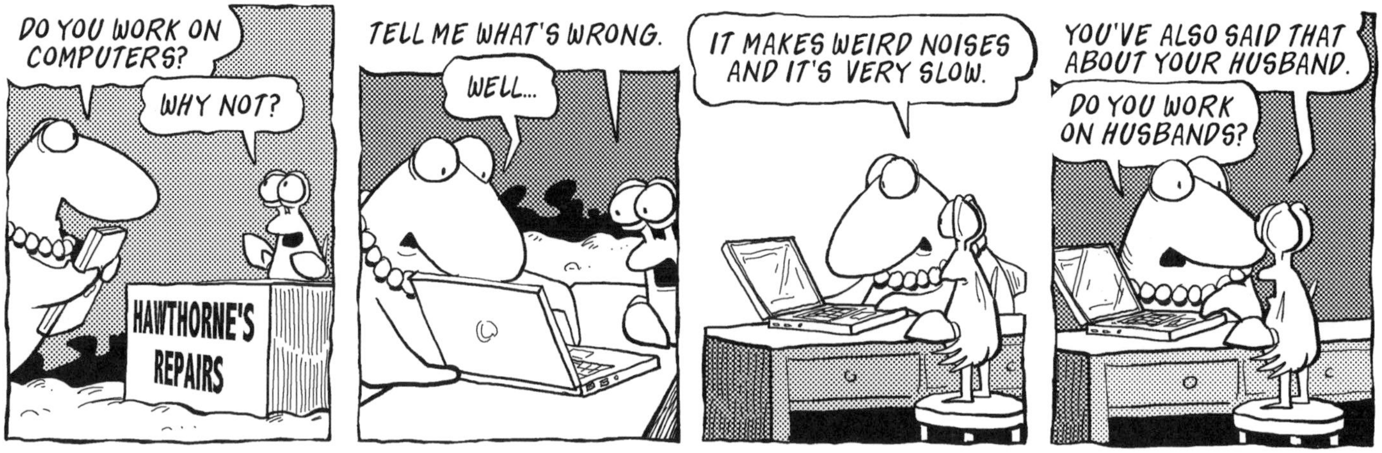
DO YOU WORK ON COMPUTERS?
WHY NOT?
HAWTHORNE'S REPAIRS
TELL ME WHAT'S WRONG.
WELL...
IT MAKES WEIRD NOISES AND IT'S VERY SLOW.
YOU'VE ALSO SAID THAT ABOUT YOUR HUSBAND.
DO YOU WORK ON HUSBANDS?

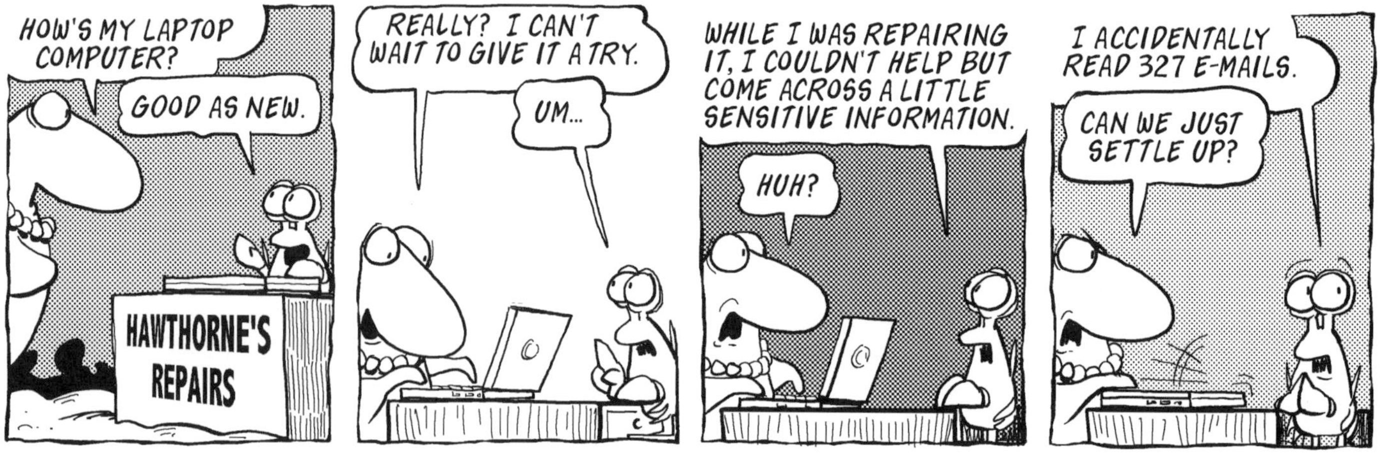
HOW'S MY LAPTOP COMPUTER?
GOOD AS NEW.
HAWTHORNE'S REPAIRS
REALLY? I CAN'T WAIT TO GIVE IT A TRY.
UM...
WHILE I WAS REPAIRING IT, I COULDN'T HELP BUT COME ACROSS A LITTLE SENSITIVE INFORMATION.
HUH?
I ACCIDENTALLY READ 327 E-MAILS.
CAN WE JUST SETTLE UP?

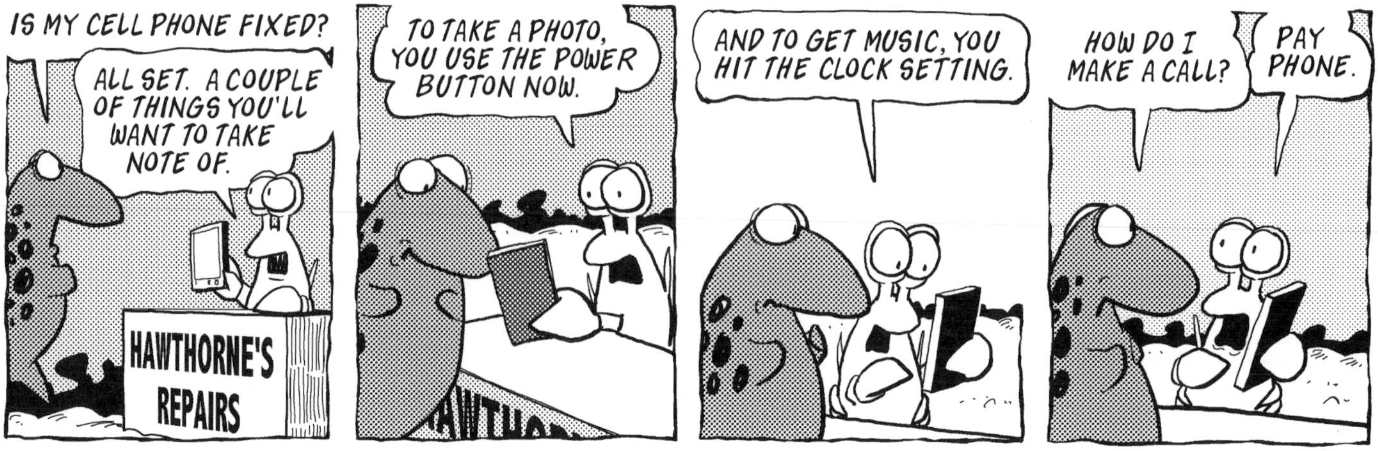
IS MY CELL PHONE FIXED?
ALL SET. A COUPLE OF THINGS YOU'LL WANT TO TAKE NOTE OF.
HAWTHORNE'S REPAIRS
TO TAKE A PHOTO, YOU USE THE POWER BUTTON NOW.
AND TO GET MUSIC, YOU HIT THE CLOCK SETTING.
HOW DO I MAKE A CALL?
PAY PHONE.

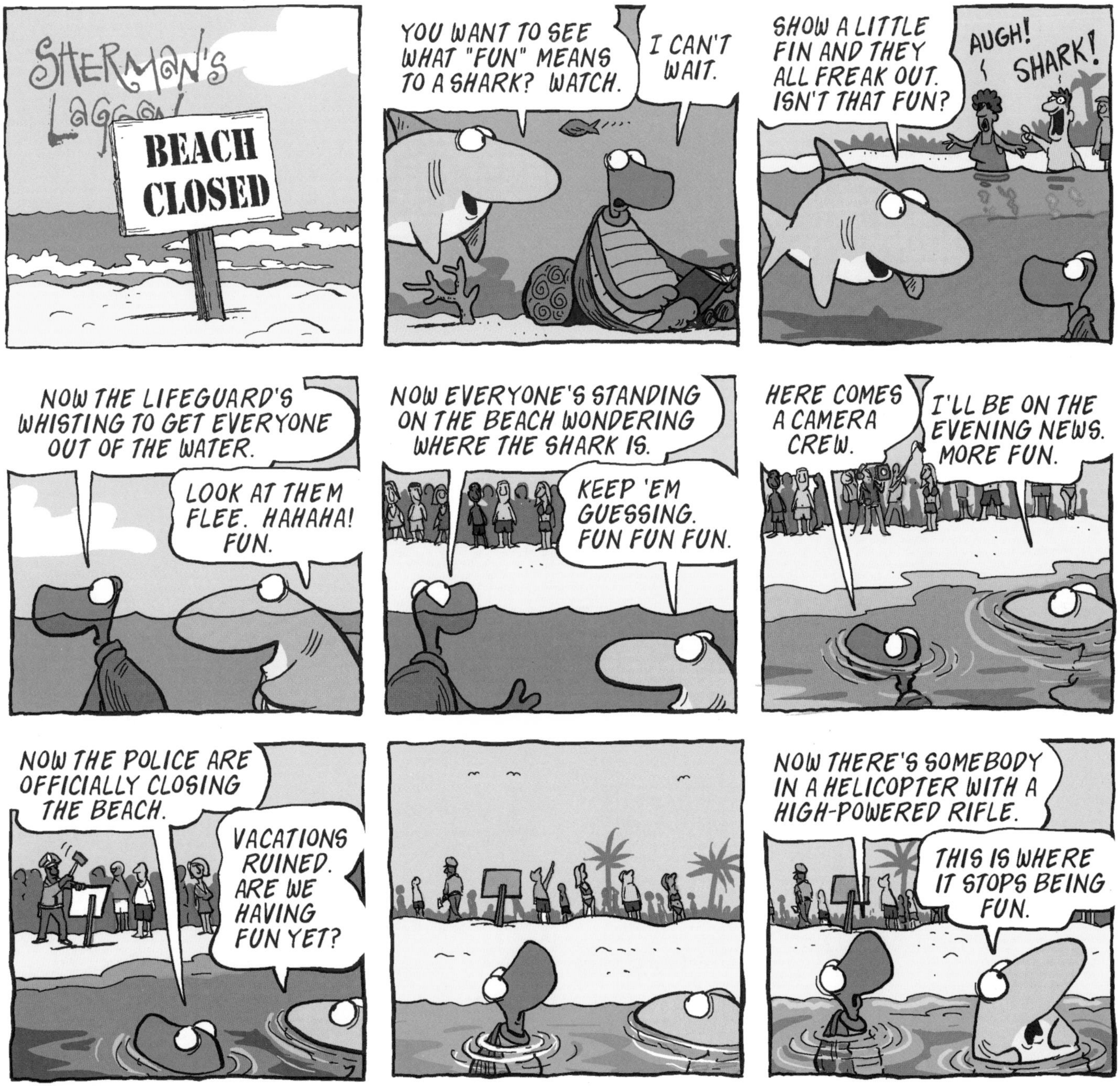
SHERMAN'S Lagoon
BEACH CLOSED
YOU WANT TO SEE WHAT "FUN" MEANS TO A SHARK? WATCH.
I CAN'T WAIT.
SHOW A LITTLE FIN AND THEY ALL FREAK OUT. ISN'T THAT FUN?
AUGH!
SHARK!
NOW THE LIFEGUARD'S WHISTING TO GET EVERYONE OUT OF THE WATER.
LOOK AT THEM FLEE. HAHAHA! FUN.
NOW EVERYONE'S STANDING ON THE BEACH WONDERING WHERE THE SHARK IS.
KEEP 'EM GUESSING. FUN FUN FUN.
HERE COMES A CAMERA CREW.
I'LL BE ON THE EVENING NEWS. MORE FUN.
NOW THE POLICE ARE OFFICIALLY CLOSING THE BEACH.
VACATIONS RUINED. ARE WE HAVING FUN YET?
NOW THERE'S SOMEBODY IN A HELICOPTER WITH A HIGH-POWERED RIFLE.
THIS IS WHERE IT STOPS BEING FUN.

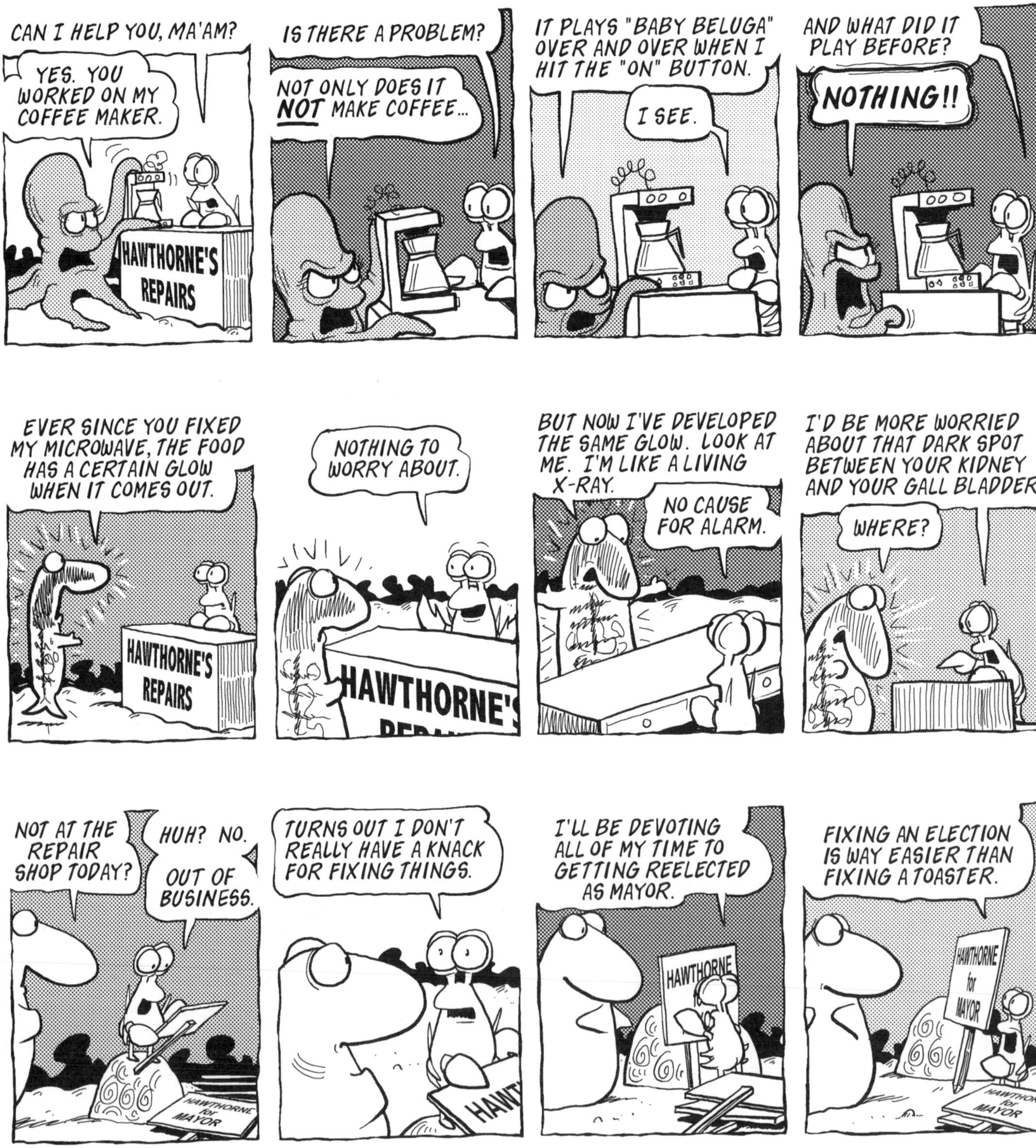
CAN I HELP YOU, MA'AM?
YES. YOU WORKED ON MY COFFEE MAKER.
HAWTHORNE'S REPAIRS
IS THERE A PROBLEM?
NOT ONLY DOES IT NOT MAKE COFFEE...
IT PLAYS "BABY BELUGA" OVER AND OVER WHEN I HIT THE "ON" BUTTON.
I SEE.
AND WHAT DID IT PLAY BEFORE?
NOTHING!!
EVER SINCE YOU FIXED MY MICROWAVE, THE FOOD HAS A CERTAIN GLOW WHEN IT COMES OUT.
HAWTHORNE'S REPAIRS
NOTHING TO WORRY ABOUT.
HAWTHORNE'S
BUT NOW I'VE DEVELOPED THE SAME GLOW. LOOK AT ME. I'M LIKE A LIVING X-RAY.
NO CAUSE FOR ALARM.
I'D BE MORE WORRIED ABOUT THAT DARK SPOT BETWEEN YOUR KIDNEY AND YOUR GALL BLADDER.
WHERE?
NOT AT THE REPAIR SHOP TODAY?
HUH? NO.
OUT OF BUSINESS.
HAWTHORNE for MAYOR
TURNS OUT I DON'T REALLY HAVE A KNACK FOR FIXING THINGS.
I'LL BE DEVOTING ALL OF MY TIME TO GETTING REELECTED AS MAYOR.
HAWTHORNE
FIXING AN ELECTION IS WAY EASIER THAN FIXING A TOASTER.
HAWTHORNE for MAYOR

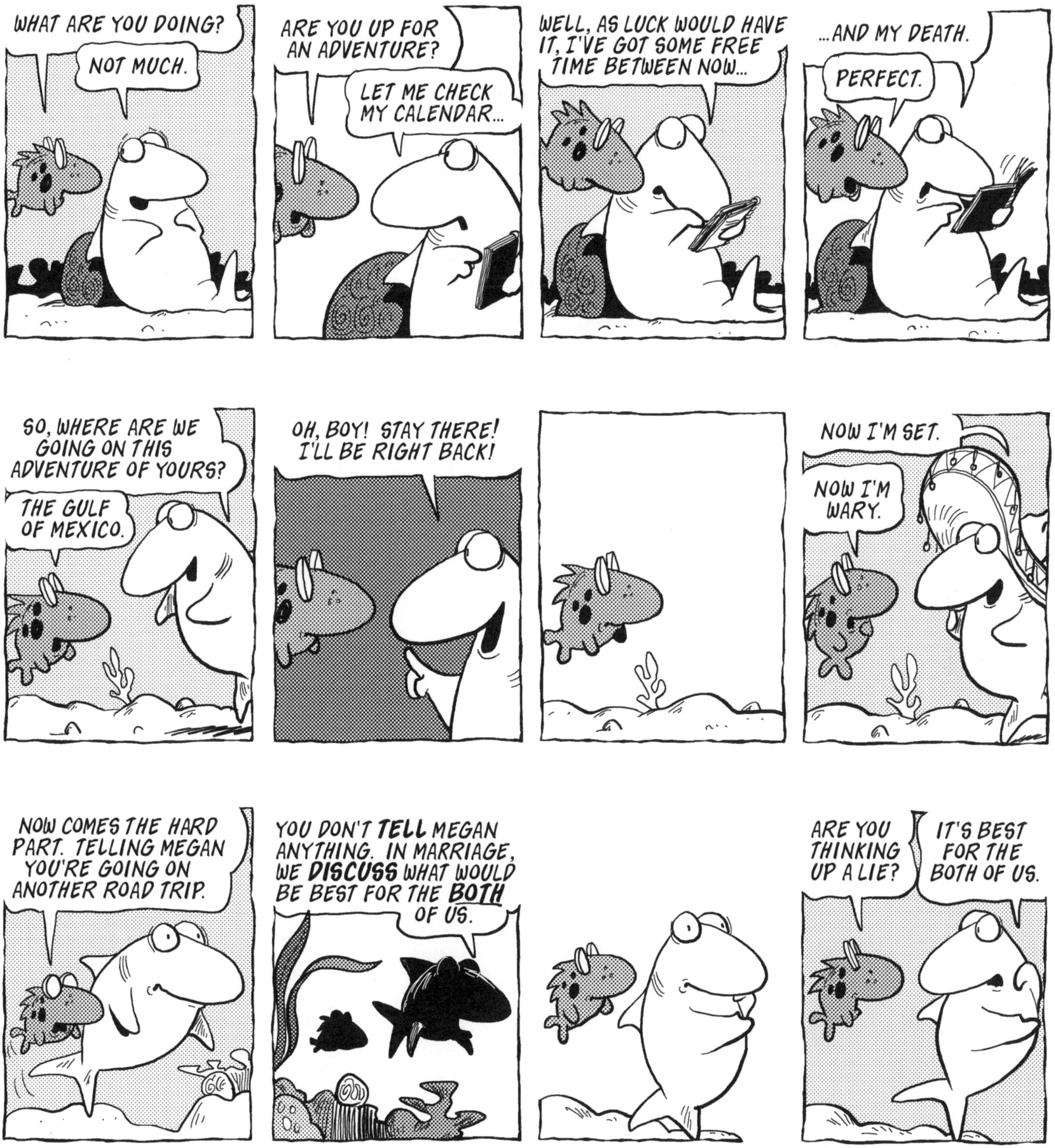
WHAT ARE YOU DOING?
NOT MUCH.
ARE YOU UP FOR AN ADVENTURE?
LET ME CHECK MY CALENDAR...
WELL, AS LUCK WOULD HAVE IT, I'VE GOT SOME FREE TIME BETWEEN NOW...
...AND MY DEATH.
PERFECT.
SO, WHERE ARE WE GOING ON THIS ADVENTURE OF YOURS?
THE GULF OF MEXICO.
OH, BOY! STAY THERE! I'LL BE RIGHT BACK!
NOW I'M SET.
NOW I'M WARY.
NOW COMES THE HARD PART. TELLING MEGAN YOU'RE GOING ON ANOTHER ROAD TRIP.
YOU DON'T TELL MEGAN ANYTHING. IN MARRIAGE, WE DISCUSS WHAT WOULD BE BEST FOR THE BOTH OF US.
ARE YOU THINKING UP A LIE?
IT'S BEST FOR THE BOTH OF US.

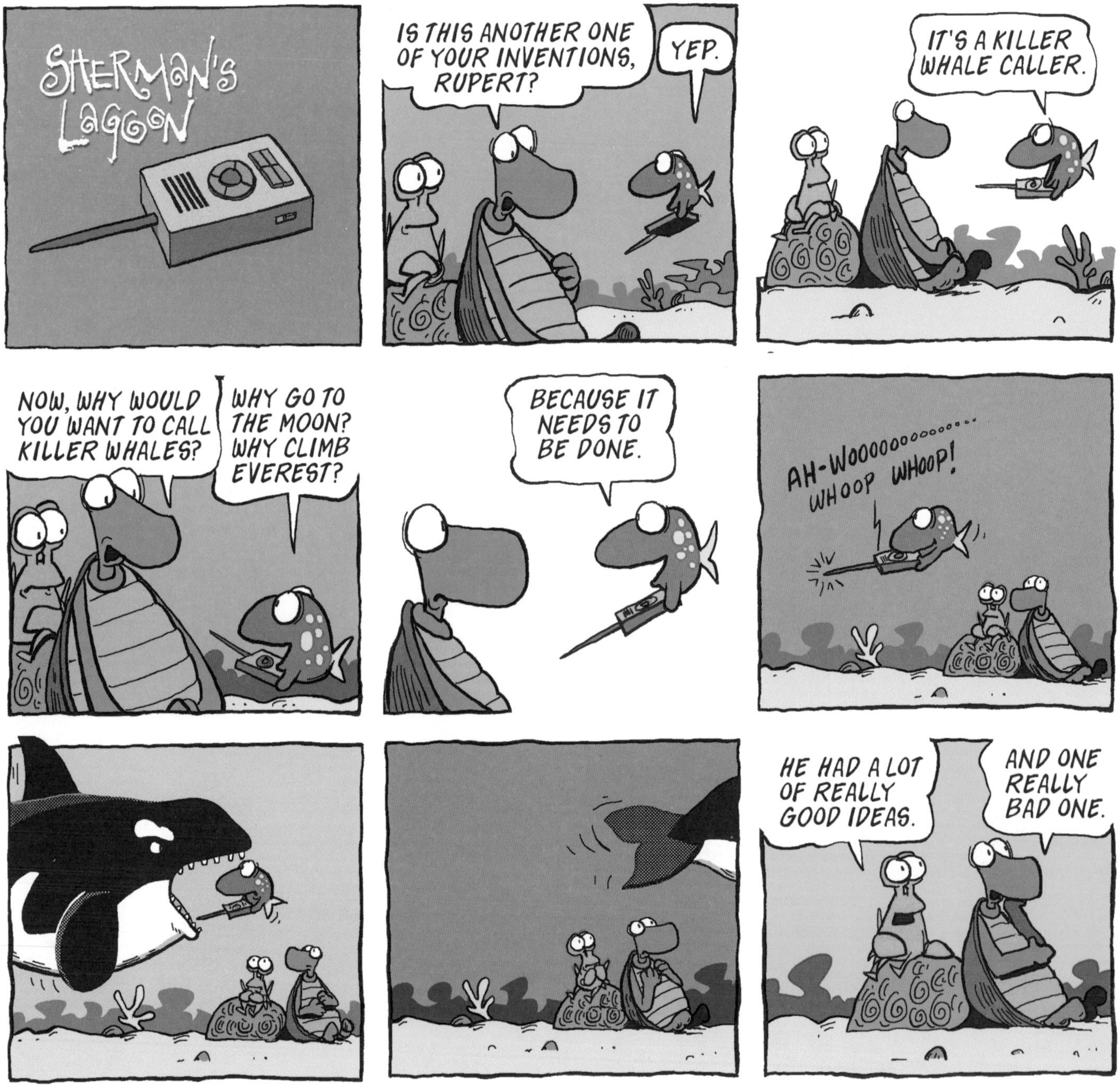
SHERMAN'S LAGOON
IS THIS ANOTHER ONE OF YOUR INVENTIONS, RUPERT?
YEP.
IT'S A KILLER WHALE CALLER.
NOW, WHY WOULD YOU WANT TO CALL KILLER WHALES?
WHY GO TO THE MOON? WHY CLIMB EVEREST?
BECAUSE IT NEEDS TO BE DONE.
AH-WOOOOOOOOOOOOOO... WHOOP WHOOP!
HE HAD A LOT OF REALLY GOOD IDEAS.
AND ONE REALLY BAD ONE.

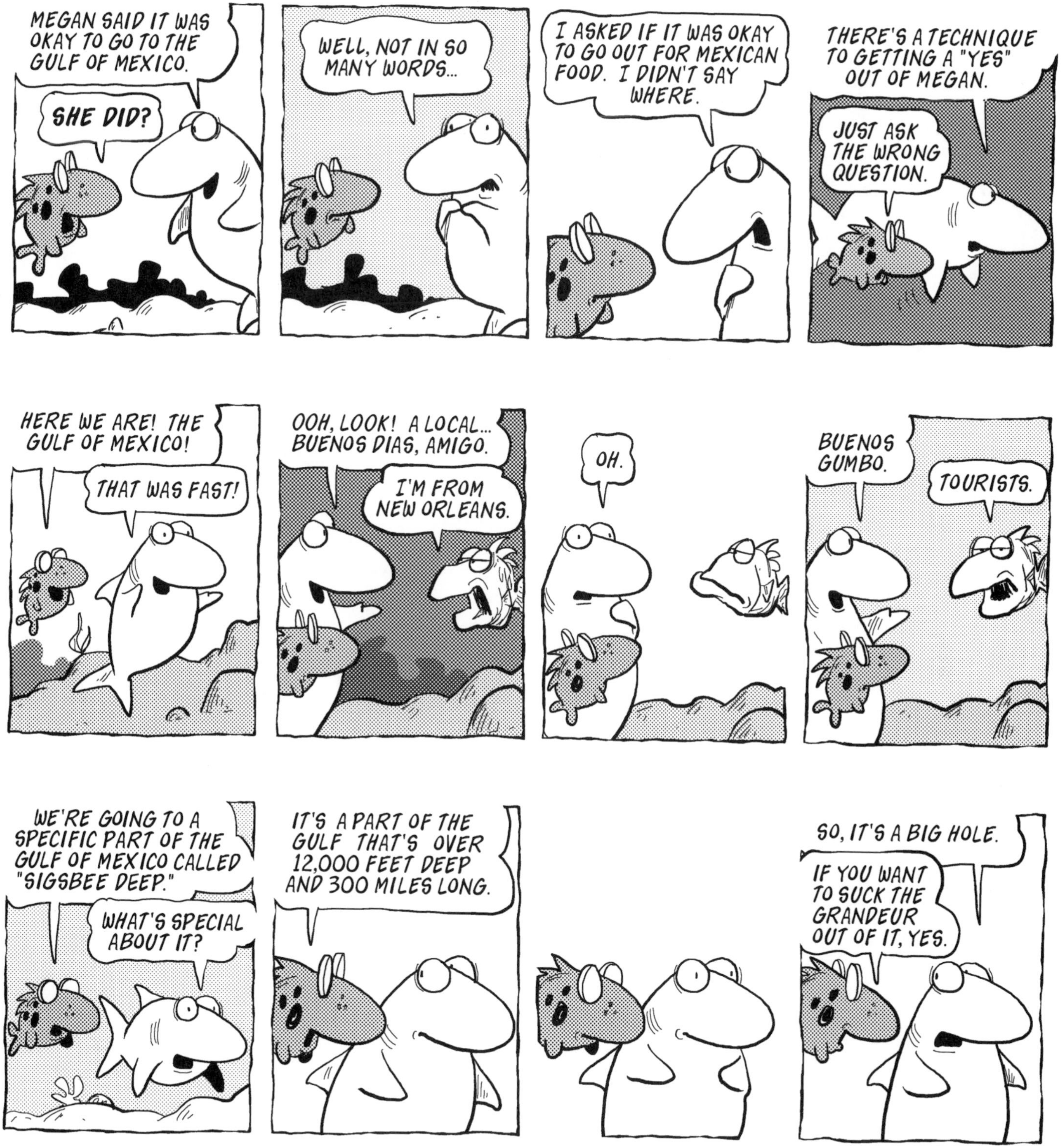
MEGAN SAID IT WAS OKAY TO GO TO THE GULF OF MEXICO.
SHE DID?
WELL, NOT IN SO MANY WORDS...
I ASKED IF IT WAS OKAY TO GO OUT FOR MEXICAN FOOD. I DIDN'T SAY WHERE.
THERE'S A TECHNIQUE TO GETTING A "YES" OUT OF MEGAN.
JUST ASK THE WRONG QUESTION.
HERE WE ARE! THE GULF OF MEXICO!
THAT WAS FAST!
OOH, LOOK! A LOCAL... BUENOS DIAS, AMIGO.
I'M FROM NEW ORLEANS.
OH.
BUENOS GUMBO.
TOURISTS.
WE'RE GOING TO A SPECIFIC PART OF THE GULF OF MEXICO CALLED "SIGSBEE DEEP."
WHAT'S SPECIAL ABOUT IT?
IT'S A PART OF THE GULF THAT'S OVER 12,000 FEET DEEP AND 300 MILES LONG.
SO, IT'S A BIG HOLE.
IF YOU WANT TO SUCK THE GRANDEUR OUT OF IT, YES.

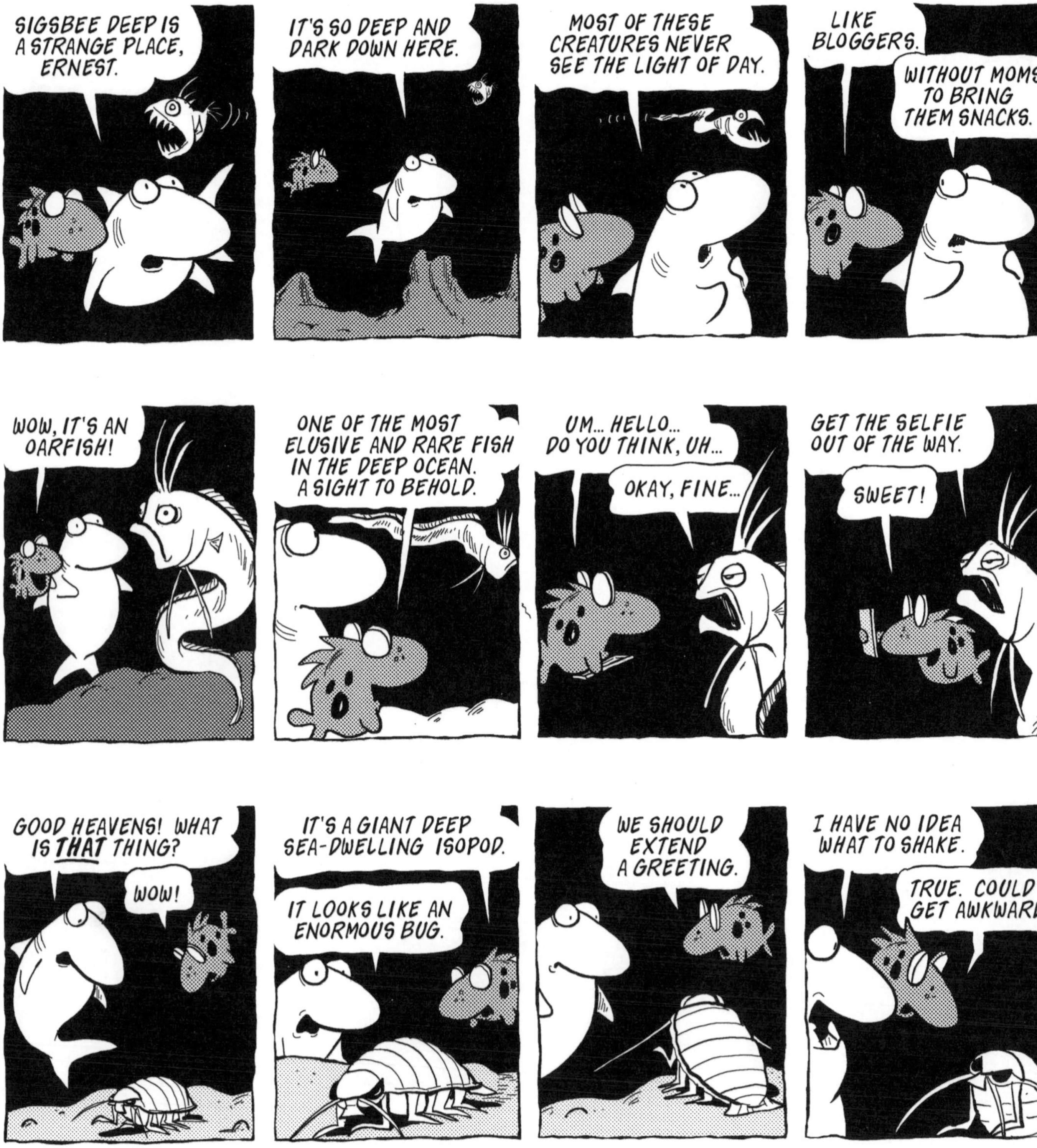
SIGSBEE DEEP IS A STRANGE PLACE, ERNEST.
IT'S SO DEEP AND DARK DOWN HERE.
MOST OF THESE CREATURES NEVER SEE THE LIGHT OF DAY.
LIKE BLOGGERS.
WITHOUT MOMS TO BRING THEM SNACKS.
WOW, IT'S AN OARFISH!
ONE OF THE MOST ELUSIVE AND RARE FISH IN THE DEEP OCEAN. A SIGHT TO BEHOLD.
UM... HELLO... DO YOU THINK, UH...
OKAY, FINE...
GET THE SELFIE OUT OF THE WAY.
SWEET!
GOOD HEAVENS! WHAT IS THAT THING?
WOW!
IT'S A GIANT DEEP SEA-DWELLING ISOPOD.
IT LOOKS LIKE AN ENORMOUS BUG.
WE SHOULD EXTEND A GREETING.
I HAVE NO IDEA WHAT TO SHAKE.
TRUE. COULD GET AWKWARD.

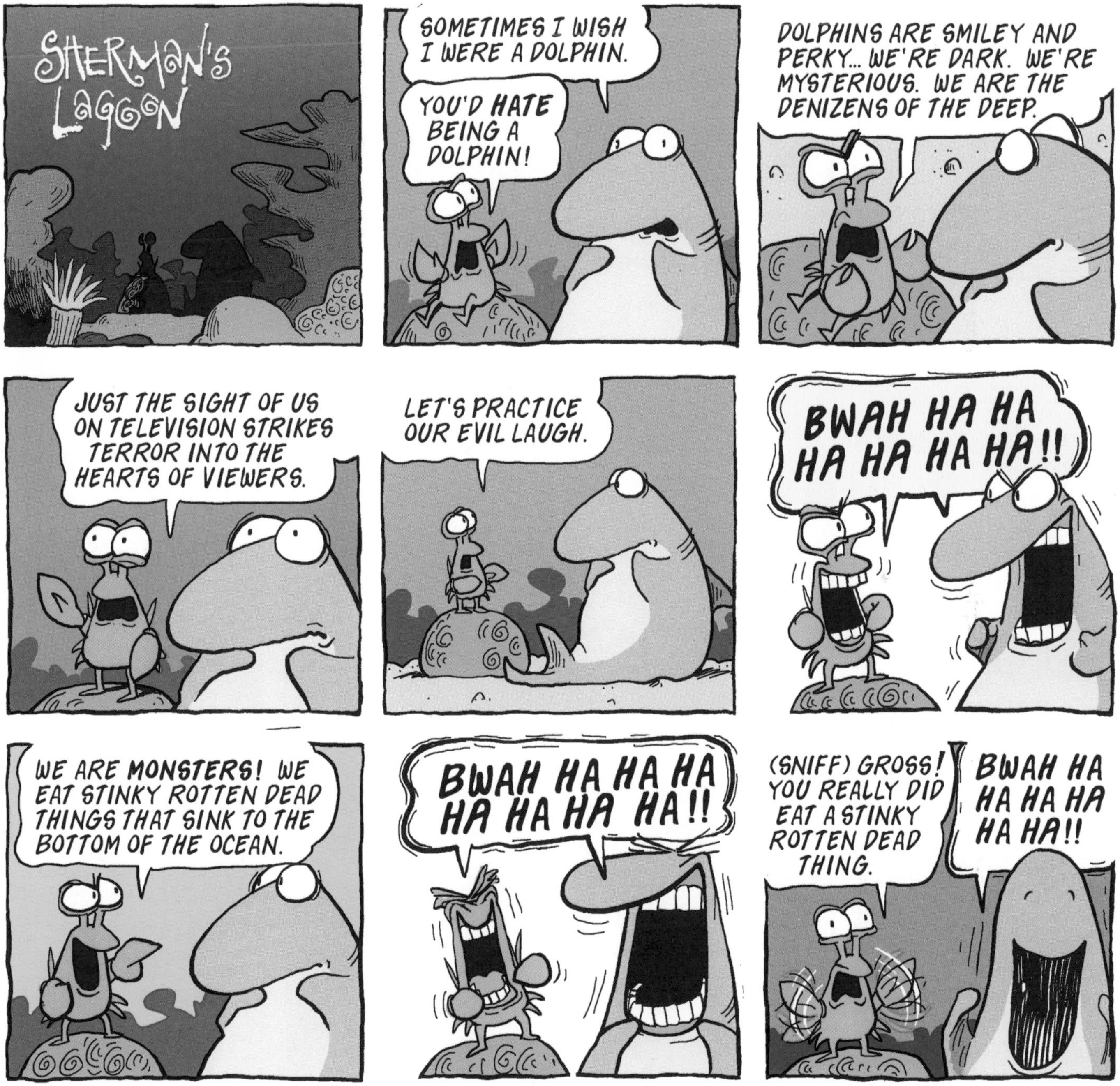
SHERMAN'S LAGOON
SOMETIMES I WISH I WERE A DOLPHIN.
YOU'D **HATE** BEING A DOLPHIN!
DOLPHINS ARE SMILEY AND PERKY... WE'RE DARK. WE'RE MYSTERIOUS. WE ARE THE DENIZENS OF THE DEEP.
JUST THE SIGHT OF US ON TELEVISION STRIKES TERROR INTO THE HEARTS OF VIEWERS.
LET'S PRACTICE OUR EVIL LAUGH.
BWAH HA HA HA HA HA HA!!
WE ARE **MONSTERS!** WE EAT STINKY ROTTEN DEAD THINGS THAT SINK TO THE BOTTOM OF THE OCEAN.
BWAH HA HA HA HA HA HA HA!!
(SNIFF) GROSS! YOU REALLY DID EAT A STINKY ROTTEN DEAD THING.
BWAH HA HA HA HA HA HA!!

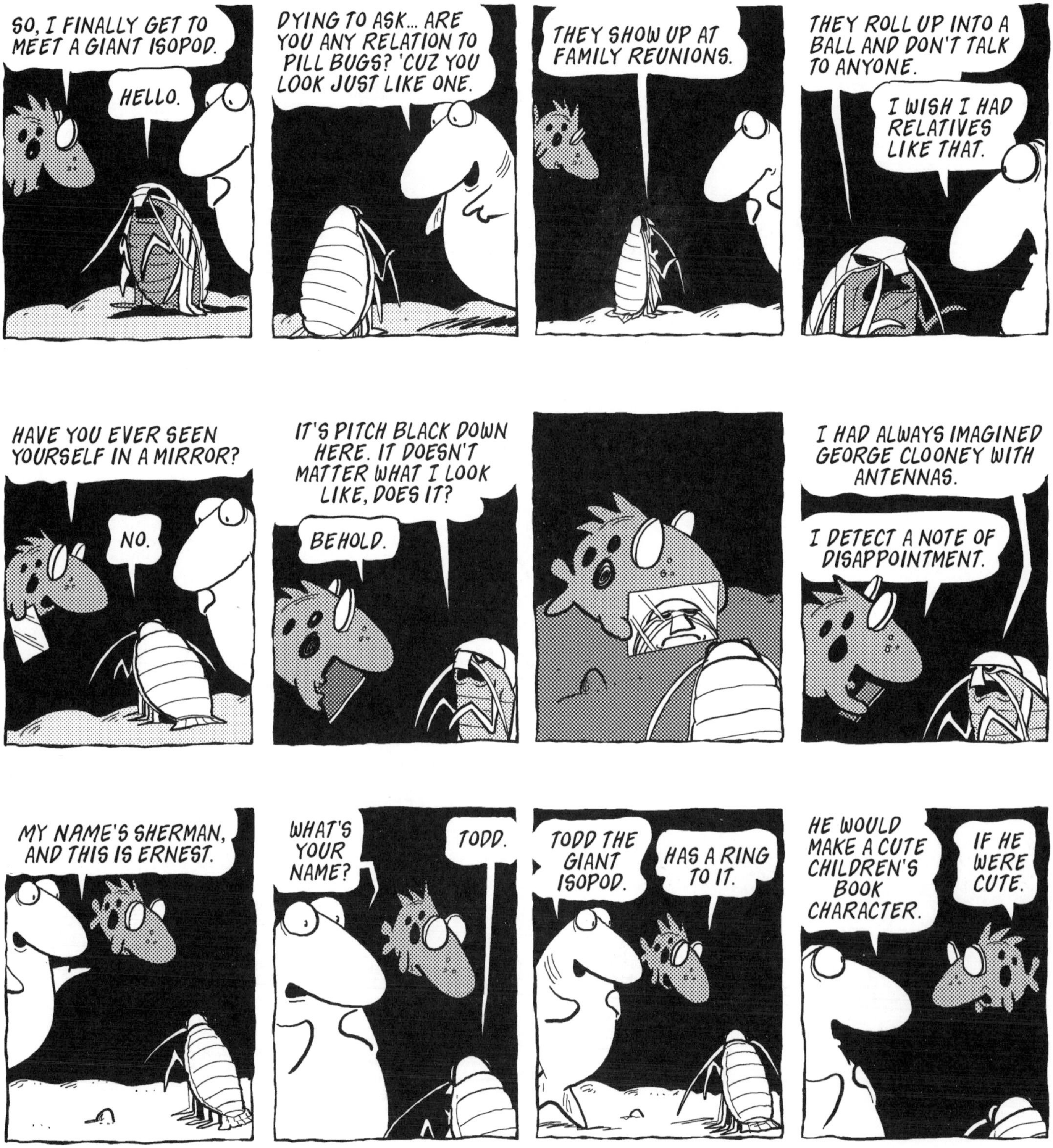
SO, I FINALLY GET TO MEET A GIANT ISOPOD.
HELLO.
DYING TO ASK... ARE YOU ANY RELATION TO PILL BUGS? 'CUZ YOU LOOK JUST LIKE ONE.
THEY SHOW UP AT FAMILY REUNIONS.
THEY ROLL UP INTO A BALL AND DON'T TALK TO ANYONE.
I WISH I HAD RELATIVES LIKE THAT.
HAVE YOU EVER SEEN YOURSELF IN A MIRROR?
NO.
IT'S PITCH BLACK DOWN HERE. IT DOESN'T MATTER WHAT I LOOK LIKE, DOES IT?
BEHOLD.
I HAD ALWAYS IMAGINED GEORGE CLOONEY WITH ANTENNAS.
I DETECT A NOTE OF DISAPPOINTMENT.
MY NAME'S SHERMAN, AND THIS IS ERNEST.
WHAT'S YOUR NAME?
TODD.
TODD THE GIANT ISOPOD.
HAS A RING TO IT.
HE WOULD MAKE A CUTE CHILDREN'S BOOK CHARACTER.
IF HE WERE CUTE.

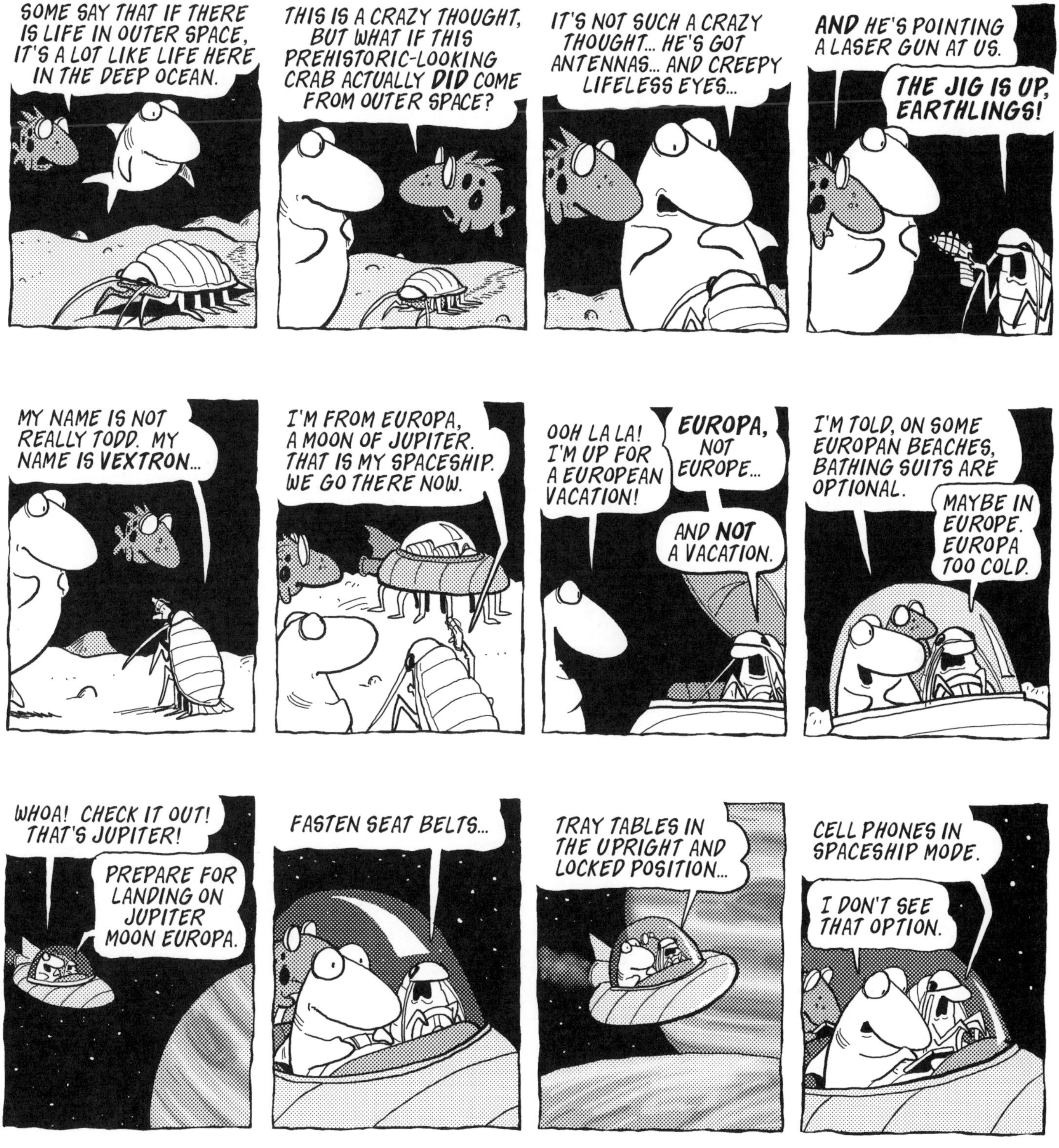
SOME SAY THAT IF THERE IS LIFE IN OUTER SPACE, IT'S A LOT LIKE LIFE HERE IN THE DEEP OCEAN.
THIS IS A CRAZY THOUGHT, BUT WHAT IF THIS PREHISTORIC-LOOKING CRAB ACTUALLY DID COME FROM OUTER SPACE?
IT'S NOT SUCH A CRAZY THOUGHT... HE'S GOT ANTENNAS... AND CREEPY LIFELESS EYES...
AND HE'S POINTING A LASER GUN AT US.
THE JIG IS UP, EARTHLINGS!
MY NAME IS NOT REALLY TODD. MY NAME IS VEXTRON...
I'M FROM EUROPA, A MOON OF JUPITER. THAT IS MY SPACESHIP. WE GO THERE NOW.
OOH LA LA! I'M UP FOR A EUROPEAN VACATION!
EUROPA, NOT EUROPE...
AND NOT A VACATION.
I'M TOLD, ON SOME EUROPAN BEACHES, BATHING SUITS ARE OPTIONAL.
MAYBE IN EUROPE. EUROPA TOO COLD.
WHOA! CHECK IT OUT! THAT'S JUPITER!
PREPARE FOR LANDING ON JUPITER MOON EUROPA.
FASTEN SEAT BELTS...
TRAY TABLES IN THE UPRIGHT AND LOCKED POSITION...
CELL PHONES IN SPACESHIP MODE.
I DON'T SEE THAT OPTION.

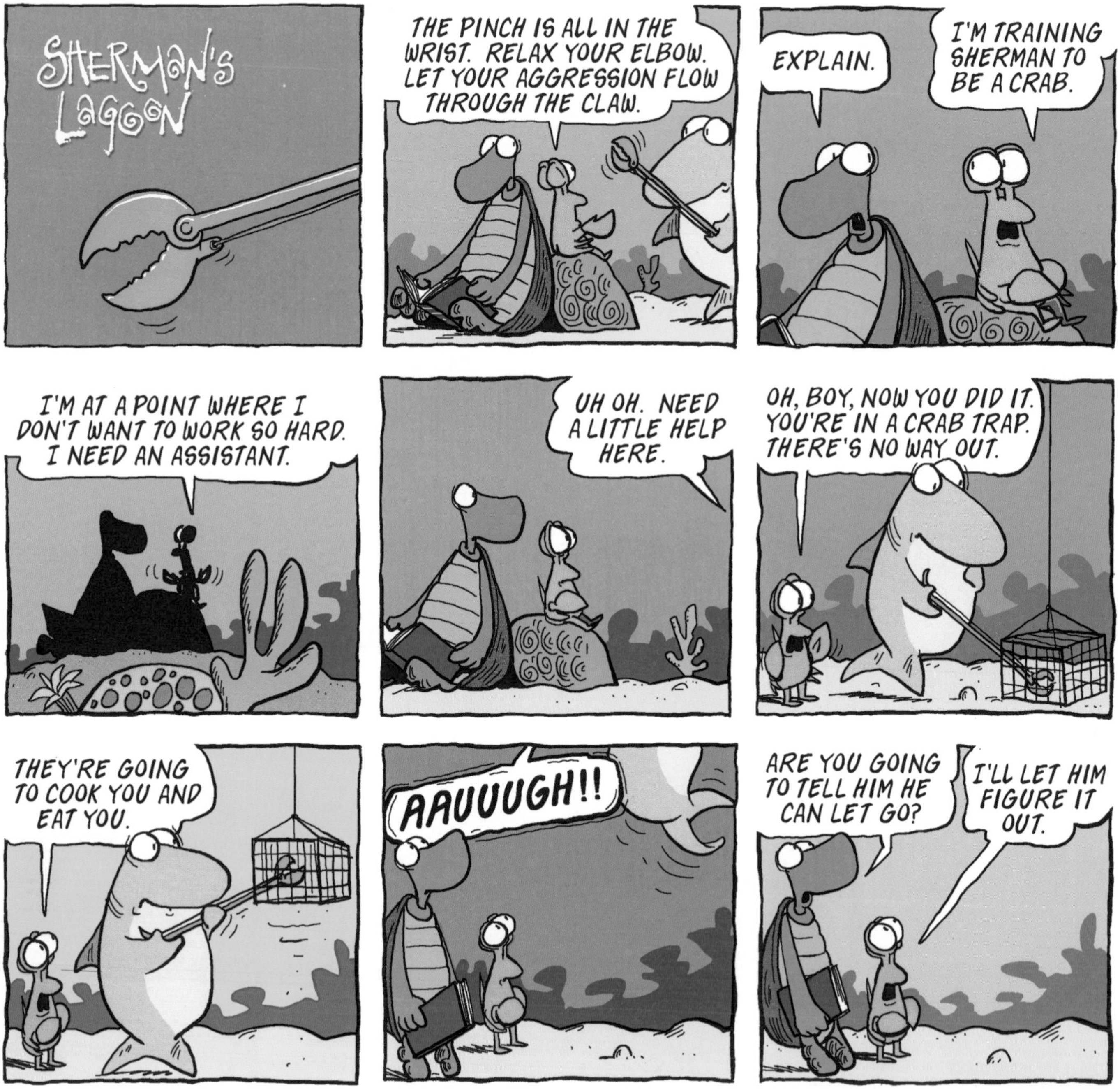
SHERMAN'S LAGOON
THE PINCH IS ALL IN THE WRIST. RELAX YOUR ELBOW. LET YOUR AGGRESSION FLOW THROUGH THE CLAW.
EXPLAIN.
I'M TRAINING SHERMAN TO BE A CRAB.
I'M AT A POINT WHERE I DON'T WANT TO WORK SO HARD. I NEED AN ASSISTANT.
UH OH. NEED A LITTLE HELP HERE.
OH, BOY, NOW YOU DID IT. YOU'RE IN A CRAB TRAP. THERE'S NO WAY OUT.
THEY'RE GOING TO COOK YOU AND EAT YOU.
AAUUUGH!!
ARE YOU GOING TO TELL HIM HE CAN LET GO?
I'LL LET HIM FIGURE IT OUT.

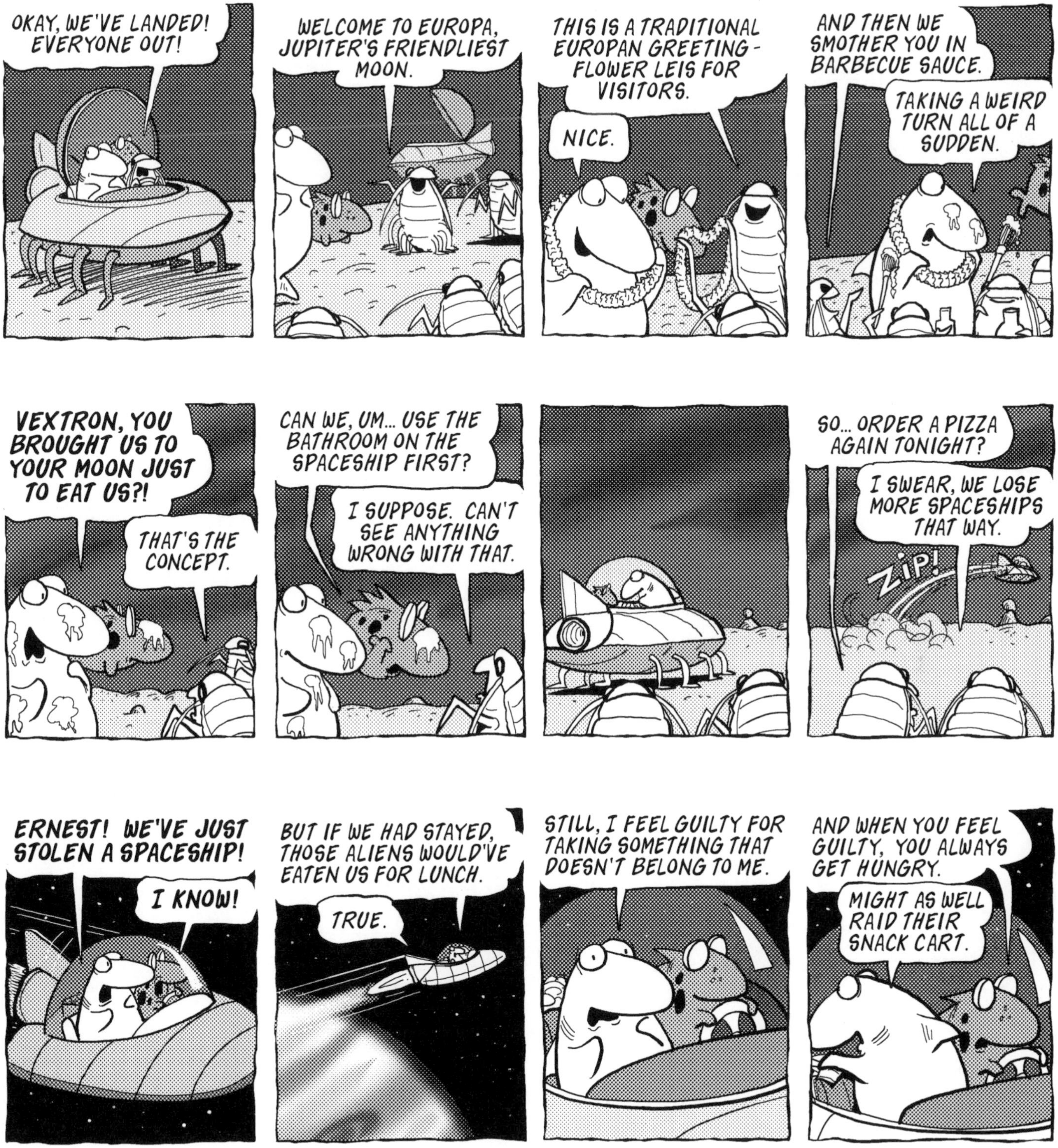
OKAY, WE'VE LANDED! EVERYONE OUT!
WELCOME TO EUROPA, JUPITER'S FRIENDLIEST MOON.
THIS IS A TRADITIONAL EUROPAN GREETING - FLOWER LEIS FOR VISITORS.
NICE.
AND THEN WE SMOTHER YOU IN BARBECUE SAUCE.
TAKING A WEIRD TURN ALL OF A SUDDEN.
VEXTRON, YOU BROUGHT US TO YOUR MOON JUST TO EAT US?!
THAT'S THE CONCEPT.
CAN WE, UM... USE THE BATHROOM ON THE SPACESHIP FIRST?
I SUPPOSE. CAN'T SEE ANYTHING WRONG WITH THAT.
SO... ORDER A PIZZA AGAIN TONIGHT?
I SWEAR, WE LOSE MORE SPACESHIPS THAT WAY.
ZIP!
ERNEST! WE'VE JUST STOLEN A SPACESHIP!
I KNOW!
BUT IF WE HAD STAYED, THOSE ALIENS WOULD'VE EATEN US FOR LUNCH.
TRUE.
STILL, I FEEL GUILTY FOR TAKING SOMETHING THAT DOESN'T BELONG TO ME.
AND WHEN YOU FEEL GUILTY, YOU ALWAYS GET HUNGRY.
MIGHT AS WELL RAID THEIR SNACK CART.

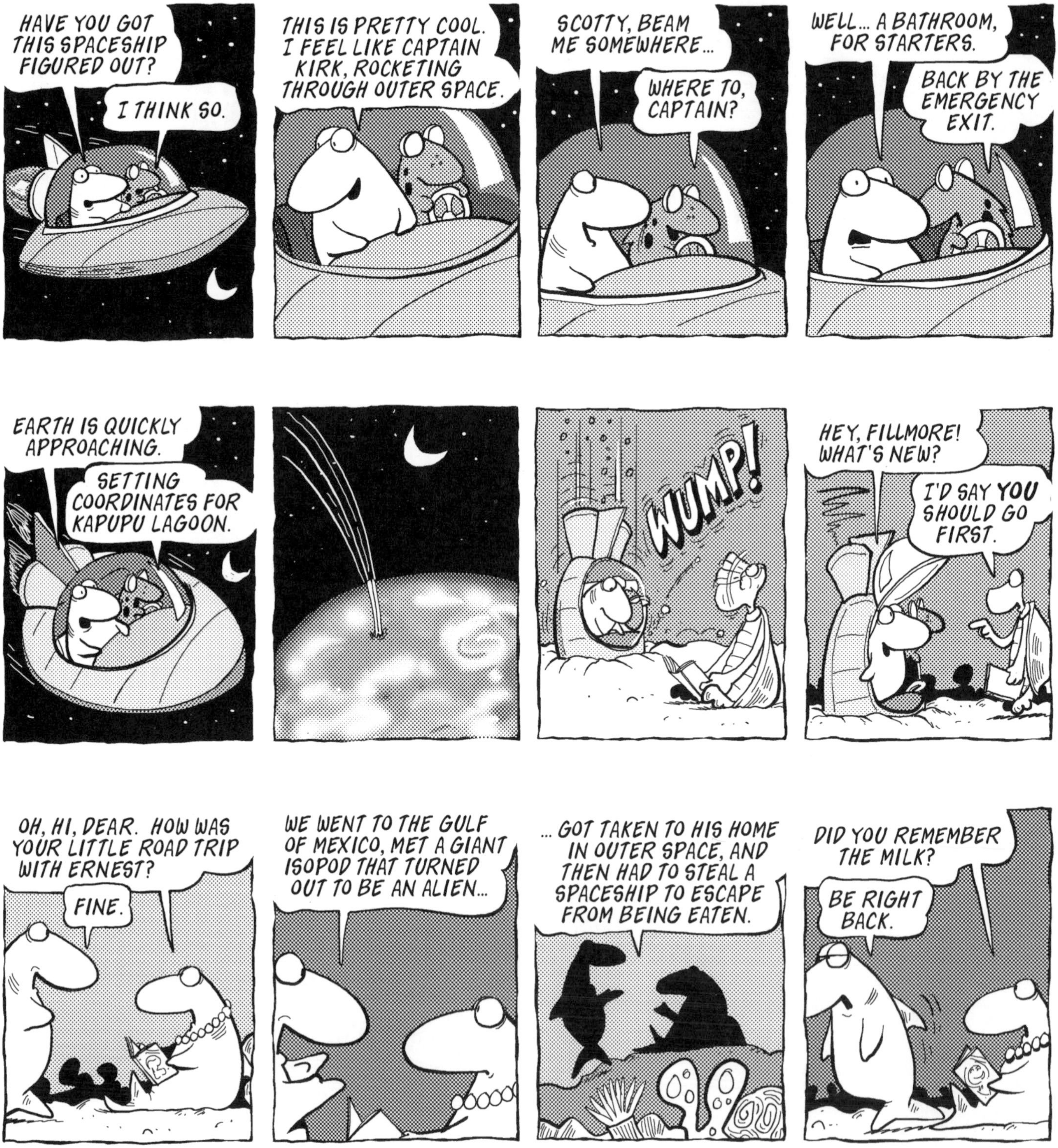
HAVE YOU GOT THIS SPACESHIP FIGURED OUT?
I THINK SO.
THIS IS PRETTY COOL. I FEEL LIKE CAPTAIN KIRK, ROCKETING THROUGH OUTER SPACE.
SCOTTY, BEAM ME SOMEWHERE...
WHERE TO, CAPTAIN?
WELL... A BATHROOM, FOR STARTERS.
BACK BY THE EMERGENCY EXIT.
EARTH IS QUICKLY APPROACHING.
SETTING COORDINATES FOR KAPUPU LAGOON.
WUMP!
HEY, FILLMORE! WHAT'S NEW?
I'D SAY YOU SHOULD GO FIRST.
OH, HI, DEAR. HOW WAS YOUR LITTLE ROAD TRIP WITH ERNEST?
FINE.
WE WENT TO THE GULF OF MEXICO, MET A GIANT ISOPOD THAT TURNED OUT TO BE AN ALIEN...
... GOT TAKEN TO HIS HOME IN OUTER SPACE, AND THEN HAD TO STEAL A SPACESHIP TO ESCAPE FROM BEING EATEN.
DID YOU REMEMBER THE MILK?
BE RIGHT BACK.

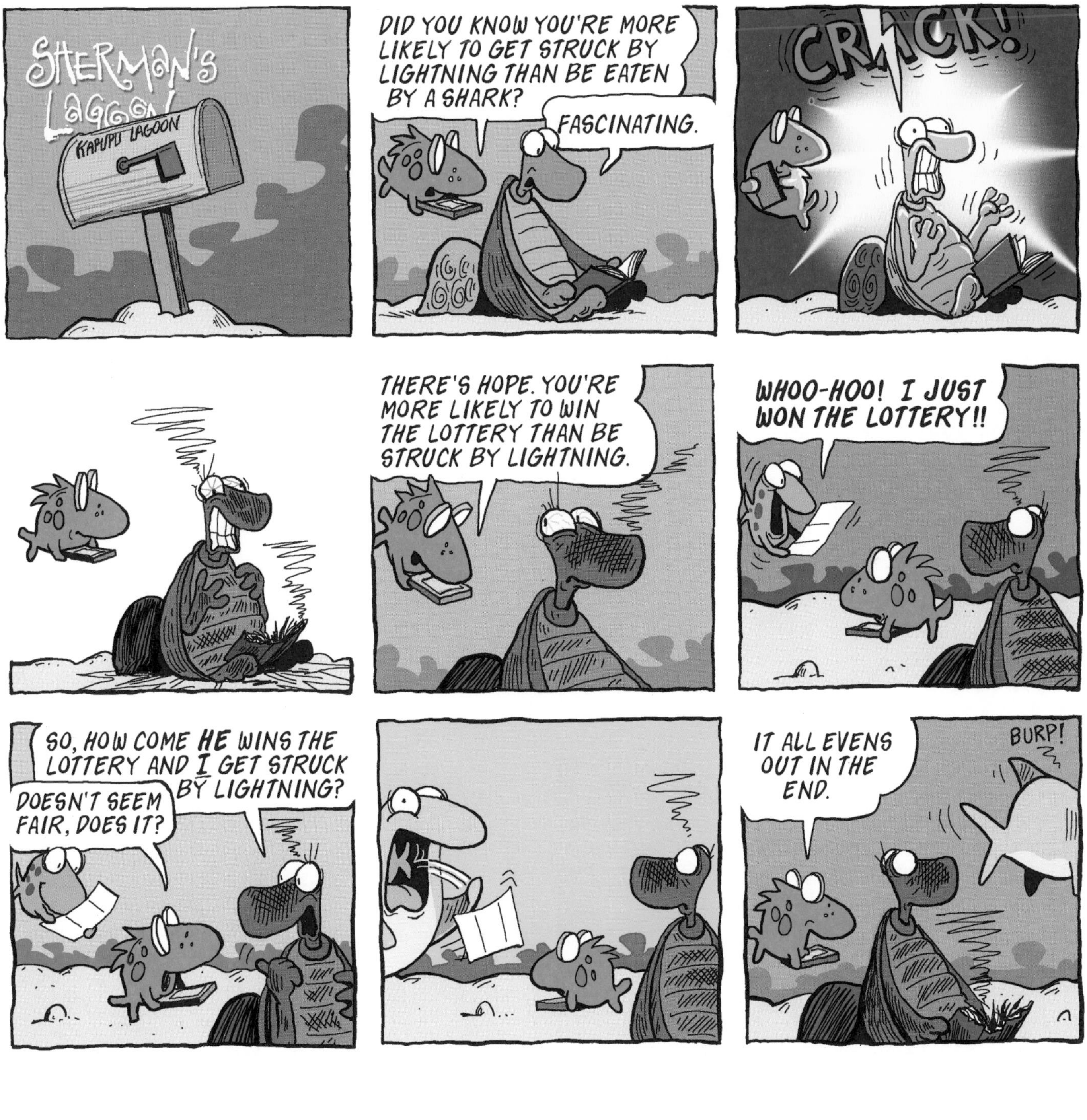
SHERMAN'S LAGOON
KAPUPU LAGOON
DID YOU KNOW YOU'RE MORE LIKELY TO GET STRUCK BY LIGHTNING THAN BE EATEN BY A SHARK?
FASCINATING.
CRACK!
THERE'S HOPE. YOU'RE MORE LIKELY TO WIN THE LOTTERY THAN BE STRUCK BY LIGHTNING.
WHOO-HOO! I JUST WON THE LOTTERY!!
SO, HOW COME HE WINS THE LOTTERY AND I GET STRUCK BY LIGHTNING?
DOESN'T SEEM FAIR, DOES IT?
IT ALL EVENS OUT IN THE END.
BURP!

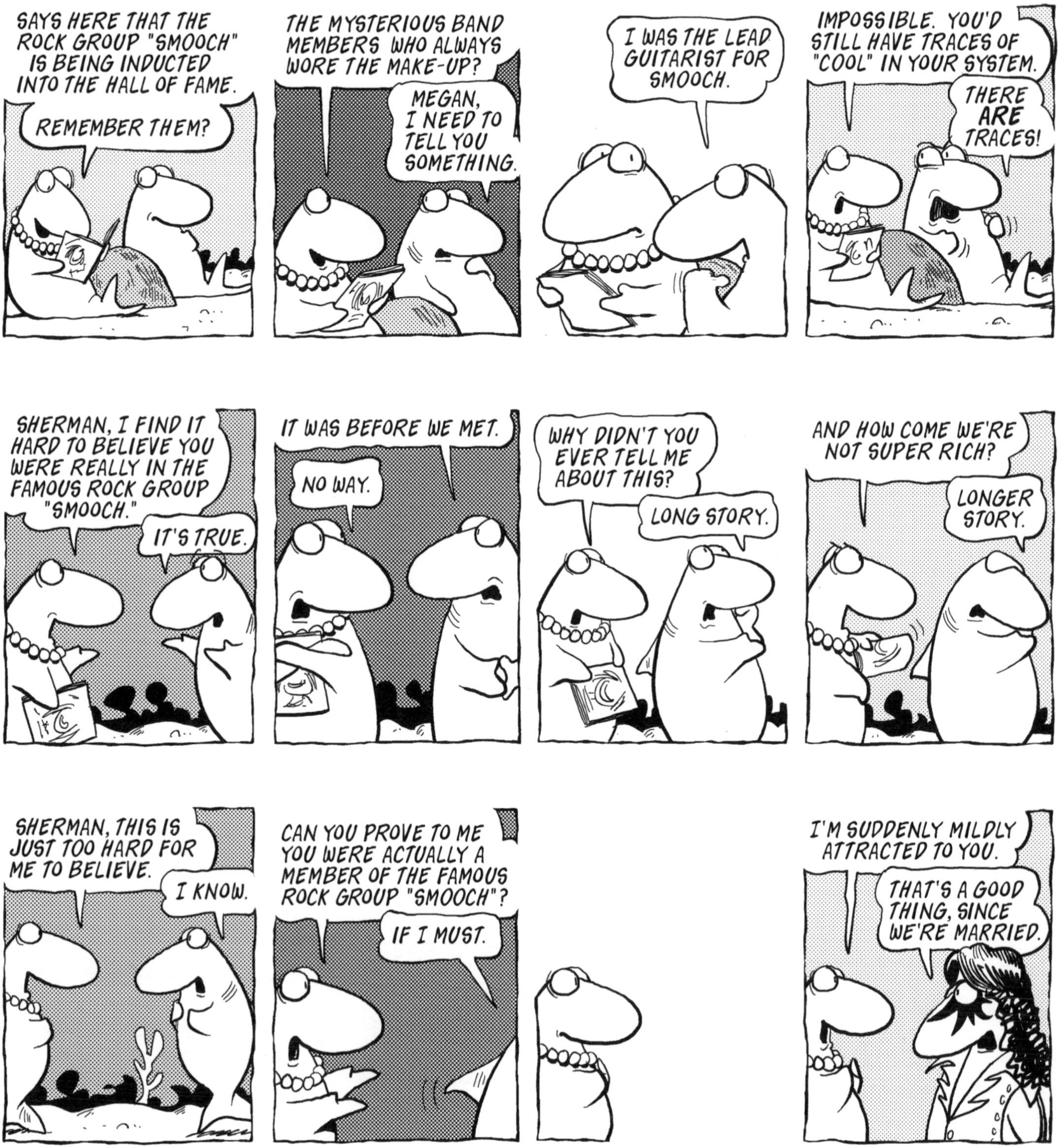
SAYS HERE THAT THE ROCK GROUP "SMOOCH" IS BEING INDUCTED INTO THE HALL OF FAME.
REMEMBER THEM?
THE MYSTERIOUS BAND MEMBERS WHO ALWAYS WORE THE MAKE-UP?
MEGAN, I NEED TO TELL YOU SOMETHING.
I WAS THE LEAD GUITARIST FOR SMOOCH.
IMPOSSIBLE. YOU'D STILL HAVE TRACES OF "COOL" IN YOUR SYSTEM.
THERE **ARE** TRACES!
SHERMAN, I FIND IT HARD TO BELIEVE YOU WERE REALLY IN THE FAMOUS ROCK GROUP "SMOOCH."
IT'S TRUE.
IT WAS BEFORE WE MET.
NO WAY.
WHY DIDN'T YOU EVER TELL ME ABOUT THIS?
LONG STORY.
AND HOW COME WE'RE NOT SUPER RICH?
LONGER STORY.
SHERMAN, THIS IS JUST TOO HARD FOR ME TO BELIEVE.
I KNOW.
CAN YOU PROVE TO ME YOU WERE ACTUALLY A MEMBER OF THE FAMOUS ROCK GROUP "SMOOCH"?
IF I MUST.
I'M SUDDENLY MILDLY ATTRACTED TO YOU.
THAT'S A GOOD THING, SINCE WE'RE MARRIED.

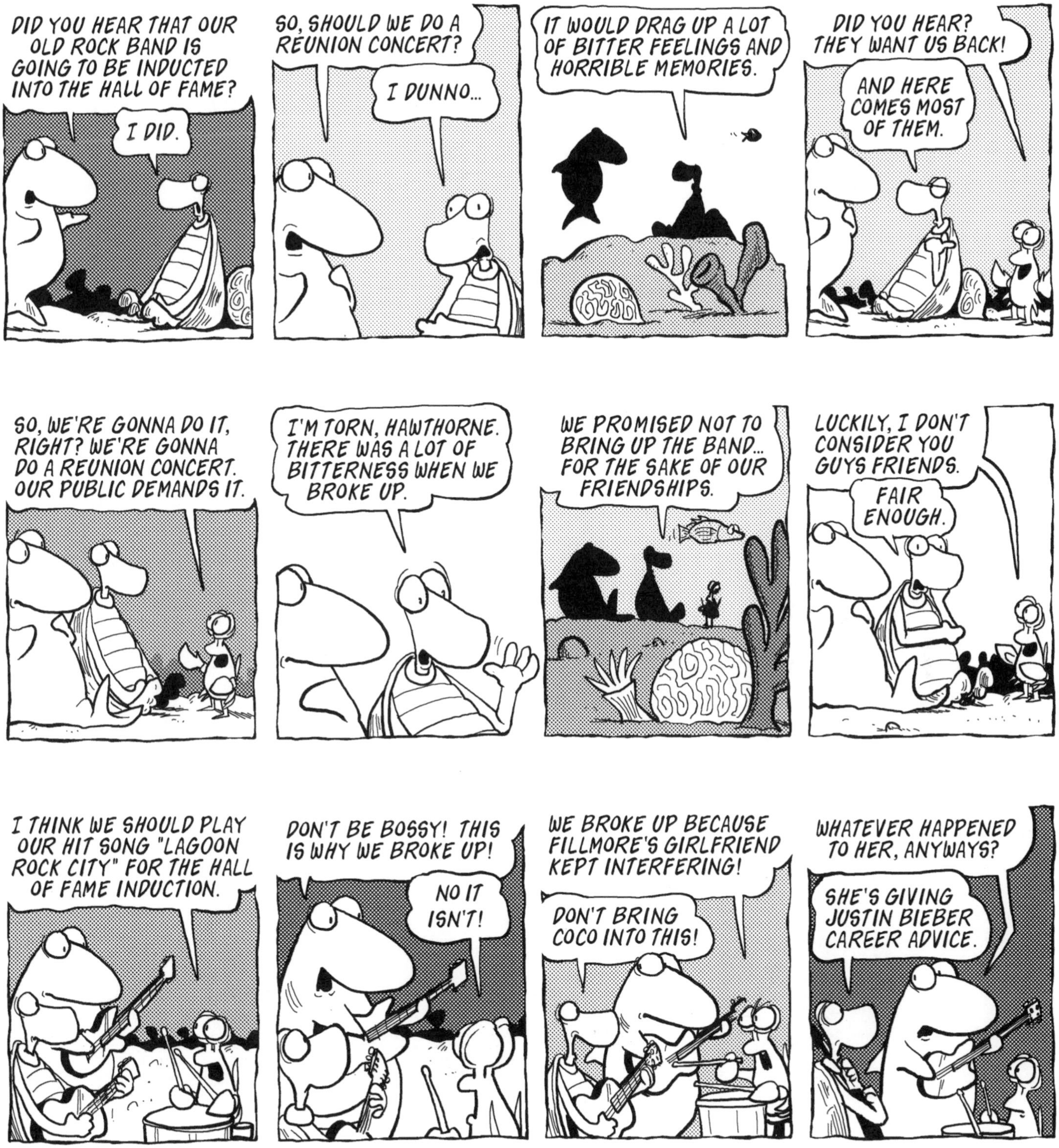
DID YOU HEAR THAT OUR OLD ROCK BAND IS GOING TO BE INDUCTED INTO THE HALL OF FAME?
I DID.
SO, SHOULD WE DO A REUNION CONCERT?
I DUNNO...
IT WOULD DRAG UP A LOT OF BITTER FEELINGS AND HORRIBLE MEMORIES.
DID YOU HEAR? THEY WANT US BACK!
AND HERE COMES MOST OF THEM.
SO, WE'RE GONNA DO IT, RIGHT? WE'RE GONNA DO A REUNION CONCERT. OUR PUBLIC DEMANDS IT.
I'M TORN, HAWTHORNE. THERE WAS A LOT OF BITTERNESS WHEN WE BROKE UP.
WE PROMISED NOT TO BRING UP THE BAND... FOR THE SAKE OF OUR FRIENDSHIPS.
LUCKILY, I DON'T CONSIDER YOU GUYS FRIENDS.
FAIR ENOUGH.
I THINK WE SHOULD PLAY OUR HIT SONG "LAGOON ROCK CITY" FOR THE HALL OF FAME INDUCTION.
DON'T BE BOSSY! THIS IS WHY WE BROKE UP!
NO IT ISN'T!
WE BROKE UP BECAUSE FILLMORE'S GIRLFRIEND KEPT INTERFERING!
DON'T BRING COCO INTO THIS!
WHATEVER HAPPENED TO HER, ANYWAYS?
SHE'S GIVING JUSTIN BIEBER CAREER ADVICE.

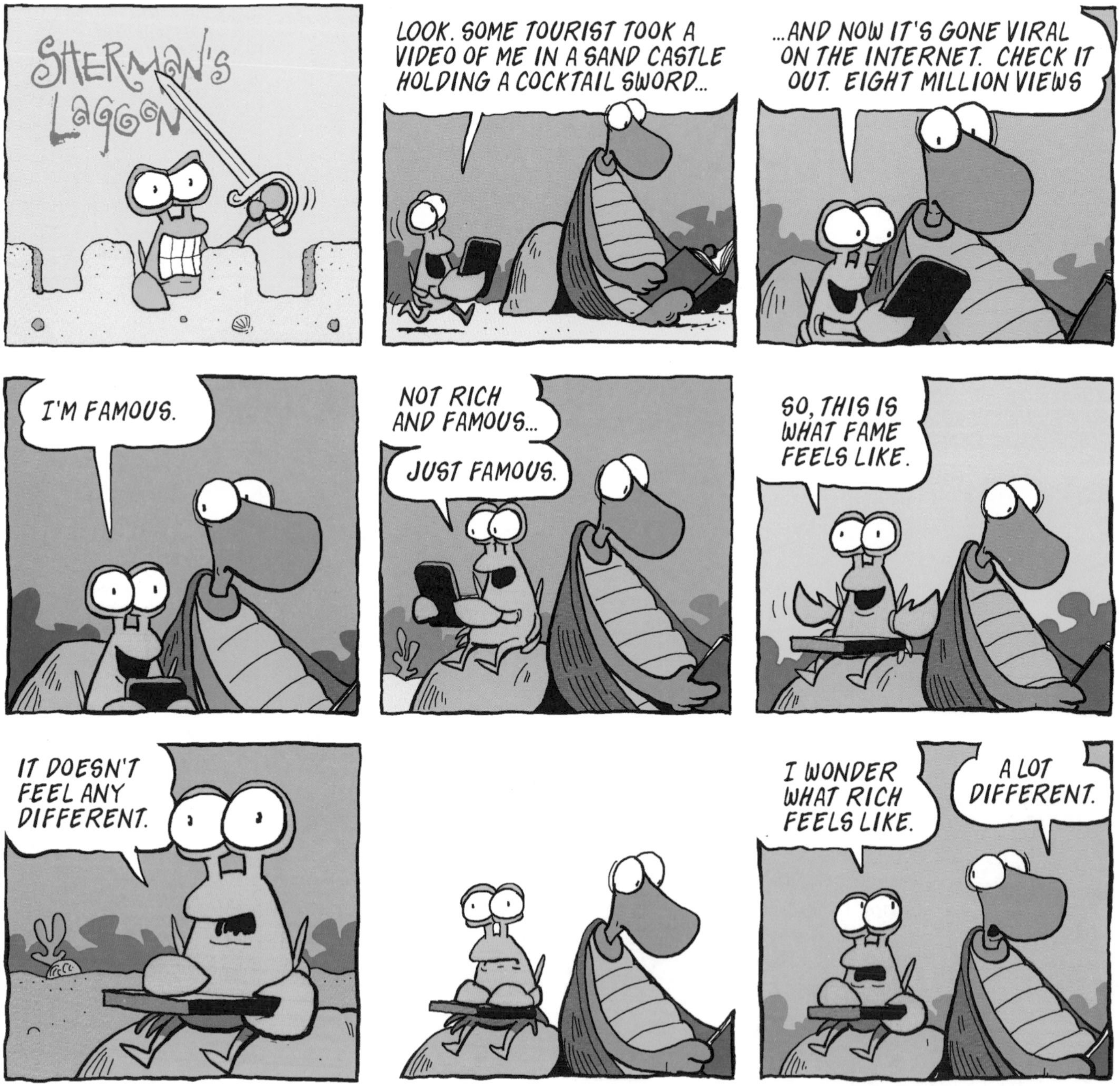
SHERMAN'S LAGOON
LOOK. SOME TOURIST TOOK A VIDEO OF ME IN A SAND CASTLE HOLDING A COCKTAIL SWORD...
...AND NOW IT'S GONE VIRAL ON THE INTERNET. CHECK IT OUT. EIGHT MILLION VIEWS
I'M FAMOUS.
NOT RICH AND FAMOUS...
JUST FAMOUS.
SO, THIS IS WHAT FAME FEELS LIKE.
IT DOESN'T FEEL ANY DIFFERENT.
I WONDER WHAT RICH FEELS LIKE.
A LOT DIFFERENT.

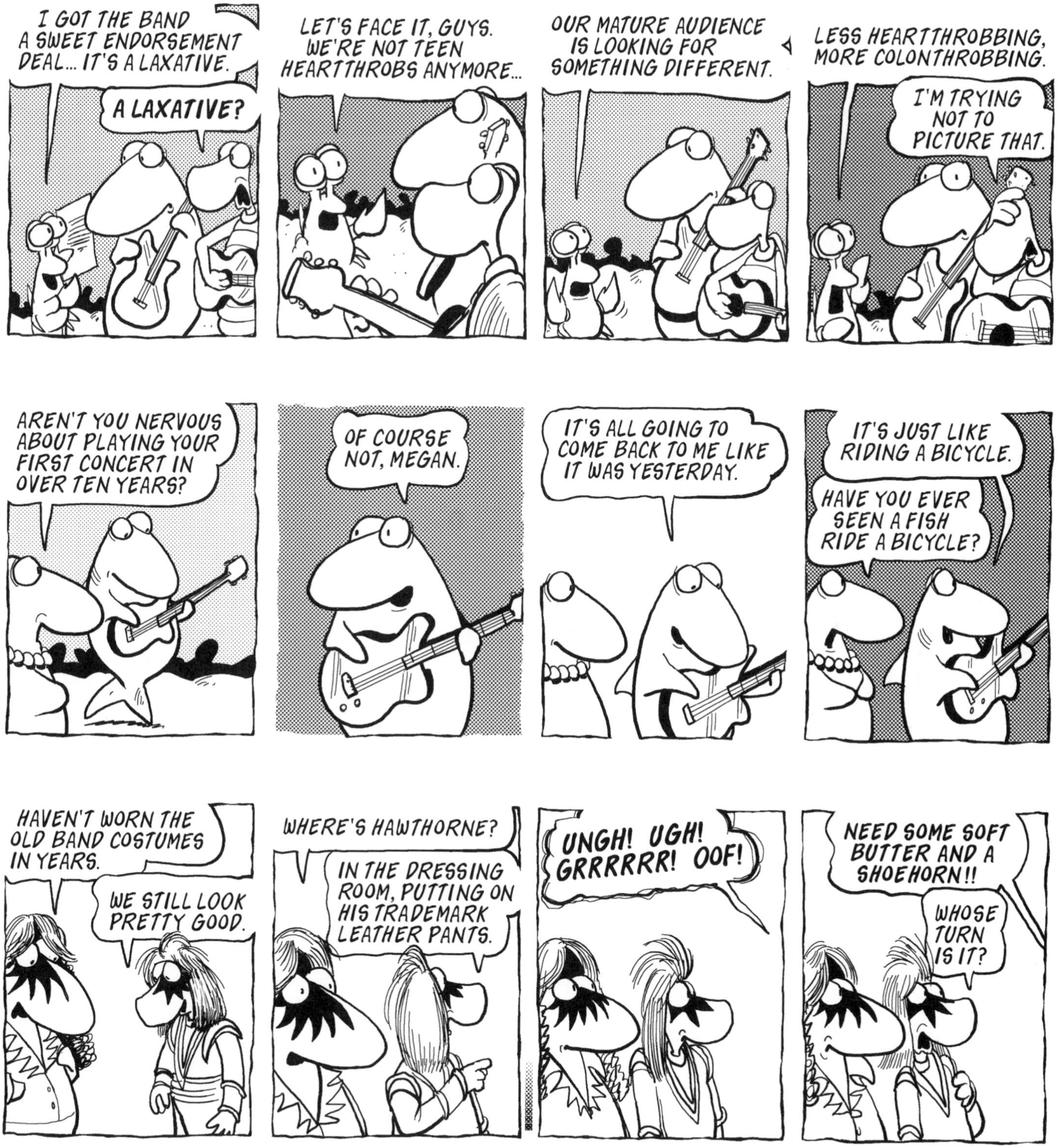
I GOT THE BAND A SWEET ENDORSEMENT DEAL... IT'S A LAXATIVE.
A LAXATIVE?
LET'S FACE IT, GUYS. WE'RE NOT TEEN HEARTTHROBS ANYMORE...
OUR MATURE AUDIENCE IS LOOKING FOR SOMETHING DIFFERENT.
LESS HEARTTHROBBING, MORE COLONTHROBBING.
I'M TRYING NOT TO PICTURE THAT.
AREN'T YOU NERVOUS ABOUT PLAYING YOUR FIRST CONCERT IN OVER TEN YEARS?
OF COURSE NOT, MEGAN.
IT'S ALL GOING TO COME BACK TO ME LIKE IT WAS YESTERDAY.
IT'S JUST LIKE RIDING A BICYCLE.
HAVE YOU EVER SEEN A FISH RIDE A BICYCLE?
HAVEN'T WORN THE OLD BAND COSTUMES IN YEARS.
WE STILL LOOK PRETTY GOOD.
WHERE'S HAWTHORNE?
IN THE DRESSING ROOM, PUTTING ON HIS TRADEMARK LEATHER PANTS.
UNGH! UGH! GRRRRRR! OOF!
NEED SOME SOFT BUTTER AND A SHOEHORN!!
WHOSE TURN IS IT?

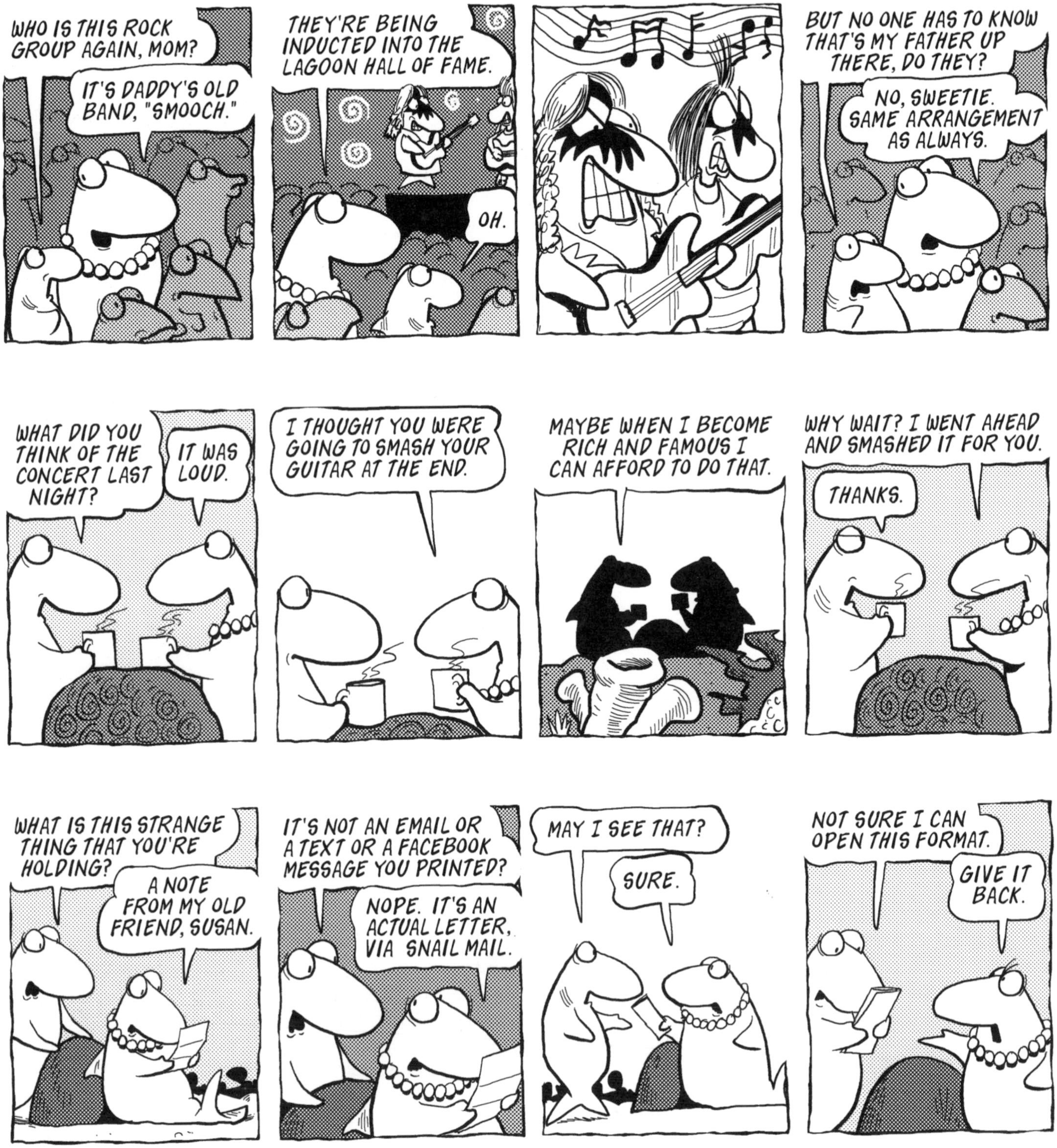
WHO IS THIS ROCK GROUP AGAIN, MOM?
IT'S DADDY'S OLD BAND, "SMOOCH."
THEY'RE BEING INDUCTED INTO THE LAGOON HALL OF FAME.
OH.
BUT NO ONE HAS TO KNOW THAT'S MY FATHER UP THERE, DO THEY?
NO, SWEETIE. SAME ARRANGEMENT AS ALWAYS.
WHAT DID YOU THINK OF THE CONCERT LAST NIGHT?
IT WAS LOUD.
I THOUGHT YOU WERE GOING TO SMASH YOUR GUITAR AT THE END.
MAYBE WHEN I BECOME RICH AND FAMOUS I CAN AFFORD TO DO THAT.
WHY WAIT? I WENT AHEAD AND SMASHED IT FOR YOU.
THANKS.
WHAT IS THIS STRANGE THING THAT YOU'RE HOLDING?
A NOTE FROM MY OLD FRIEND, SUSAN.
IT'S NOT AN EMAIL OR A TEXT OR A FACEBOOK MESSAGE YOU PRINTED?
NOPE. IT'S AN ACTUAL LETTER, VIA SNAIL MAIL.
MAY I SEE THAT?
SURE.
NOT SURE I CAN OPEN THIS FORMAT.
GIVE IT BACK.

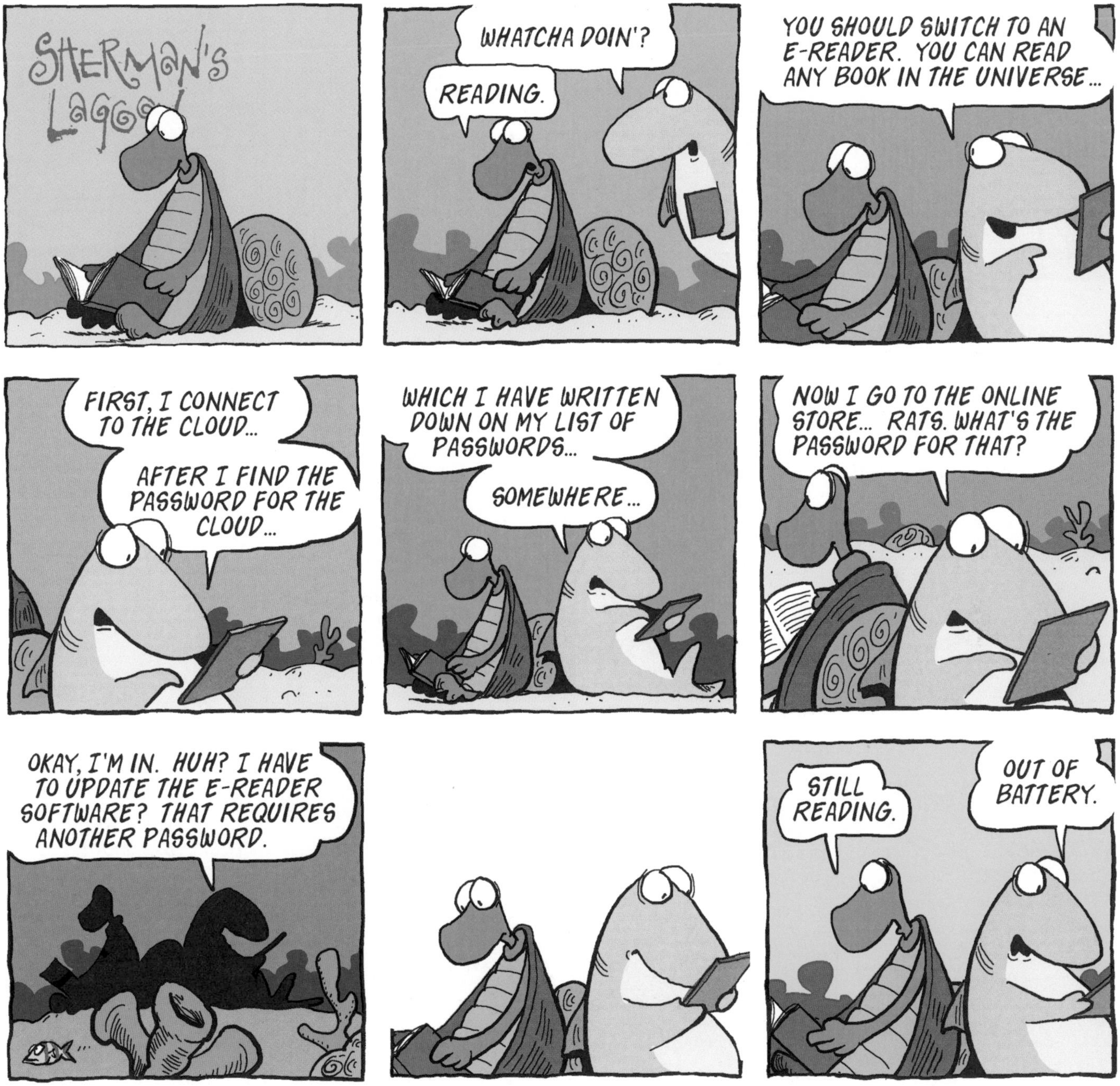
SHERMAN'S Lagoon
WHATCHA DOIN'?
READING.
YOU SHOULD SWITCH TO AN E-READER. YOU CAN READ ANY BOOK IN THE UNIVERSE...
FIRST, I CONNECT TO THE CLOUD...
AFTER I FIND THE PASSWORD FOR THE CLOUD...
WHICH I HAVE WRITTEN DOWN ON MY LIST OF PASSWORDS...
SOMEWHERE...
NOW I GO TO THE ONLINE STORE... RATS. WHAT'S THE PASSWORD FOR THAT?
OKAY, I'M IN. HUH? I HAVE TO UPDATE THE E-READER SOFTWARE? THAT REQUIRES ANOTHER PASSWORD.
STILL READING.
OUT OF BATTERY.

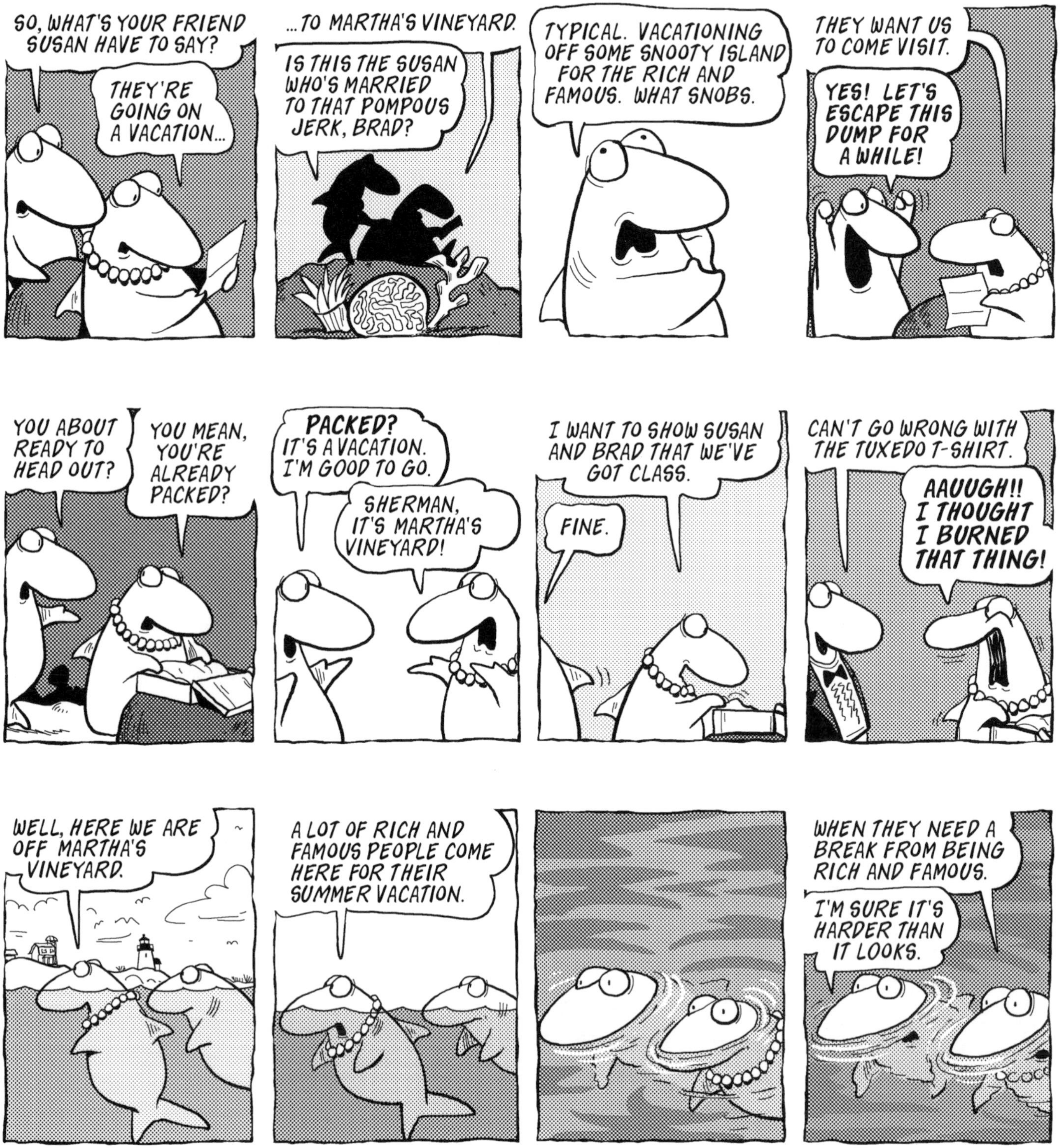
SO, WHAT'S YOUR FRIEND SUSAN HAVE TO SAY?
THEY'RE GOING ON A VACATION...
...TO MARTHA'S VINEYARD.
IS THIS THE SUSAN WHO'S MARRIED TO THAT POMPOUS JERK, BRAD?
TYPICAL. VACATIONING OFF SOME SNOOTY ISLAND FOR THE RICH AND FAMOUS. WHAT SNOBS.
THEY WANT US TO COME VISIT.
YES! LET'S ESCAPE THIS DUMP FOR A WHILE!
YOU ABOUT READY TO HEAD OUT?
YOU MEAN, YOU'RE ALREADY PACKED?
PACKED? IT'S A VACATION. I'M GOOD TO GO.
SHERMAN, IT'S MARTHA'S VINEYARD!
I WANT TO SHOW SUSAN AND BRAD THAT WE'VE GOT CLASS.
FINE.
CAN'T GO WRONG WITH THE TUXEDO T-SHIRT.
AAUUGH!! I THOUGHT I BURNED THAT THING!
WELL, HERE WE ARE OFF MARTHA'S VINEYARD.
A LOT OF RICH AND FAMOUS PEOPLE COME HERE FOR THEIR SUMMER VACATION.
WHEN THEY NEED A BREAK FROM BEING RICH AND FAMOUS.
I'M SURE IT'S HARDER THAN IT LOOKS.

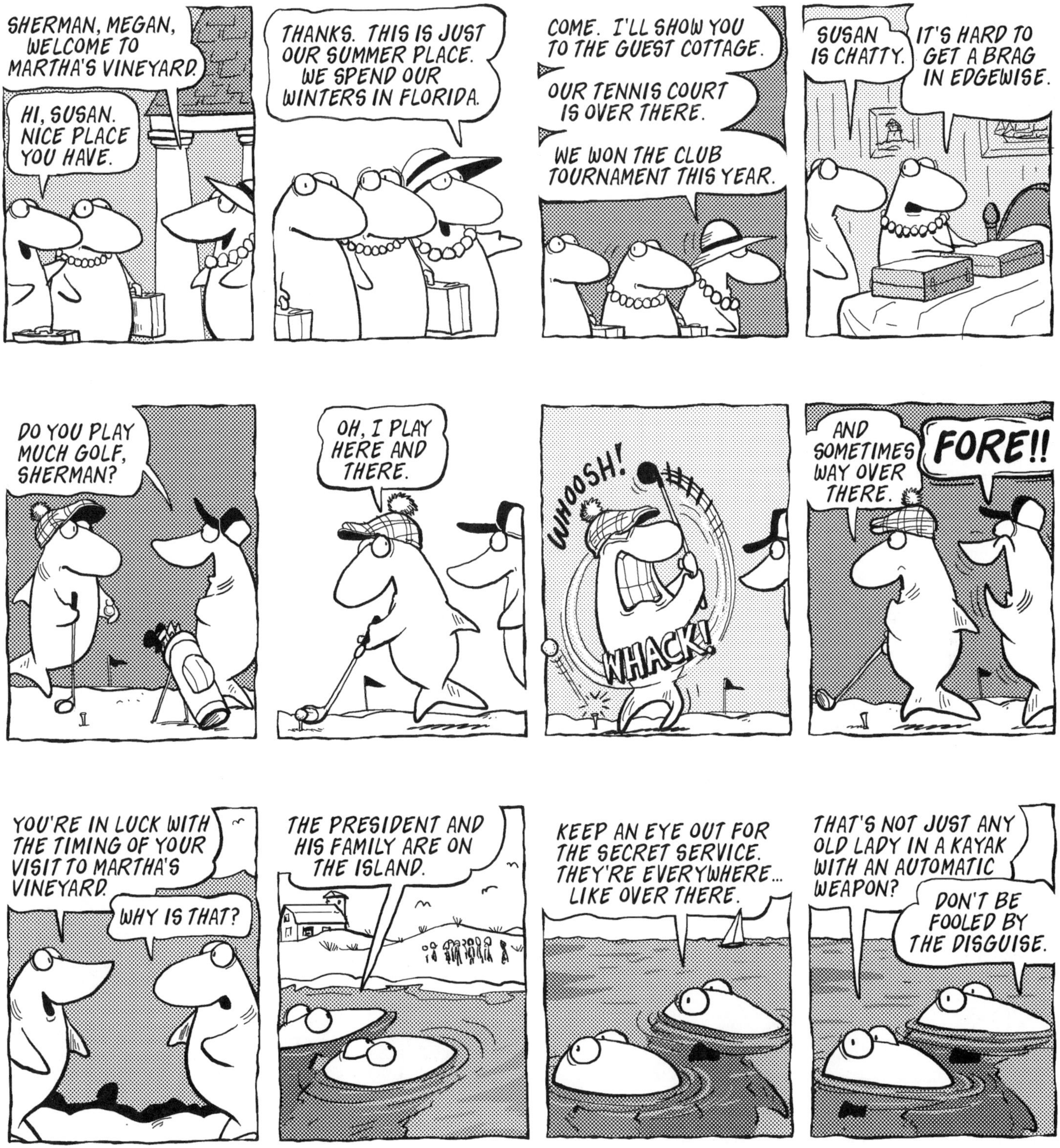
SHERMAN, MEGAN, WELCOME TO MARTHA'S VINEYARD.
HI, SUSAN. NICE PLACE YOU HAVE.
THANKS. THIS IS JUST OUR SUMMER PLACE. WE SPEND OUR WINTERS IN FLORIDA.
COME. I'LL SHOW YOU TO THE GUEST COTTAGE.
OUR TENNIS COURT IS OVER THERE.
WE WON THE CLUB TOURNAMENT THIS YEAR.
SUSAN IS CHATTY.
IT'S HARD TO GET A BRAG IN EDGEWISE.
DO YOU PLAY MUCH GOLF, SHERMAN?
OH, I PLAY HERE AND THERE.
WHOOSH!
WHACK!
AND SOMETIMES WAY OVER THERE.
FORE!!
YOU'RE IN LUCK WITH THE TIMING OF YOUR VISIT TO MARTHA'S VINEYARD.
WHY IS THAT?
THE PRESIDENT AND HIS FAMILY ARE ON THE ISLAND.
KEEP AN EYE OUT FOR THE SECRET SERVICE. THEY'RE EVERYWHERE... LIKE OVER THERE.
THAT'S NOT JUST ANY OLD LADY IN A KAYAK WITH AN AUTOMATIC WEAPON?
DON'T BE FOOLED BY THE DISGUISE.

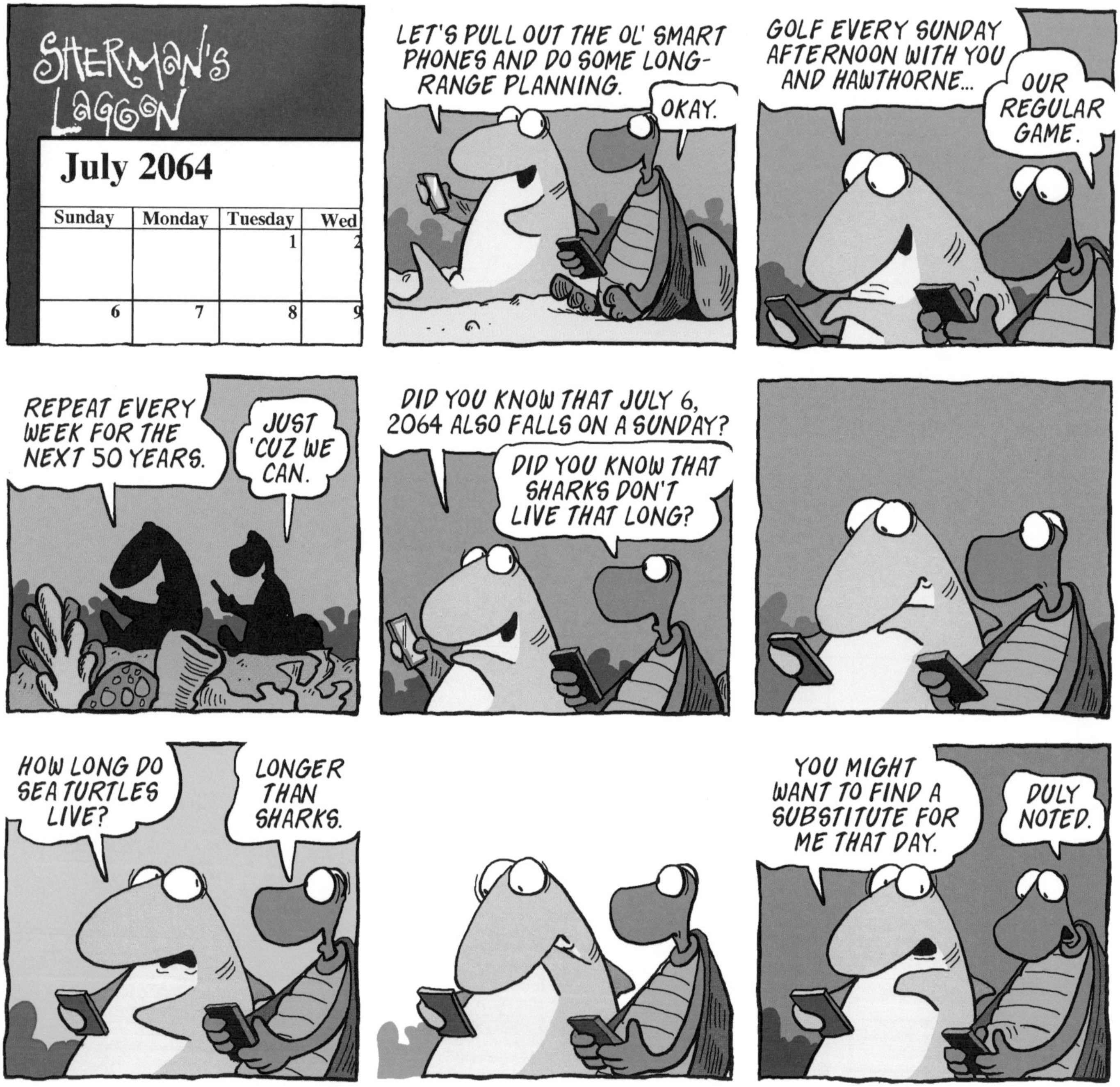
SHERMAN'S LAGOON
July 2064
Sunday Monday Tuesday Wed
1 2
6 7 8 9
LET'S PULL OUT THE OL' SMART PHONES AND DO SOME LONG-RANGE PLANNING.
OKAY.
GOLF EVERY SUNDAY AFTERNOON WITH YOU AND HAWTHORNE...
OUR REGULAR GAME.
REPEAT EVERY WEEK FOR THE NEXT 50 YEARS.
JUST 'CUZ WE CAN.
DID YOU KNOW THAT JULY 6, 2064 ALSO FALLS ON A SUNDAY?
DID YOU KNOW THAT SHARKS DON'T LIVE THAT LONG?
HOW LONG DO SEA TURTLES LIVE?
LONGER THAN SHARKS.
YOU MIGHT WANT TO FIND A SUBSTITUTE FOR ME THAT DAY.
DULY NOTED.

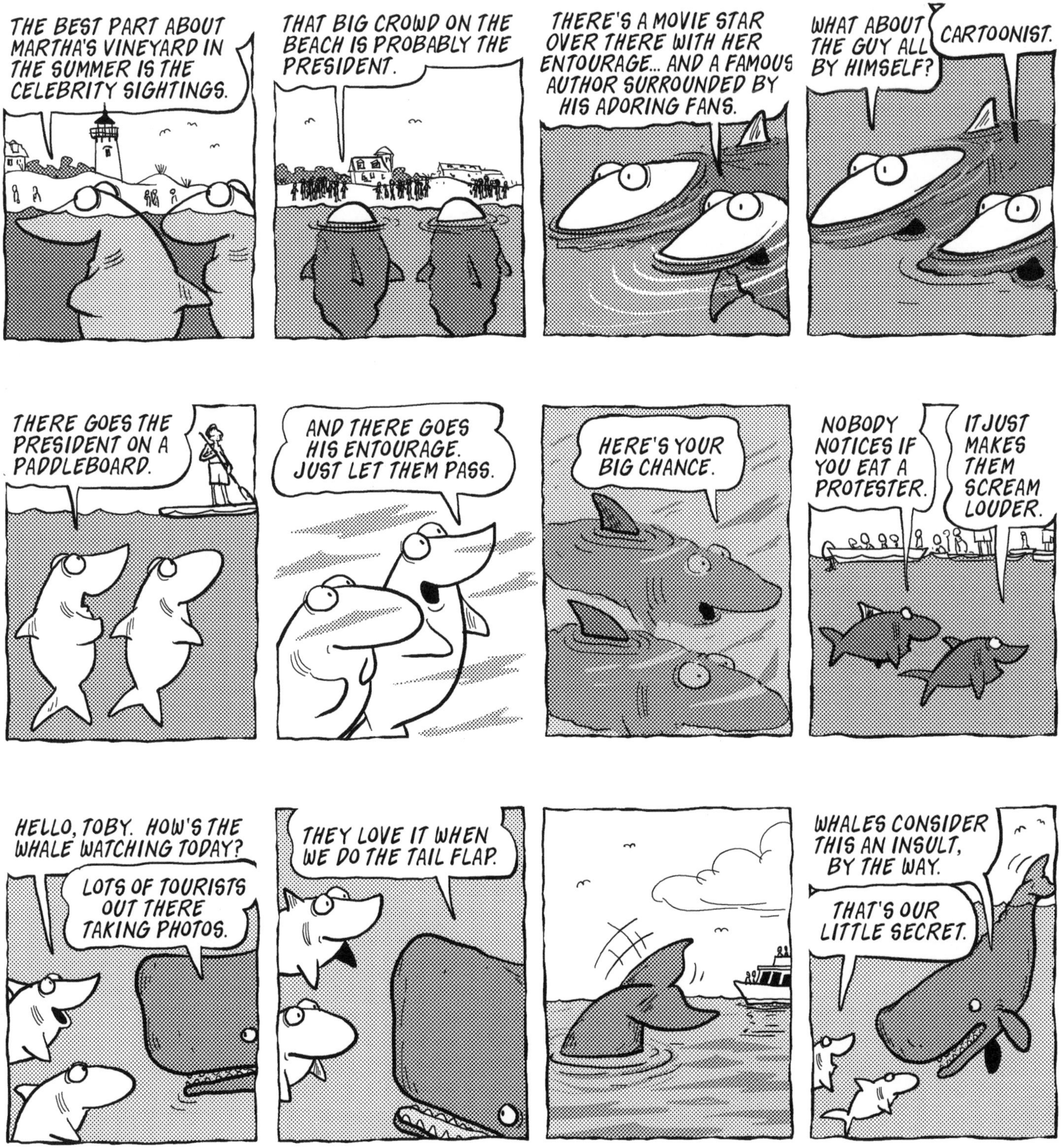
THE BEST PART ABOUT MARTHA'S VINEYARD IN THE SUMMER IS THE CELEBRITY SIGHTINGS.
THAT BIG CROWD ON THE BEACH IS PROBABLY THE PRESIDENT.
THERE'S A MOVIE STAR OVER THERE WITH HER ENTOURAGE... AND A FAMOUS AUTHOR SURROUNDED BY HIS ADORING FANS.
WHAT ABOUT THE GUY ALL BY HIMSELF?
CARTOONIST.
THERE GOES THE PRESIDENT ON A PADDLEBOARD.
AND THERE GOES HIS ENTOURAGE. JUST LET THEM PASS.
HERE'S YOUR BIG CHANCE.
NOBODY NOTICES IF YOU EAT A PROTESTER.
IT JUST MAKES THEM SCREAM LOUDER.
HELLO, TOBY. HOW'S THE WHALE WATCHING TODAY?
LOTS OF TOURISTS OUT THERE TAKING PHOTOS.
THEY LOVE IT WHEN WE DO THE TAIL FLAP.
WHALES CONSIDER THIS AN INSULT, BY THE WAY.
THAT'S OUR LITTLE SECRET.

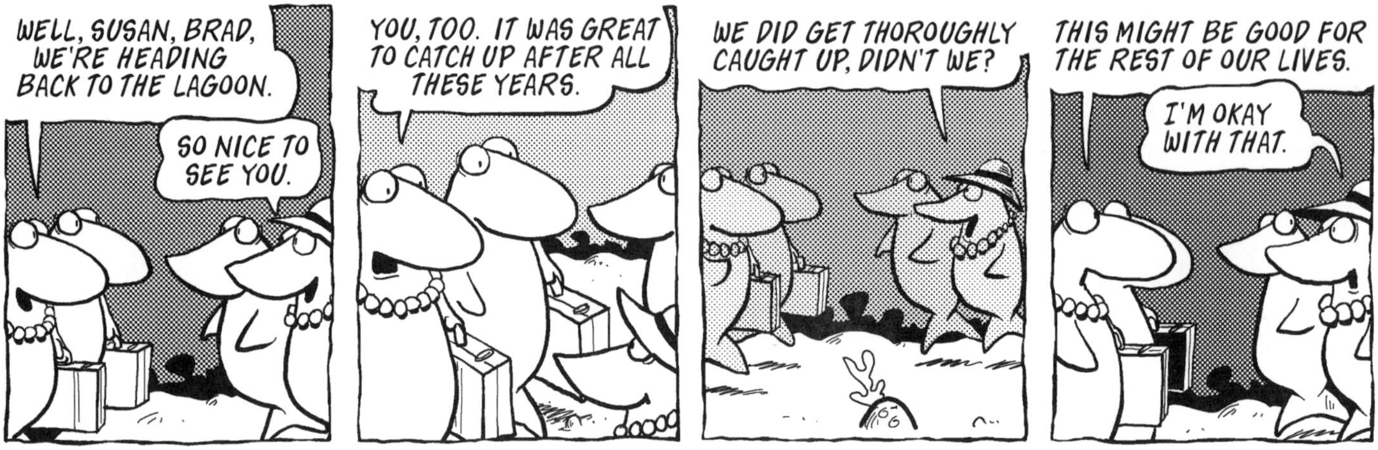
WELL, SUSAN, BRAD, WE'RE HEADING BACK TO THE LAGOON.
SO NICE TO SEE YOU.
YOU, TOO. IT WAS GREAT TO CATCH UP AFTER ALL THESE YEARS.
WE DID GET THOROUGHLY CAUGHT UP, DIDN'T WE?
THIS MIGHT BE GOOD FOR THE REST OF OUR LIVES.
I'M OKAY WITH THAT.

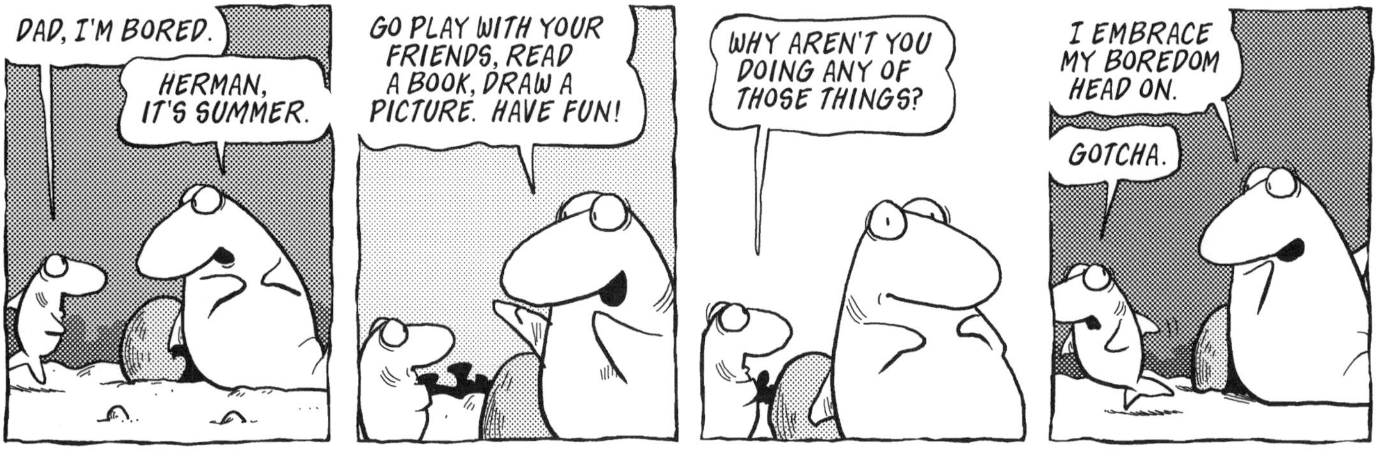
DAD, I'M BORED.
HERMAN, IT'S SUMMER.
GO PLAY WITH YOUR FRIENDS, READ A BOOK, DRAW A PICTURE. HAVE FUN!
WHY AREN'T YOU DOING ANY OF THOSE THINGS?
I EMBRACE MY BOREDOM HEAD ON.
GOTCHA.

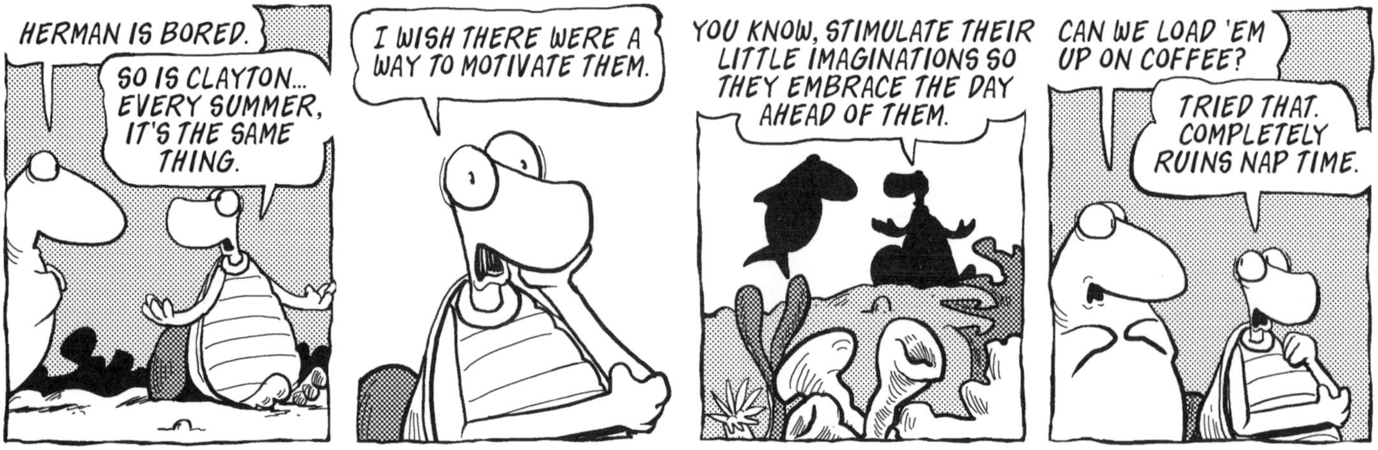
HERMAN IS BORED.
SO IS CLAYTON... EVERY SUMMER, IT'S THE SAME THING.
I WISH THERE WERE A WAY TO MOTIVATE THEM.
YOU KNOW, STIMULATE THEIR LITTLE IMAGINATIONS SO THEY EMBRACE THE DAY AHEAD OF THEM.
CAN WE LOAD 'EM UP ON COFFEE?
TRIED THAT. COMPLETELY RUINS NAP TIME.

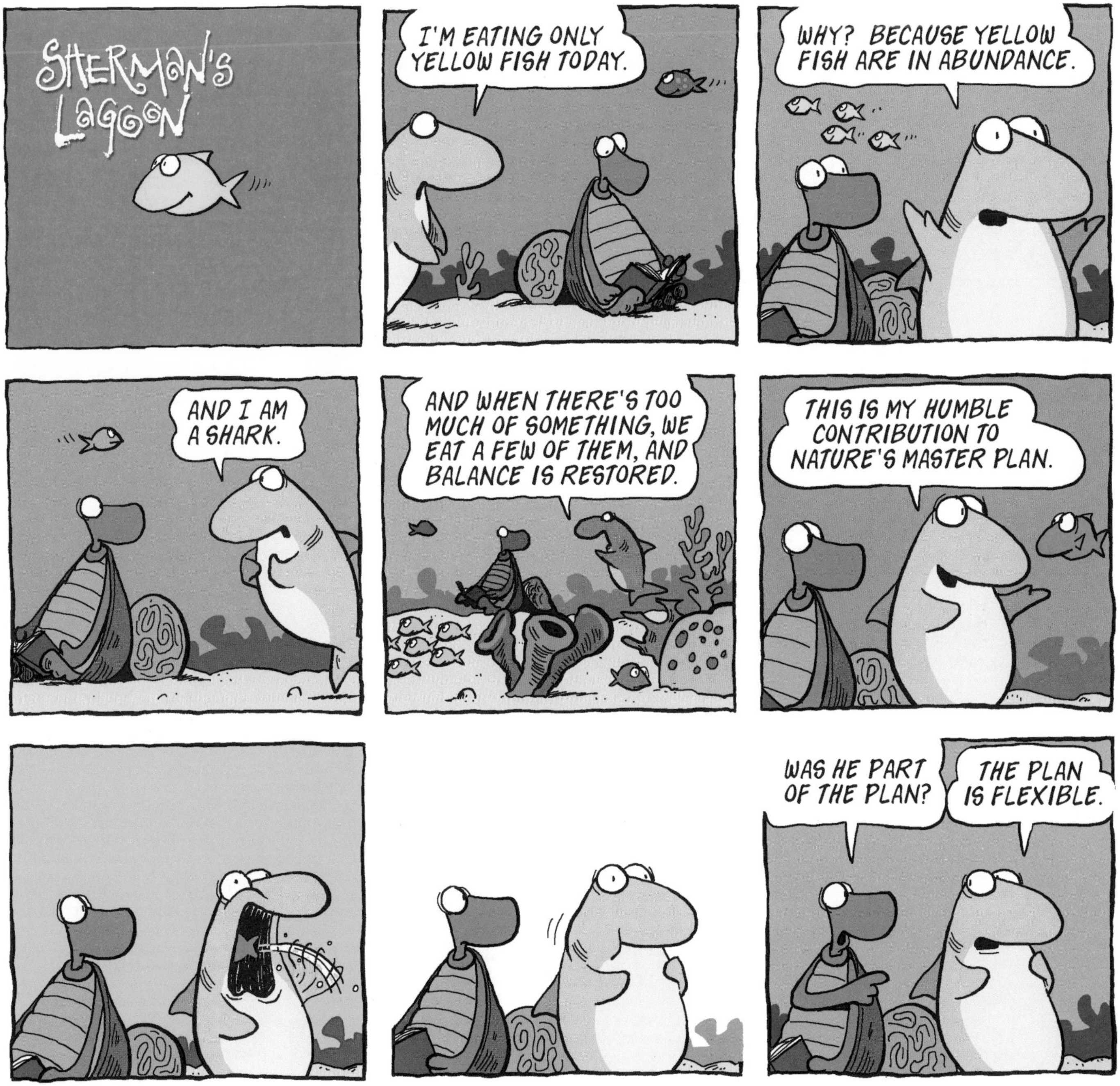
SHERMAN'S LAGOON
I'M EATING ONLY YELLOW FISH TODAY.
WHY? BECAUSE YELLOW FISH ARE IN ABUNDANCE.
AND I AM A SHARK.
AND WHEN THERE'S TOO MUCH OF SOMETHING, WE EAT A FEW OF THEM, AND BALANCE IS RESTORED.
THIS IS MY HUMBLE CONTRIBUTION TO NATURE'S MASTER PLAN.
WAS HE PART OF THE PLAN?
THE PLAN IS FLEXIBLE.

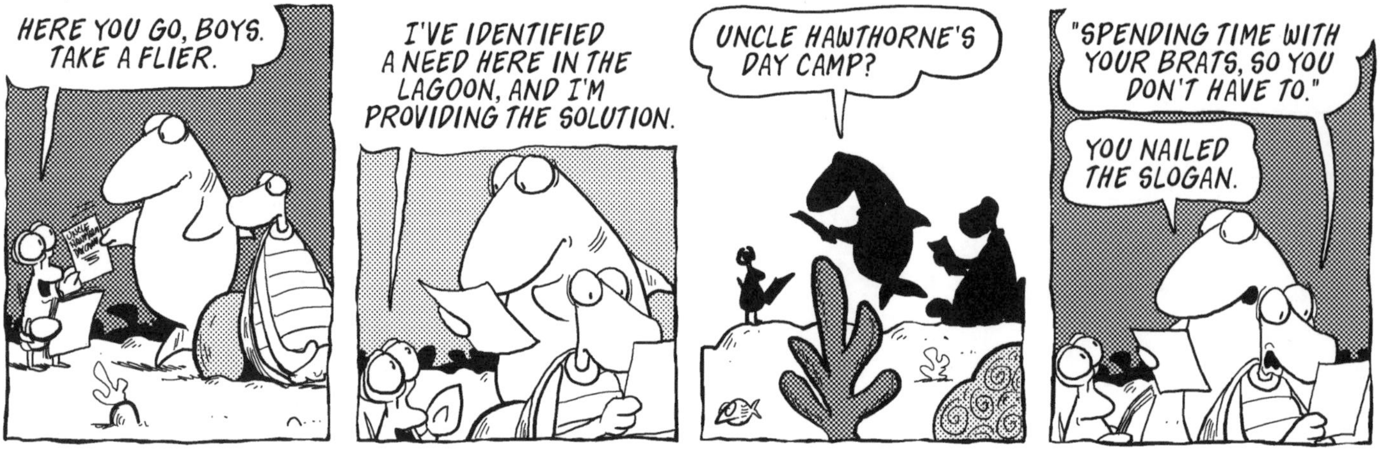
HERE YOU GO, BOYS. TAKE A FLIER.
I'VE IDENTIFIED A NEED HERE IN THE LAGOON, AND I'M PROVIDING THE SOLUTION.
UNCLE HAWTHORNE'S DAY CAMP?
"SPENDING TIME WITH YOUR BRATS, SO YOU DON'T HAVE TO."
YOU NAILED THE SLOGAN.

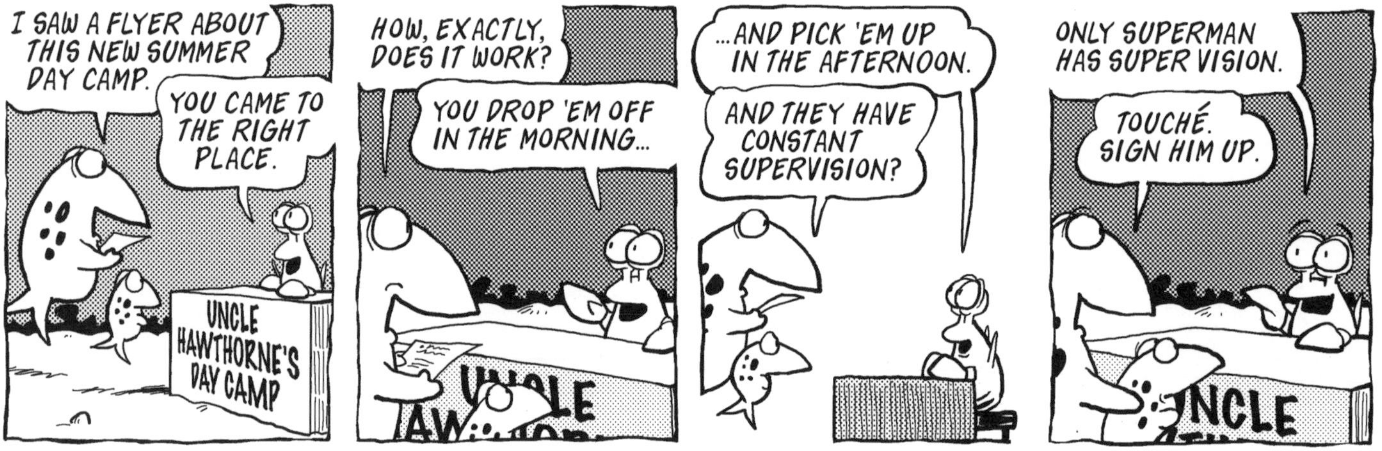
I SAW A FLYER ABOUT THIS NEW SUMMER DAY CAMP.
YOU CAME TO THE RIGHT PLACE.
UNCLE HAWTHORNE'S DAY CAMP
HOW, EXACTLY, DOES IT WORK?
YOU DROP 'EM OFF IN THE MORNING...
...AND PICK 'EM UP IN THE AFTERNOON.
AND THEY HAVE CONSTANT SUPERVISION?
ONLY SUPERMAN HAS SUPER VISION.
TOUCHÉ. SIGN HIM UP.

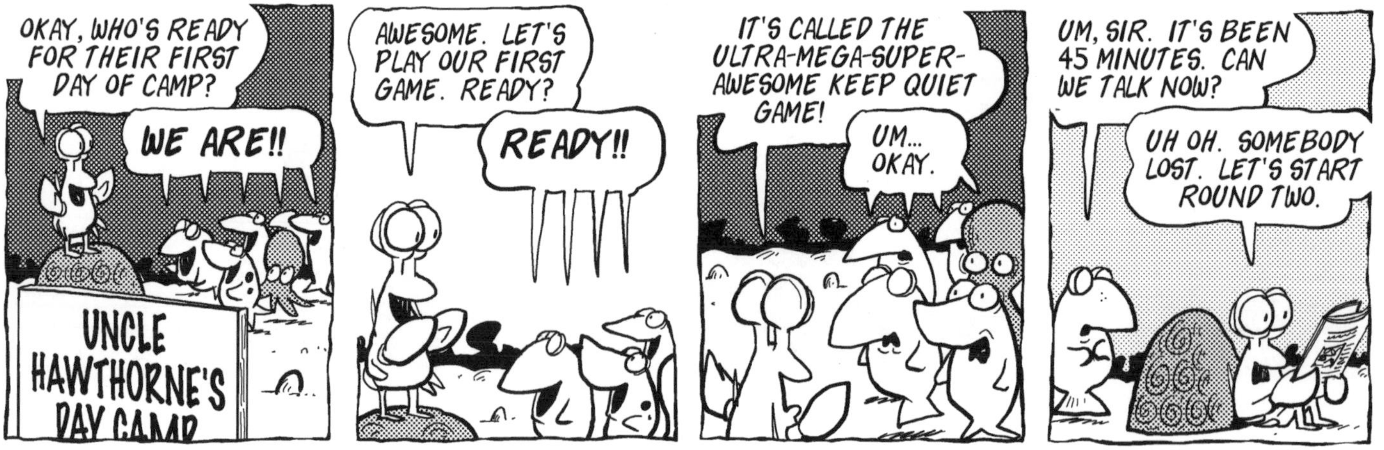
OKAY, WHO'S READY FOR THEIR FIRST DAY OF CAMP?
WE ARE!!
UNCLE HAWTHORNE'S DAY CAMP
AWESOME. LET'S PLAY OUR FIRST GAME. READY?
READY!!
IT'S CALLED THE ULTRA-MEGA-SUPER-AWESOME KEEP QUIET GAME!
UM... OKAY.
UM, SIR. IT'S BEEN 45 MINUTES. CAN WE TALK NOW?
UH OH. SOMEBODY LOST. LET'S START ROUND TWO.

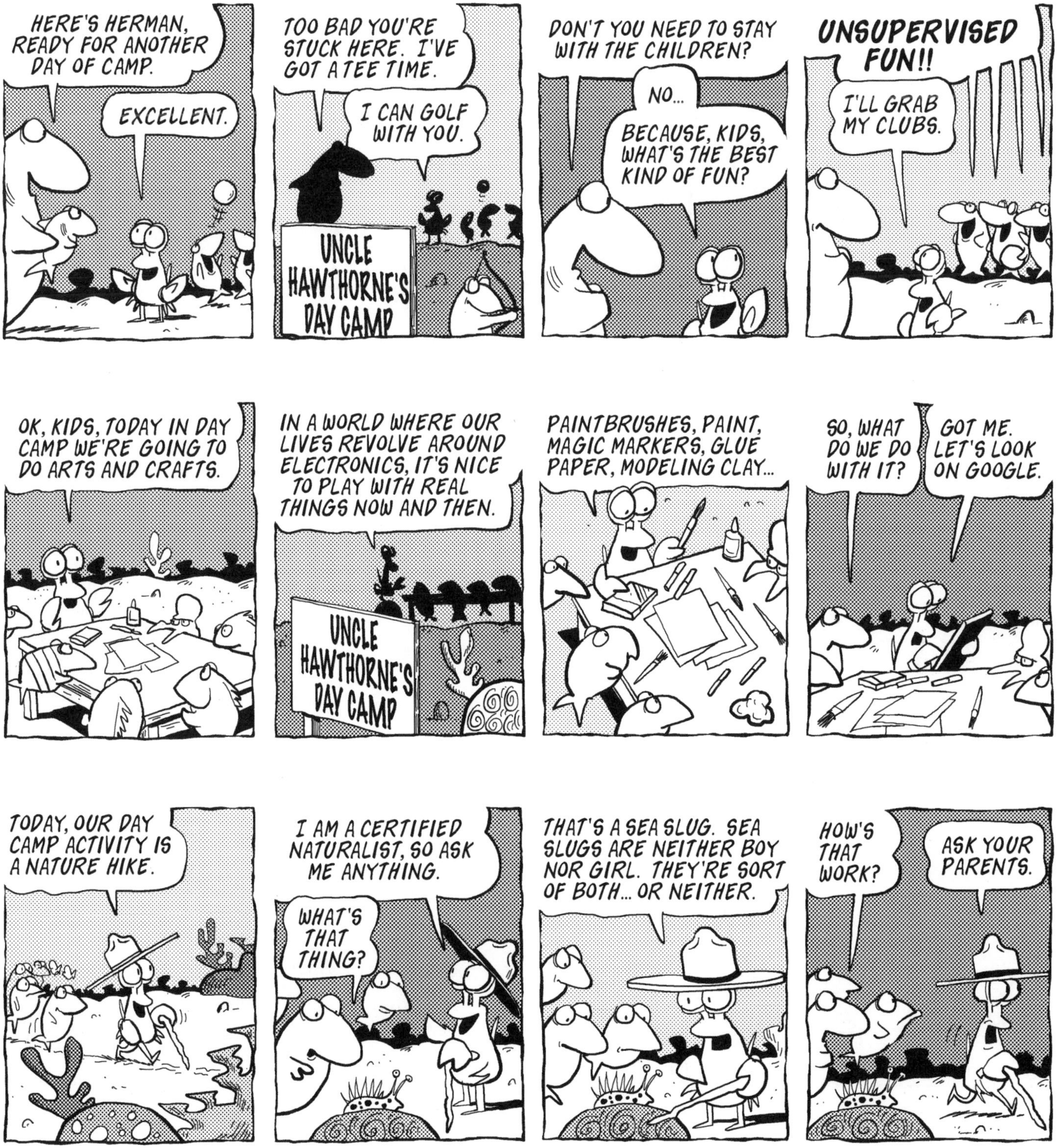
HERE'S HERMAN, READY FOR ANOTHER DAY OF CAMP.
EXCELLENT.
TOO BAD YOU'RE STUCK HERE. I'VE GOT A TEE TIME.
I CAN GOLF WITH YOU.
UNCLE HAWTHORNE'S DAY CAMP
DON'T YOU NEED TO STAY WITH THE CHILDREN?
NO...
BECAUSE, KIDS, WHAT'S THE BEST KIND OF FUN?
UNSUPERVISED FUN!!
I'LL GRAB MY CLUBS.
OK, KIDS, TODAY IN DAY CAMP WE'RE GOING TO DO ARTS AND CRAFTS.
IN A WORLD WHERE OUR LIVES REVOLVE AROUND ELECTRONICS, IT'S NICE TO PLAY WITH REAL THINGS NOW AND THEN.
UNCLE HAWTHORNE'S DAY CAMP
PAINTBRUSHES, PAINT, MAGIC MARKERS, GLUE PAPER, MODELING CLAY...
SO, WHAT DO WE DO WITH IT?
GOT ME. LET'S LOOK ON GOOGLE.
TODAY, OUR DAY CAMP ACTIVITY IS A NATURE HIKE.
I AM A CERTIFIED NATURALIST, SO ASK ME ANYTHING.
WHAT'S THAT THING?
THAT'S A SEA SLUG. SEA SLUGS ARE NEITHER BOY NOR GIRL. THEY'RE SORT OF BOTH... OR NEITHER.
HOW'S THAT WORK?
ASK YOUR PARENTS.

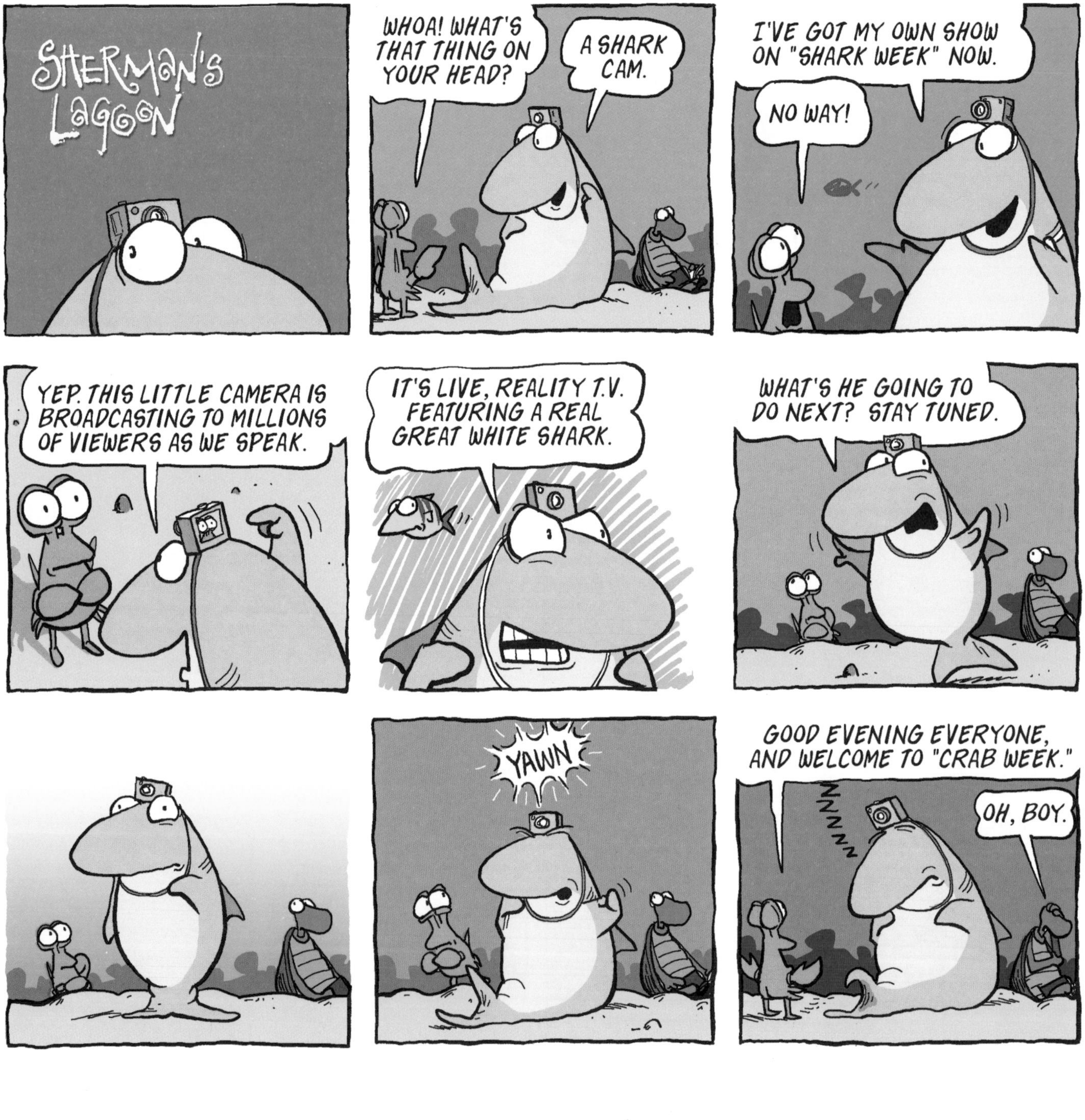
Sherman's Lagoon
WHOA! WHAT'S THAT THING ON YOUR HEAD?
A SHARK CAM.
I'VE GOT MY OWN SHOW ON "SHARK WEEK" NOW.
NO WAY!
YEP. THIS LITTLE CAMERA IS BROADCASTING TO MILLIONS OF VIEWERS AS WE SPEAK.
IT'S LIVE, REALITY T.V. FEATURING A REAL GREAT WHITE SHARK.
WHAT'S HE GOING TO DO NEXT? STAY TUNED.
YAWN
GOOD EVENING EVERYONE, AND WELCOME TO "CRAB WEEK."
ZZZZZZ
OH, BOY.

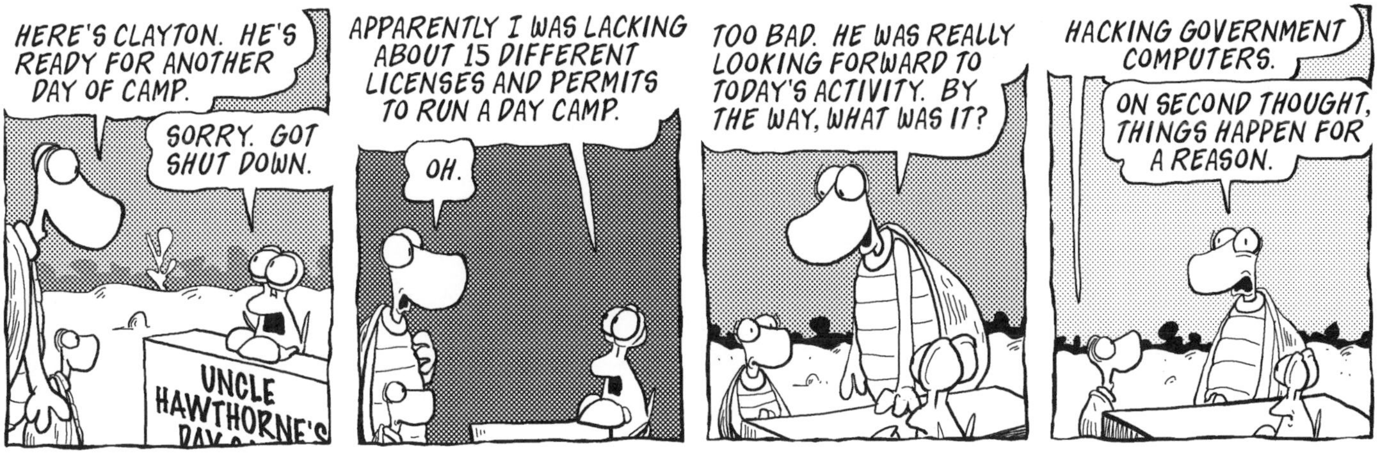
HERE'S CLAYTON. HE'S READY FOR ANOTHER DAY OF CAMP.
SORRY. GOT SHUT DOWN.
UNCLE HAWTHORNE'S
APPARENTLY I WAS LACKING ABOUT 15 DIFFERENT LICENSES AND PERMITS TO RUN A DAY CAMP.
OH.
TOO BAD. HE WAS REALLY LOOKING FORWARD TO TODAY'S ACTIVITY. BY THE WAY, WHAT WAS IT?
HACKING GOVERNMENT COMPUTERS.
ON SECOND THOUGHT, THINGS HAPPEN FOR A REASON.

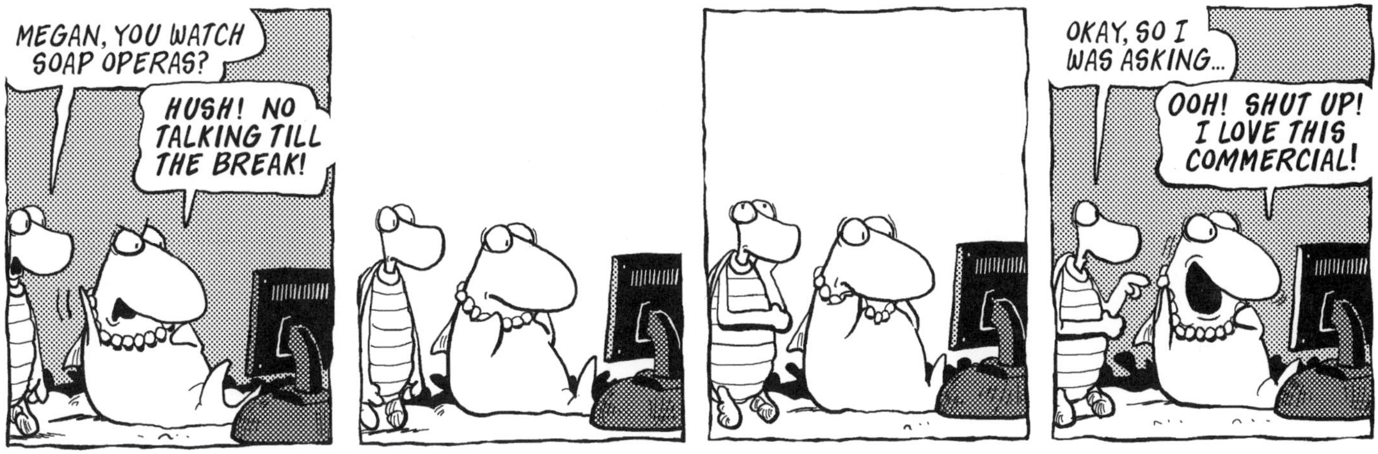
MEGAN, YOU WATCH SOAP OPERAS?
HUSH! NO TALKING TILL THE BREAK!
OKAY, SO I WAS ASKING...
OOH! SHUT UP! I LOVE THIS COMMERCIAL!

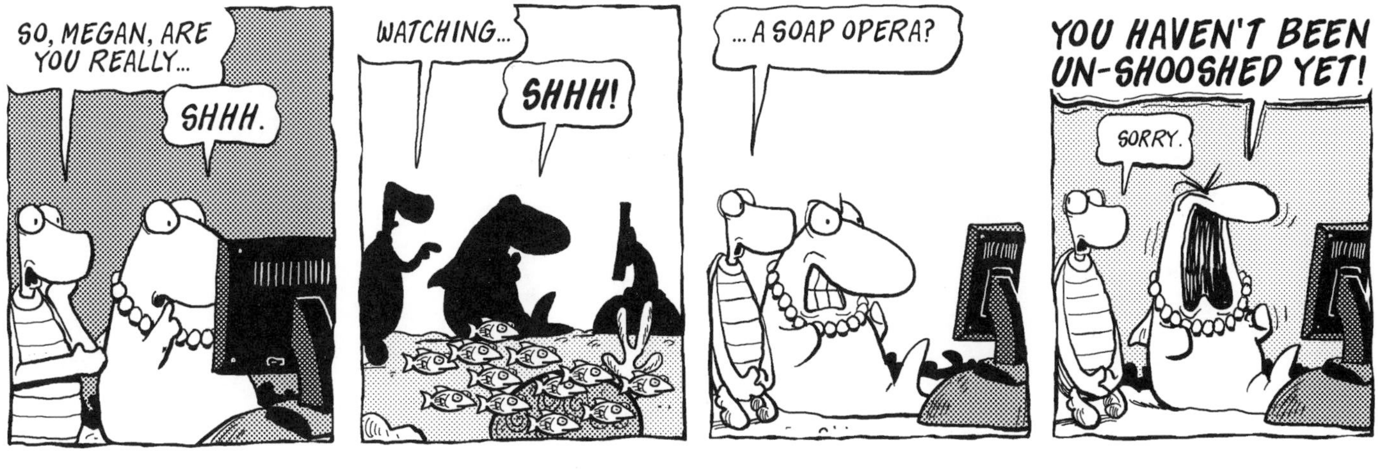
SO, MEGAN, ARE YOU REALLY...
SHHH.
WATCHING...
SHHH!
...A SOAP OPERA?
YOU HAVEN'T BEEN UN-SHOOSHED YET!
SORRY.

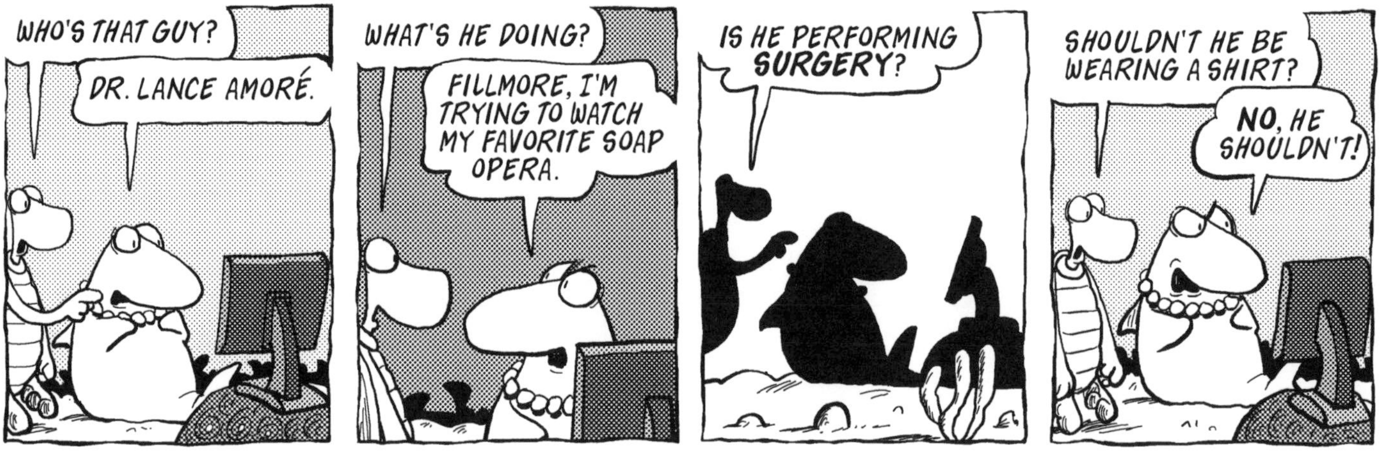
WHO'S THAT GUY?
DR. LANCE AMORÉ.
WHAT'S HE DOING?
FILLMORE, I'M TRYING TO WATCH MY FAVORITE SOAP OPERA.
IS HE PERFORMING SURGERY?
SHOULDN'T HE BE WEARING A SHIRT?
NO, HE SHOULDN'T!

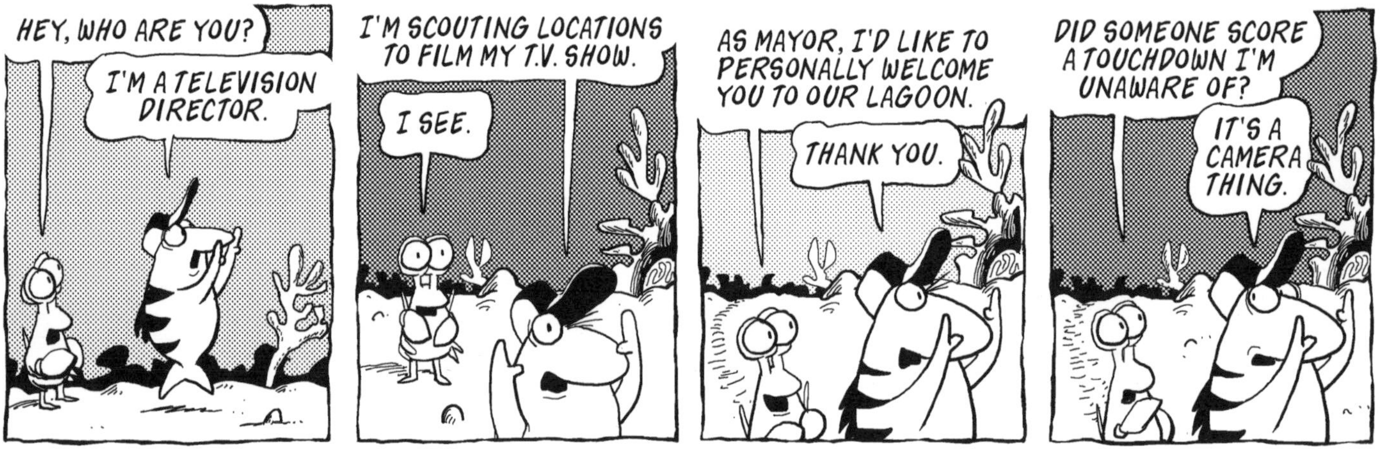
HEY, WHO ARE YOU?
I'M A TELEVISION DIRECTOR.
I'M SCOUTING LOCATIONS TO FILM MY T.V. SHOW.
I SEE.
AS MAYOR, I'D LIKE TO PERSONALLY WELCOME YOU TO OUR LAGOON.
THANK YOU.
DID SOMEONE SCORE A TOUCHDOWN I'M UNAWARE OF?
IT'S A CAMERA THING.

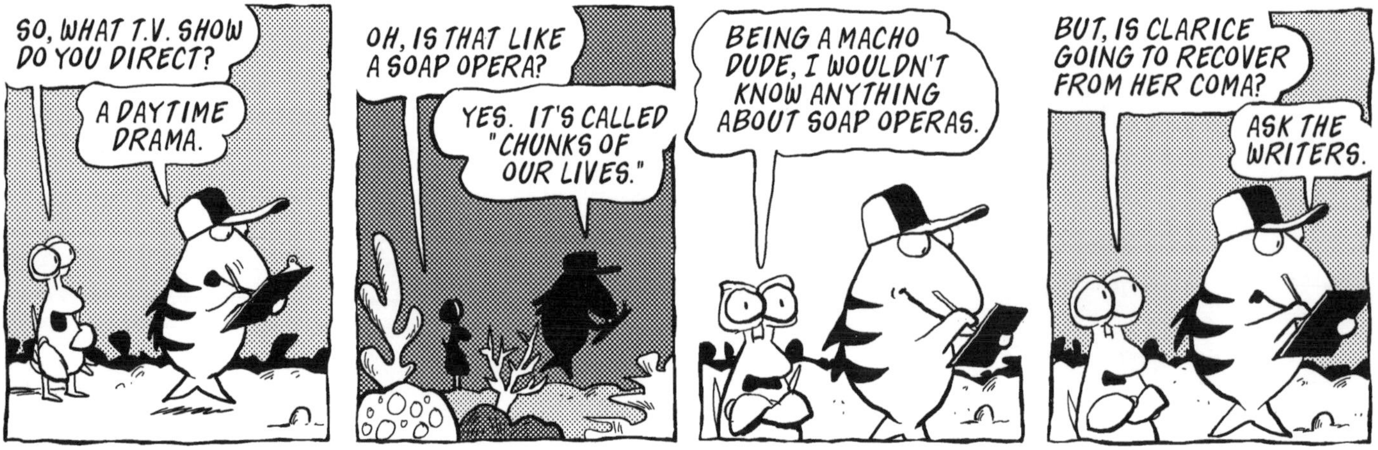
SO, WHAT T.V. SHOW DO YOU DIRECT?
A DAYTIME DRAMA.
OH, IS THAT LIKE A SOAP OPERA?
YES. IT'S CALLED "CHUNKS OF OUR LIVES."
BEING A MACHO DUDE, I WOULDN'T KNOW ANYTHING ABOUT SOAP OPERAS.
BUT, IS CLARICE GOING TO RECOVER FROM HER COMA?
ASK THE WRITERS.

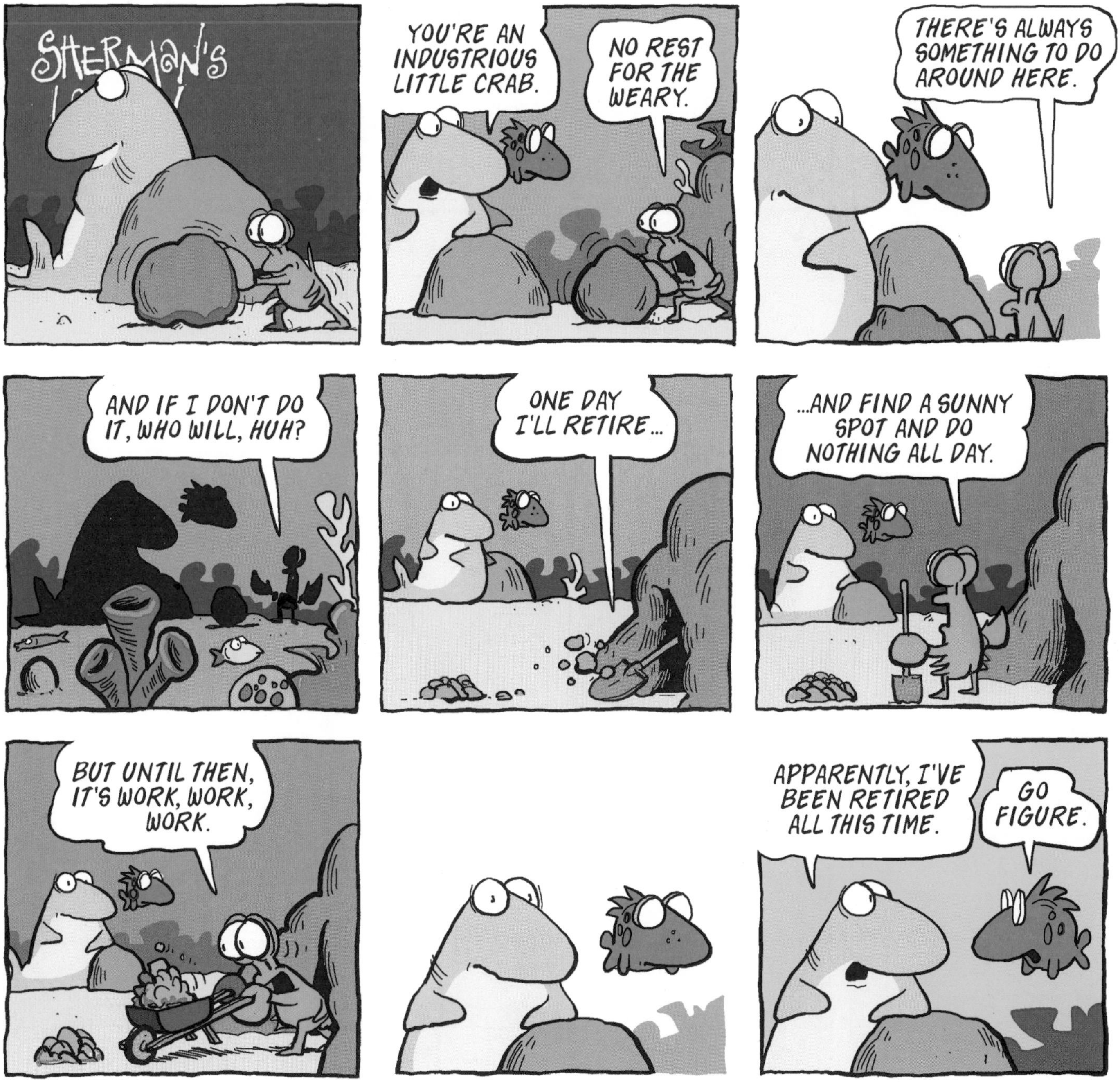
SHERMAN'S
YOU'RE AN INDUSTRIOUS LITTLE CRAB.
NO REST FOR THE WEARY.
THERE'S ALWAYS SOMETHING TO DO AROUND HERE.
AND IF I DON'T DO IT, WHO WILL, HUH?
ONE DAY I'LL RETIRE...
...AND FIND A SUNNY SPOT AND DO NOTHING ALL DAY.
BUT UNTIL THEN, IT'S WORK, WORK, WORK.
APPARENTLY, I'VE BEEN RETIRED ALL THIS TIME.
GO FIGURE.

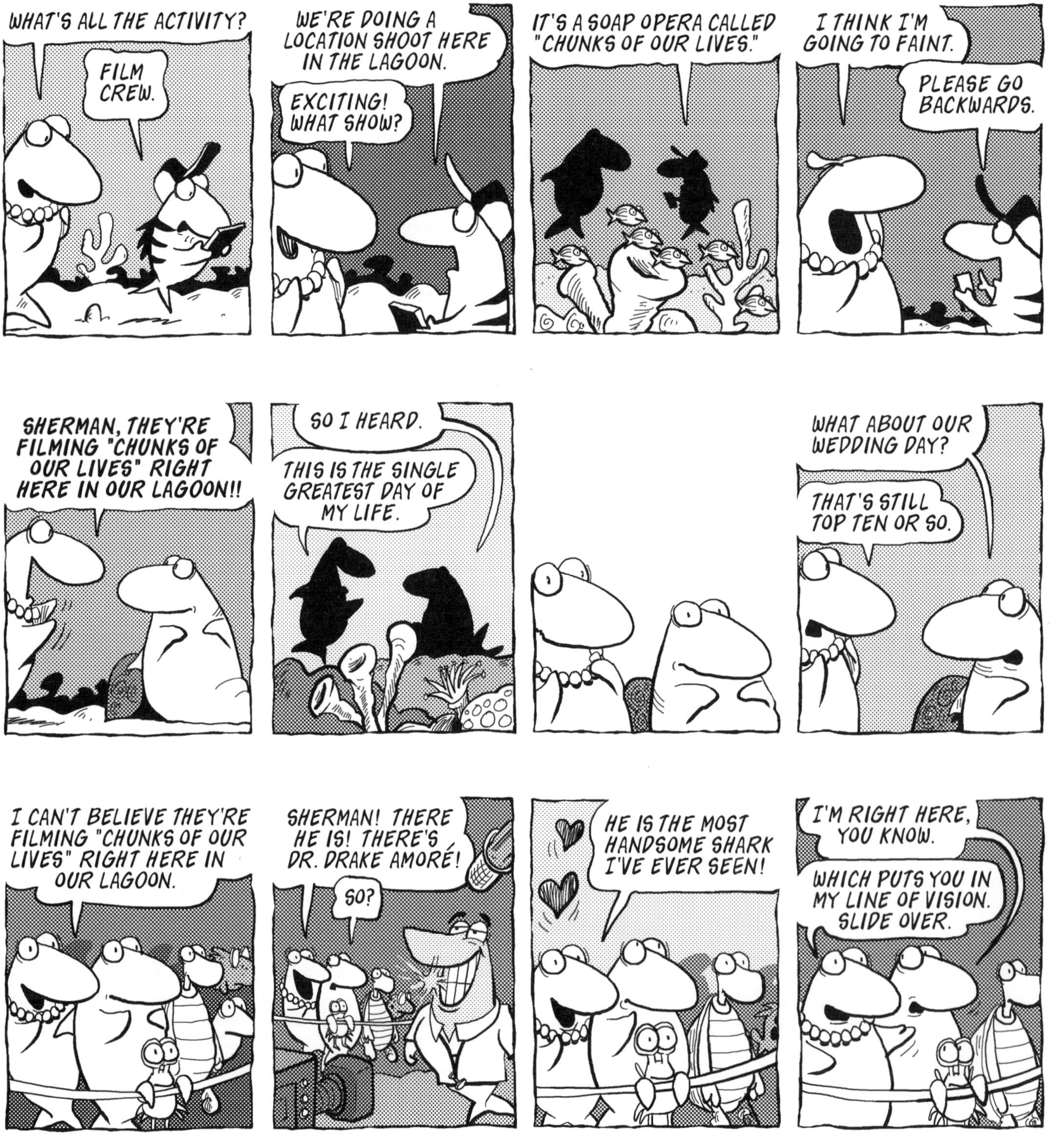
WHAT'S ALL THE ACTIVITY?
FILM CREW.
WE'RE DOING A LOCATION SHOOT HERE IN THE LAGOON.
EXCITING! WHAT SHOW?
IT'S A SOAP OPERA CALLED "CHUNKS OF OUR LIVES."
I THINK I'M GOING TO FAINT.
PLEASE GO BACKWARDS.
SHERMAN, THEY'RE FILMING "CHUNKS OF OUR LIVES" RIGHT HERE IN OUR LAGOON!!
SO I HEARD.
THIS IS THE SINGLE GREATEST DAY OF MY LIFE.
WHAT ABOUT OUR WEDDING DAY?
THAT'S STILL TOP TEN OR SO.
I CAN'T BELIEVE THEY'RE FILMING "CHUNKS OF OUR LIVES" RIGHT HERE IN OUR LAGOON.
SHERMAN! THERE HE IS! THERE'S DR. DRAKE AMORÉ!
SO?
HE IS THE MOST HANDSOME SHARK I'VE EVER SEEN!
I'M RIGHT HERE, YOU KNOW.
WHICH PUTS YOU IN MY LINE OF VISION. SLIDE OVER.

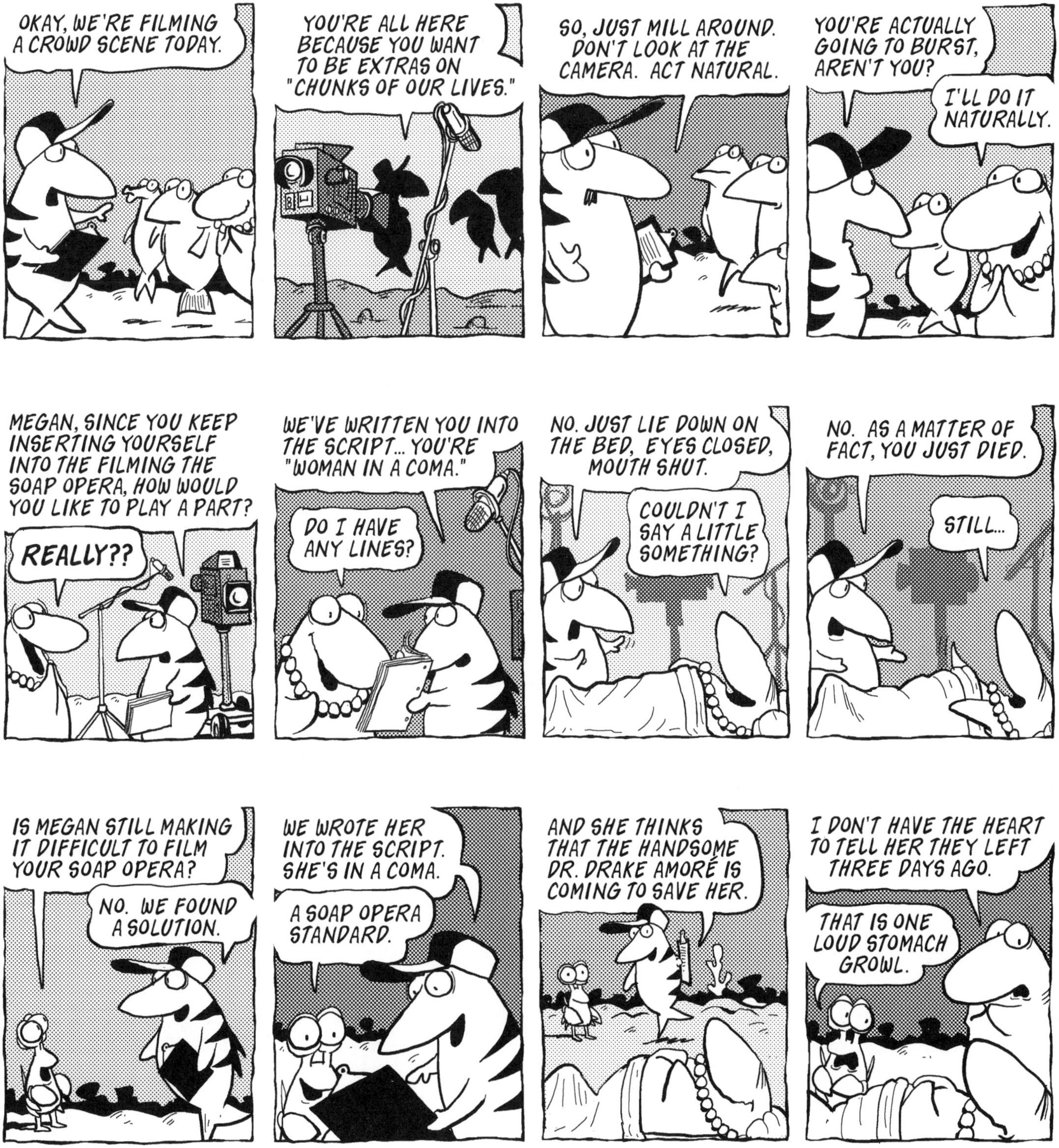
OKAY, WE'RE FILMING A CROWD SCENE TODAY.
YOU'RE ALL HERE BECAUSE YOU WANT TO BE EXTRAS ON "CHUNKS OF OUR LIVES."
SO, JUST MILL AROUND. DON'T LOOK AT THE CAMERA. ACT NATURAL.
YOU'RE ACTUALLY GOING TO BURST, AREN'T YOU?
I'LL DO IT NATURALLY.
MEGAN, SINCE YOU KEEP INSERTING YOURSELF INTO THE FILMING THE SOAP OPERA, HOW WOULD YOU LIKE TO PLAY A PART?
REALLY??
WE'VE WRITTEN YOU INTO THE SCRIPT... YOU'RE "WOMAN IN A COMA."
DO I HAVE ANY LINES?
NO. JUST LIE DOWN ON THE BED, EYES CLOSED, MOUTH SHUT.
COULDN'T I SAY A LITTLE SOMETHING?
NO. AS A MATTER OF FACT, YOU JUST DIED.
STILL...
IS MEGAN STILL MAKING IT DIFFICULT TO FILM YOUR SOAP OPERA?
NO. WE FOUND A SOLUTION.
WE WROTE HER INTO THE SCRIPT. SHE'S IN A COMA.
A SOAP OPERA STANDARD.
AND SHE THINKS THAT THE HANDSOME DR. DRAKE AMORÉ IS COMING TO SAVE HER.
I DON'T HAVE THE HEART TO TELL HER THEY LEFT THREE DAYS AGO.
THAT IS ONE LOUD STOMACH GROWL.

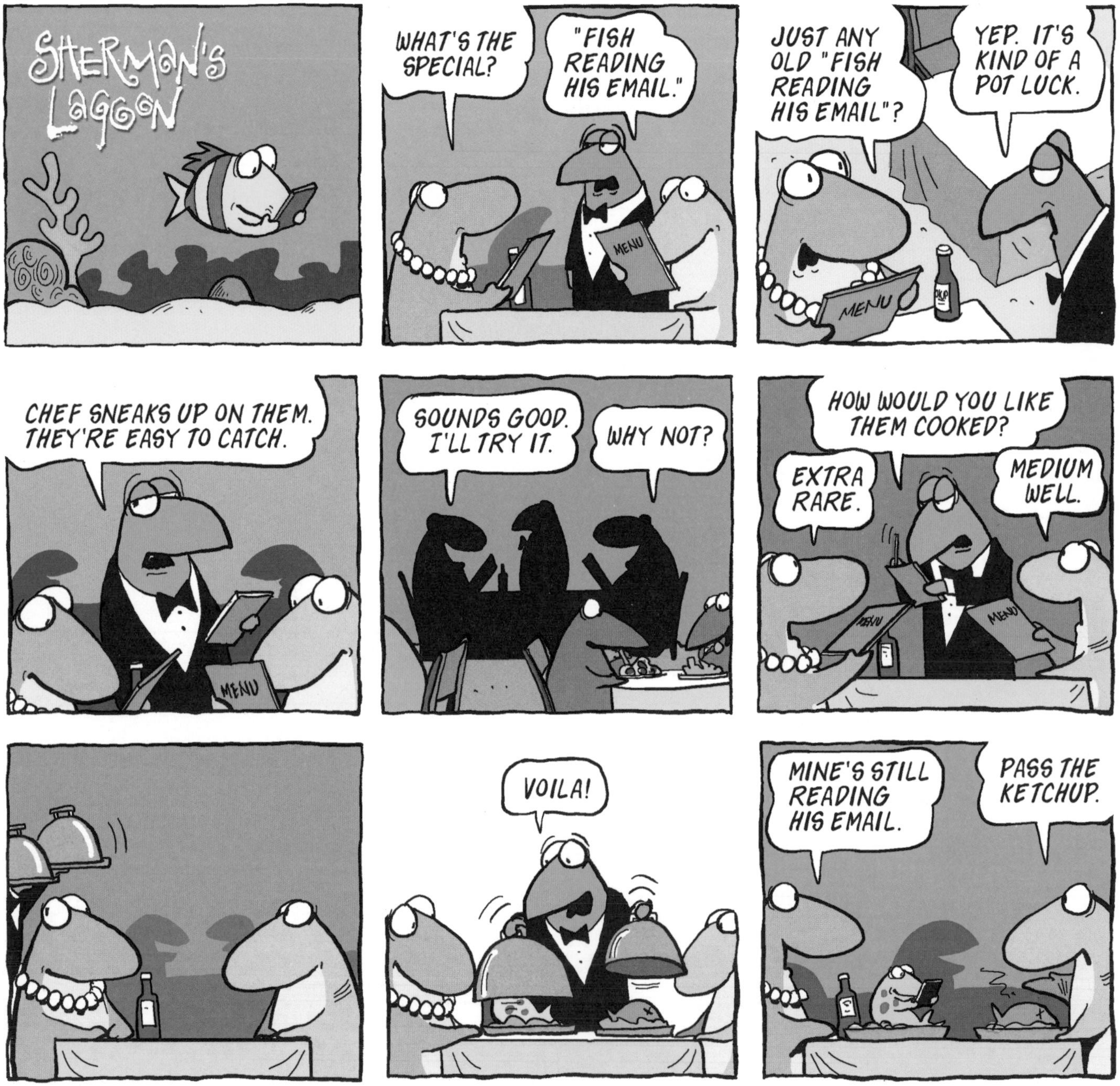
SHERMAN'S LAGOON
WHAT'S THE SPECIAL?
"FISH READING HIS EMAIL."
JUST ANY OLD "FISH READING HIS EMAIL"?
YEP. IT'S KIND OF A POT LUCK.
CHEF SNEAKS UP ON THEM. THEY'RE EASY TO CATCH.
SOUNDS GOOD. I'LL TRY IT.
WHY NOT?
HOW WOULD YOU LIKE THEM COOKED?
EXTRA RARE.
MEDIUM WELL.
VOILA!
MINE'S STILL READING HIS EMAIL.
PASS THE KETCHUP.

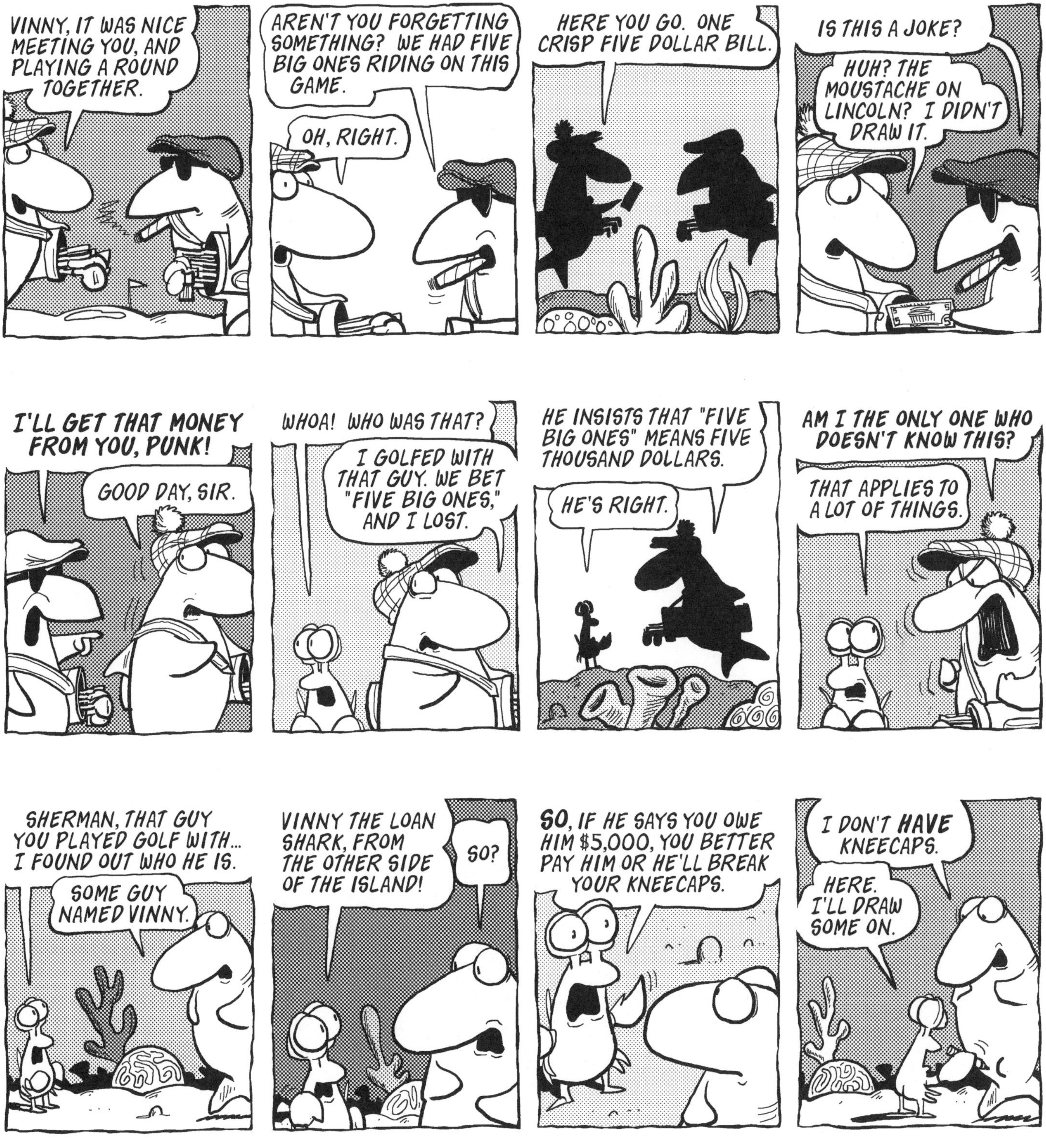
VINNY, IT WAS NICE MEETING YOU, AND PLAYING A ROUND TOGETHER.
AREN'T YOU FORGETTING SOMETHING? WE HAD FIVE BIG ONES RIDING ON THIS GAME.
OH, RIGHT.
HERE YOU GO. ONE CRISP FIVE DOLLAR BILL.
IS THIS A JOKE?
HUH? THE MOUSTACHE ON LINCOLN? I DIDN'T DRAW IT.
I'LL GET THAT MONEY FROM YOU, PUNK!
GOOD DAY, SIR.
WHOA! WHO WAS THAT?
I GOLFED WITH THAT GUY. WE BET "FIVE BIG ONES," AND I LOST.
HE INSISTS THAT "FIVE BIG ONES" MEANS FIVE THOUSAND DOLLARS.
HE'S RIGHT.
AM I THE ONLY ONE WHO DOESN'T KNOW THIS?
THAT APPLIES TO A LOT OF THINGS.
SHERMAN, THAT GUY YOU PLAYED GOLF WITH... I FOUND OUT WHO HE IS.
SOME GUY NAMED VINNY.
VINNY THE LOAN SHARK, FROM THE OTHER SIDE OF THE ISLAND!
SO?
SO, IF HE SAYS YOU OWE HIM $5,000, YOU BETTER PAY HIM OR HE'LL BREAK YOUR KNEECAPS.
I DON'T HAVE KNEECAPS.
HERE. I'LL DRAW SOME ON.

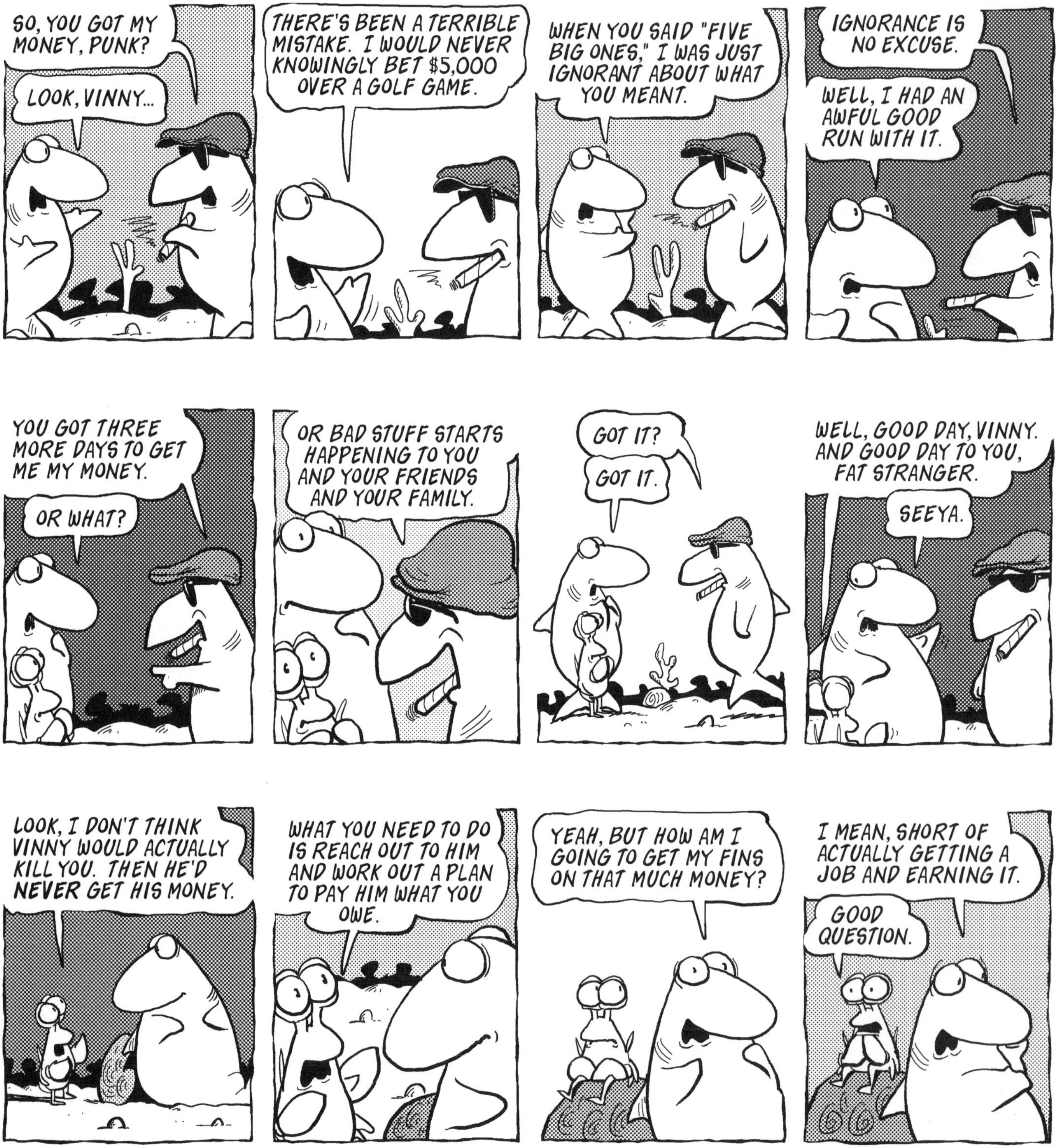
SO, YOU GOT MY MONEY, PUNK?
LOOK, VINNY...
THERE'S BEEN A TERRIBLE MISTAKE. I WOULD NEVER KNOWINGLY BET $5,000 OVER A GOLF GAME.
WHEN YOU SAID "FIVE BIG ONES," I WAS JUST IGNORANT ABOUT WHAT YOU MEANT.
IGNORANCE IS NO EXCUSE.
WELL, I HAD AN AWFUL GOOD RUN WITH IT.
YOU GOT THREE MORE DAYS TO GET ME MY MONEY.
OR WHAT?
OR BAD STUFF STARTS HAPPENING TO YOU AND YOUR FRIENDS AND YOUR FAMILY.
GOT IT?
GOT IT.
WELL, GOOD DAY, VINNY. AND GOOD DAY TO YOU, FAT STRANGER.
SEEYA.
LOOK, I DON'T THINK VINNY WOULD ACTUALLY KILL YOU. THEN HE'D NEVER GET HIS MONEY.
WHAT YOU NEED TO DO IS REACH OUT TO HIM AND WORK OUT A PLAN TO PAY HIM WHAT YOU OWE.
YEAH, BUT HOW AM I GOING TO GET MY FINS ON THAT MUCH MONEY?
I MEAN, SHORT OF ACTUALLY GETTING A JOB AND EARNING IT.
GOOD QUESTION.

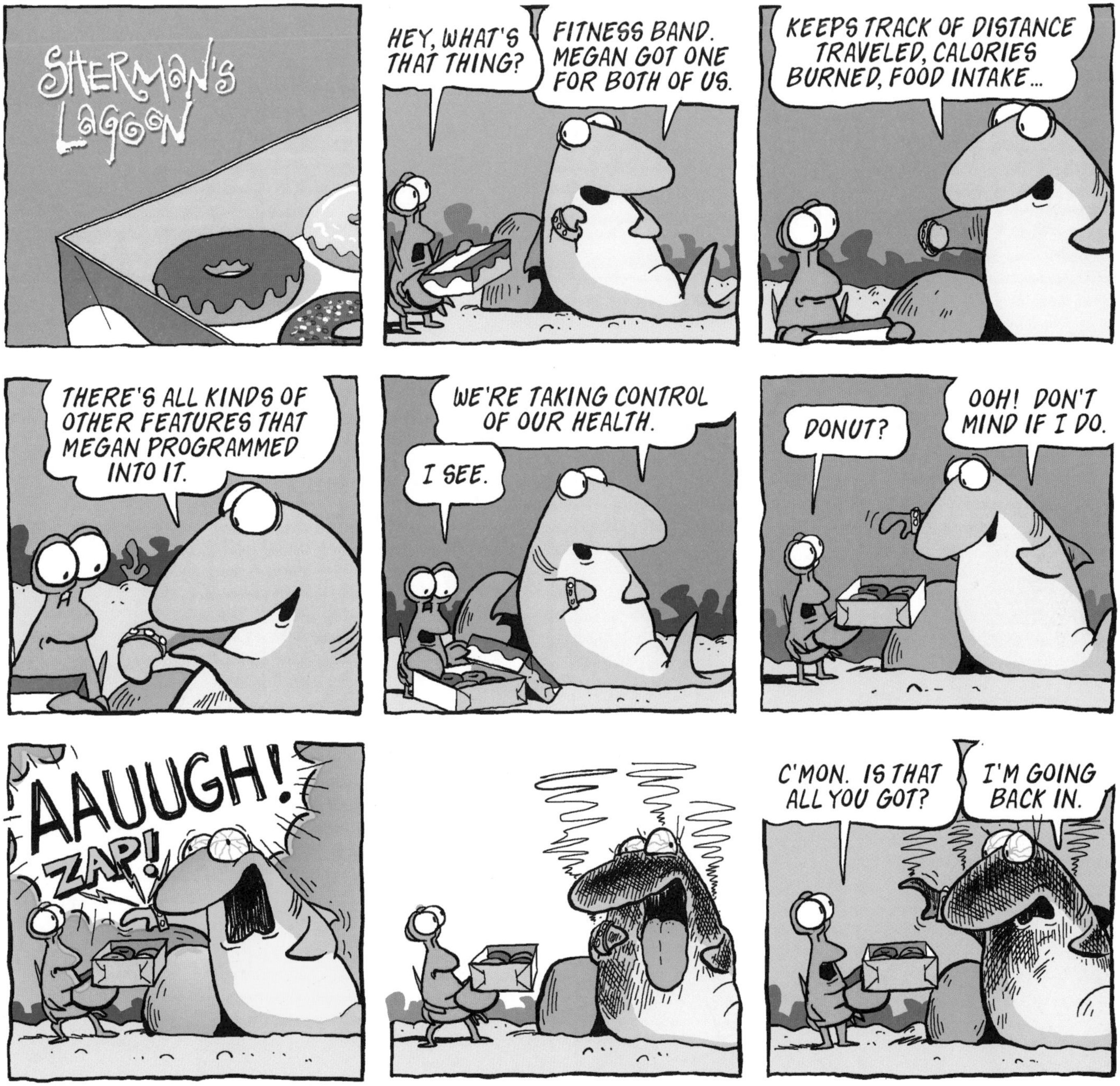
SHERMAN'S LAGOON
HEY, WHAT'S THAT THING?
FITNESS BAND. MEGAN GOT ONE FOR BOTH OF US.
KEEPS TRACK OF DISTANCE TRAVELED, CALORIES BURNED, FOOD INTAKE...
THERE'S ALL KINDS OF OTHER FEATURES THAT MEGAN PROGRAMMED INTO IT.
WE'RE TAKING CONTROL OF OUR HEALTH.
I SEE.
DONUT?
OOH! DON'T MIND IF I DO.
AAUUGH!
ZAP!
C'MON. IS THAT ALL YOU GOT?
I'M GOING BACK IN.

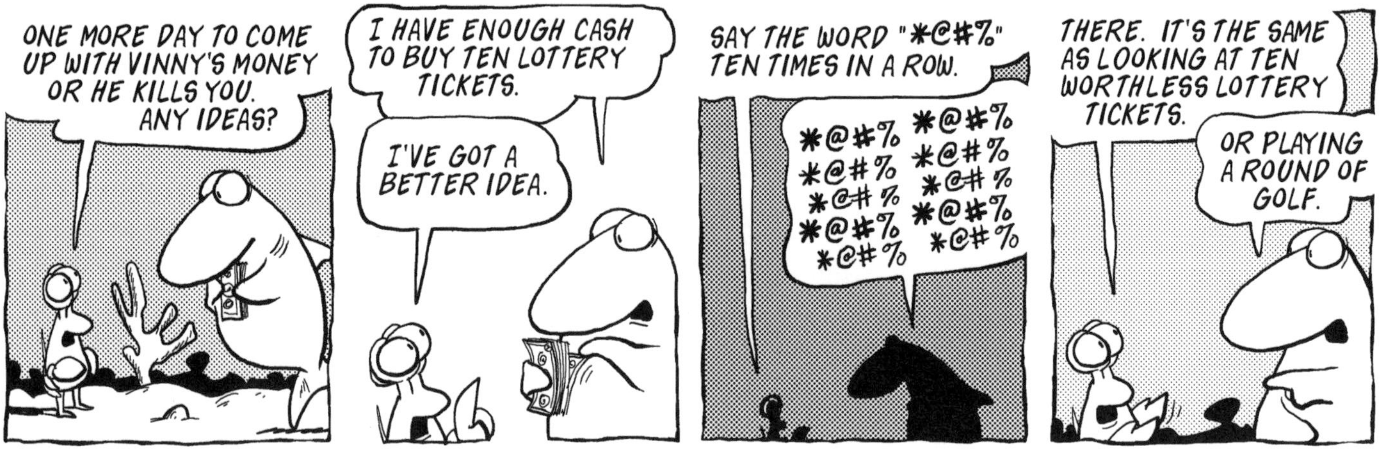
ONE MORE DAY TO COME UP WITH VINNY'S MONEY OR HE KILLS YOU. ANY IDEAS?
I HAVE ENOUGH CASH TO BUY TEN LOTTERY TICKETS.
I'VE GOT A BETTER IDEA.
SAY THE WORD "*@#%" TEN TIMES IN A ROW.
*@#% *@#% *@#% *@#% *@#% *@#% *@#% *@#% *@#% *@#%
THERE. IT'S THE SAME AS LOOKING AT TEN WORTHLESS LOTTERY TICKETS.
OR PLAYING A ROUND OF GOLF.

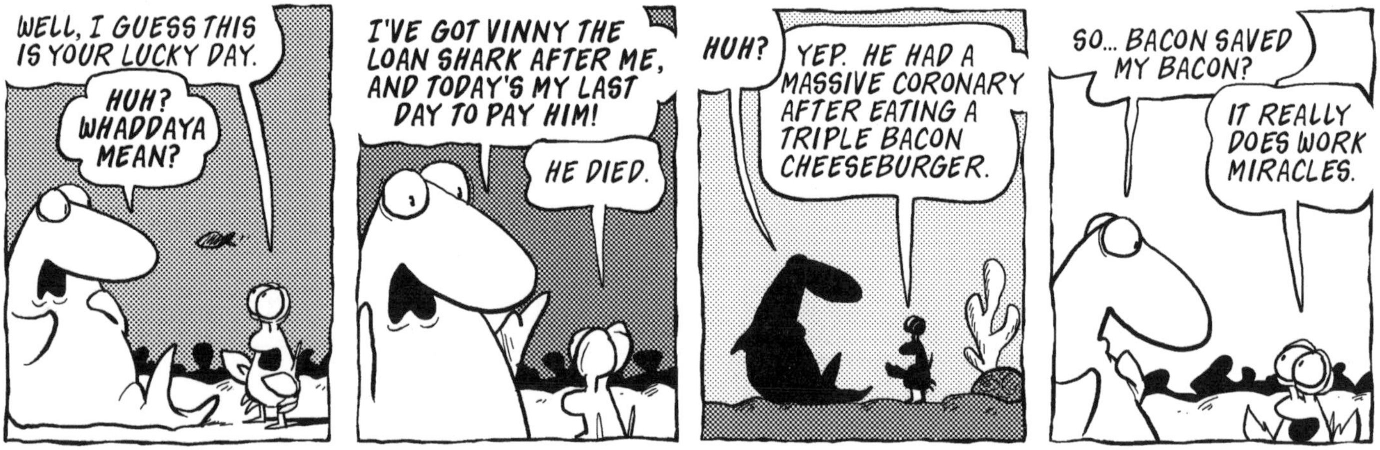
WELL, I GUESS THIS IS YOUR LUCKY DAY.
HUH? WHADDAYA MEAN?
I'VE GOT VINNY THE LOAN SHARK AFTER ME, AND TODAY'S MY LAST DAY TO PAY HIM!
HE DIED.
HUH?
YEP. HE HAD A MASSIVE CORONARY AFTER EATING A TRIPLE BACON CHEESEBURGER.
SO... BACON SAVED MY BACON?
IT REALLY DOES WORK MIRACLES.

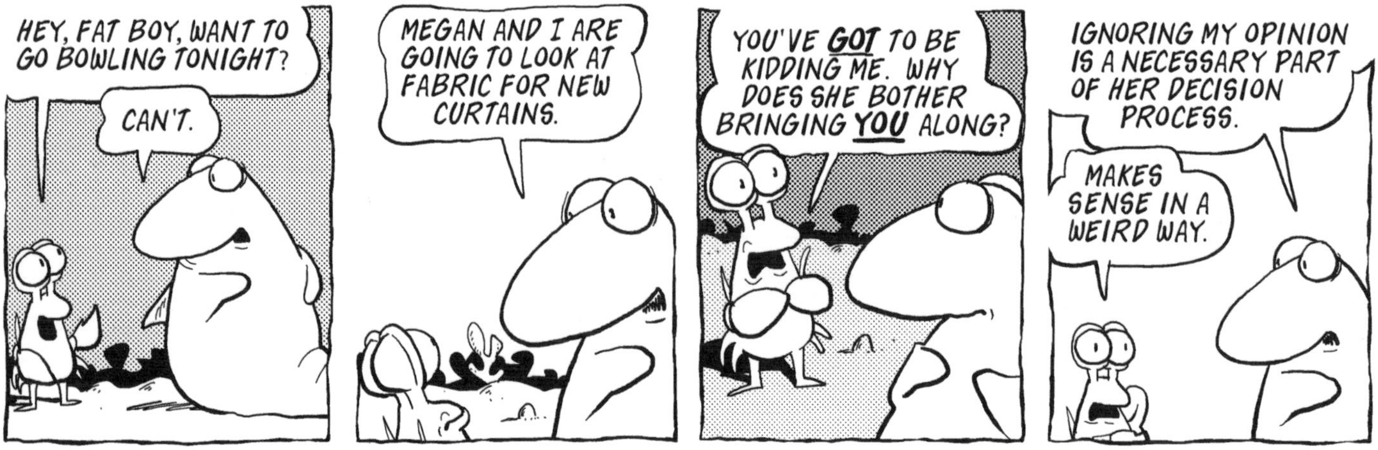
HEY, FAT BOY, WANT TO GO BOWLING TONIGHT?
CAN'T.
MEGAN AND I ARE GOING TO LOOK AT FABRIC FOR NEW CURTAINS.
YOU'VE GOT TO BE KIDDING ME. WHY DOES SHE BOTHER BRINGING YOU ALONG?
IGNORING MY OPINION IS A NECESSARY PART OF HER DECISION PROCESS.
MAKES SENSE IN A WEIRD WAY.

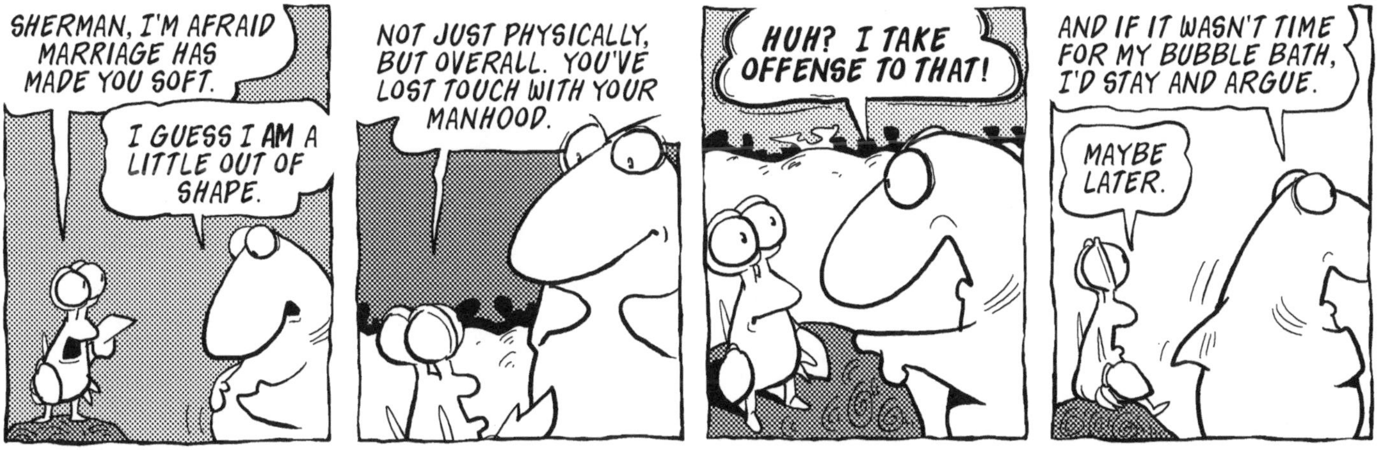
SHERMAN, I'M AFRAID MARRIAGE HAS MADE YOU SOFT.
I GUESS I AM A LITTLE OUT OF SHAPE.
NOT JUST PHYSICALLY, BUT OVERALL. YOU'VE LOST TOUCH WITH YOUR MANHOOD.
HUH? I TAKE OFFENSE TO THAT!
AND IF IT WASN'T TIME FOR MY BUBBLE BATH, I'D STAY AND ARGUE.
MAYBE LATER.

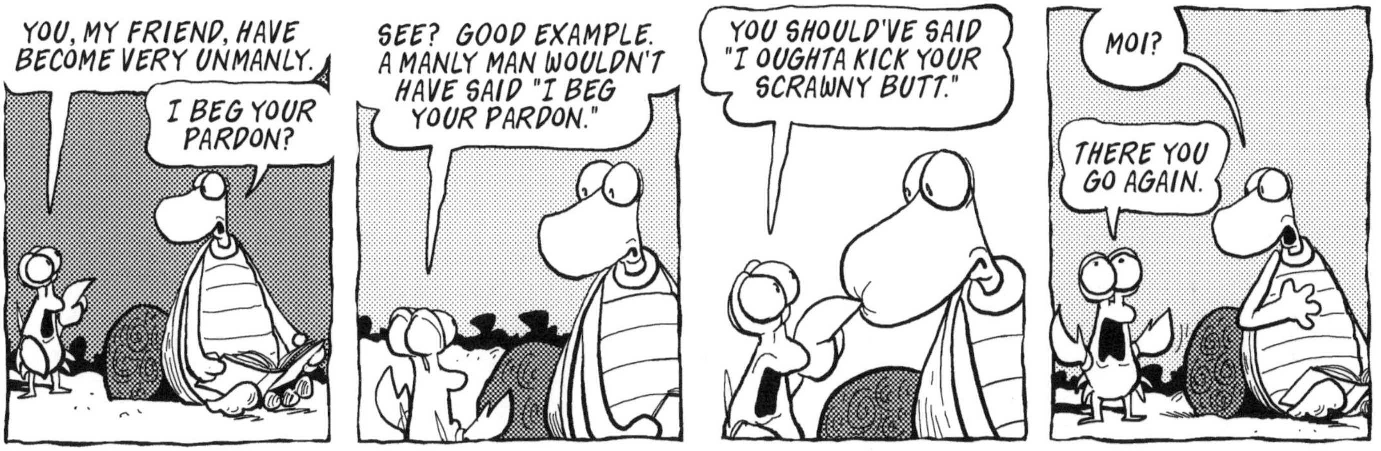
YOU, MY FRIEND, HAVE BECOME VERY UNMANLY.
I BEG YOUR PARDON?
SEE? GOOD EXAMPLE. A MANLY MAN WOULDN'T HAVE SAID "I BEG YOUR PARDON."
YOU SHOULD'VE SAID "I OUGHTA KICK YOUR SCRAWNY BUTT."
MOI?
THERE YOU GO AGAIN.

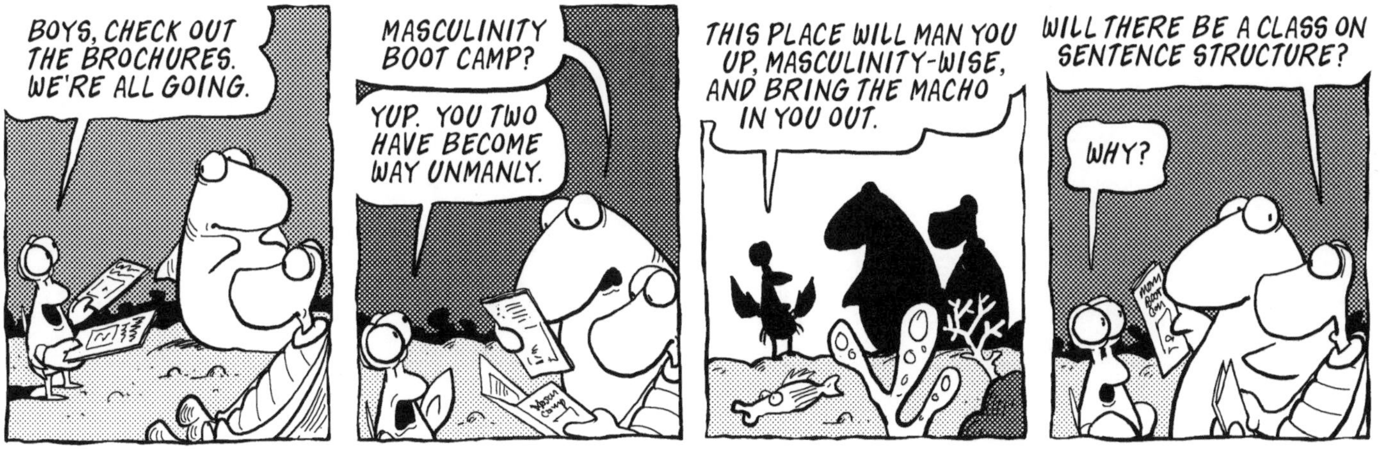
BOYS, CHECK OUT THE BROCHURES. WE'RE ALL GOING.
MASCULINITY BOOT CAMP?
YUP. YOU TWO HAVE BECOME WAY UNMANLY.
THIS PLACE WILL MAN YOU UP, MASCULINITY-WISE, AND BRING THE MACHO IN YOU OUT.
WILL THERE BE A CLASS ON SENTENCE STRUCTURE?
WHY?

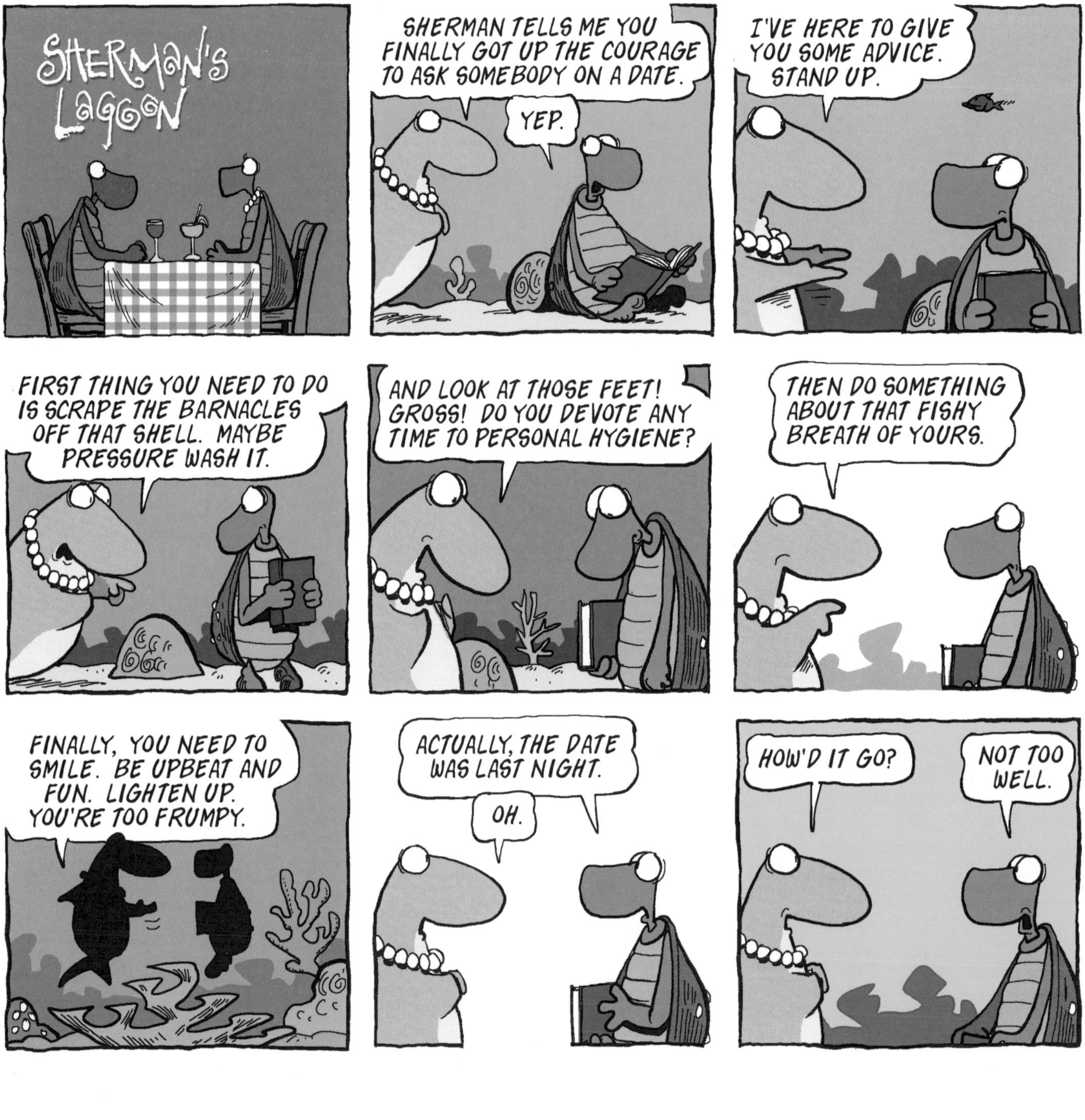
SHERMAN'S LAGOON
SHERMAN TELLS ME YOU FINALLY GOT UP THE COURAGE TO ASK SOMEBODY ON A DATE.
YEP.
I'VE HERE TO GIVE YOU SOME ADVICE. STAND UP.
FIRST THING YOU NEED TO DO IS SCRAPE THE BARNACLES OFF THAT SHELL. MAYBE PRESSURE WASH IT.
AND LOOK AT THOSE FEET! GROSS! DO YOU DEVOTE ANY TIME TO PERSONAL HYGIENE?
THEN DO SOMETHING ABOUT THAT FISHY BREATH OF YOURS.
FINALLY, YOU NEED TO SMILE. BE UPBEAT AND FUN. LIGHTEN UP. YOU'RE TOO FRUMPY.
ACTUALLY, THE DATE WAS LAST NIGHT.
OH.
HOW'D IT GO?
NOT TOO WELL.

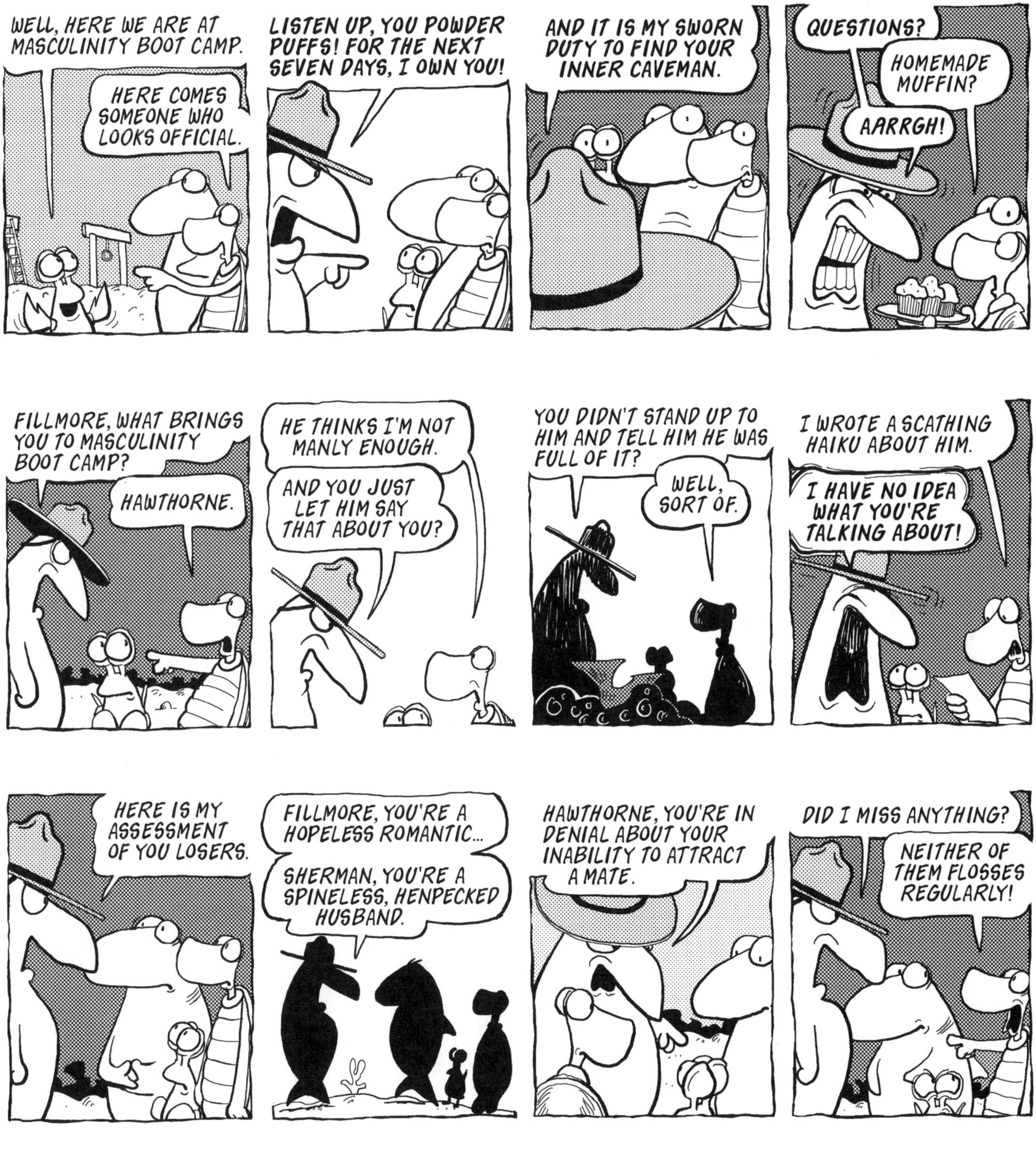
WELL, HERE WE ARE AT MASCULINITY BOOT CAMP.
HERE COMES SOMEONE WHO LOOKS OFFICIAL.
LISTEN UP, YOU POWDER PUFFS! FOR THE NEXT SEVEN DAYS, I OWN YOU!
AND IT IS MY SWORN DUTY TO FIND YOUR INNER CAVEMAN.
QUESTIONS?
HOMEMADE MUFFIN?
AARRGH!
FILLMORE, WHAT BRINGS YOU TO MASCULINITY BOOT CAMP?
HAWTHORNE.
HE THINKS I'M NOT MANLY ENOUGH.
AND YOU JUST LET HIM SAY THAT ABOUT YOU?
YOU DIDN'T STAND UP TO HIM AND TELL HIM HE WAS FULL OF IT?
WELL, SORT OF.
I WROTE A SCATHING HAIKU ABOUT HIM.
I HAVE NO IDEA WHAT YOU'RE TALKING ABOUT!
HERE IS MY ASSESSMENT OF YOU LOSERS.
FILLMORE, YOU'RE A HOPELESS ROMANTIC...
SHERMAN, YOU'RE A SPINELESS, HENPECKED HUSBAND.
HAWTHORNE, YOU'RE IN DENIAL ABOUT YOUR INABILITY TO ATTRACT A MATE.
DID I MISS ANYTHING?
NEITHER OF THEM FLOSSES REGULARLY!

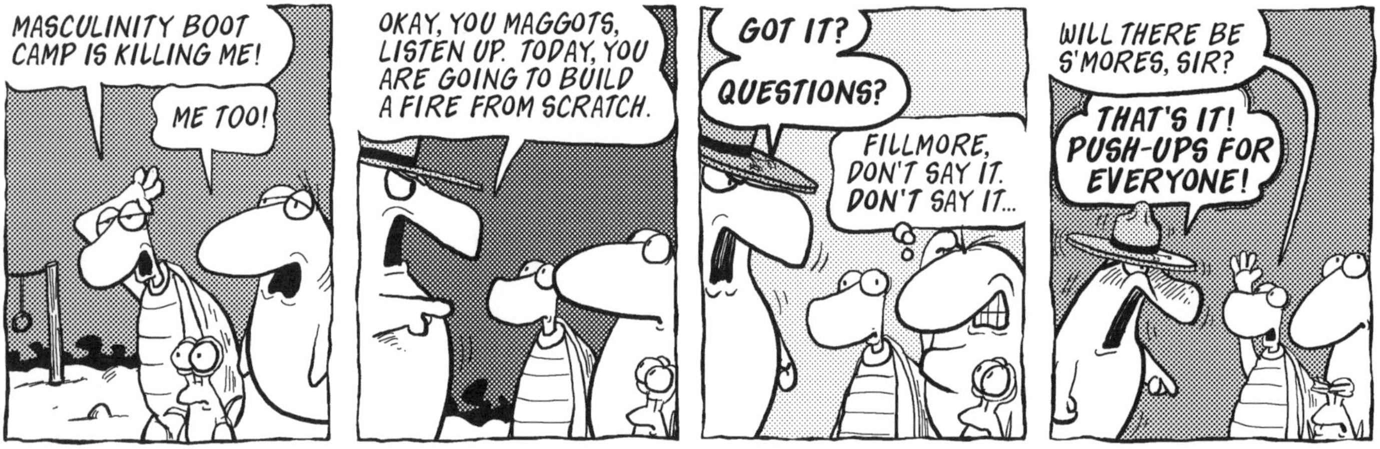
MASCULINITY BOOT CAMP IS KILLING ME!
ME TOO!
OKAY, YOU MAGGOTS, LISTEN UP. TODAY, YOU ARE GOING TO BUILD A FIRE FROM SCRATCH.
GOT IT?
QUESTIONS?
FILLMORE, DON'T SAY IT. DON'T SAY IT...
WILL THERE BE S'MORES, SIR?
THAT'S IT! PUSH-UPS FOR EVERYONE!

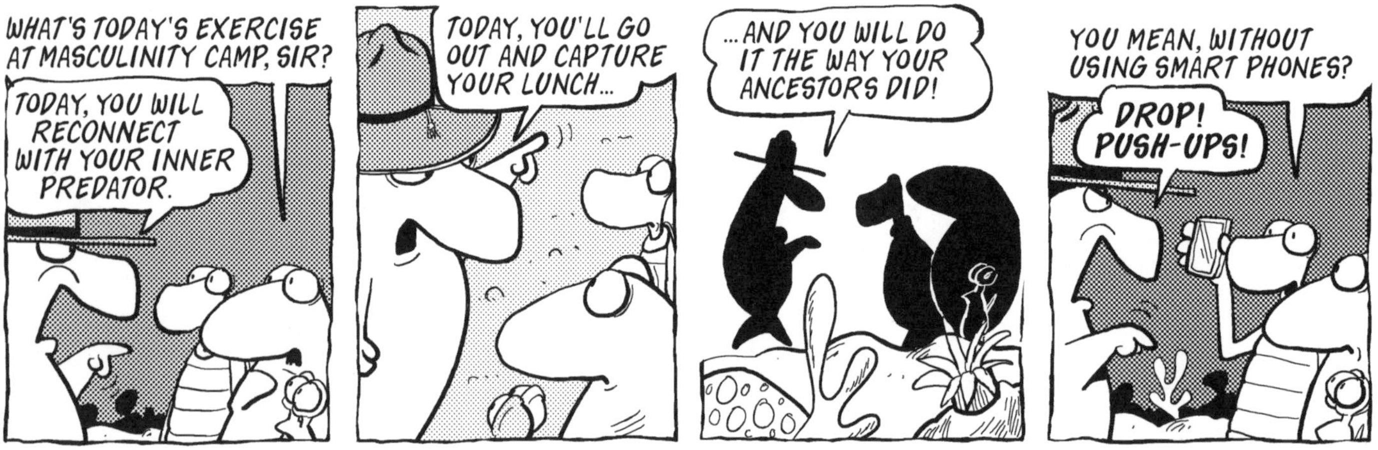
WHAT'S TODAY'S EXERCISE AT MASCULINITY CAMP, SIR?
TODAY, YOU WILL RECONNECT WITH YOUR INNER PREDATOR.
TODAY, YOU'LL GO OUT AND CAPTURE YOUR LUNCH...
...AND YOU WILL DO IT THE WAY YOUR ANCESTORS DID!
YOU MEAN, WITHOUT USING SMART PHONES?
DROP! PUSH-UPS!

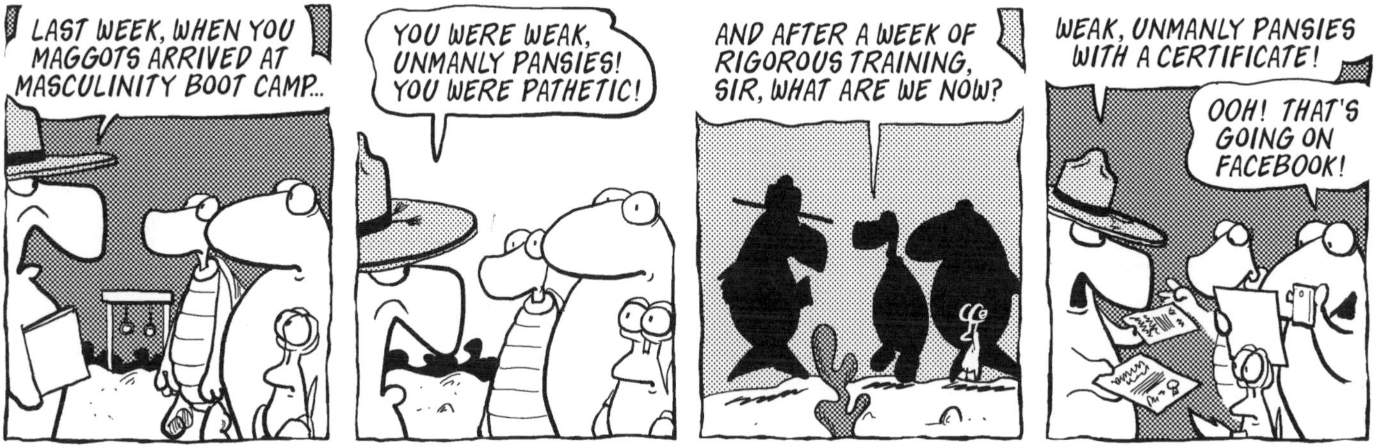
LAST WEEK, WHEN YOU MAGGOTS ARRIVED AT MASCULINITY BOOT CAMP...
YOU WERE WEAK, UNMANLY PANSIES! YOU WERE PATHETIC!
AND AFTER A WEEK OF RIGOROUS TRAINING, SIR, WHAT ARE WE NOW?
WEAK, UNMANLY PANSIES WITH A CERTIFICATE!
OOH! THAT'S GOING ON FACEBOOK!

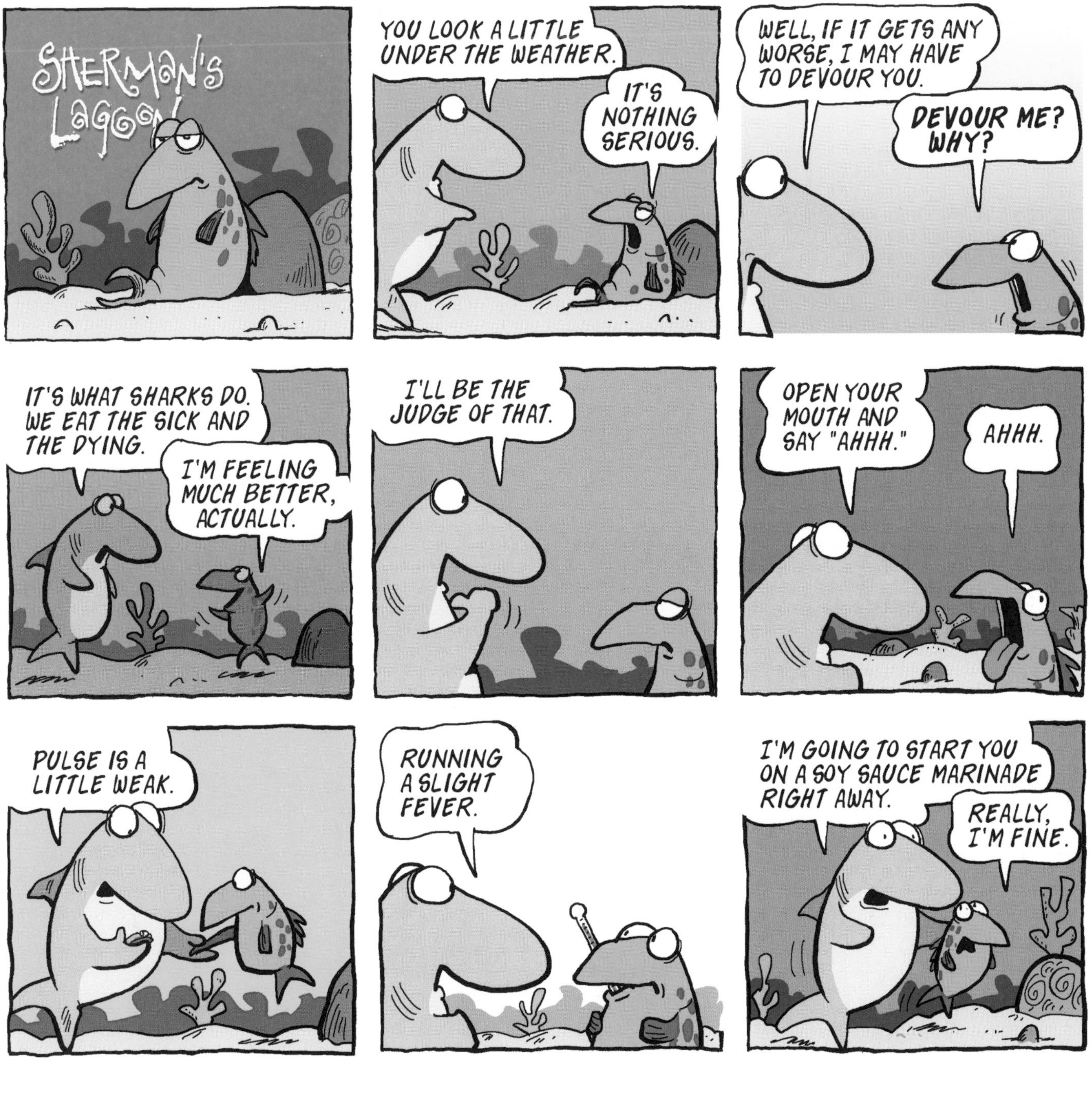
SHERMAN'S LAGOON
YOU LOOK A LITTLE UNDER THE WEATHER.
IT'S NOTHING SERIOUS.
WELL, IF IT GETS ANY WORSE, I MAY HAVE TO DEVOUR YOU.
DEVOUR ME? WHY?
IT'S WHAT SHARKS DO. WE EAT THE SICK AND THE DYING.
I'M FEELING MUCH BETTER, ACTUALLY.
I'LL BE THE JUDGE OF THAT.
OPEN YOUR MOUTH AND SAY "AHHH."
AHHH.
PULSE IS A LITTLE WEAK.
RUNNING A SLIGHT FEVER.
I'M GOING TO START YOU ON A SOY SAUCE MARINADE RIGHT AWAY.
REALLY, I'M FINE.

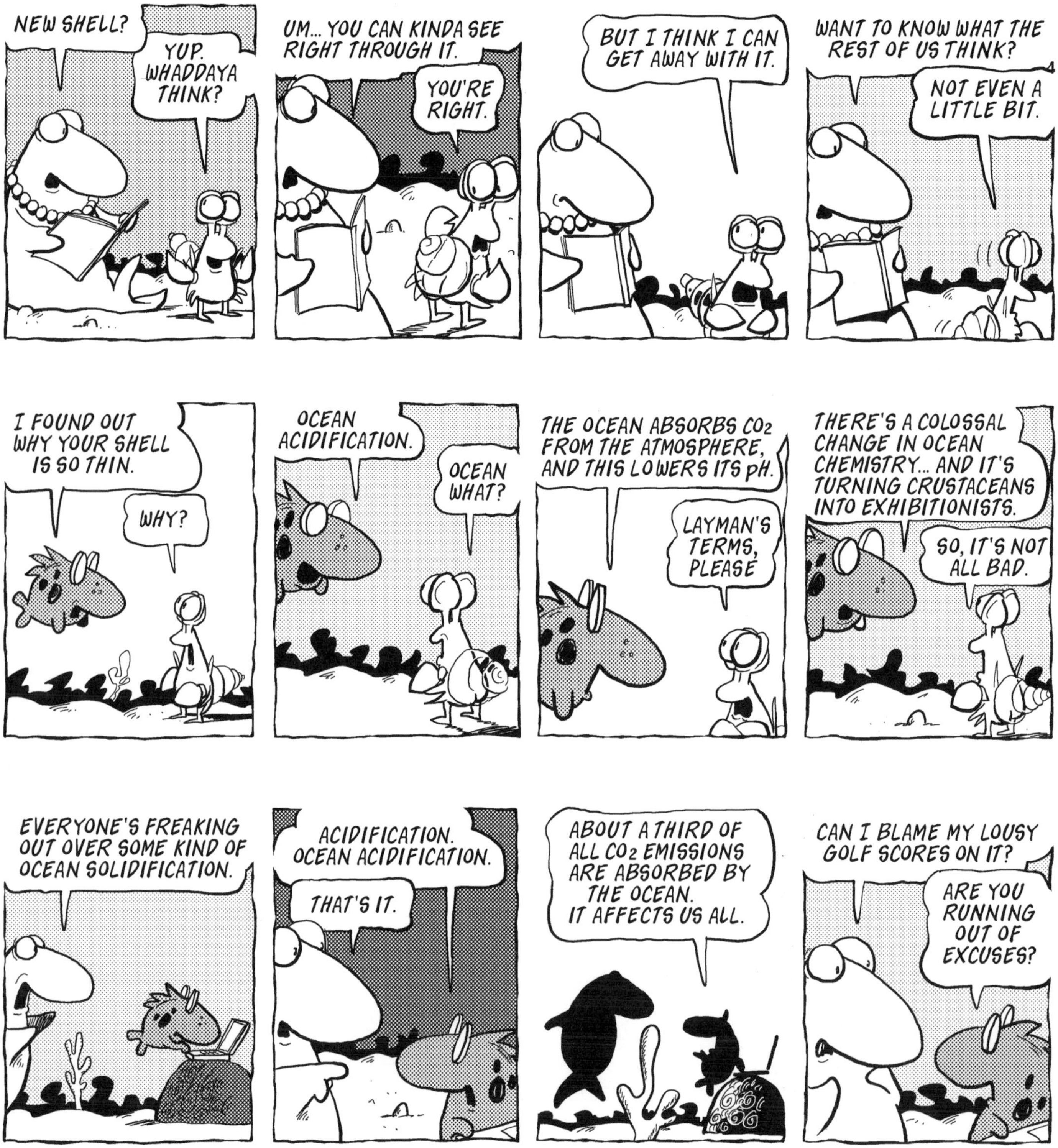
NEW SHELL?
YUP. WHADDAYA THINK?
UM... YOU CAN KINDA SEE RIGHT THROUGH IT.
YOU'RE RIGHT.
BUT I THINK I CAN GET AWAY WITH IT.
WANT TO KNOW WHAT THE REST OF US THINK?
NOT EVEN A LITTLE BIT.
I FOUND OUT WHY YOUR SHELL IS SO THIN.
WHY?
OCEAN ACIDIFICATION.
OCEAN WHAT?
THE OCEAN ABSORBS CO_2 FROM THE ATMOSPHERE, AND THIS LOWERS ITS pH.
LAYMAN'S TERMS, PLEASE
THERE'S A COLOSSAL CHANGE IN OCEAN CHEMISTRY... AND IT'S TURNING CRUSTACEANS INTO EXHIBITIONISTS.
SO, IT'S NOT ALL BAD.
EVERYONE'S FREAKING OUT OVER SOME KIND OF OCEAN SOLIDIFICATION.
ACIDIFICATION. OCEAN ACIDIFICATION.
THAT'S IT.
ABOUT A THIRD OF ALL CO_2 EMISSIONS ARE ABSORBED BY THE OCEAN. IT AFFECTS US ALL.
CAN I BLAME MY LOUSY GOLF SCORES ON IT?
ARE YOU RUNNING OUT OF EXCUSES?

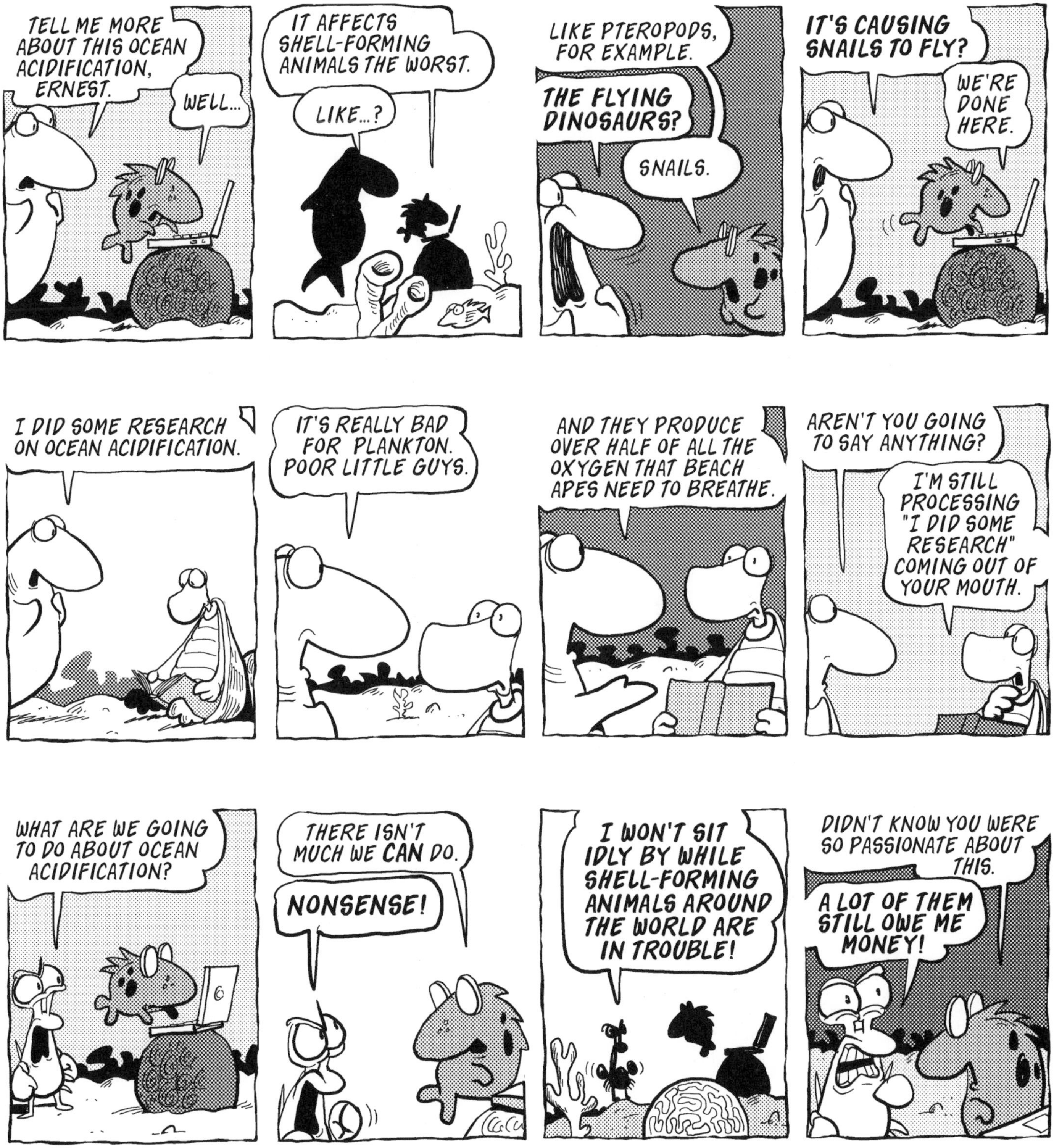
TELL ME MORE ABOUT THIS OCEAN ACIDIFICATION, ERNEST.
WELL...
IT AFFECTS SHELL-FORMING ANIMALS THE WORST.
LIKE...?
LIKE PTEROPODS, FOR EXAMPLE.
THE FLYING DINOSAURS?
SNAILS.
IT'S CAUSING SNAILS TO FLY?
WE'RE DONE HERE.
I DID SOME RESEARCH ON OCEAN ACIDIFICATION.
IT'S REALLY BAD FOR PLANKTON. POOR LITTLE GUYS.
AND THEY PRODUCE OVER HALF OF ALL THE OXYGEN THAT BEACH APES NEED TO BREATHE.
AREN'T YOU GOING TO SAY ANYTHING?
I'M STILL PROCESSING "I DID SOME RESEARCH" COMING OUT OF YOUR MOUTH.
WHAT ARE WE GOING TO DO ABOUT OCEAN ACIDIFICATION?
THERE ISN'T MUCH WE CAN DO.
NONSENSE!
I WON'T SIT IDLY BY WHILE SHELL-FORMING ANIMALS AROUND THE WORLD ARE IN TROUBLE!
DIDN'T KNOW YOU WERE SO PASSIONATE ABOUT THIS.
A LOT OF THEM STILL OWE ME MONEY!

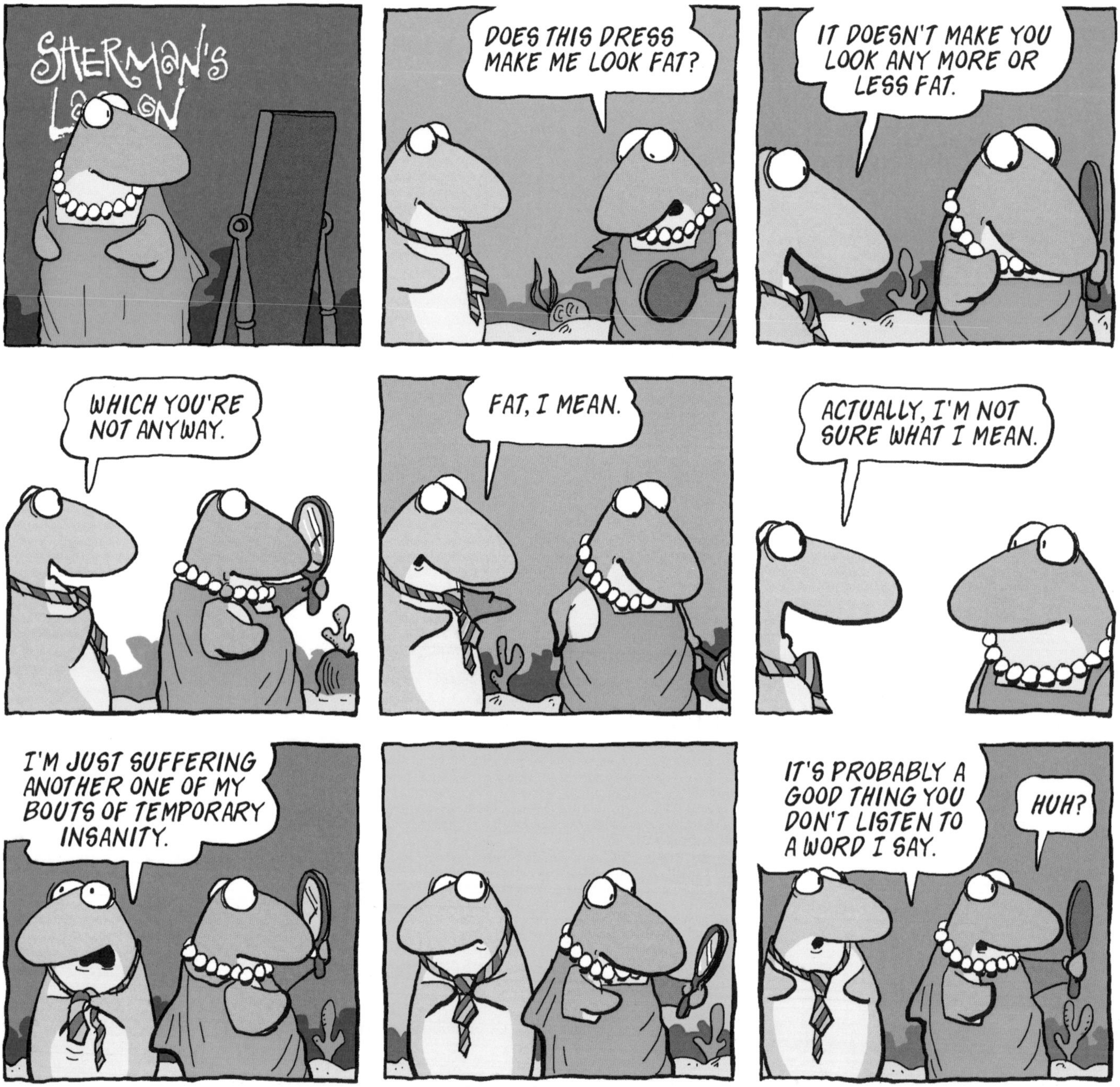
SHERMAN'S LAGOON
DOES THIS DRESS MAKE ME LOOK FAT?
IT DOESN'T MAKE YOU LOOK ANY MORE OR LESS FAT.
WHICH YOU'RE NOT ANYWAY.
FAT, I MEAN.
ACTUALLY, I'M NOT SURE WHAT I MEAN.
I'M JUST SUFFERING ANOTHER ONE OF MY BOUTS OF TEMPORARY INSANITY.
IT'S PROBABLY A GOOD THING YOU DON'T LISTEN TO A WORD I SAY.
HUH?

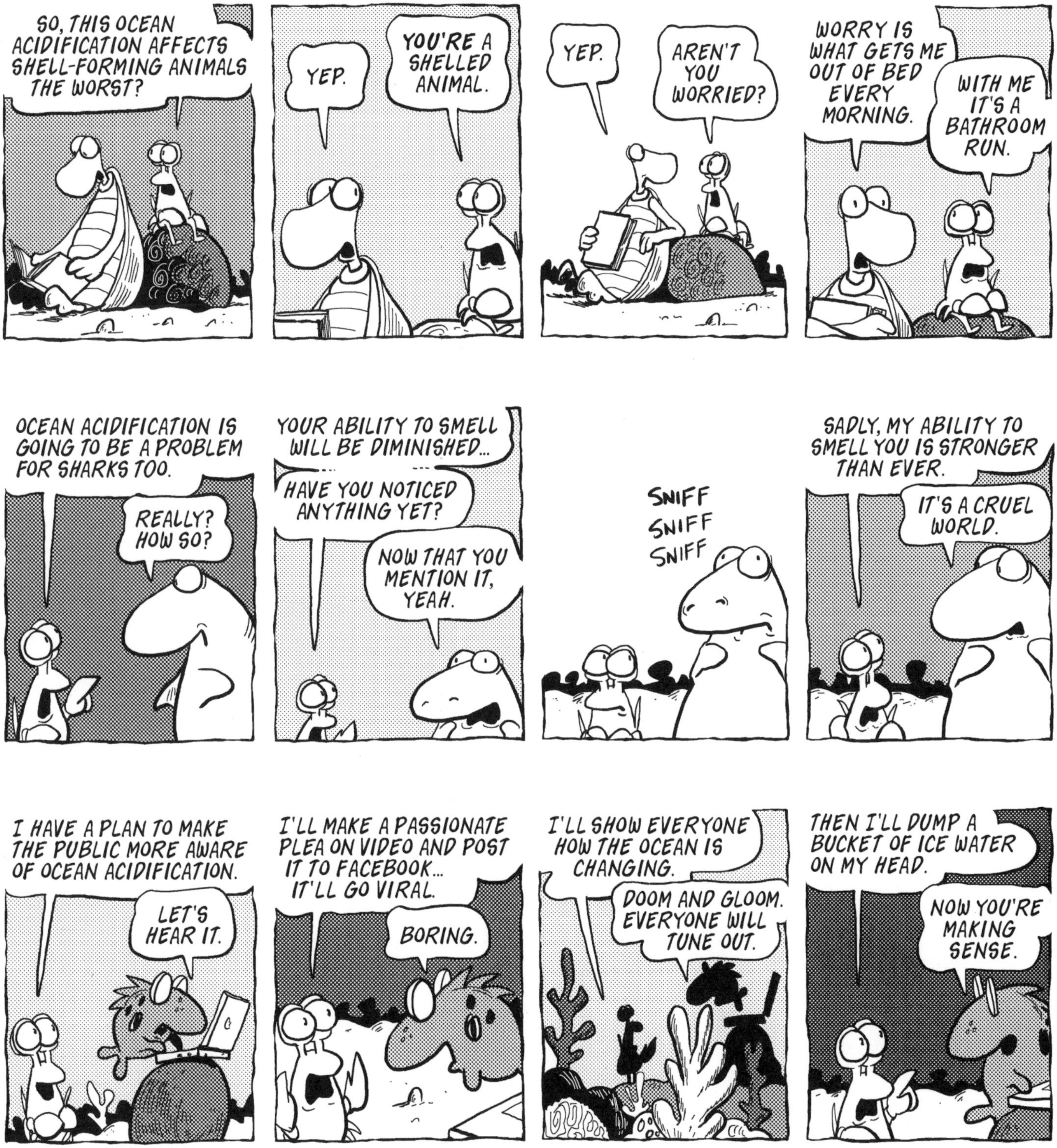

SO, THIS OCEAN ACIDIFICATION AFFECTS SHELL-FORMING ANIMALS THE WORST?
YEP.
YOU'RE A SHELLED ANIMAL.
YEP.
AREN'T YOU WORRIED?
WORRY IS WHAT GETS ME OUT OF BED EVERY MORNING.
WITH ME IT'S A BATHROOM RUN.
OCEAN ACIDIFICATION IS GOING TO BE A PROBLEM FOR SHARKS TOO.
REALLY? HOW SO?
YOUR ABILITY TO SMELL WILL BE DIMINISHED...
HAVE YOU NOTICED ANYTHING YET?
NOW THAT YOU MENTION IT, YEAH.
SNIFF
SNIFF
SNIFF
SADLY, MY ABILITY TO SMELL YOU IS STRONGER THAN EVER.
IT'S A CRUEL WORLD.
I HAVE A PLAN TO MAKE THE PUBLIC MORE AWARE OF OCEAN ACIDIFICATION.
LET'S HEAR IT.
I'LL MAKE A PASSIONATE PLEA ON VIDEO AND POST IT TO FACEBOOK... IT'LL GO VIRAL.
BORING.
I'LL SHOW EVERYONE HOW THE OCEAN IS CHANGING.
DOOM AND GLOOM. EVERYONE WILL TUNE OUT.
THEN I'LL DUMP A BUCKET OF ICE WATER ON MY HEAD.
NOW YOU'RE MAKING SENSE.

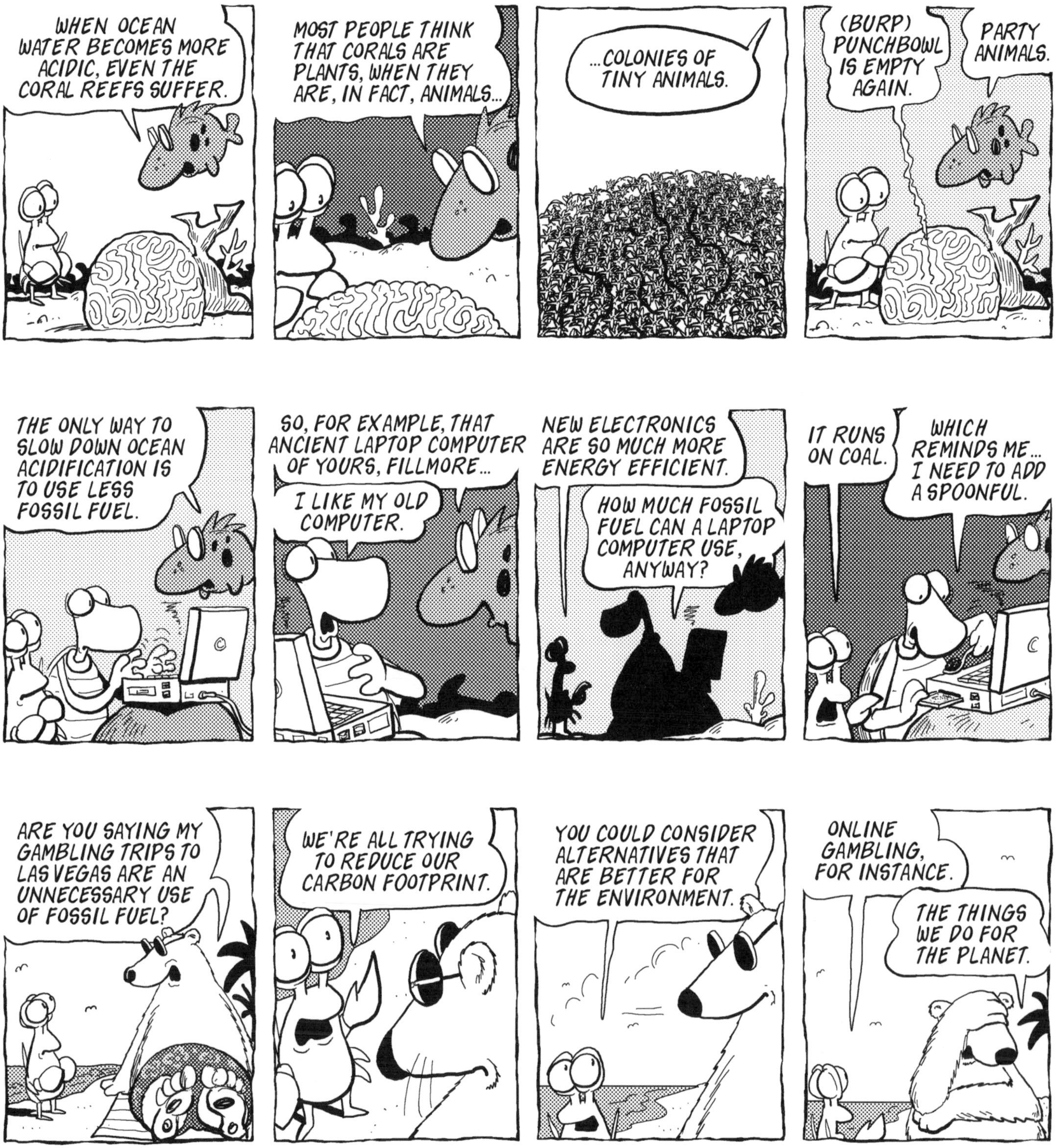
WHEN OCEAN WATER BECOMES MORE ACIDIC, EVEN THE CORAL REEFS SUFFER.
MOST PEOPLE THINK THAT CORALS ARE PLANTS, WHEN THEY ARE, IN FACT, ANIMALS...
...COLONIES OF TINY ANIMALS.
(BURP) PUNCHBOWL IS EMPTY AGAIN.
PARTY ANIMALS.
THE ONLY WAY TO SLOW DOWN OCEAN ACIDIFICATION IS TO USE LESS FOSSIL FUEL.
SO, FOR EXAMPLE, THAT ANCIENT LAPTOP COMPUTER OF YOURS, FILLMORE...
I LIKE MY OLD COMPUTER.
NEW ELECTRONICS ARE SO MUCH MORE ENERGY EFFICIENT.
HOW MUCH FOSSIL FUEL CAN A LAPTOP COMPUTER USE, ANYWAY?
IT RUNS ON COAL.
WHICH REMINDS ME... I NEED TO ADD A SPOONFUL.
ARE YOU SAYING MY GAMBLING TRIPS TO LAS VEGAS ARE AN UNNECESSARY USE OF FOSSIL FUEL?
WE'RE ALL TRYING TO REDUCE OUR CARBON FOOTPRINT.
YOU COULD CONSIDER ALTERNATIVES THAT ARE BETTER FOR THE ENVIRONMENT.
ONLINE GAMBLING, FOR INSTANCE.
THE THINGS WE DO FOR THE PLANET.

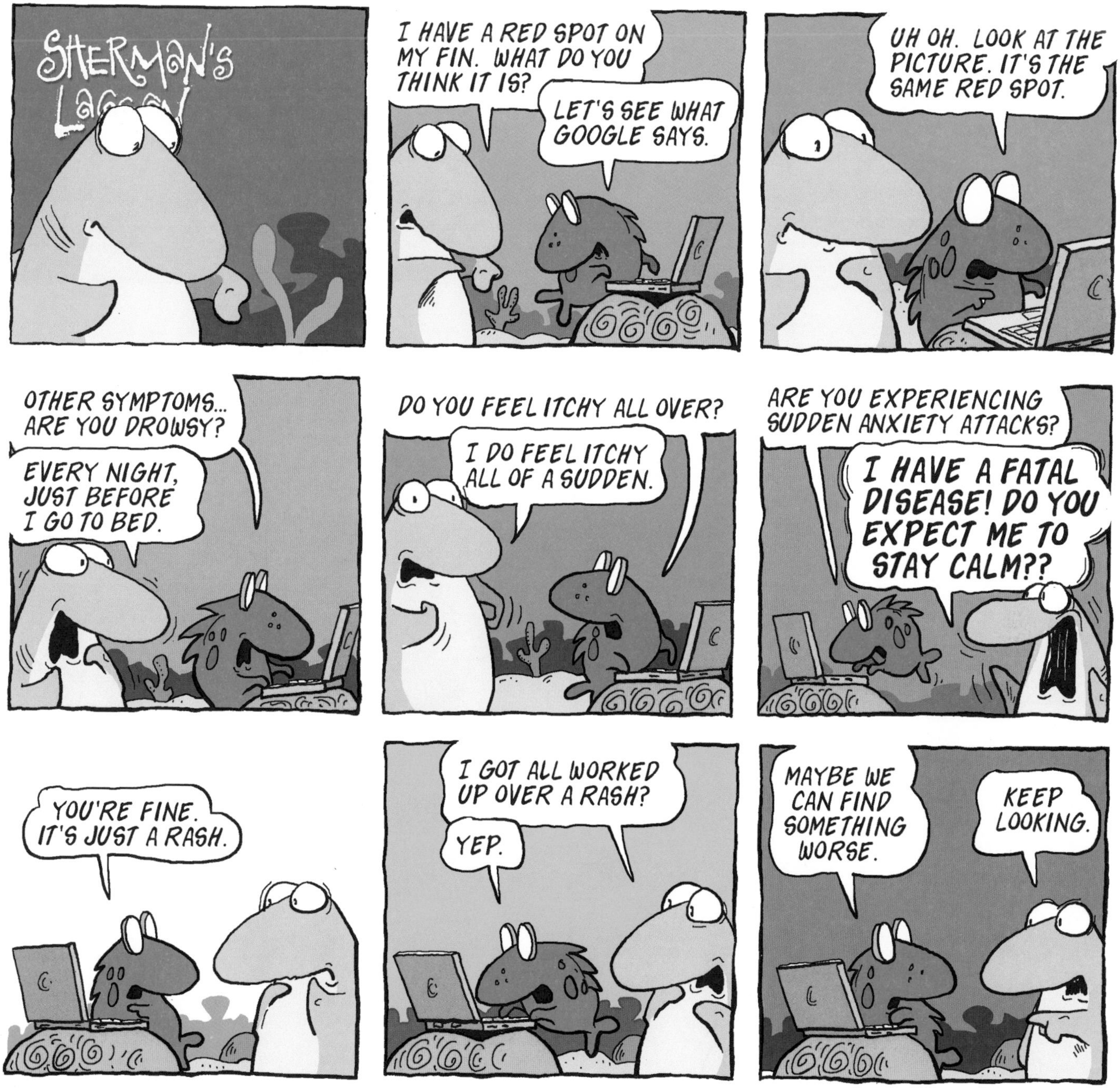
SHERMAN'S LAGOON
I HAVE A RED SPOT ON MY FIN. WHAT DO YOU THINK IT IS?
LET'S SEE WHAT GOOGLE SAYS.
UH OH. LOOK AT THE PICTURE. IT'S THE SAME RED SPOT.
OTHER SYMPTOMS... ARE YOU DROWSY?
EVERY NIGHT, JUST BEFORE I GO TO BED.
DO YOU FEEL ITCHY ALL OVER?
I DO FEEL ITCHY ALL OF A SUDDEN.
ARE YOU EXPERIENCING SUDDEN ANXIETY ATTACKS?
I HAVE A FATAL DISEASE! DO YOU EXPECT ME TO STAY CALM??
YOU'RE FINE. IT'S JUST A RASH.
I GOT ALL WORKED UP OVER A RASH?
YEP.
MAYBE WE CAN FIND SOMETHING WORSE.
KEEP LOOKING.

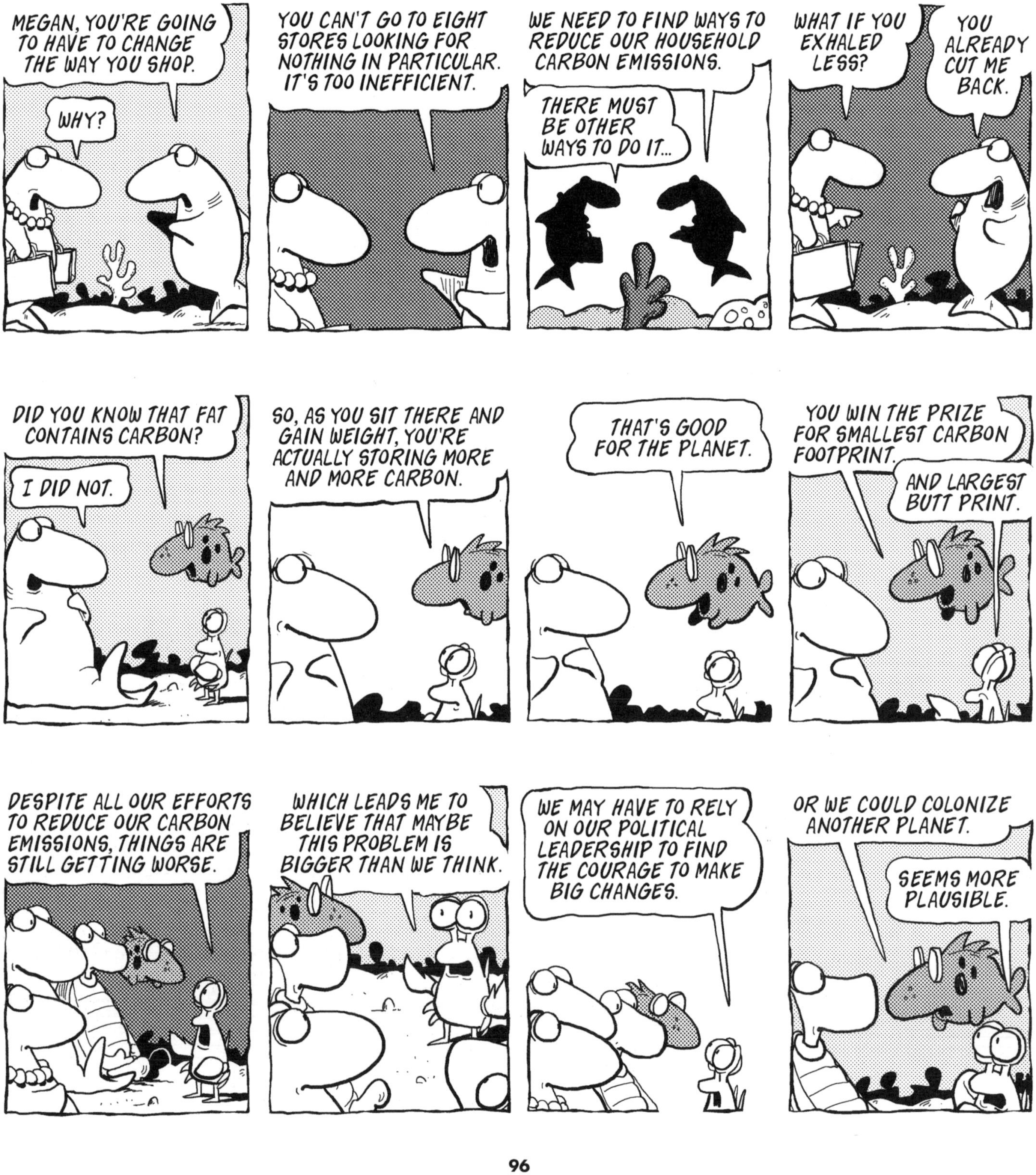
MEGAN, YOU'RE GOING TO HAVE TO CHANGE THE WAY YOU SHOP.
WHY?
YOU CAN'T GO TO EIGHT STORES LOOKING FOR NOTHING IN PARTICULAR. IT'S TOO INEFFICIENT.
WE NEED TO FIND WAYS TO REDUCE OUR HOUSEHOLD CARBON EMISSIONS.
THERE MUST BE OTHER WAYS TO DO IT...
WHAT IF YOU EXHALED LESS?
YOU ALREADY CUT ME BACK.
DID YOU KNOW THAT FAT CONTAINS CARBON?
I DID NOT.
SO, AS YOU SIT THERE AND GAIN WEIGHT, YOU'RE ACTUALLY STORING MORE AND MORE CARBON.
THAT'S GOOD FOR THE PLANET.
YOU WIN THE PRIZE FOR SMALLEST CARBON FOOTPRINT.
AND LARGEST BUTT PRINT.
DESPITE ALL OUR EFFORTS TO REDUCE OUR CARBON EMISSIONS, THINGS ARE STILL GETTING WORSE.
WHICH LEADS ME TO BELIEVE THAT MAYBE THIS PROBLEM IS BIGGER THAN WE THINK.
WE MAY HAVE TO RELY ON OUR POLITICAL LEADERSHIP TO FIND THE COURAGE TO MAKE BIG CHANGES.
OR WE COULD COLONIZE ANOTHER PLANET.
SEEMS MORE PLAUSIBLE.

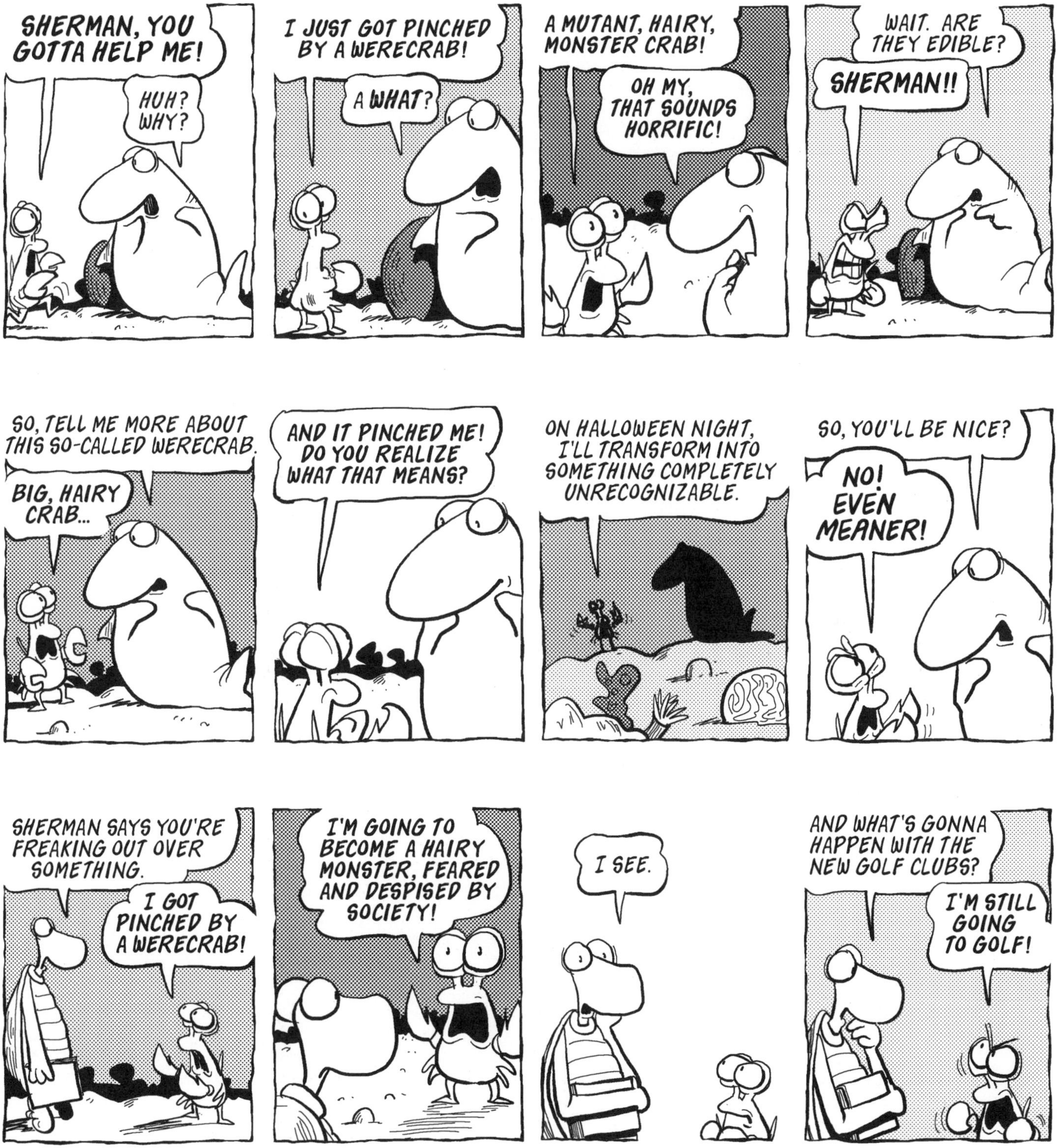

SHERMAN, YOU GOTTA HELP ME!
HUH? WHY?
I JUST GOT PINCHED BY A WERECRAB!
A WHAT?
A MUTANT, HAIRY, MONSTER CRAB!
OH MY, THAT SOUNDS HORRIFIC!
WAIT. ARE THEY EDIBLE?
SHERMAN!!
SO, TELL ME MORE ABOUT THIS SO-CALLED WERECRAB.
BIG, HAIRY CRAB...
AND IT PINCHED ME! DO YOU REALIZE WHAT THAT MEANS?
ON HALLOWEEN NIGHT, I'LL TRANSFORM INTO SOMETHING COMPLETELY UNRECOGNIZABLE.
SO, YOU'LL BE NICE?
NO! EVEN MEANER!
SHERMAN SAYS YOU'RE FREAKING OUT OVER SOMETHING.
I GOT PINCHED BY A WERECRAB!
I'M GOING TO BECOME A HAIRY MONSTER, FEARED AND DESPISED BY SOCIETY!
I SEE.
AND WHAT'S GONNA HAPPEN WITH THE NEW GOLF CLUBS?
I'M STILL GOING TO GOLF!

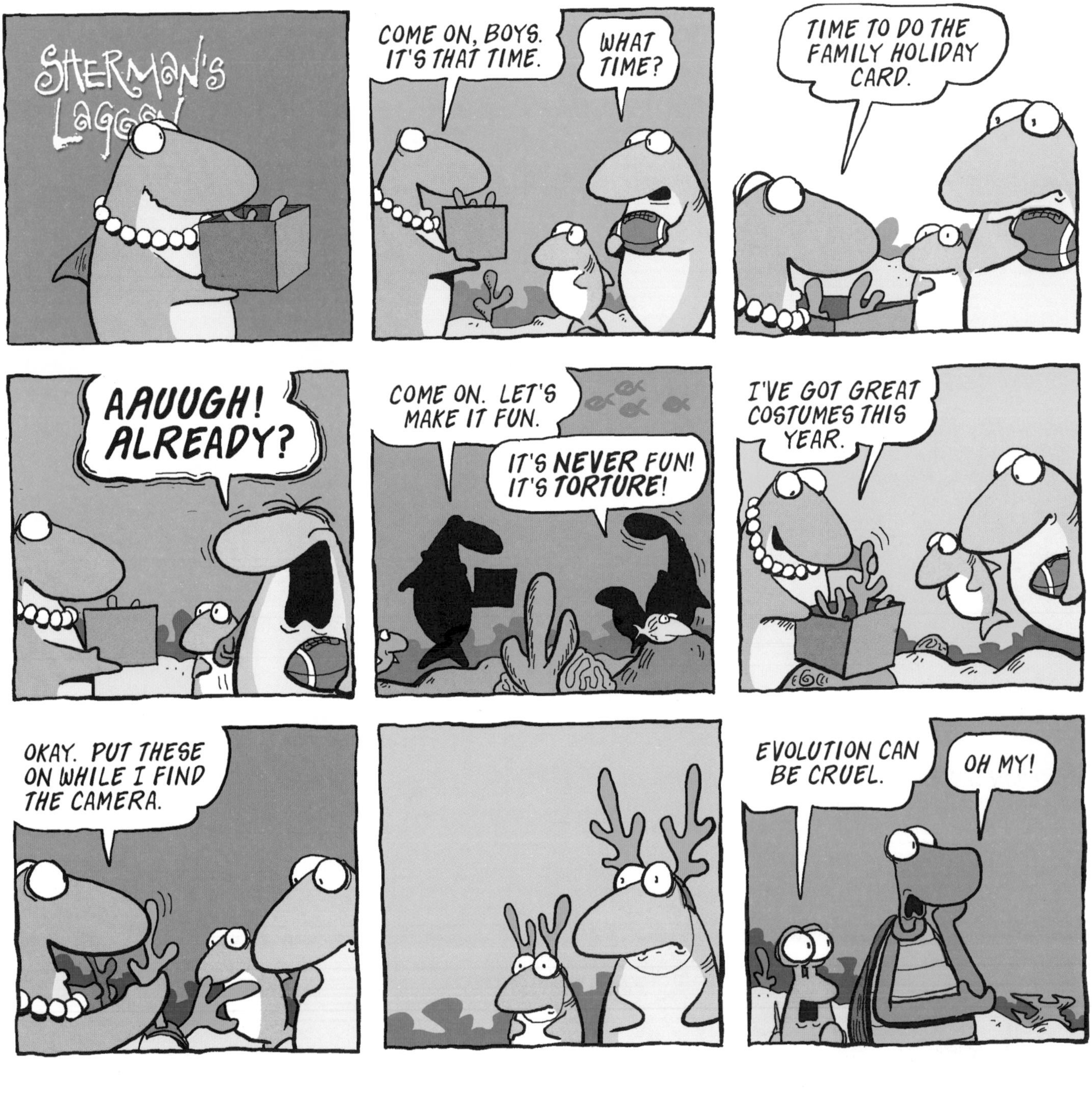
SHERMAN'S LAGOON
COME ON, BOYS. IT'S THAT TIME.
WHAT TIME?
TIME TO DO THE FAMILY HOLIDAY CARD.
AAUUGH! ALREADY?
COME ON. LET'S MAKE IT FUN.
IT'S NEVER FUN! IT'S TORTURE!
I'VE GOT GREAT COSTUMES THIS YEAR.
OKAY. PUT THESE ON WHILE I FIND THE CAMERA.
EVOLUTION CAN BE CRUEL.
OH MY!

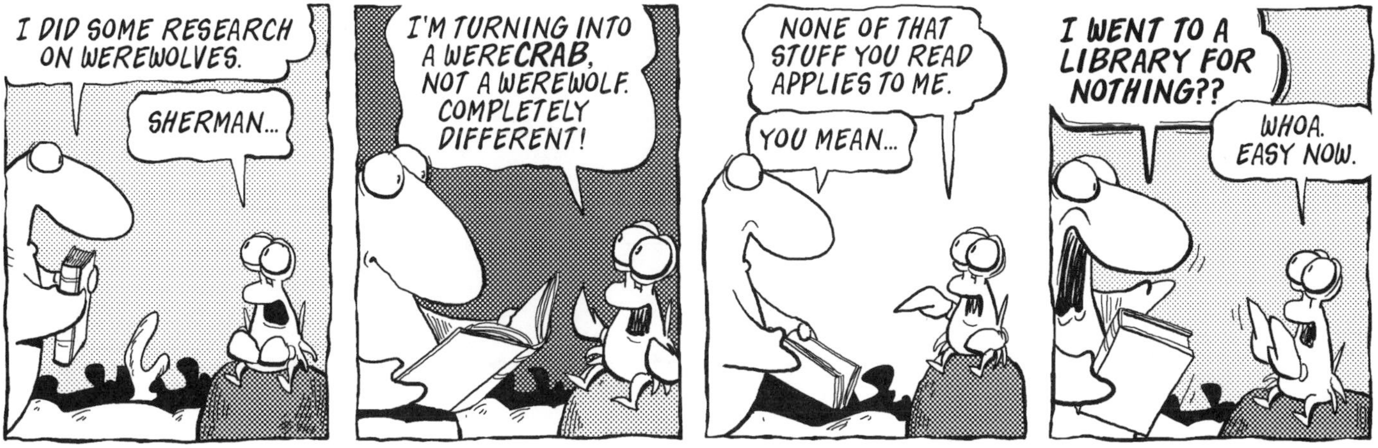
I DID SOME RESEARCH ON WEREWOLVES.
SHERMAN...
I'M TURNING INTO A WERECRAB, NOT A WEREWOLF. COMPLETELY DIFFERENT!
NONE OF THAT STUFF YOU READ APPLIES TO ME.
YOU MEAN...
I WENT TO A LIBRARY FOR NOTHING??
WHOA. EASY NOW.

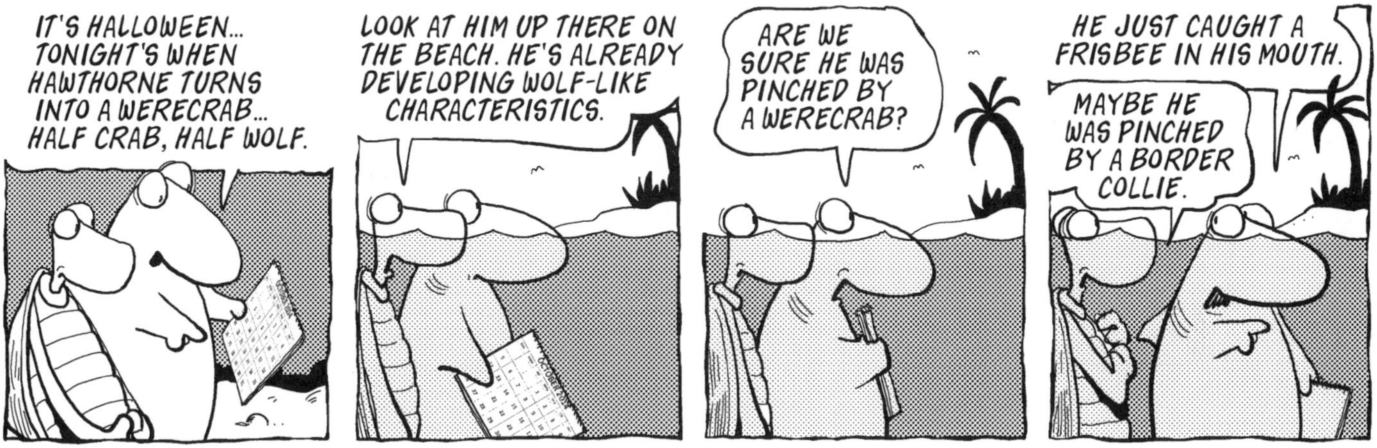
IT'S HALLOWEEN... TONIGHT'S WHEN HAWTHORNE TURNS INTO A WERECRAB... HALF CRAB, HALF WOLF.
LOOK AT HIM UP THERE ON THE BEACH. HE'S ALREADY DEVELOPING WOLF-LIKE CHARACTERISTICS.
ARE WE SURE HE WAS PINCHED BY A WERECRAB?
HE JUST CAUGHT A FRISBEE IN HIS MOUTH.
MAYBE HE WAS PINCHED BY A BORDER COLLIE.

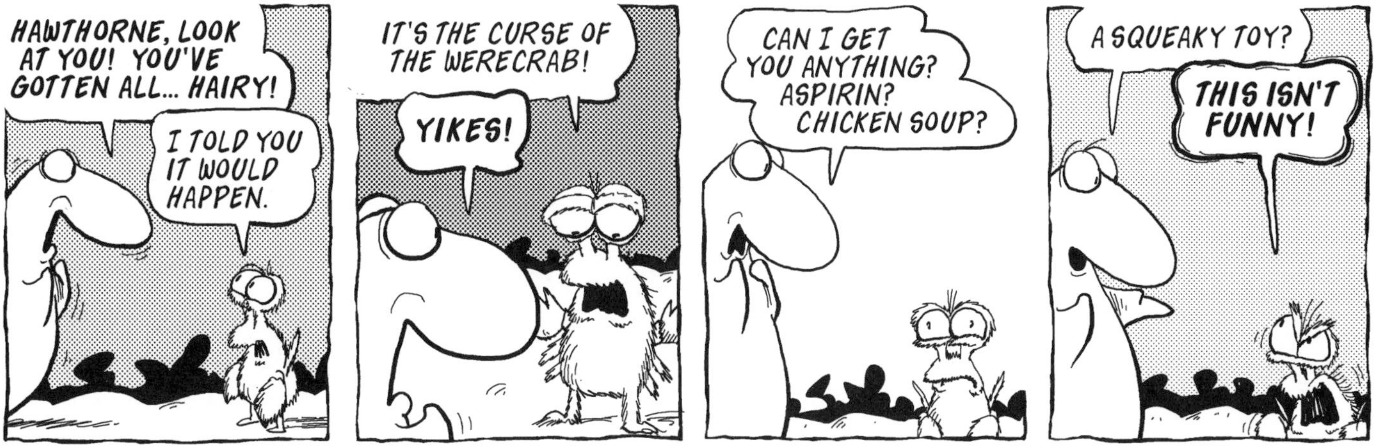
HAWTHORNE, LOOK AT YOU! YOU'VE GOTTEN ALL... HAIRY!
I TOLD YOU IT WOULD HAPPEN.
IT'S THE CURSE OF THE WERECRAB!
YIKES!
CAN I GET YOU ANYTHING? ASPIRIN? CHICKEN SOUP?
A SQUEAKY TOY?
THIS ISN'T FUNNY!

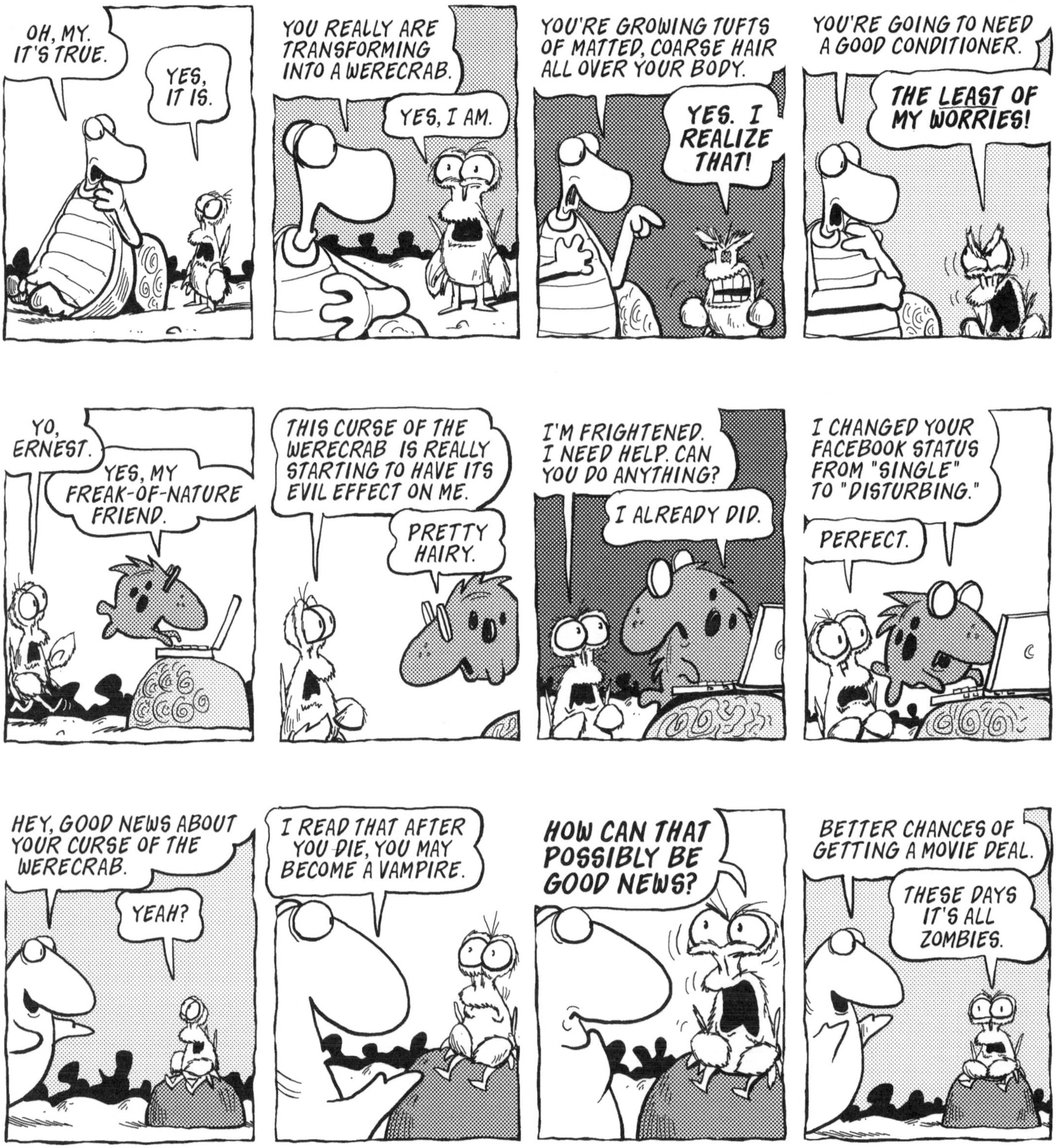
OH, MY. IT'S TRUE.
YES, IT IS.
YOU REALLY ARE TRANSFORMING INTO A WERECRAB.
YES, I AM.
YOU'RE GROWING TUFTS OF MATTED, COARSE HAIR ALL OVER YOUR BODY.
YES. I REALIZE THAT!
YOU'RE GOING TO NEED A GOOD CONDITIONER.
THE LEAST OF MY WORRIES!
YO, ERNEST.
YES, MY FREAK-OF-NATURE FRIEND.
THIS CURSE OF THE WERECRAB IS REALLY STARTING TO HAVE ITS EVIL EFFECT ON ME.
PRETTY HAIRY.
I'M FRIGHTENED. I NEED HELP. CAN YOU DO ANYTHING?
I ALREADY DID.
I CHANGED YOUR FACEBOOK STATUS FROM "SINGLE" TO "DISTURBING."
PERFECT.
HEY, GOOD NEWS ABOUT YOUR CURSE OF THE WERECRAB.
YEAH?
I READ THAT AFTER YOU DIE, YOU MAY BECOME A VAMPIRE.
HOW CAN THAT POSSIBLY BE GOOD NEWS?
BETTER CHANCES OF GETTING A MOVIE DEAL.
THESE DAYS IT'S ALL ZOMBIES.

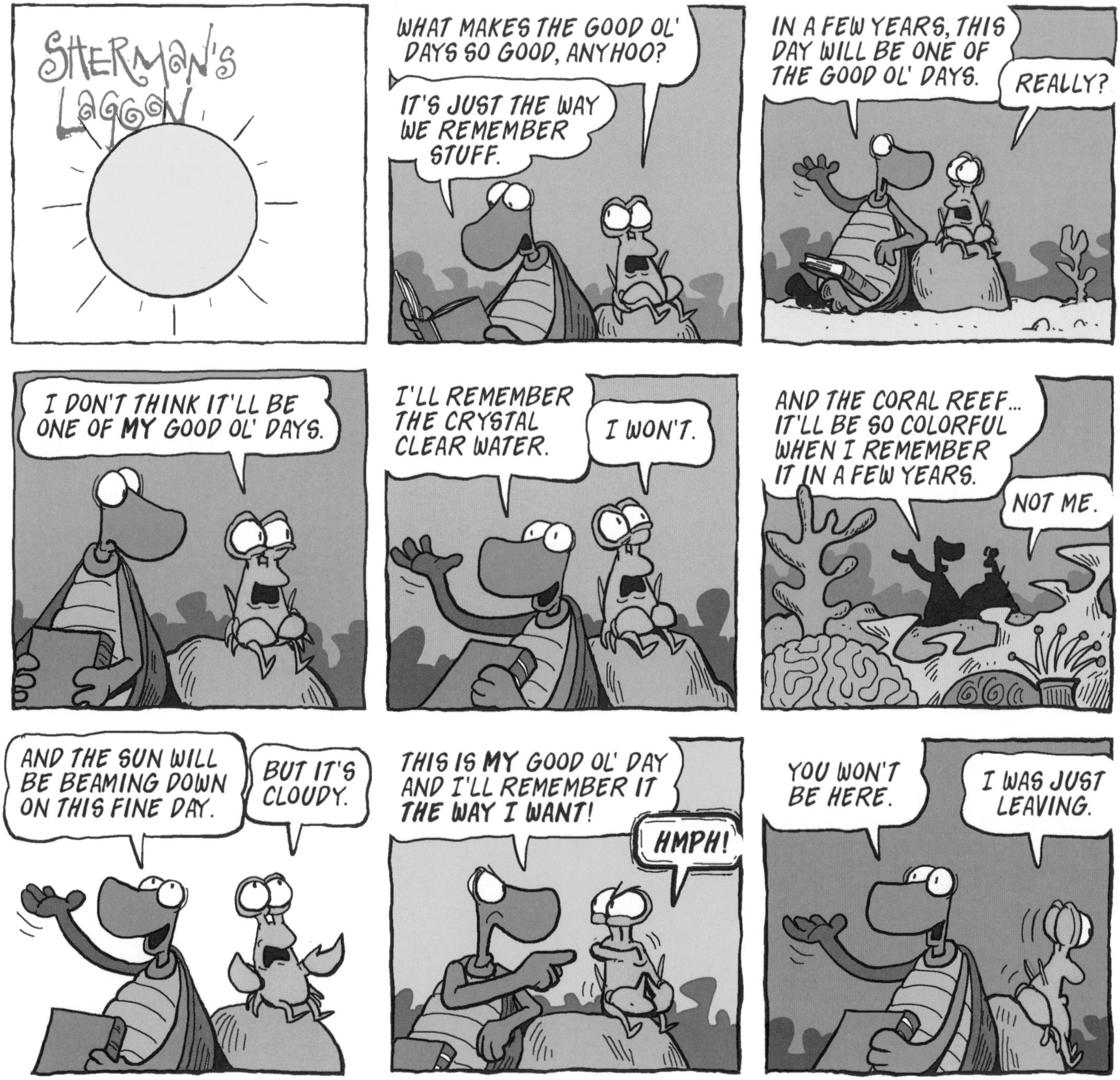
SHERMAN'S LAGOON
WHAT MAKES THE GOOD OL' DAYS SO GOOD, ANYHOO?
IT'S JUST THE WAY WE REMEMBER STUFF.
IN A FEW YEARS, THIS DAY WILL BE ONE OF THE GOOD OL' DAYS.
REALLY?
I DON'T THINK IT'LL BE ONE OF MY GOOD OL' DAYS.
I'LL REMEMBER THE CRYSTAL CLEAR WATER.
I WON'T.
AND THE CORAL REEF... IT'LL BE SO COLORFUL WHEN I REMEMBER IT IN A FEW YEARS.
NOT ME.
AND THE SUN WILL BE BEAMING DOWN ON THIS FINE DAY.
BUT IT'S CLOUDY.
THIS IS MY GOOD OL' DAY AND I'LL REMEMBER IT THE WAY I WANT!
HMPH!
YOU WON'T BE HERE.
I WAS JUST LEAVING.

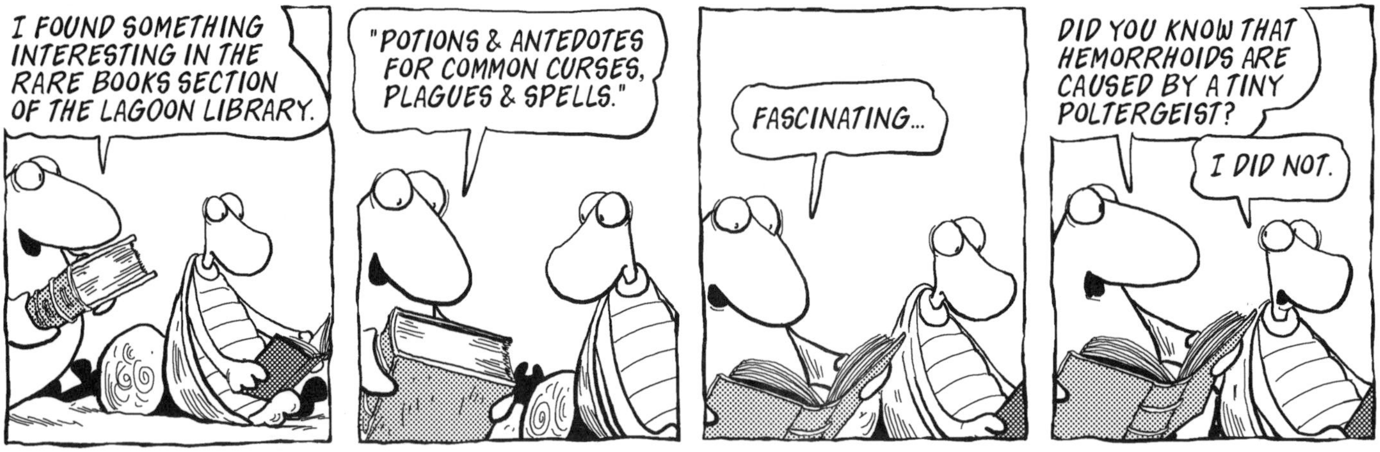
I FOUND SOMETHING INTERESTING IN THE RARE BOOKS SECTION OF THE LAGOON LIBRARY.
"POTIONS & ANTEDOTES FOR COMMON CURSES, PLAGUES & SPELLS."
FASCINATING...
DID YOU KNOW THAT HEMORRHOIDS ARE CAUSED BY A TINY POLTERGEIST?
I DID NOT.

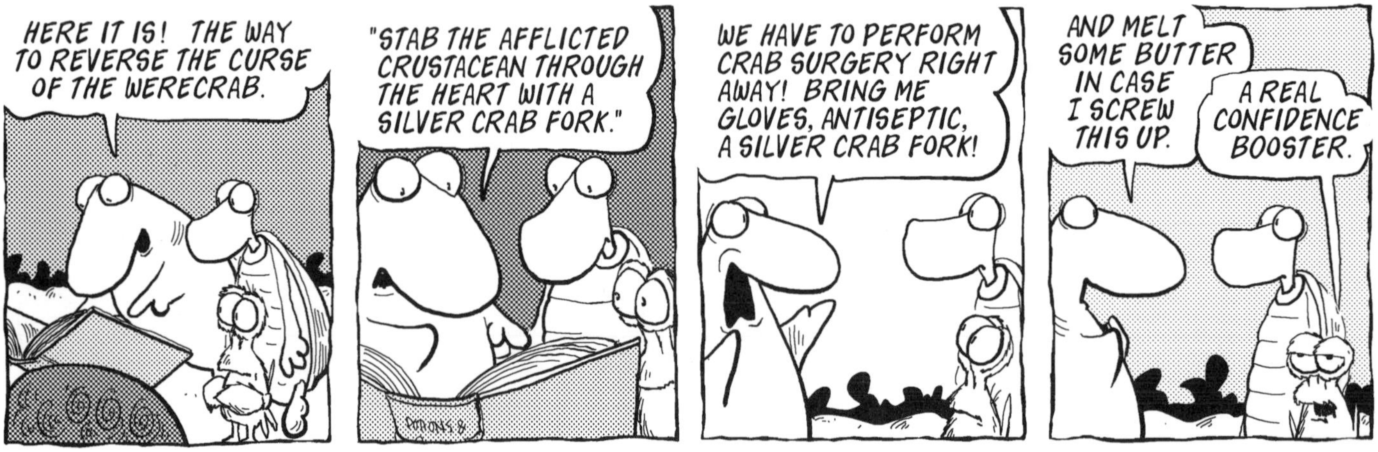
HERE IT IS! THE WAY TO REVERSE THE CURSE OF THE WERECRAB.
"STAB THE AFFLICTED CRUSTACEAN THROUGH THE HEART WITH A SILVER CRAB FORK."
WE HAVE TO PERFORM CRAB SURGERY RIGHT AWAY! BRING ME GLOVES, ANTISEPTIC, A SILVER CRAB FORK!
AND MELT SOME BUTTER IN CASE I SCREW THIS UP.
A REAL CONFIDENCE BOOSTER.

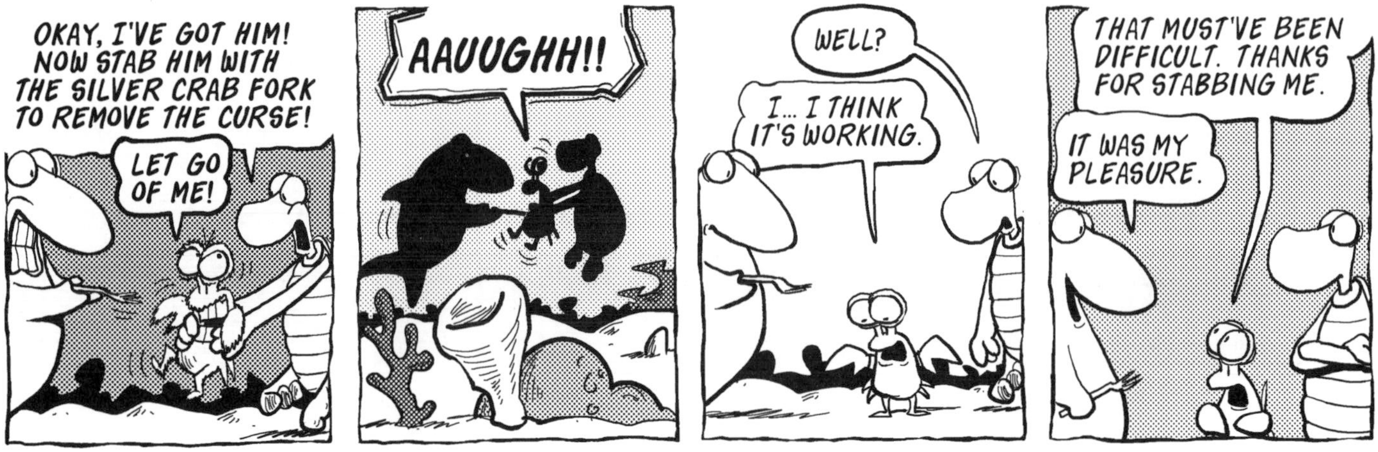
OKAY, I'VE GOT HIM! NOW STAB HIM WITH THE SILVER CRAB FORK TO REMOVE THE CURSE!
LET GO OF ME!
AAUUGHH!!
WELL?
I... I THINK IT'S WORKING.
THAT MUST'VE BEEN DIFFICULT. THANKS FOR STABBING ME.
IT WAS MY PLEASURE.

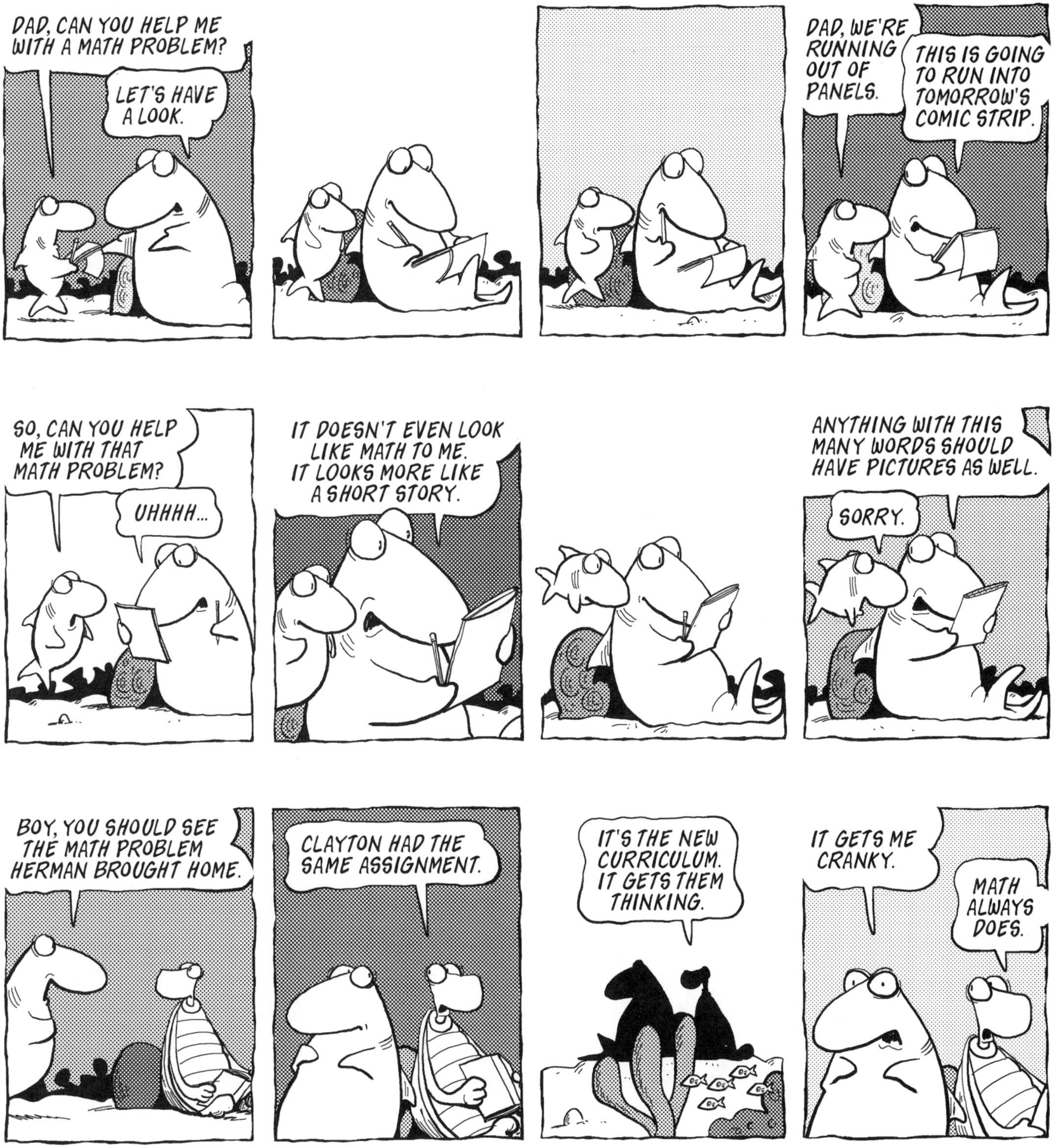
DAD, CAN YOU HELP ME WITH A MATH PROBLEM?
LET'S HAVE A LOOK.
DAD, WE'RE RUNNING OUT OF PANELS.
THIS IS GOING TO RUN INTO TOMORROW'S COMIC STRIP.
SO, CAN YOU HELP ME WITH THAT MATH PROBLEM?
UHHHH...
IT DOESN'T EVEN LOOK LIKE MATH TO ME. IT LOOKS MORE LIKE A SHORT STORY.
ANYTHING WITH THIS MANY WORDS SHOULD HAVE PICTURES AS WELL.
SORRY.
BOY, YOU SHOULD SEE THE MATH PROBLEM HERMAN BROUGHT HOME.
CLAYTON HAD THE SAME ASSIGNMENT.
IT'S THE NEW CURRICULUM. IT GETS THEM THINKING.
IT GETS ME CRANKY.
MATH ALWAYS DOES.

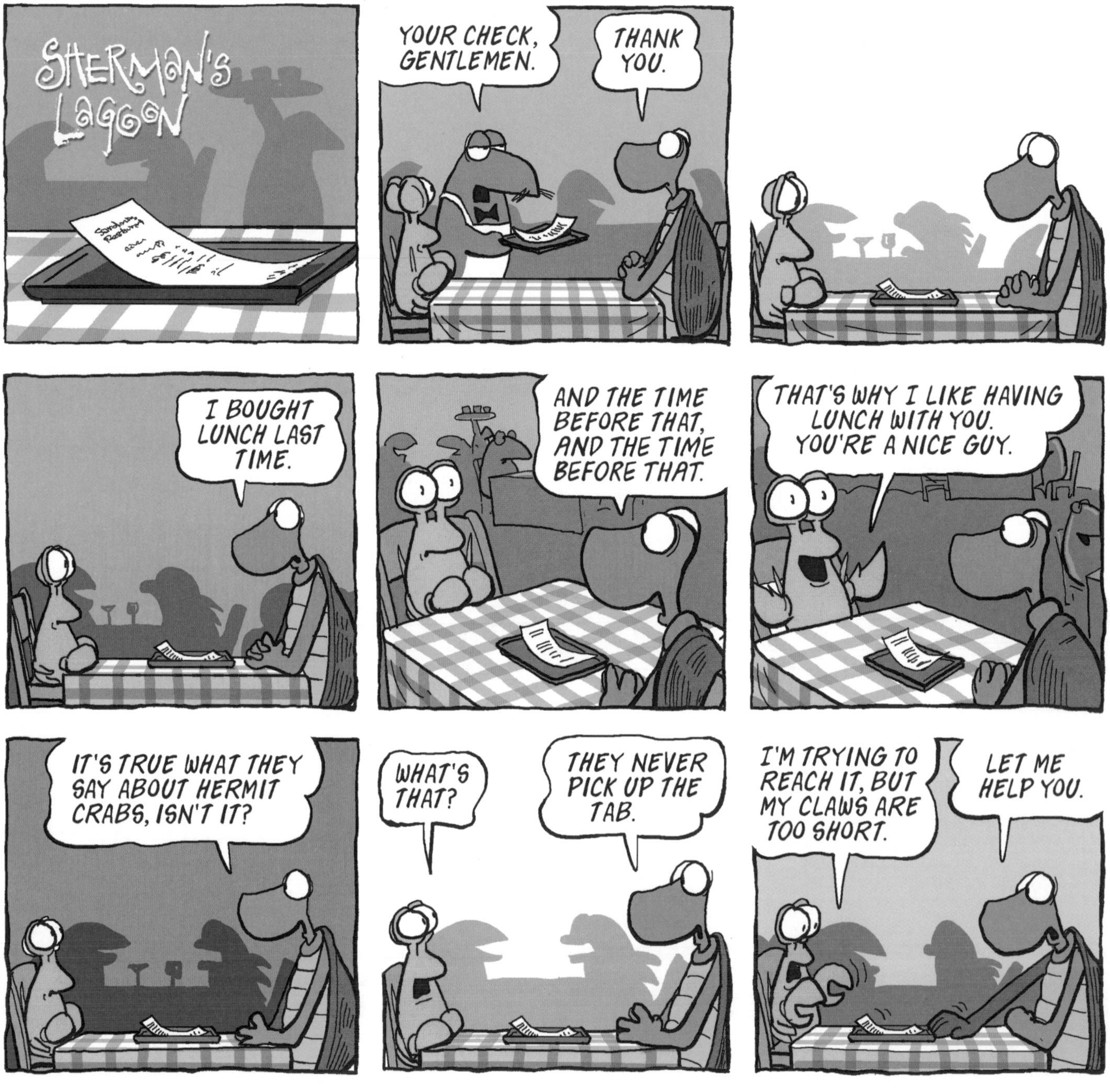
SHERMAN'S LAGOON
YOUR CHECK, GENTLEMEN.
THANK YOU.
I BOUGHT LUNCH LAST TIME.
AND THE TIME BEFORE THAT, AND THE TIME BEFORE THAT.
THAT'S WHY I LIKE HAVING LUNCH WITH YOU. YOU'RE A NICE GUY.
IT'S TRUE WHAT THEY SAY ABOUT HERMIT CRABS, ISN'T IT?
WHAT'S THAT?
THEY NEVER PICK UP THE TAB.
I'M TRYING TO REACH IT, BUT MY CLAWS ARE TOO SHORT.
LET ME HELP YOU.

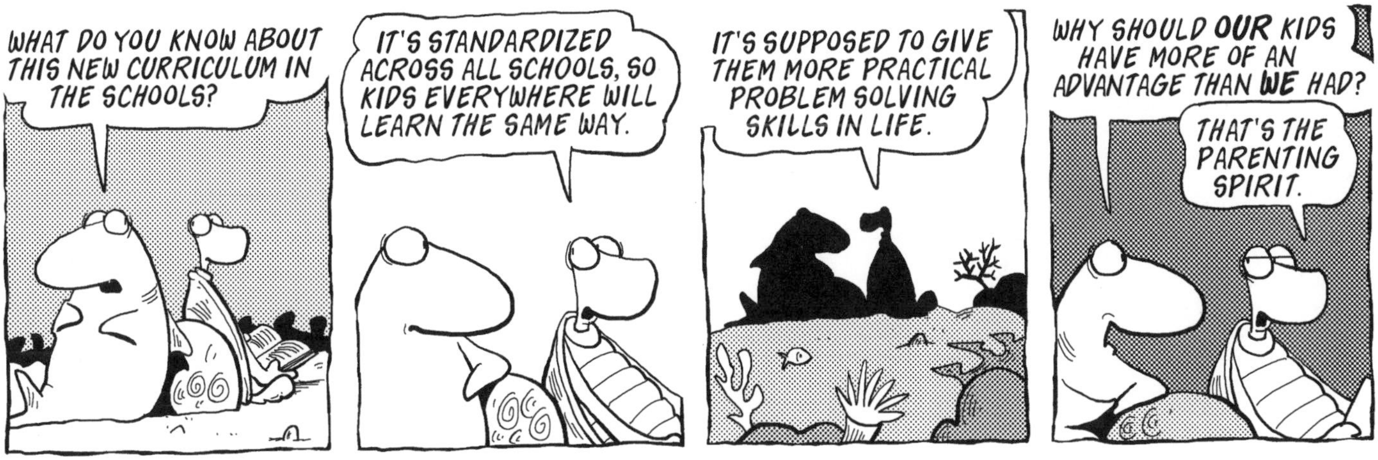
WHAT DO YOU KNOW ABOUT THIS NEW CURRICULUM IN THE SCHOOLS?
IT'S STANDARDIZED ACROSS ALL SCHOOLS, SO KIDS EVERYWHERE WILL LEARN THE SAME WAY.
IT'S SUPPOSED TO GIVE THEM MORE PRACTICAL PROBLEM SOLVING SKILLS IN LIFE.
WHY SHOULD **OUR** KIDS HAVE MORE OF AN ADVANTAGE THAN **WE** HAD?
THAT'S THE PARENTING SPIRIT.

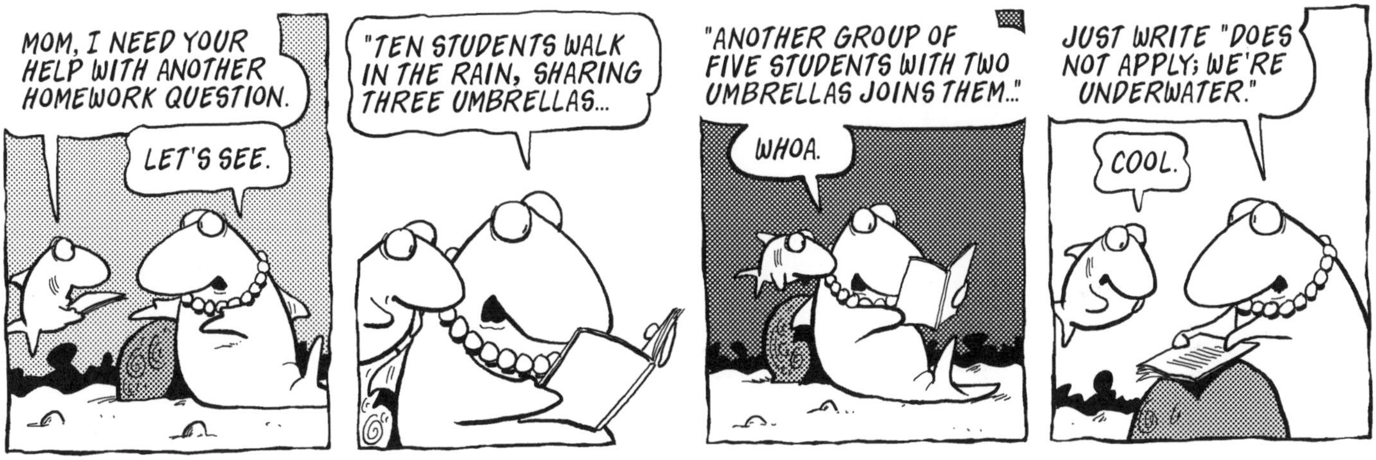
MOM, I NEED YOUR HELP WITH ANOTHER HOMEWORK QUESTION.
LET'S SEE.
"TEN STUDENTS WALK IN THE RAIN, SHARING THREE UMBRELLAS...
"ANOTHER GROUP OF FIVE STUDENTS WITH TWO UMBRELLAS JOINS THEM..."
WHOA.
JUST WRITE "DOES NOT APPLY; WE'RE UNDERWATER."
COOL.

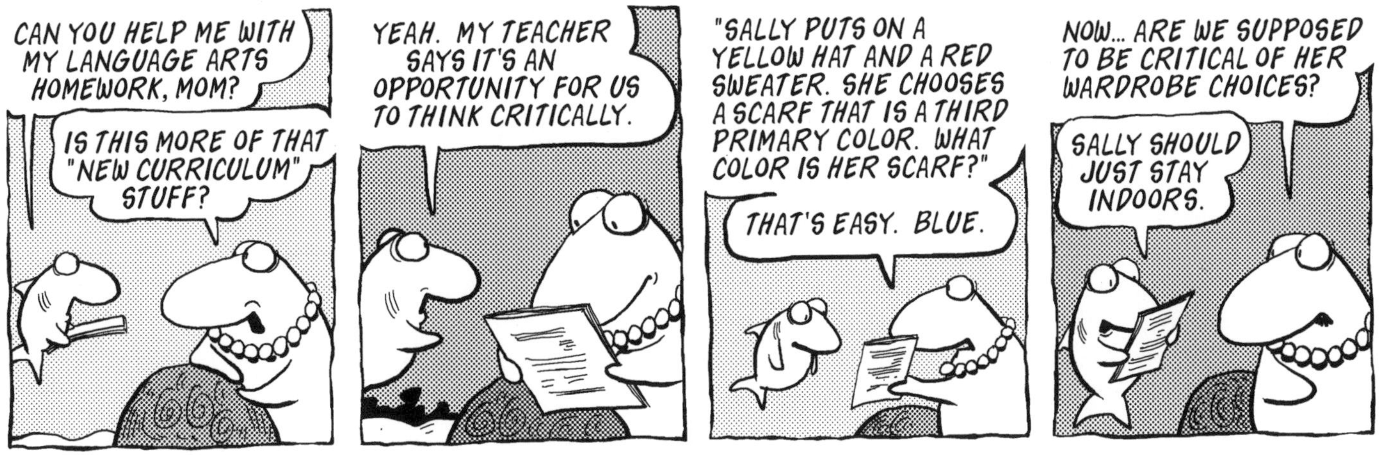
CAN YOU HELP ME WITH MY LANGUAGE ARTS HOMEWORK, MOM?
IS THIS MORE OF THAT "NEW CURRICULUM" STUFF?
YEAH. MY TEACHER SAYS IT'S AN OPPORTUNITY FOR US TO THINK CRITICALLY.
"SALLY PUTS ON A YELLOW HAT AND A RED SWEATER. SHE CHOOSES A SCARF THAT IS A THIRD PRIMARY COLOR. WHAT COLOR IS HER SCARF?"
THAT'S EASY. BLUE.
NOW... ARE WE SUPPOSED TO BE CRITICAL OF HER WARDROBE CHOICES?
SALLY SHOULD JUST STAY INDOORS.

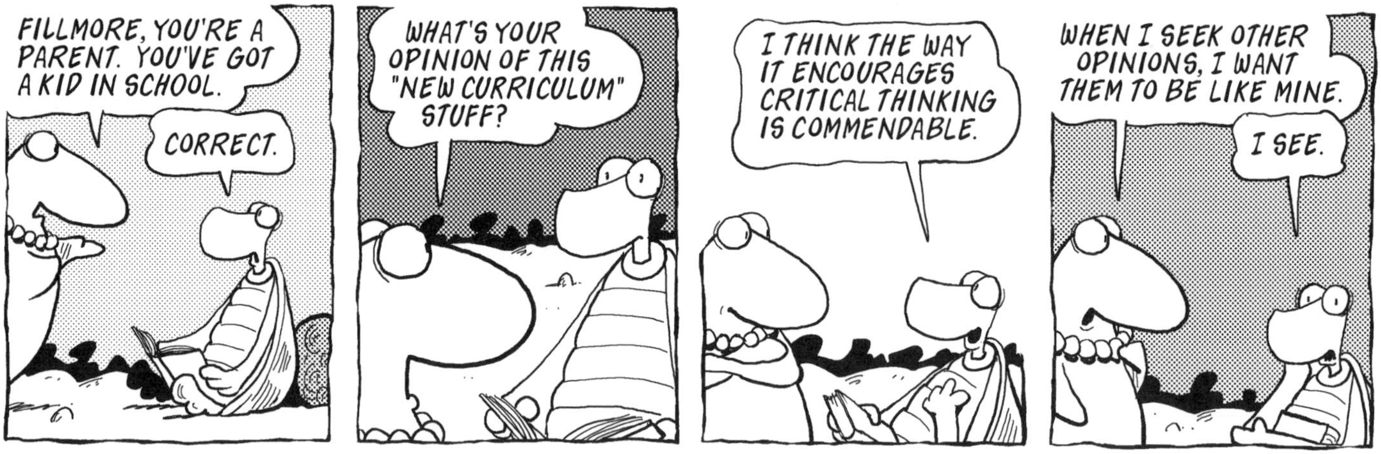
FILLMORE, YOU'RE A PARENT. YOU'VE GOT A KID IN SCHOOL.
CORRECT.
WHAT'S YOUR OPINION OF THIS "NEW CURRICULUM" STUFF?
I THINK THE WAY IT ENCOURAGES CRITICAL THINKING IS COMMENDABLE.
WHEN I SEEK OTHER OPINIONS, I WANT THEM TO BE LIKE MINE.
I SEE.

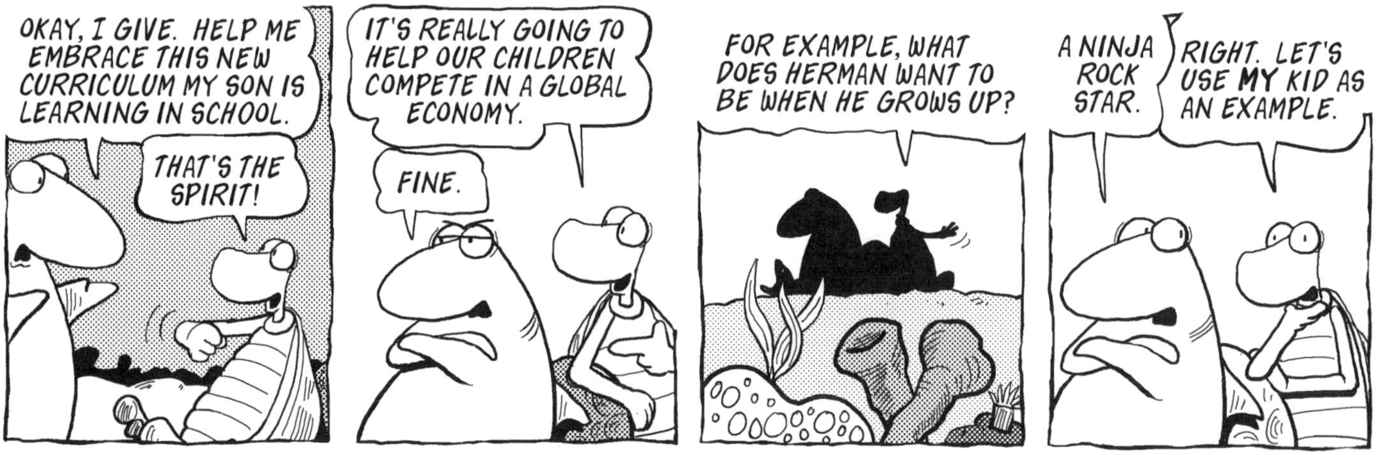
OKAY, I GIVE. HELP ME EMBRACE THIS NEW CURRICULUM MY SON IS LEARNING IN SCHOOL.
THAT'S THE SPIRIT!
IT'S REALLY GOING TO HELP OUR CHILDREN COMPETE IN A GLOBAL ECONOMY.
FINE.
FOR EXAMPLE, WHAT DOES HERMAN WANT TO BE WHEN HE GROWS UP?
A NINJA ROCK STAR.
RIGHT. LET'S USE MY KID AS AN EXAMPLE.

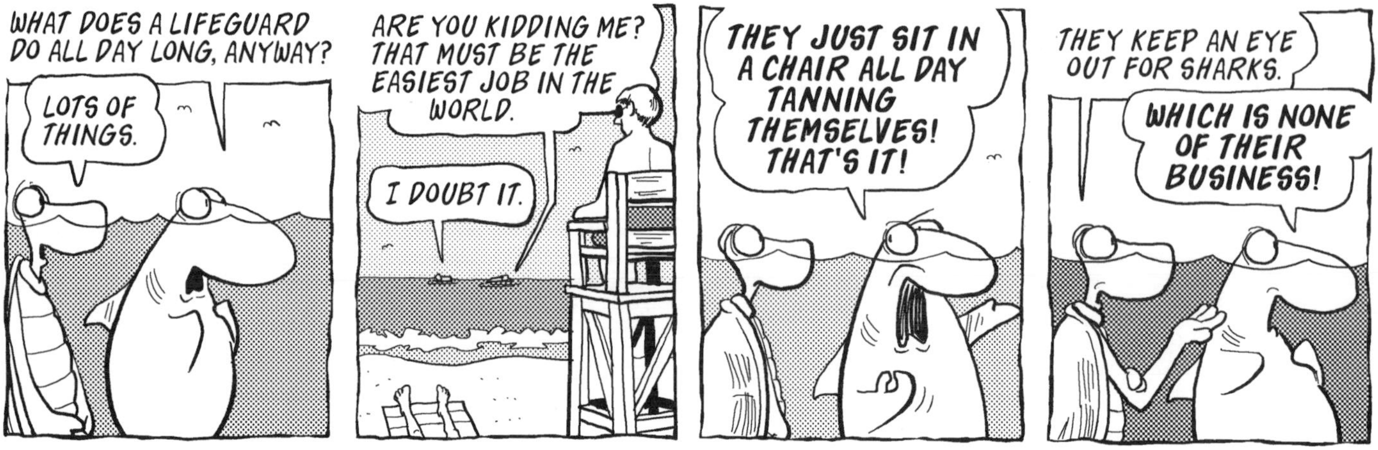
WHAT DOES A LIFEGUARD DO ALL DAY LONG, ANYWAY?
LOTS OF THINGS.
ARE YOU KIDDING ME? THAT MUST BE THE EASIEST JOB IN THE WORLD.
I DOUBT IT.
THEY JUST SIT IN A CHAIR ALL DAY TANNING THEMSELVES! THAT'S IT!
THEY KEEP AN EYE OUT FOR SHARKS.
WHICH IS NONE OF THEIR BUSINESS!

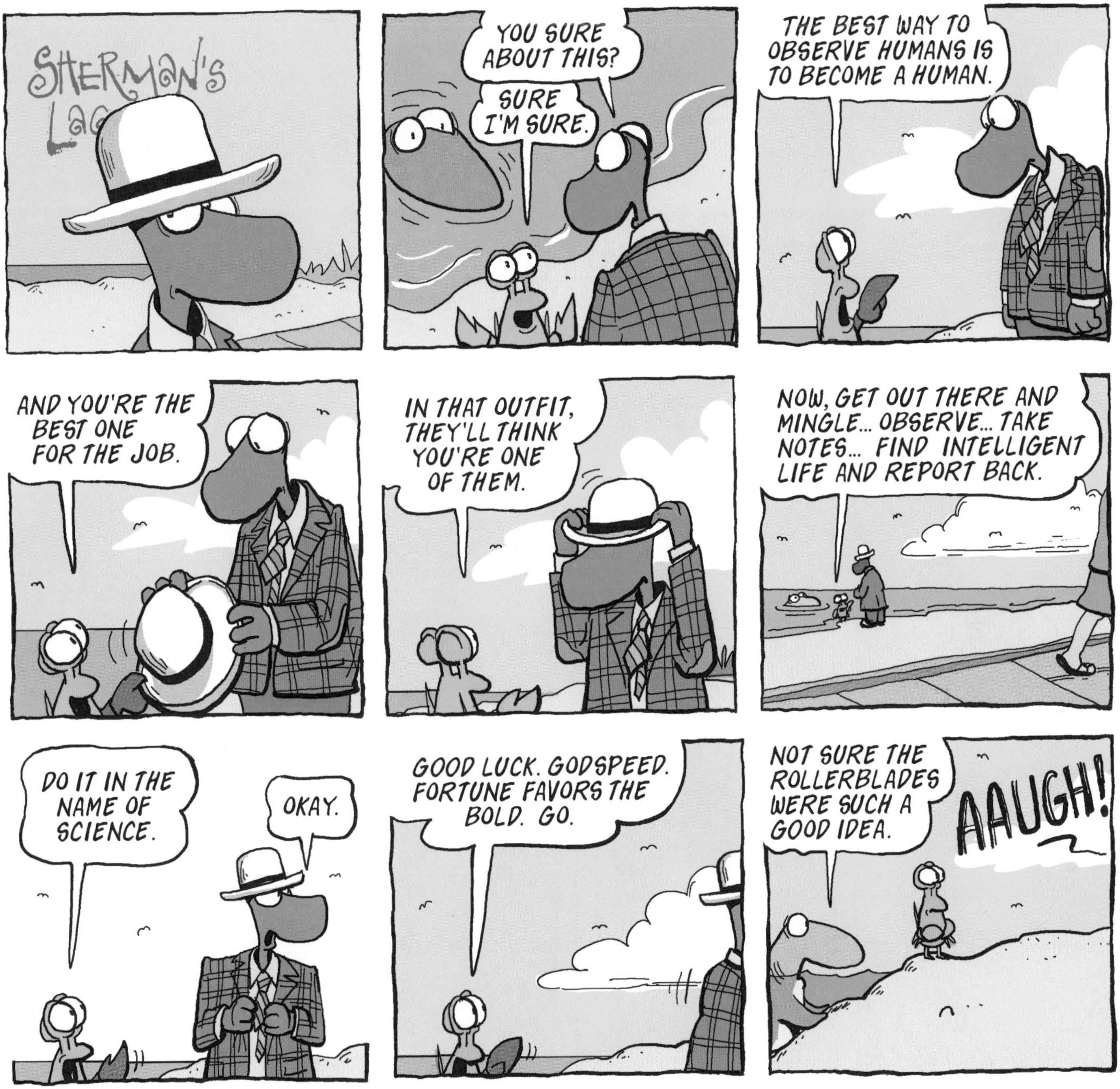
SHERMAN'S LAG
YOU SURE ABOUT THIS?
SURE I'M SURE.
THE BEST WAY TO OBSERVE HUMANS IS TO BECOME A HUMAN.
AND YOU'RE THE BEST ONE FOR THE JOB.
IN THAT OUTFIT, THEY'LL THINK YOU'RE ONE OF THEM.
NOW, GET OUT THERE AND MINGLE... OBSERVE... TAKE NOTES... FIND INTELLIGENT LIFE AND REPORT BACK.
DO IT IN THE NAME OF SCIENCE.
OKAY.
GOOD LUCK. GODSPEED. FORTUNE FAVORS THE BOLD. GO.
NOT SURE THE ROLLERBLADES WERE SUCH A GOOD IDEA.
AAUGH!

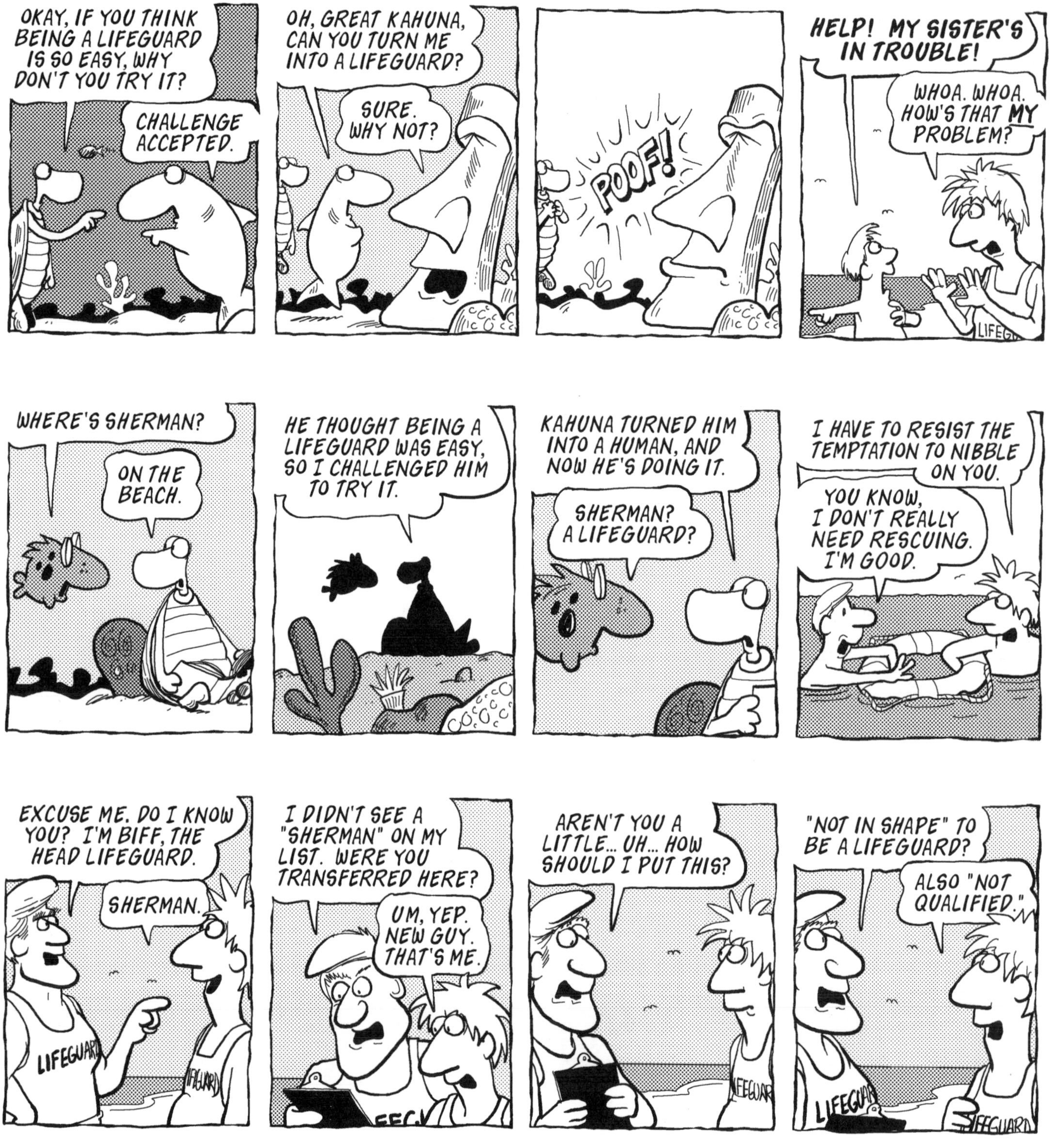

OKAY, IF YOU THINK BEING A LIFEGUARD IS SO EASY, WHY DON'T YOU TRY IT?
CHALLENGE ACCEPTED.
OH, GREAT KAHUNA, CAN YOU TURN ME INTO A LIFEGUARD?
SURE. WHY NOT?
POOF!
HELP! MY SISTER'S IN TROUBLE!
WHOA. WHOA. HOW'S THAT MY PROBLEM?
LIFEG
WHERE'S SHERMAN?
ON THE BEACH.
HE THOUGHT BEING A LIFEGUARD WAS EASY, SO I CHALLENGED HIM TO TRY IT.
KAHUNA TURNED HIM INTO A HUMAN, AND NOW HE'S DOING IT.
SHERMAN? A LIFEGUARD?
I HAVE TO RESIST THE TEMPTATION TO NIBBLE ON YOU.
YOU KNOW, I DON'T REALLY NEED RESCUING. I'M GOOD.
EXCUSE ME. DO I KNOW YOU? I'M BIFF, THE HEAD LIFEGUARD.
SHERMAN.
LIFEGUARD
LIFEGUARD
I DIDN'T SEE A "SHERMAN" ON MY LIST. WERE YOU TRANSFERRED HERE?
UM, YEP. NEW GUY. THAT'S ME.
AREN'T YOU A LITTLE... UH... HOW SHOULD I PUT THIS?
"NOT IN SHAPE" TO BE A LIFEGUARD?
ALSO "NOT QUALIFIED."
LIFEGUARD
LIFEGUARD

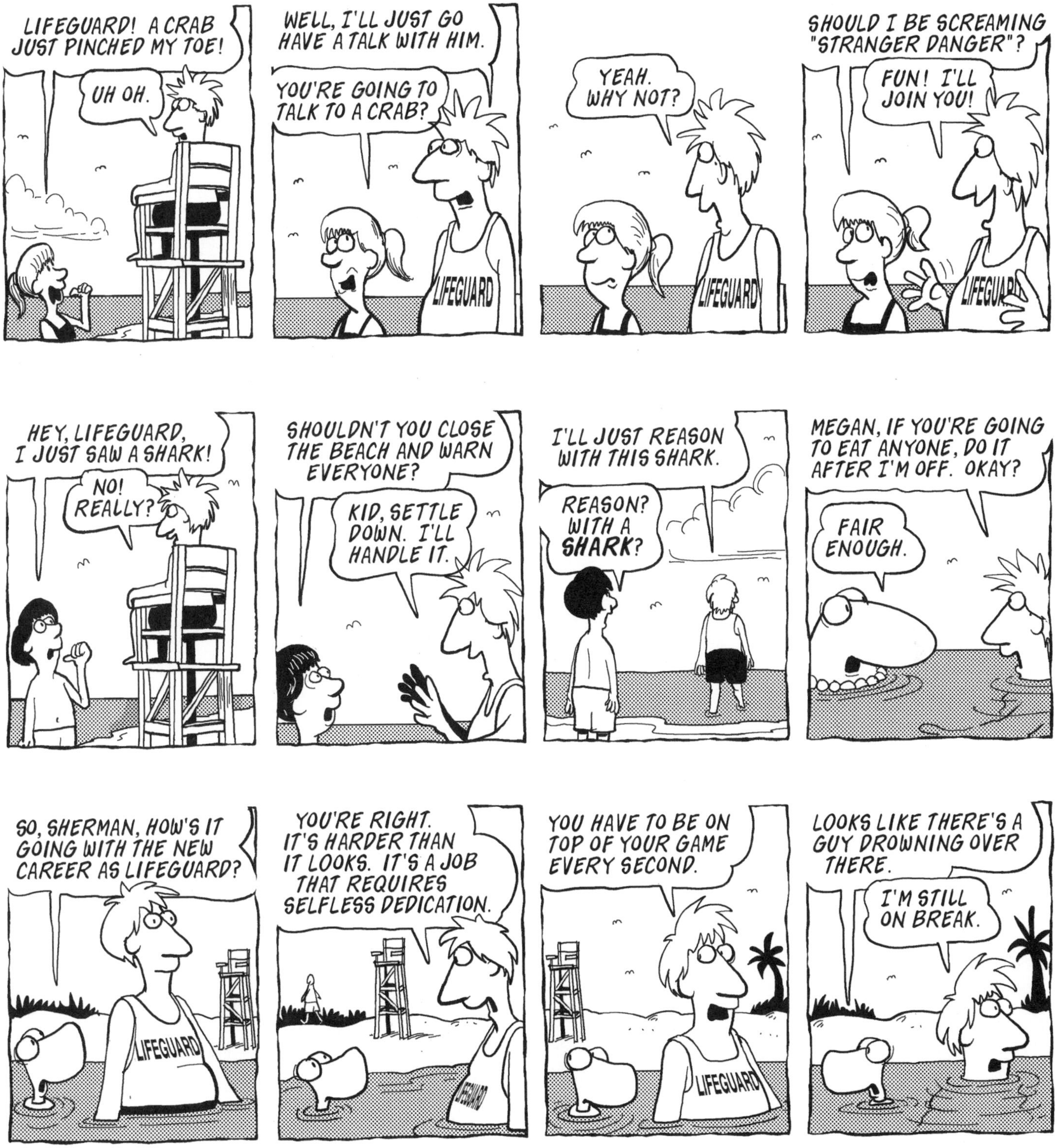
LIFEGUARD! A CRAB JUST PINCHED MY TOE!
UH OH.
WELL, I'LL JUST GO HAVE A TALK WITH HIM.
YOU'RE GOING TO TALK TO A CRAB?
LIFEGUARD
YEAH. WHY NOT?
LIFEGUARD
SHOULD I BE SCREAMING "STRANGER DANGER"?
FUN! I'LL JOIN YOU!
HEY, LIFEGUARD, I JUST SAW A SHARK!
NO! REALLY?
SHOULDN'T YOU CLOSE THE BEACH AND WARN EVERYONE?
KID, SETTLE DOWN. I'LL HANDLE IT.
I'LL JUST REASON WITH THIS SHARK.
REASON? WITH A SHARK?
MEGAN, IF YOU'RE GOING TO EAT ANYONE, DO IT AFTER I'M OFF. OKAY?
FAIR ENOUGH.
SO, SHERMAN, HOW'S IT GOING WITH THE NEW CAREER AS LIFEGUARD?
LIFEGUARD
YOU'RE RIGHT. IT'S HARDER THAN IT LOOKS. IT'S A JOB THAT REQUIRES SELFLESS DEDICATION.
YOU HAVE TO BE ON TOP OF YOUR GAME EVERY SECOND.
LIFEGUARD
LOOKS LIKE THERE'S A GUY DROWNING OVER THERE.
I'M STILL ON BREAK.

SHERMAN'S LAGOON

I HAVE A PLAN. IT'S AN INGENIOUS PLAN. **BWAHAHAHAHA!**

YEAH?

PICTURE THIS... YOU'RE A HAIRLESS BEACH APE OUT FOR A NICE RELAXING SWIM...

WHEN ALL OF A SUDDEN FROM EVERY DIRECTION YOU SEE SHARK FINS COMING AT YOU.

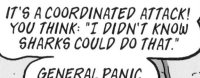

IT'S A COORDINATED ATTACK! YOU THINK: "I DIDN'T KNOW SHARKS COULD DO THAT."

GENERAL PANIC ENSUES.

SOON, WORD SPREADS THAT SHARKS ARE THE MASTERMINDS BEHIND AN UPRISING BY ANIMALS ALL OVER THE PLANET.

ALL HUMANITY SEES NATURE DIFFERENTLY. AND THEY ALL PAY TRIBUTE TO THE GREAT AND POWERFUL SHARK.

SO, WE THOUGHT IT MIGHT BE NICE TO HAVE A REAL SHARK.

YOU GUYS HAVE IT COVERED.

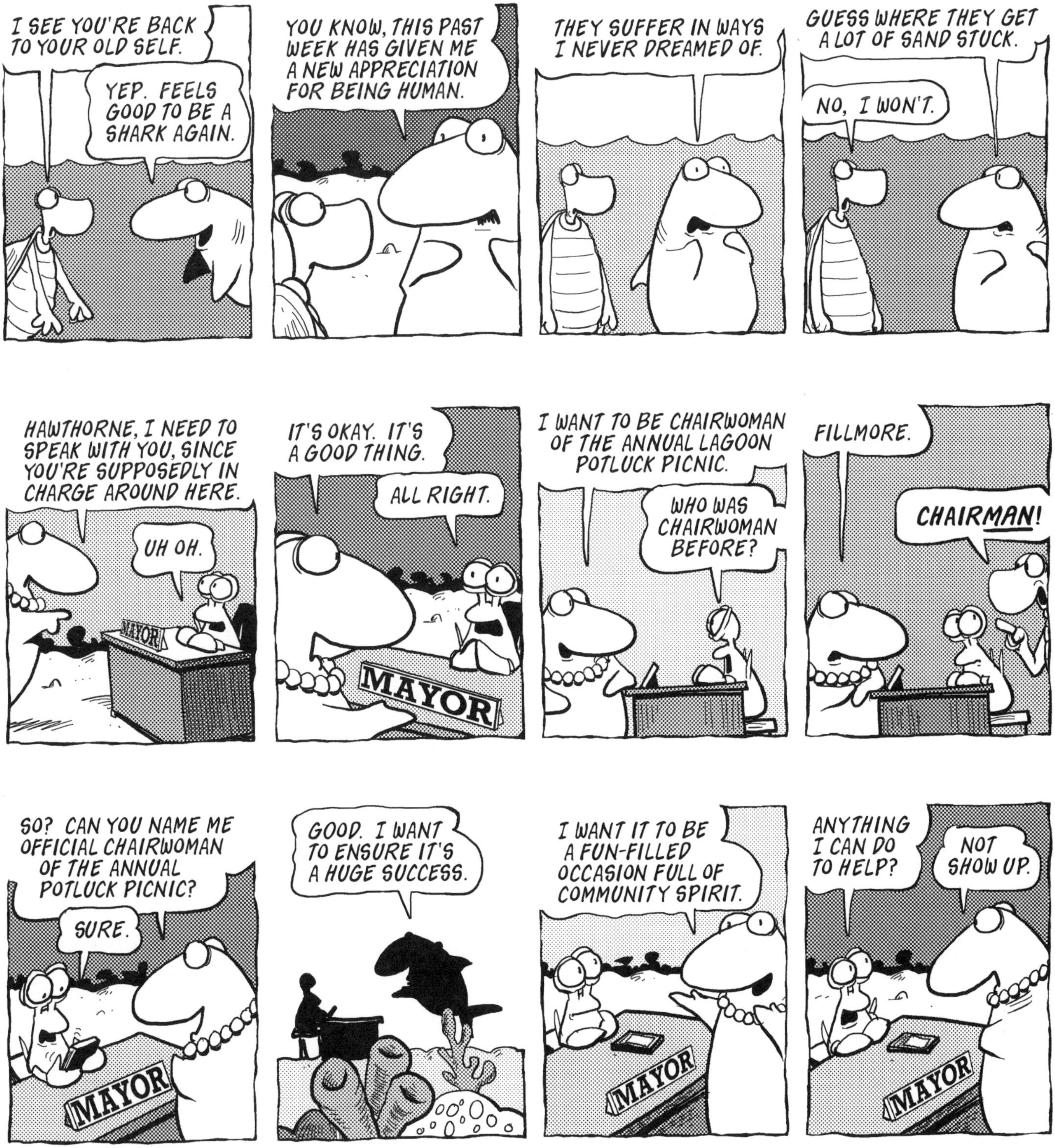
I SEE YOU'RE BACK TO YOUR OLD SELF.
YEP. FEELS GOOD TO BE A SHARK AGAIN.
YOU KNOW, THIS PAST WEEK HAS GIVEN ME A NEW APPRECIATION FOR BEING HUMAN.
THEY SUFFER IN WAYS I NEVER DREAMED OF.
GUESS WHERE THEY GET A LOT OF SAND STUCK.
NO, I WON'T.
HAWTHORNE, I NEED TO SPEAK WITH YOU, SINCE YOU'RE SUPPOSEDLY IN CHARGE AROUND HERE.
UH OH.
MAYOR
IT'S OKAY. IT'S A GOOD THING.
ALL RIGHT.
MAYOR
I WANT TO BE CHAIRWOMAN OF THE ANNUAL LAGOON POTLUCK PICNIC.
WHO WAS CHAIRWOMAN BEFORE?
FILLMORE.
CHAIRMAN!
SO? CAN YOU NAME ME OFFICIAL CHAIRWOMAN OF THE ANNUAL POTLUCK PICNIC?
SURE.
MAYOR
GOOD. I WANT TO ENSURE IT'S A HUGE SUCCESS.
I WANT IT TO BE A FUN-FILLED OCCASION FULL OF COMMUNITY SPIRIT.
MAYOR
ANYTHING I CAN DO TO HELP?
NOT SHOW UP.
MAYOR

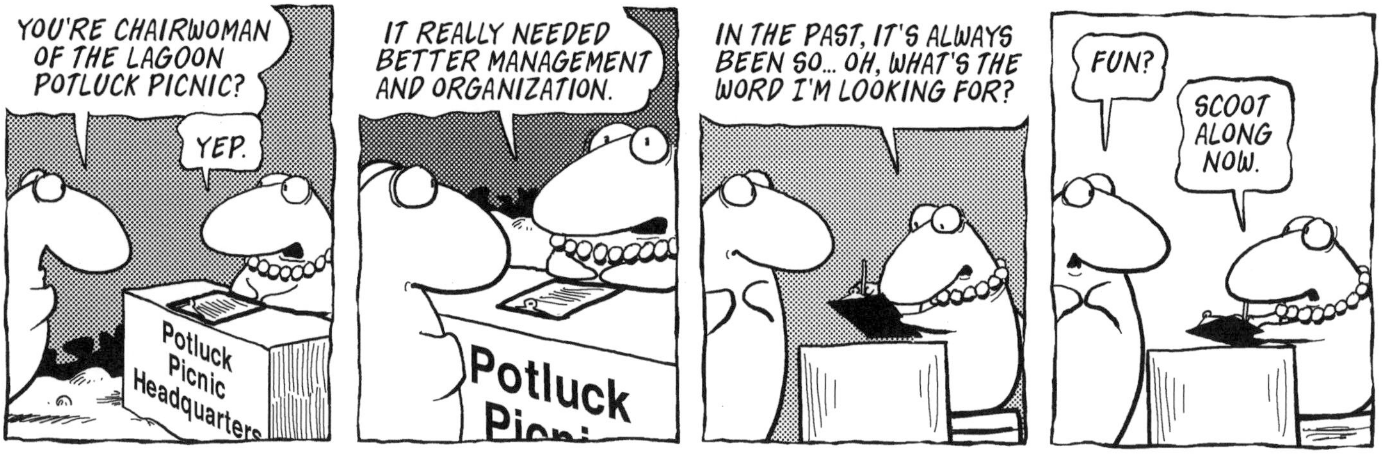
YOU'RE CHAIRWOMAN OF THE LAGOON POTLUCK PICNIC?
YEP.
Potluck Picnic Headquarters
IT REALLY NEEDED BETTER MANAGEMENT AND ORGANIZATION.
Potluck Picni
IN THE PAST, IT'S ALWAYS BEEN SO... OH, WHAT'S THE WORD I'M LOOKING FOR?
FUN?
SCOOT ALONG NOW.

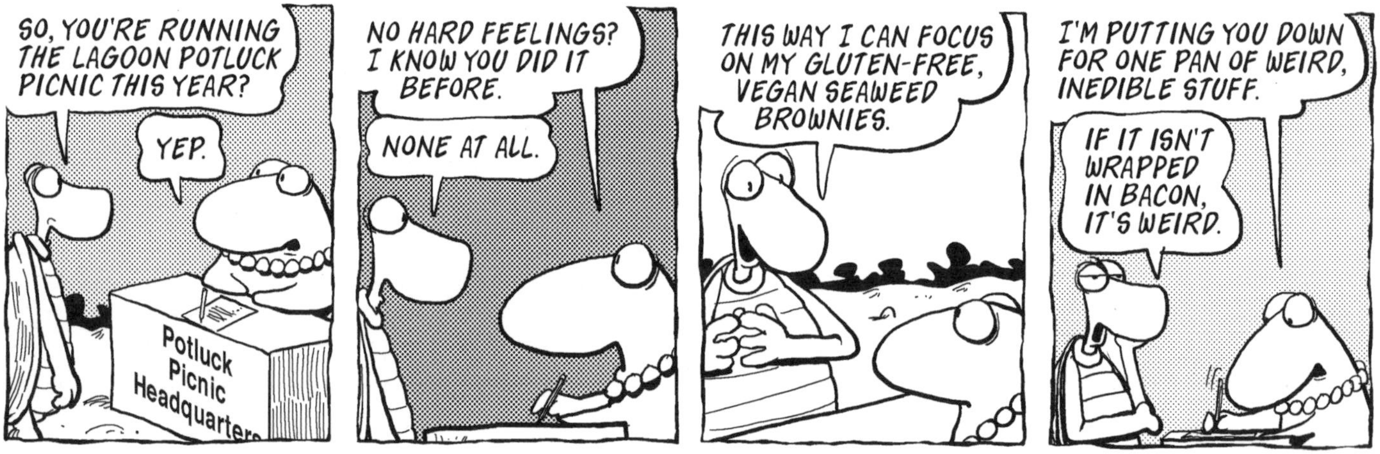
SO, YOU'RE RUNNING THE LAGOON POTLUCK PICNIC THIS YEAR?
YEP.
Potluck Picnic Headquarters
NO HARD FEELINGS? I KNOW YOU DID IT BEFORE.
NONE AT ALL.
THIS WAY I CAN FOCUS ON MY GLUTEN-FREE, VEGAN SEAWEED BROWNIES.
I'M PUTTING YOU DOWN FOR ONE PAN OF WEIRD, INEDIBLE STUFF.
IF IT ISN'T WRAPPED IN BACON, IT'S WEIRD.

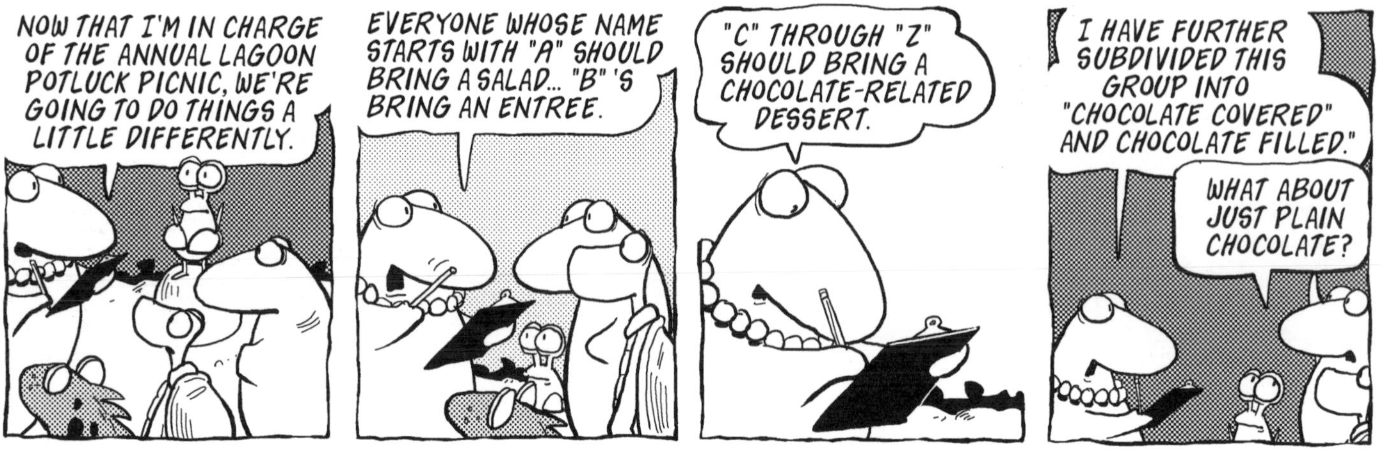
NOW THAT I'M IN CHARGE OF THE ANNUAL LAGOON POTLUCK PICNIC, WE'RE GOING TO DO THINGS A LITTLE DIFFERENTLY.
EVERYONE WHOSE NAME STARTS WITH "A" SHOULD BRING A SALAD... "B" 'S BRING AN ENTREE.
"C" THROUGH "Z" SHOULD BRING A CHOCOLATE-RELATED DESSERT.
I HAVE FURTHER SUBDIVIDED THIS GROUP INTO "CHOCOLATE COVERED" AND CHOCOLATE FILLED."
WHAT ABOUT JUST PLAIN CHOCOLATE?

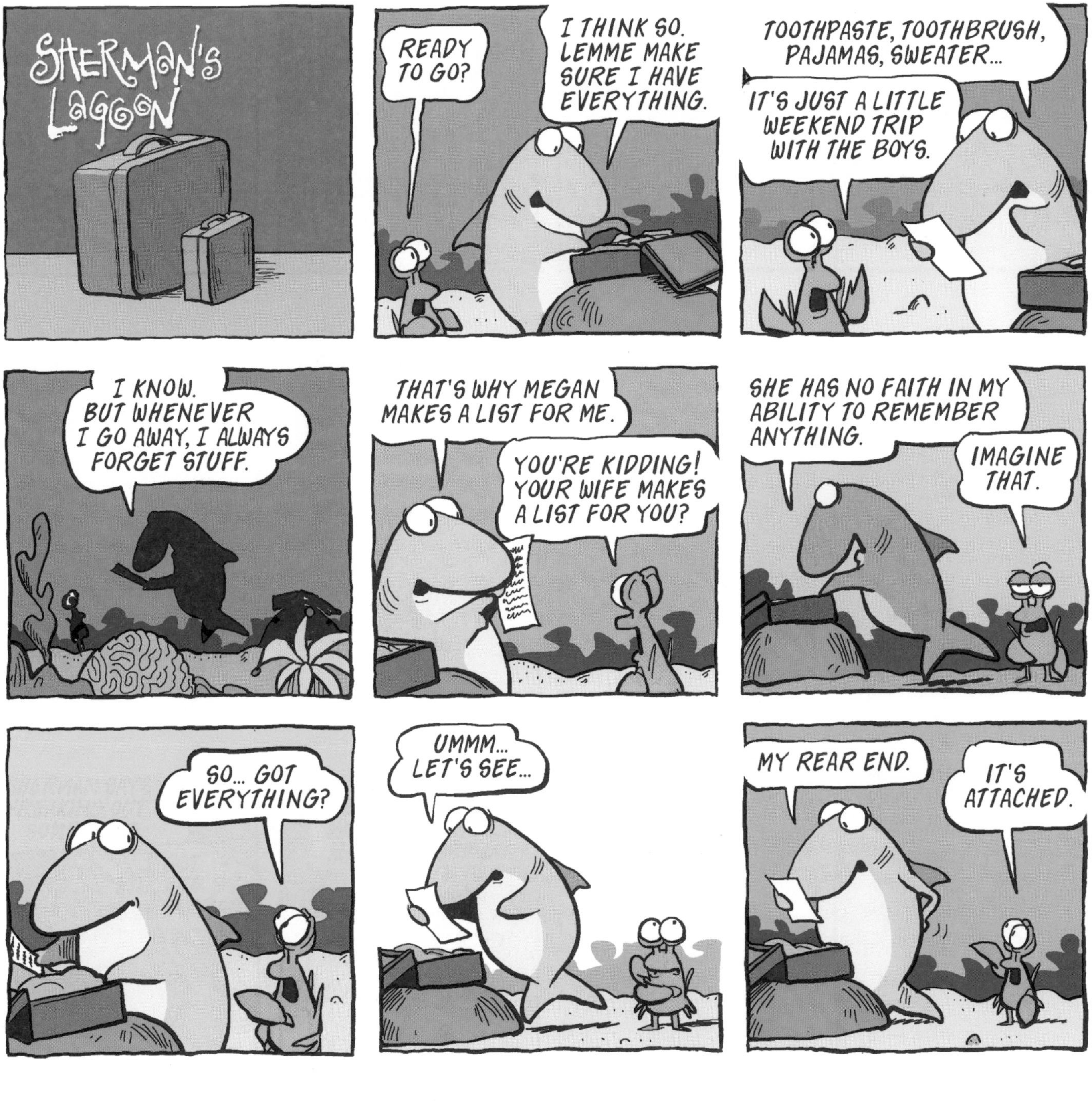
SHERMAN'S LAGOON
READY TO GO?
I THINK SO. LEMME MAKE SURE I HAVE EVERYTHING.
TOOTHPASTE, TOOTHBRUSH, PAJAMAS, SWEATER...
IT'S JUST A LITTLE WEEKEND TRIP WITH THE BOYS.
I KNOW. BUT WHENEVER I GO AWAY, I ALWAYS FORGET STUFF.
THAT'S WHY MEGAN MAKES A LIST FOR ME.
YOU'RE KIDDING! YOUR WIFE MAKES A LIST FOR YOU?
SHE HAS NO FAITH IN MY ABILITY TO REMEMBER ANYTHING.
IMAGINE THAT.
SO... GOT EVERYTHING?
UMMM... LET'S SEE...
MY REAR END.
IT'S ATTACHED.

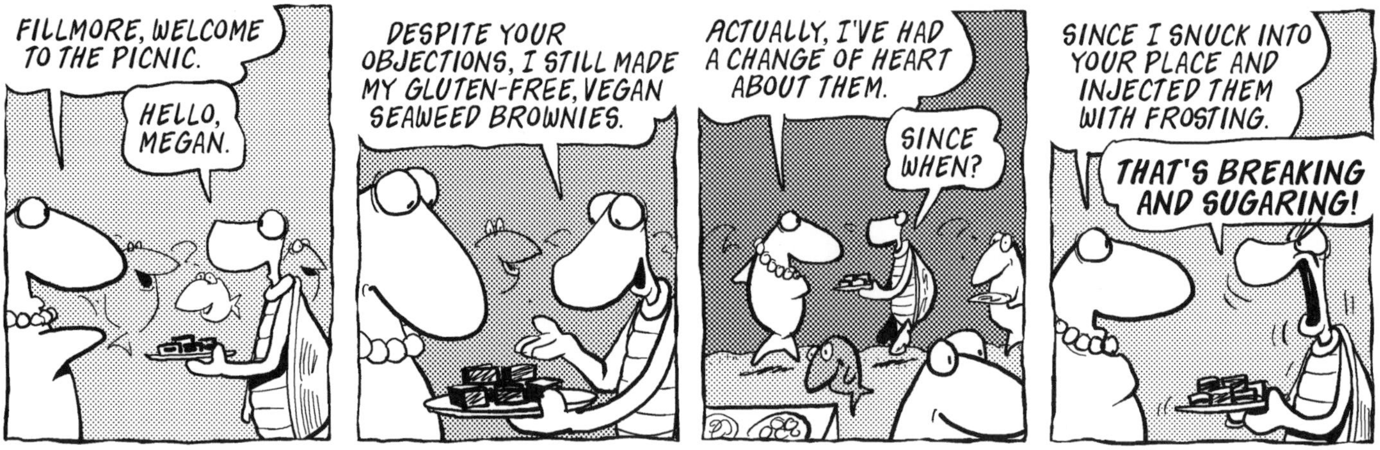
FILLMORE, WELCOME TO THE PICNIC.
HELLO, MEGAN.
DESPITE YOUR OBJECTIONS, I STILL MADE MY GLUTEN-FREE, VEGAN SEAWEED BROWNIES.
ACTUALLY, I'VE HAD A CHANGE OF HEART ABOUT THEM.
SINCE WHEN?
SINCE I SNUCK INTO YOUR PLACE AND INJECTED THEM WITH FROSTING.
THAT'S BREAKING AND SUGARING!

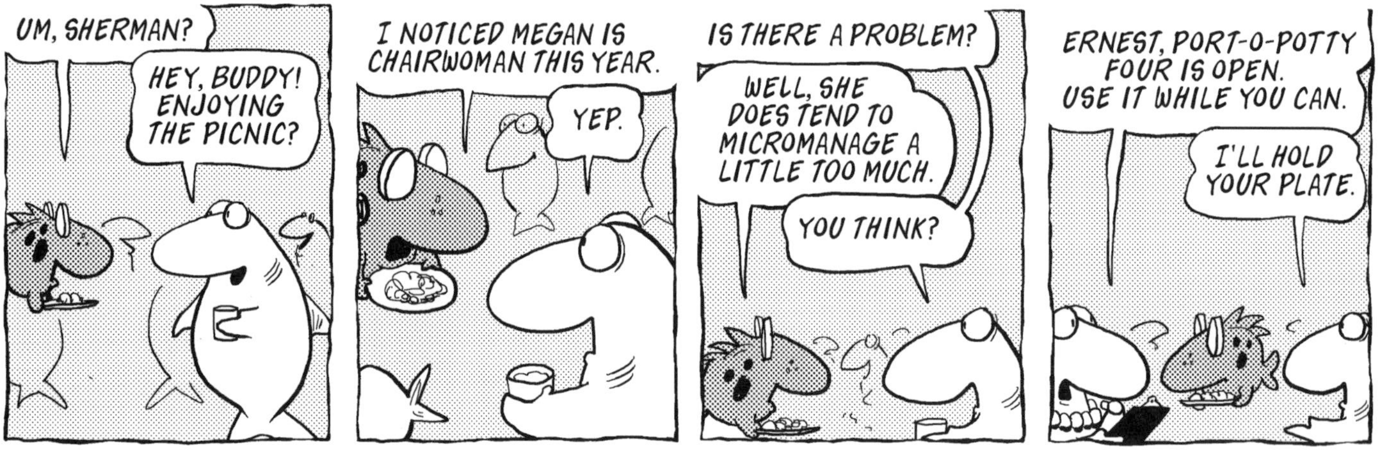
UM, SHERMAN?
HEY, BUDDY! ENJOYING THE PICNIC?
I NOTICED MEGAN IS CHAIRWOMAN THIS YEAR.
YEP.
IS THERE A PROBLEM?
WELL, SHE DOES TEND TO MICROMANAGE A LITTLE TOO MUCH.
YOU THINK?
ERNEST, PORT-O-POTTY FOUR IS OPEN. USE IT WHILE YOU CAN.
I'LL HOLD YOUR PLATE.

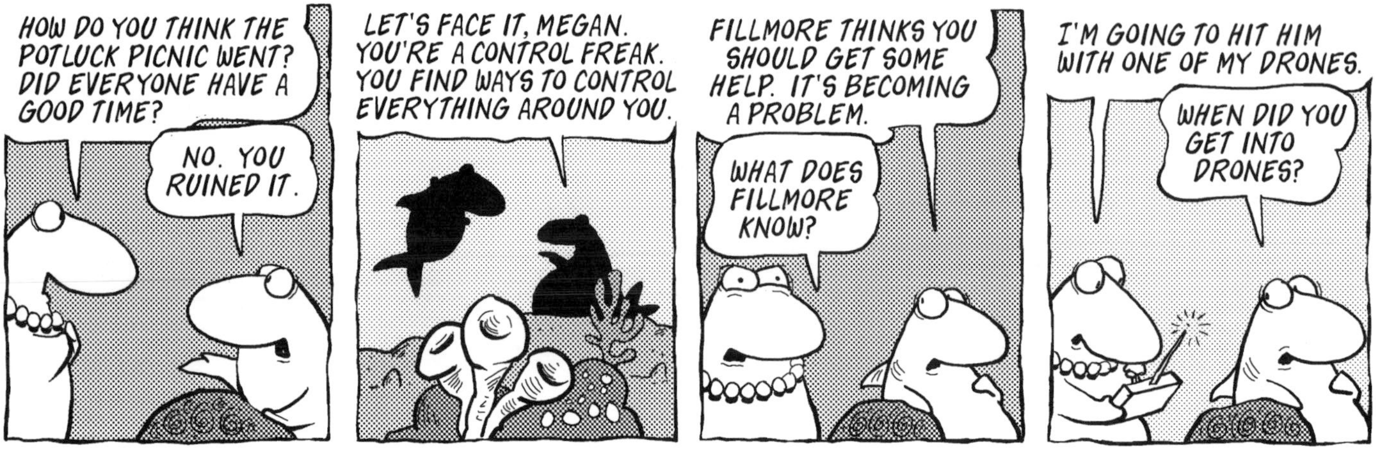
HOW DO YOU THINK THE POTLUCK PICNIC WENT? DID EVERYONE HAVE A GOOD TIME?
NO. YOU RUINED IT.
LET'S FACE IT, MEGAN. YOU'RE A CONTROL FREAK. YOU FIND WAYS TO CONTROL EVERYTHING AROUND YOU.
FILLMORE THINKS YOU SHOULD GET SOME HELP. IT'S BECOMING A PROBLEM.
WHAT DOES FILLMORE KNOW?
I'M GOING TO HIT HIM WITH ONE OF MY DRONES.
WHEN DID YOU GET INTO DRONES?

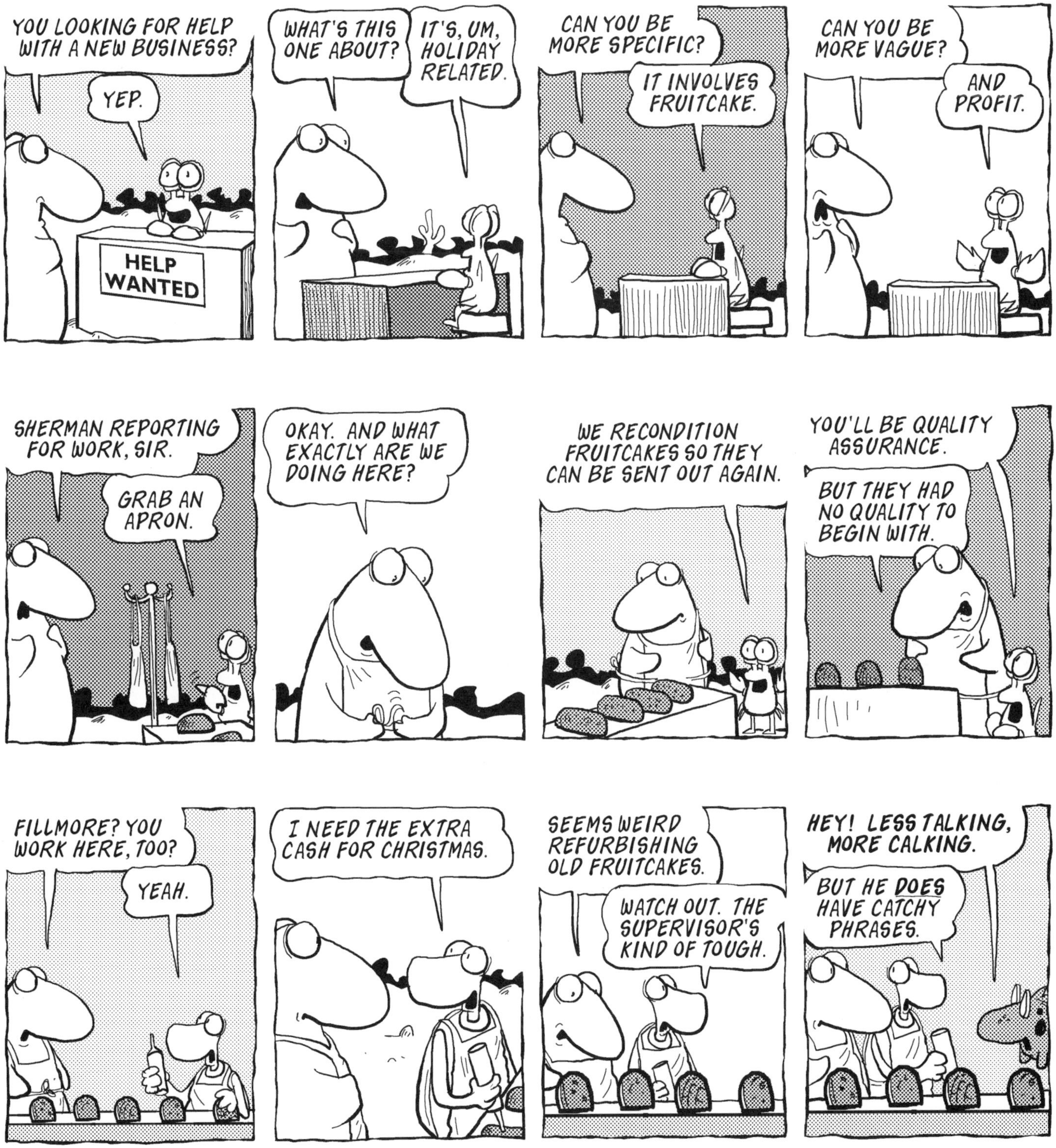
YOU LOOKING FOR HELP WITH A NEW BUSINESS?
YEP.
HELP WANTED
WHAT'S THIS ONE ABOUT?
IT'S, UM, HOLIDAY RELATED.
CAN YOU BE MORE SPECIFIC?
IT INVOLVES FRUITCAKE.
CAN YOU BE MORE VAGUE?
AND PROFIT.
SHERMAN REPORTING FOR WORK, SIR.
GRAB AN APRON.
OKAY. AND WHAT EXACTLY ARE WE DOING HERE?
WE RECONDITION FRUITCAKES SO THEY CAN BE SENT OUT AGAIN.
YOU'LL BE QUALITY ASSURANCE.
BUT THEY HAD NO QUALITY TO BEGIN WITH.
FILLMORE? YOU WORK HERE, TOO?
YEAH.
I NEED THE EXTRA CASH FOR CHRISTMAS.
SEEMS WEIRD REFURBISHING OLD FRUITCAKES.
WATCH OUT. THE SUPERVISOR'S KIND OF TOUGH.
HEY! LESS TALKING, MORE CALKING.
BUT HE DOES HAVE CATCHY PHRASES.

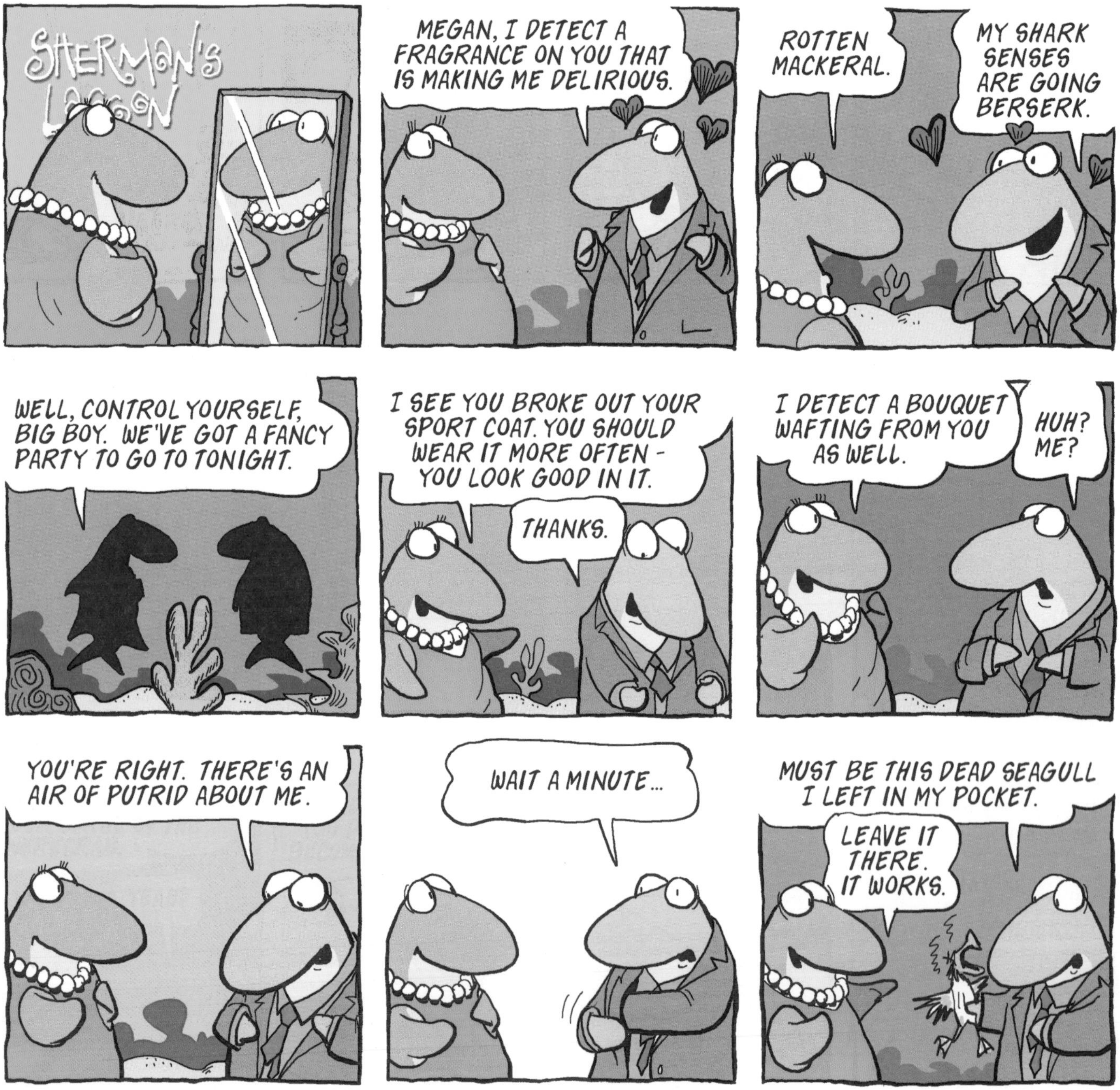
SHERMAN'S LAGOON
MEGAN, I DETECT A FRAGRANCE ON YOU THAT IS MAKING ME DELIRIOUS.
ROTTEN MACKERAL.
MY SHARK SENSES ARE GOING BERSERK.
WELL, CONTROL YOURSELF, BIG BOY. WE'VE GOT A FANCY PARTY TO GO TO TONIGHT.
I SEE YOU BROKE OUT YOUR SPORT COAT. YOU SHOULD WEAR IT MORE OFTEN - YOU LOOK GOOD IN IT.
THANKS.
I DETECT A BOUQUET WAFTING FROM YOU AS WELL.
HUH? ME?
YOU'RE RIGHT. THERE'S AN AIR OF PUTRID ABOUT ME.
WAIT A MINUTE...
MUST BE THIS DEAD SEAGULL I LEFT IN MY POCKET.
LEAVE IT THERE. IT WORKS.

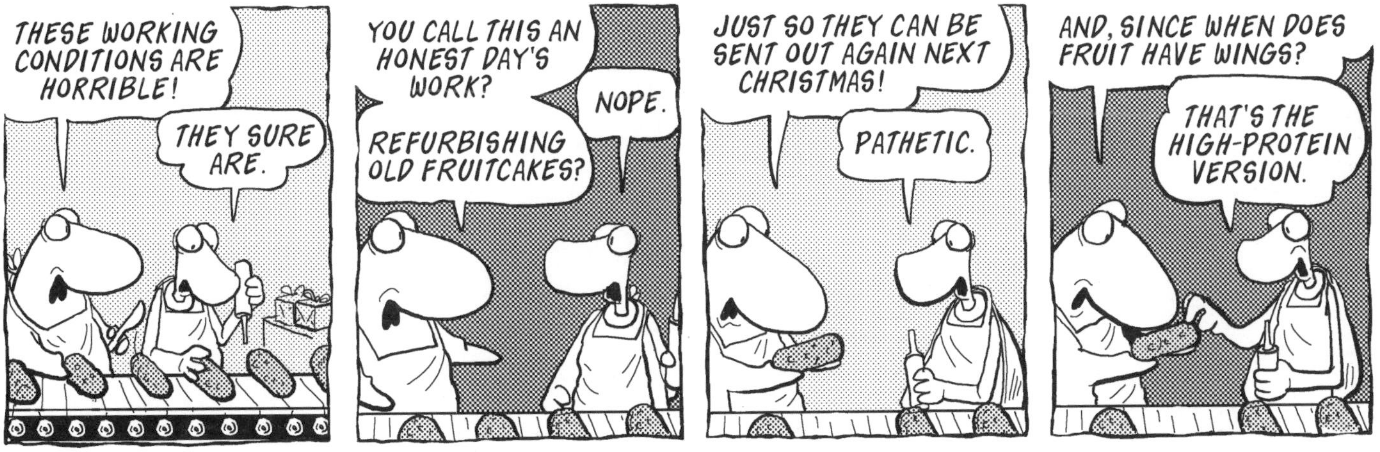
THESE WORKING CONDITIONS ARE HORRIBLE!
THEY SURE ARE.
YOU CALL THIS AN HONEST DAY'S WORK?
REFURBISHING OLD FRUITCAKES?
NOPE.
JUST SO THEY CAN BE SENT OUT AGAIN NEXT CHRISTMAS!
PATHETIC.
AND, SINCE WHEN DOES FRUIT HAVE WINGS?
THAT'S THE HIGH-PROTEIN VERSION.

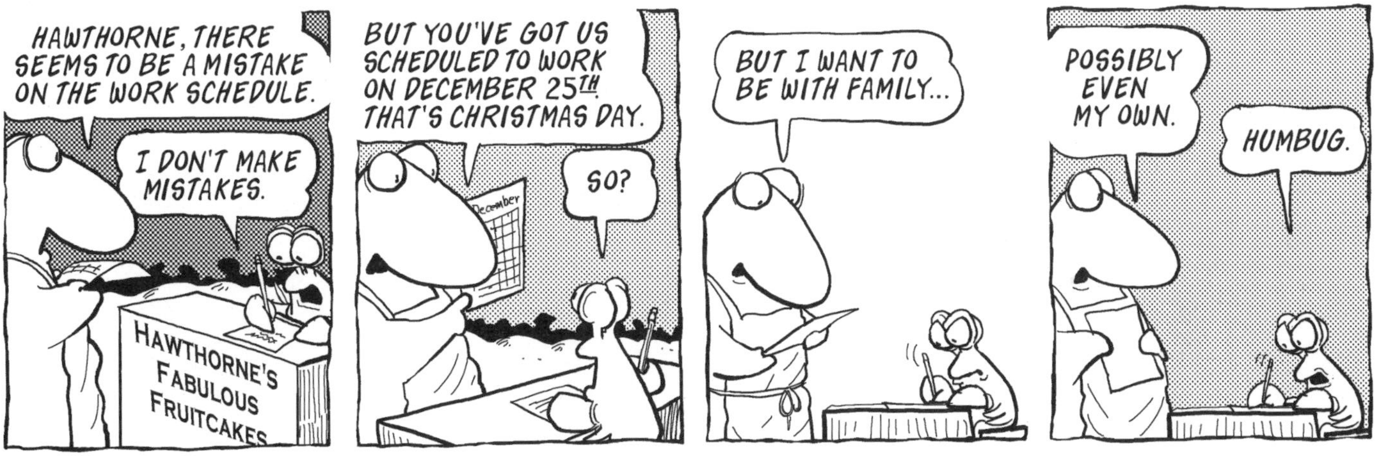
HAWTHORNE, THERE SEEMS TO BE A MISTAKE ON THE WORK SCHEDULE.
I DON'T MAKE MISTAKES.
HAWTHORNE'S FABULOUS FRUITCAKES
BUT YOU'VE GOT US SCHEDULED TO WORK ON DECEMBER 25TH. THAT'S CHRISTMAS DAY.
December
SO?
BUT I WANT TO BE WITH FAMILY...
POSSIBLY EVEN MY OWN.
HUMBUG.

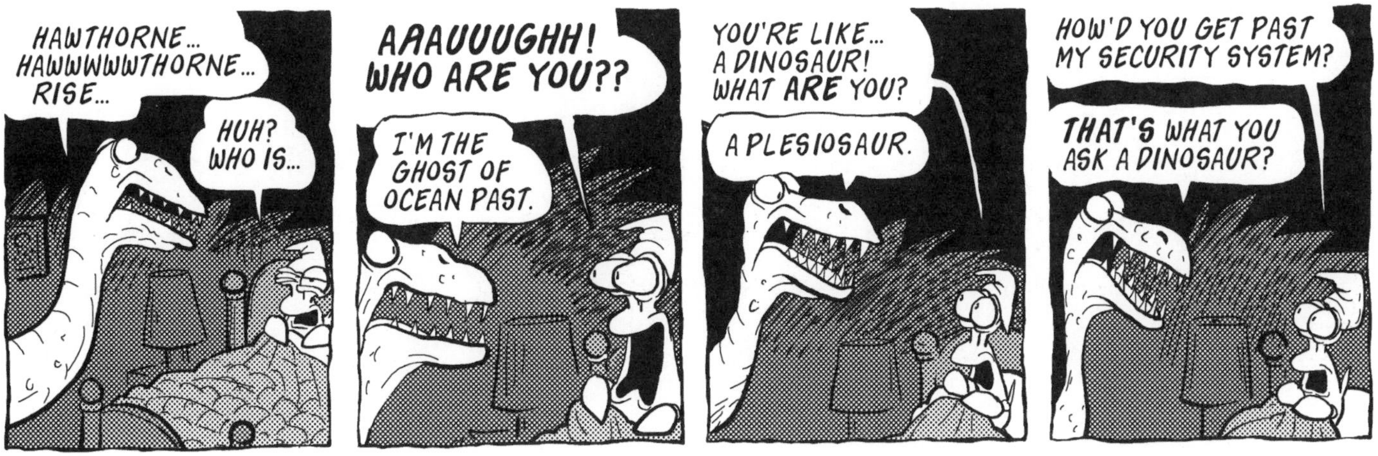
HAWTHORNE... HAWWWWWTHORNE... RISE...
HUH? WHO IS...
AAAUUUGHH! WHO ARE YOU??
I'M THE GHOST OF OCEAN PAST.
YOU'RE LIKE... A DINOSAUR! WHAT ARE YOU?
A PLESIOSAUR.
HOW'D YOU GET PAST MY SECURITY SYSTEM?
THAT'S WHAT YOU ASK A DINOSAUR?

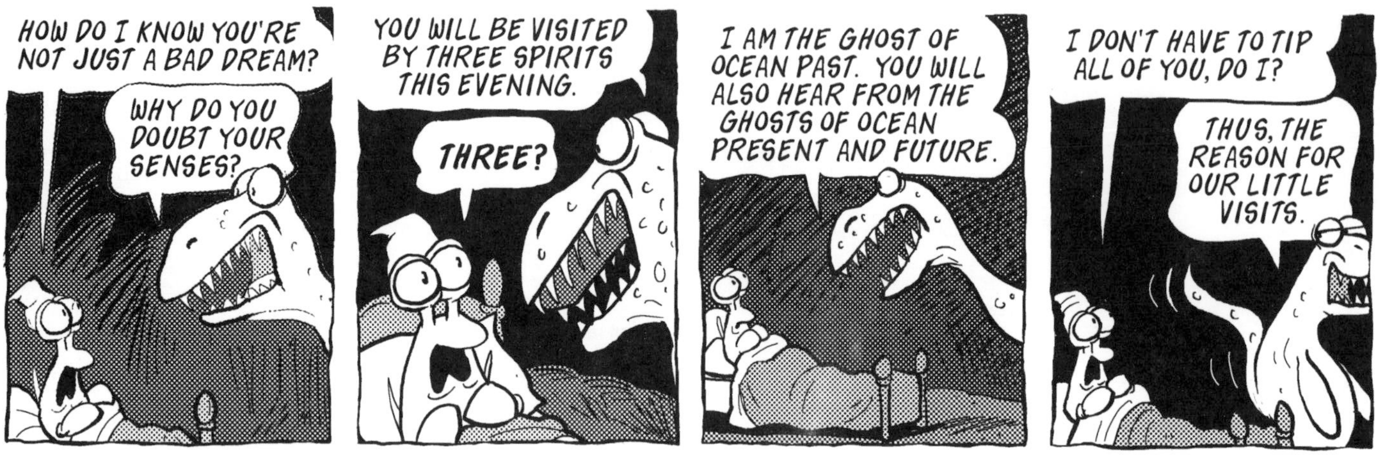
HOW DO I KNOW YOU'RE NOT JUST A BAD DREAM?
WHY DO YOU DOUBT YOUR SENSES?
YOU WILL BE VISITED BY THREE SPIRITS THIS EVENING.
THREE?
I AM THE GHOST OF OCEAN PAST. YOU WILL ALSO HEAR FROM THE GHOSTS OF OCEAN PRESENT AND FUTURE.
I DON'T HAVE TO TIP ALL OF YOU, DO I?
THUS, THE REASON FOR OUR LITTLE VISITS.

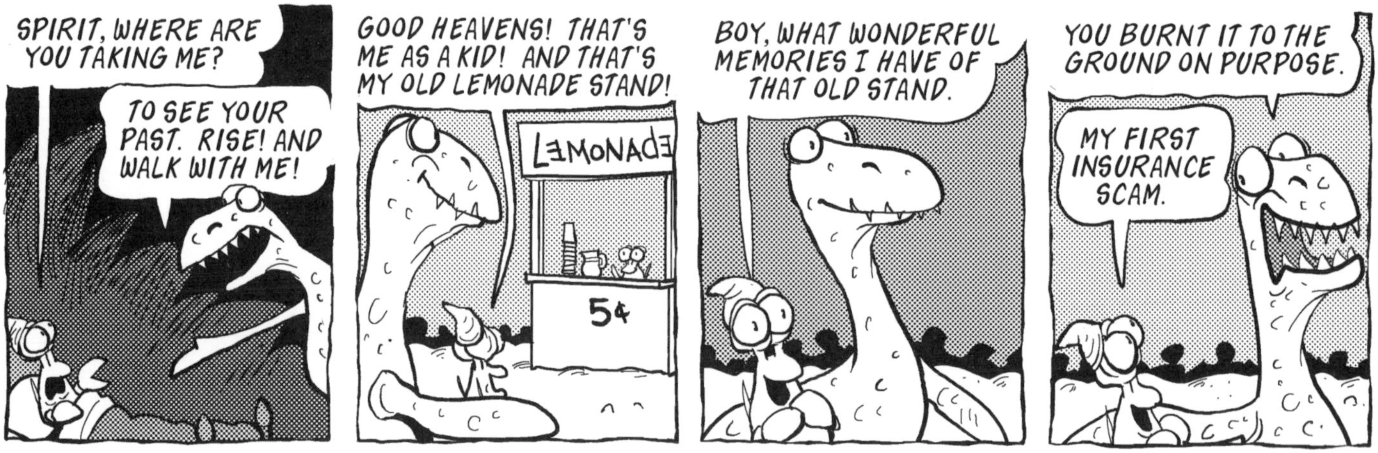
SPIRIT, WHERE ARE YOU TAKING ME?
TO SEE YOUR PAST. RISE! AND WALK WITH ME!
GOOD HEAVENS! THAT'S ME AS A KID! AND THAT'S MY OLD LEMONADE STAND!
LEMONADE
5¢
BOY, WHAT WONDERFUL MEMORIES I HAVE OF THAT OLD STAND.
YOU BURNT IT TO THE GROUND ON PURPOSE.
MY FIRST INSURANCE SCAM.

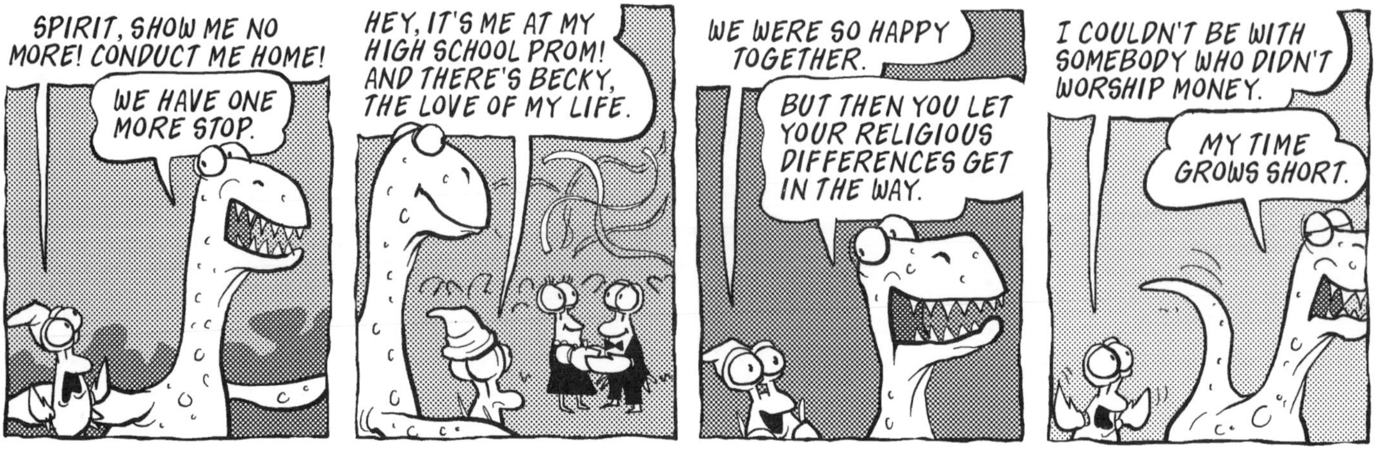
SPIRIT, SHOW ME NO MORE! CONDUCT ME HOME!
WE HAVE ONE MORE STOP.
HEY, IT'S ME AT MY HIGH SCHOOL PROM! AND THERE'S BECKY, THE LOVE OF MY LIFE.
WE WERE SO HAPPY TOGETHER.
BUT THEN YOU LET YOUR RELIGIOUS DIFFERENCES GET IN THE WAY.
I COULDN'T BE WITH SOMEBODY WHO DIDN'T WORSHIP MONEY.
MY TIME GROWS SHORT.

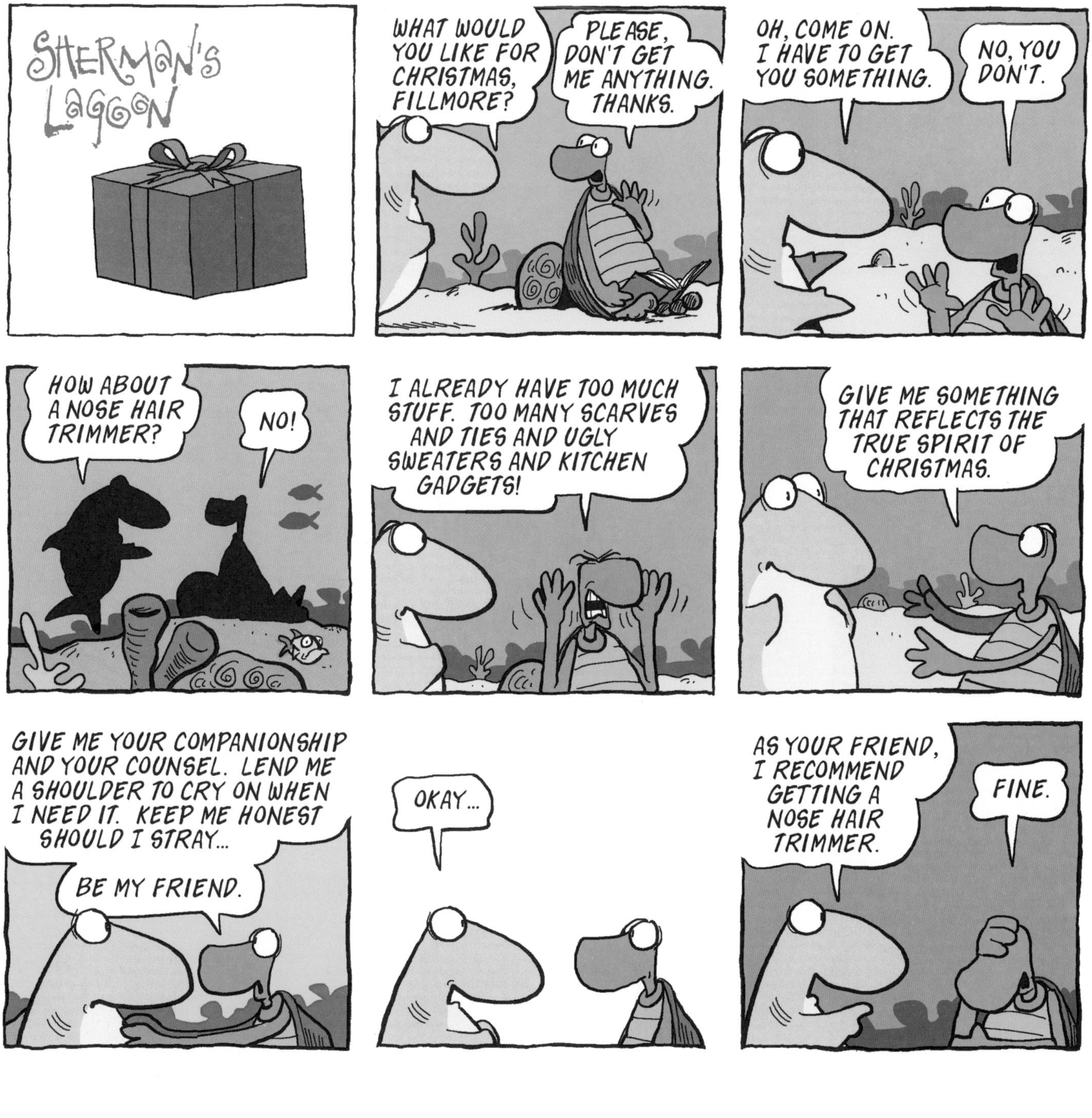
SHERMAN'S LAGOON
WHAT WOULD YOU LIKE FOR CHRISTMAS, FILLMORE?
PLEASE, DON'T GET ME ANYTHING. THANKS.
OH, COME ON. I HAVE TO GET YOU SOMETHING.
NO, YOU DON'T.
HOW ABOUT A NOSE HAIR TRIMMER?
NO!
I ALREADY HAVE TOO MUCH STUFF. TOO MANY SCARVES AND TIES AND UGLY SWEATERS AND KITCHEN GADGETS!
GIVE ME SOMETHING THAT REFLECTS THE TRUE SPIRIT OF CHRISTMAS.
GIVE ME YOUR COMPANIONSHIP AND YOUR COUNSEL. LEND ME A SHOULDER TO CRY ON WHEN I NEED IT. KEEP ME HONEST SHOULD I STRAY...
BE MY FRIEND.
OKAY...
AS YOUR FRIEND, I RECOMMEND GETTING A NOSE HAIR TRIMMER.
FINE.

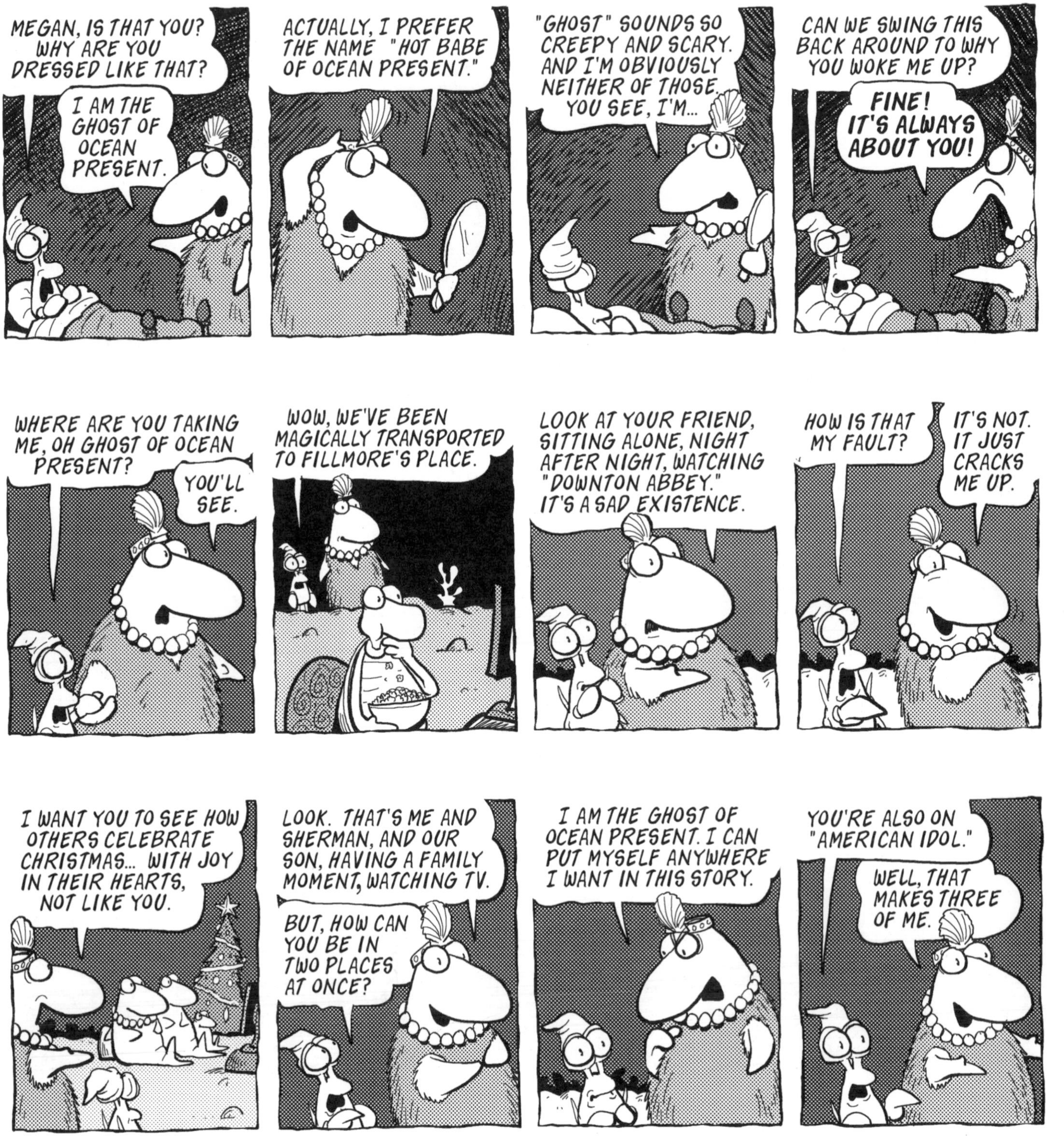
MEGAN, IS THAT YOU? WHY ARE YOU DRESSED LIKE THAT?
I AM THE GHOST OF OCEAN PRESENT.
ACTUALLY, I PREFER THE NAME "HOT BABE OF OCEAN PRESENT."
"GHOST" SOUNDS SO CREEPY AND SCARY. AND I'M OBVIOUSLY NEITHER OF THOSE. YOU SEE, I'M...
CAN WE SWING THIS BACK AROUND TO WHY YOU WOKE ME UP?
FINE! IT'S ALWAYS ABOUT YOU!
WHERE ARE YOU TAKING ME, OH GHOST OF OCEAN PRESENT?
YOU'LL SEE.
WOW, WE'VE BEEN MAGICALLY TRANSPORTED TO FILLMORE'S PLACE.
LOOK AT YOUR FRIEND, SITTING ALONE, NIGHT AFTER NIGHT, WATCHING "DOWNTON ABBEY." IT'S A SAD EXISTENCE.
HOW IS THAT MY FAULT?
IT'S NOT. IT JUST CRACKS ME UP.
I WANT YOU TO SEE HOW OTHERS CELEBRATE CHRISTMAS... WITH JOY IN THEIR HEARTS, NOT LIKE YOU.
LOOK. THAT'S ME AND SHERMAN, AND OUR SON, HAVING A FAMILY MOMENT, WATCHING TV.
BUT, HOW CAN YOU BE IN TWO PLACES AT ONCE?
I AM THE GHOST OF OCEAN PRESENT. I CAN PUT MYSELF ANYWHERE I WANT IN THIS STORY.
YOU'RE ALSO ON "AMERICAN IDOL."
WELL, THAT MAKES THREE OF ME.

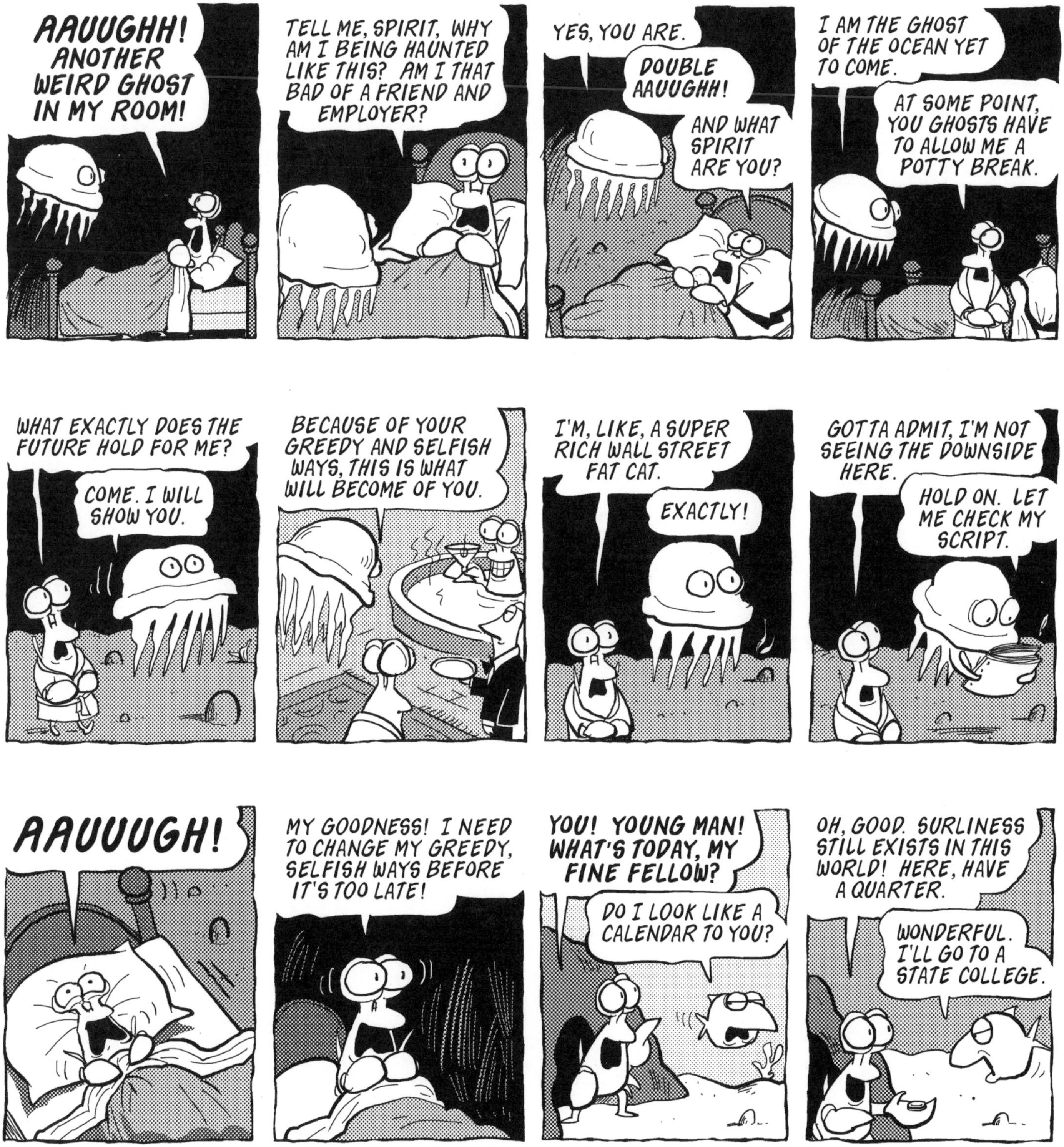
AAUUGHH! ANOTHER WEIRD GHOST IN MY ROOM!
TELL ME, SPIRIT, WHY AM I BEING HAUNTED LIKE THIS? AM I THAT BAD OF A FRIEND AND EMPLOYER?
YES, YOU ARE.
DOUBLE AAUUGHH!
AND WHAT SPIRIT ARE YOU?
I AM THE GHOST OF THE OCEAN YET TO COME.
AT SOME POINT, YOU GHOSTS HAVE TO ALLOW ME A POTTY BREAK.
WHAT EXACTLY DOES THE FUTURE HOLD FOR ME?
COME. I WILL SHOW YOU.
BECAUSE OF YOUR GREEDY AND SELFISH WAYS, THIS IS WHAT WILL BECOME OF YOU.
I'M, LIKE, A SUPER RICH WALL STREET FAT CAT.
EXACTLY!
GOTTA ADMIT, I'M NOT SEEING THE DOWNSIDE HERE.
HOLD ON. LET ME CHECK MY SCRIPT.
AAUUUGH!
MY GOODNESS! I NEED TO CHANGE MY GREEDY, SELFISH WAYS BEFORE IT'S TOO LATE!
YOU! YOUNG MAN! WHAT'S TODAY, MY FINE FELLOW?
DO I LOOK LIKE A CALENDAR TO YOU?
OH, GOOD. SURLINESS STILL EXISTS IN THIS WORLD! HERE, HAVE A QUARTER.
WONDERFUL. I'LL GO TO A STATE COLLEGE.

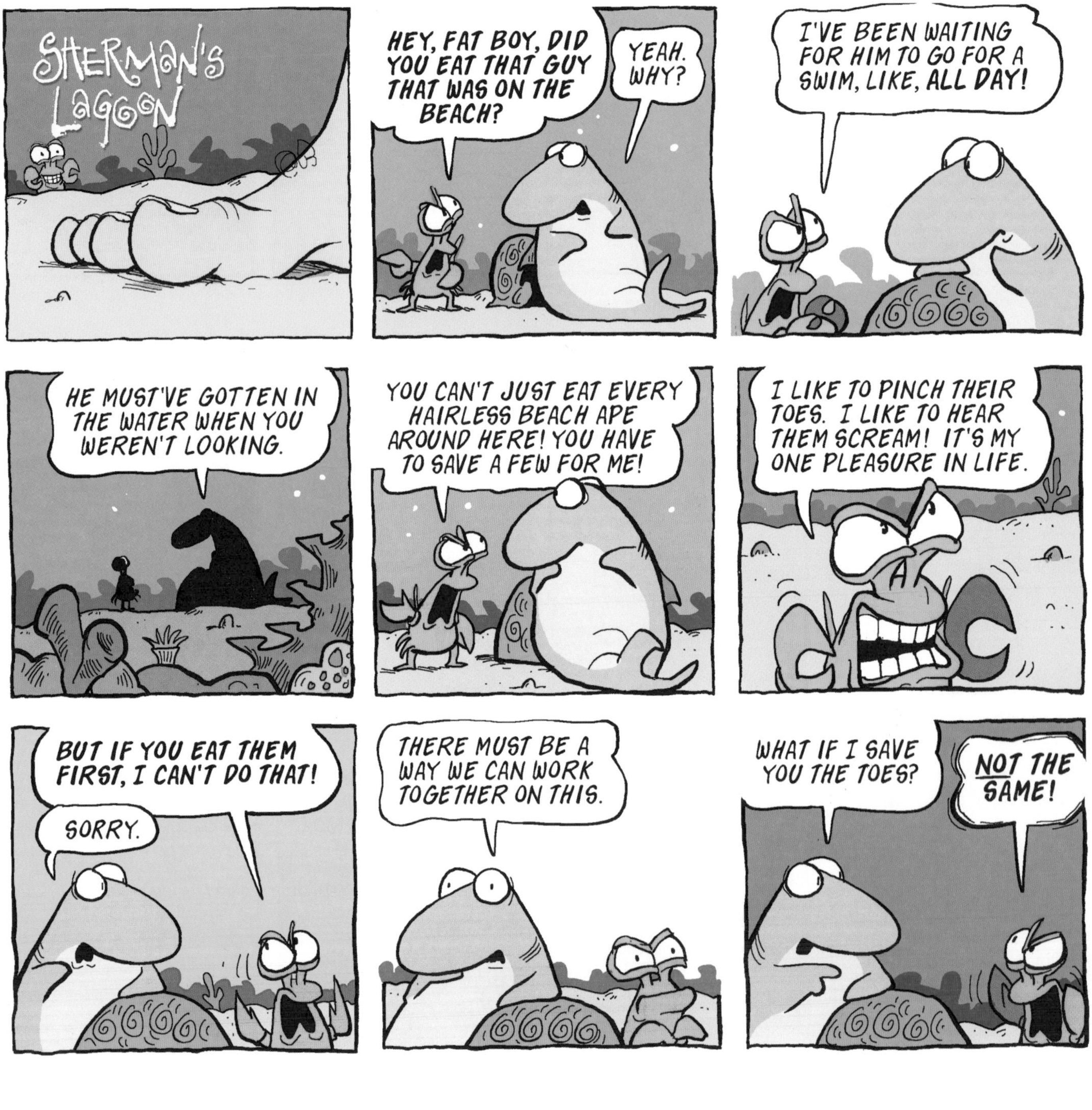
SHERMAN'S LAGOON
HEY, FAT BOY, DID YOU EAT THAT GUY THAT WAS ON THE BEACH?
YEAH. WHY?
I'VE BEEN WAITING FOR HIM TO GO FOR A SWIM, LIKE, ALL DAY!
HE MUST'VE GOTTEN IN THE WATER WHEN YOU WEREN'T LOOKING.
YOU CAN'T JUST EAT EVERY HAIRLESS BEACH APE AROUND HERE! YOU HAVE TO SAVE A FEW FOR ME!
I LIKE TO PINCH THEIR TOES. I LIKE TO HEAR THEM SCREAM! IT'S MY ONE PLEASURE IN LIFE.
BUT IF YOU EAT THEM FIRST, I CAN'T DO THAT!
SORRY.
THERE MUST BE A WAY WE CAN WORK TOGETHER ON THIS.
WHAT IF I SAVE YOU THE TOES?
NOT THE SAME!

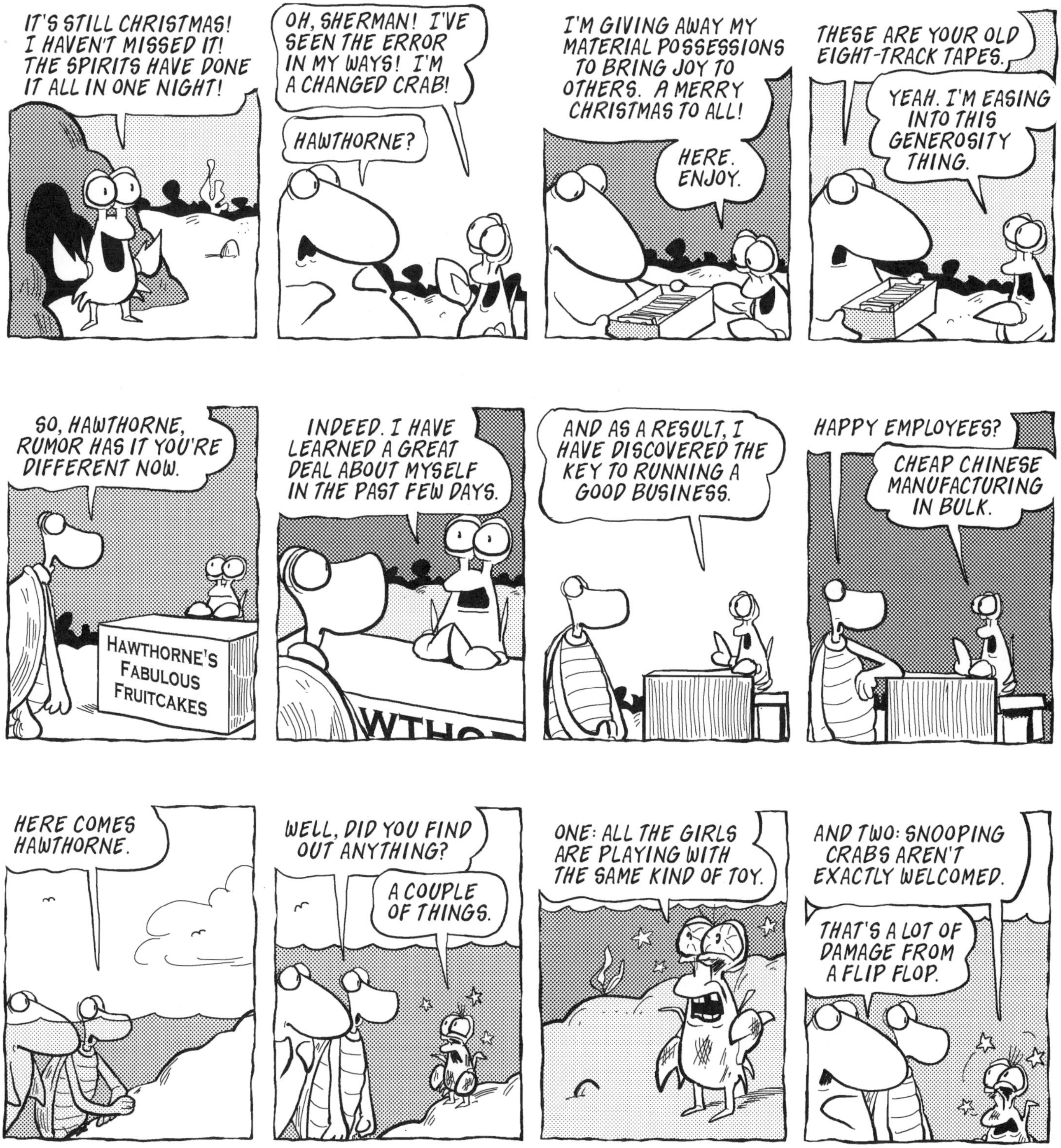
IT'S STILL CHRISTMAS! I HAVEN'T MISSED IT! THE SPIRITS HAVE DONE IT ALL IN ONE NIGHT!
OH, SHERMAN! I'VE SEEN THE ERROR IN MY WAYS! I'M A CHANGED CRAB!
HAWTHORNE?
I'M GIVING AWAY MY MATERIAL POSSESSIONS TO BRING JOY TO OTHERS. A MERRY CHRISTMAS TO ALL!
HERE. ENJOY.
THESE ARE YOUR OLD EIGHT-TRACK TAPES.
YEAH. I'M EASING INTO THIS GENEROSITY THING.
SO, HAWTHORNE, RUMOR HAS IT YOU'RE DIFFERENT NOW.
HAWTHORNE'S FABULOUS FRUITCAKES
INDEED. I HAVE LEARNED A GREAT DEAL ABOUT MYSELF IN THE PAST FEW DAYS.
AND AS A RESULT, I HAVE DISCOVERED THE KEY TO RUNNING A GOOD BUSINESS.
HAPPY EMPLOYEES?
CHEAP CHINESE MANUFACTURING IN BULK.
HERE COMES HAWTHORNE.
WELL, DID YOU FIND OUT ANYTHING?
A COUPLE OF THINGS.
ONE: ALL THE GIRLS ARE PLAYING WITH THE SAME KIND OF TOY.
AND TWO: SNOOPING CRABS AREN'T EXACTLY WELCOMED.
THAT'S A LOT OF DAMAGE FROM A FLIP FLOP.

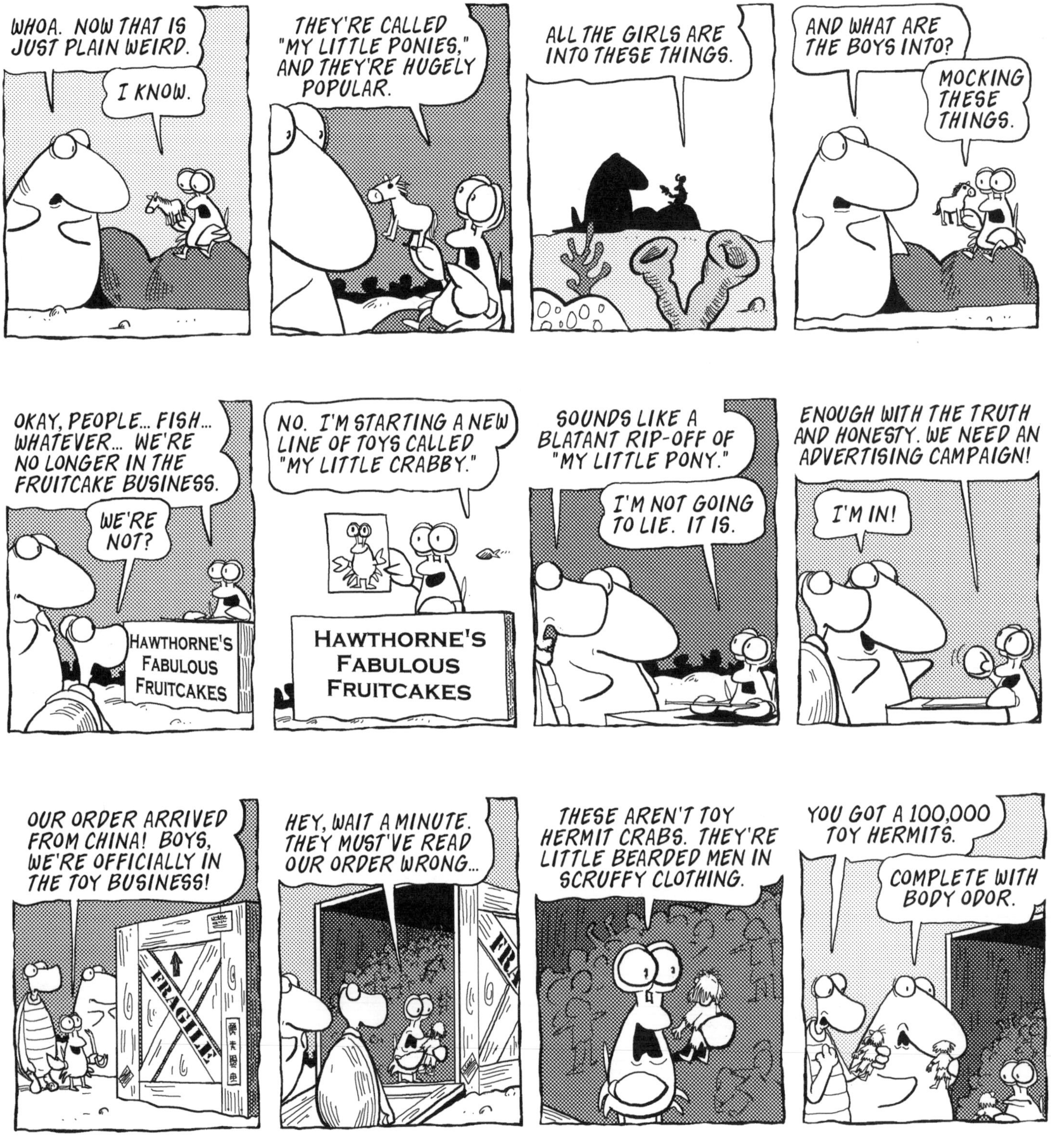
WHOA. NOW THAT IS JUST PLAIN WEIRD.
I KNOW.
THEY'RE CALLED "MY LITTLE PONIES," AND THEY'RE HUGELY POPULAR.
ALL THE GIRLS ARE INTO THESE THINGS.
AND WHAT ARE THE BOYS INTO?
MOCKING THESE THINGS.
OKAY, PEOPLE... FISH... WHATEVER... WE'RE NO LONGER IN THE FRUITCAKE BUSINESS.
WE'RE NOT?
HAWTHORNE'S FABULOUS FRUITCAKES
NO. I'M STARTING A NEW LINE OF TOYS CALLED "MY LITTLE CRABBY."
HAWTHORNE'S FABULOUS FRUITCAKES
SOUNDS LIKE A BLATANT RIP-OFF OF "MY LITTLE PONY."
I'M NOT GOING TO LIE. IT IS.
ENOUGH WITH THE TRUTH AND HONESTY. WE NEED AN ADVERTISING CAMPAIGN!
I'M IN!
OUR ORDER ARRIVED FROM CHINA! BOYS, WE'RE OFFICIALLY IN THE TOY BUSINESS!
FRAGILE
HEY, WAIT A MINUTE. THEY MUST'VE READ OUR ORDER WRONG...
THESE AREN'T TOY HERMIT CRABS. THEY'RE LITTLE BEARDED MEN IN SCRUFFY CLOTHING.
YOU GOT A 100,000 TOY HERMITS.
COMPLETE WITH BODY ODOR.

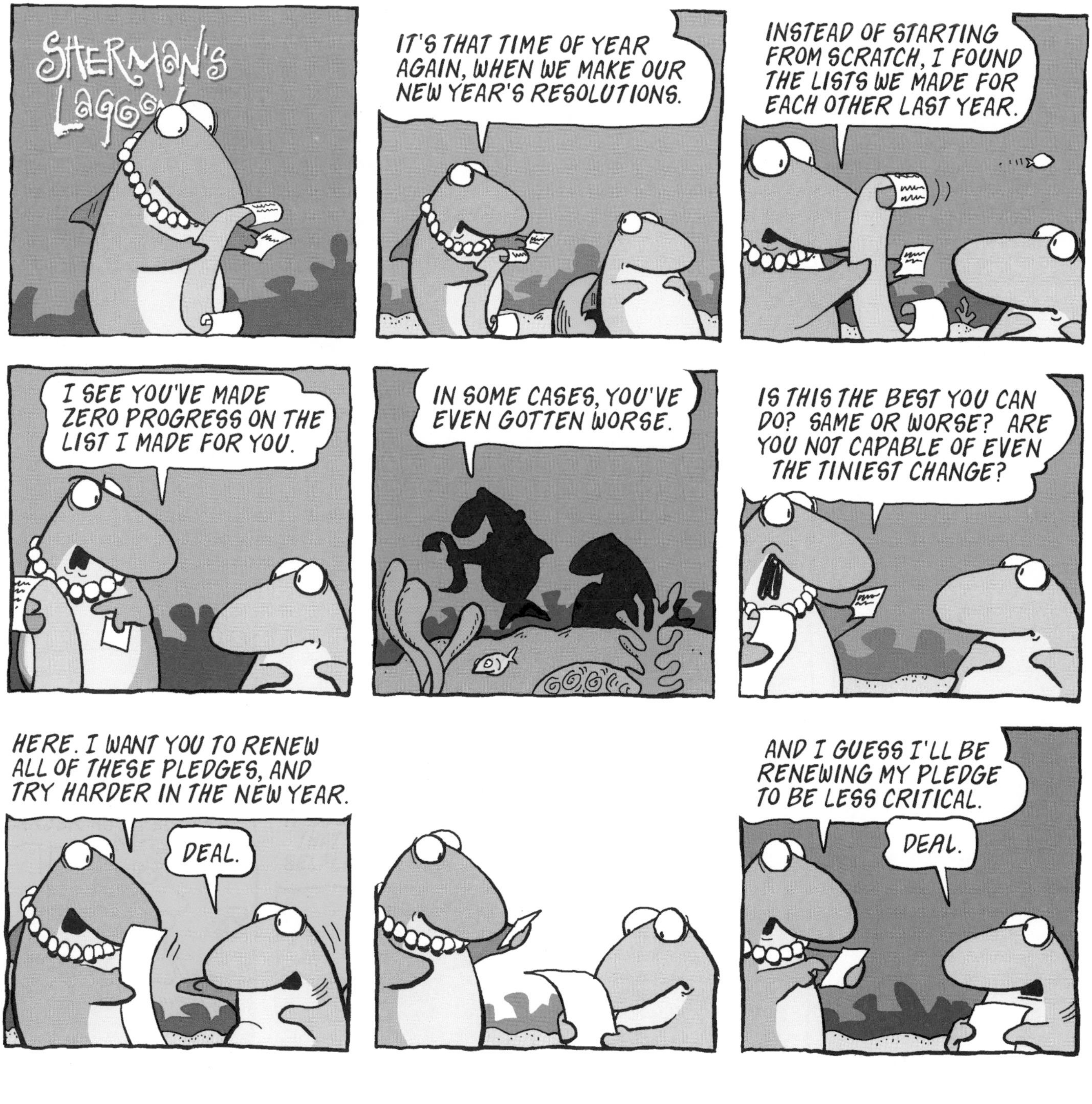
SHERMAN'S LAGOON
IT'S THAT TIME OF YEAR AGAIN, WHEN WE MAKE OUR NEW YEAR'S RESOLUTIONS.
INSTEAD OF STARTING FROM SCRATCH, I FOUND THE LISTS WE MADE FOR EACH OTHER LAST YEAR.
I SEE YOU'VE MADE ZERO PROGRESS ON THE LIST I MADE FOR YOU.
IN SOME CASES, YOU'VE EVEN GOTTEN WORSE.
IS THIS THE BEST YOU CAN DO? SAME OR WORSE? ARE YOU NOT CAPABLE OF EVEN THE TINIEST CHANGE?
HERE. I WANT YOU TO RENEW ALL OF THESE PLEDGES, AND TRY HARDER IN THE NEW YEAR.
DEAL.
AND I GUESS I'LL BE RENEWING MY PLEDGE TO BE LESS CRITICAL.
DEAL.

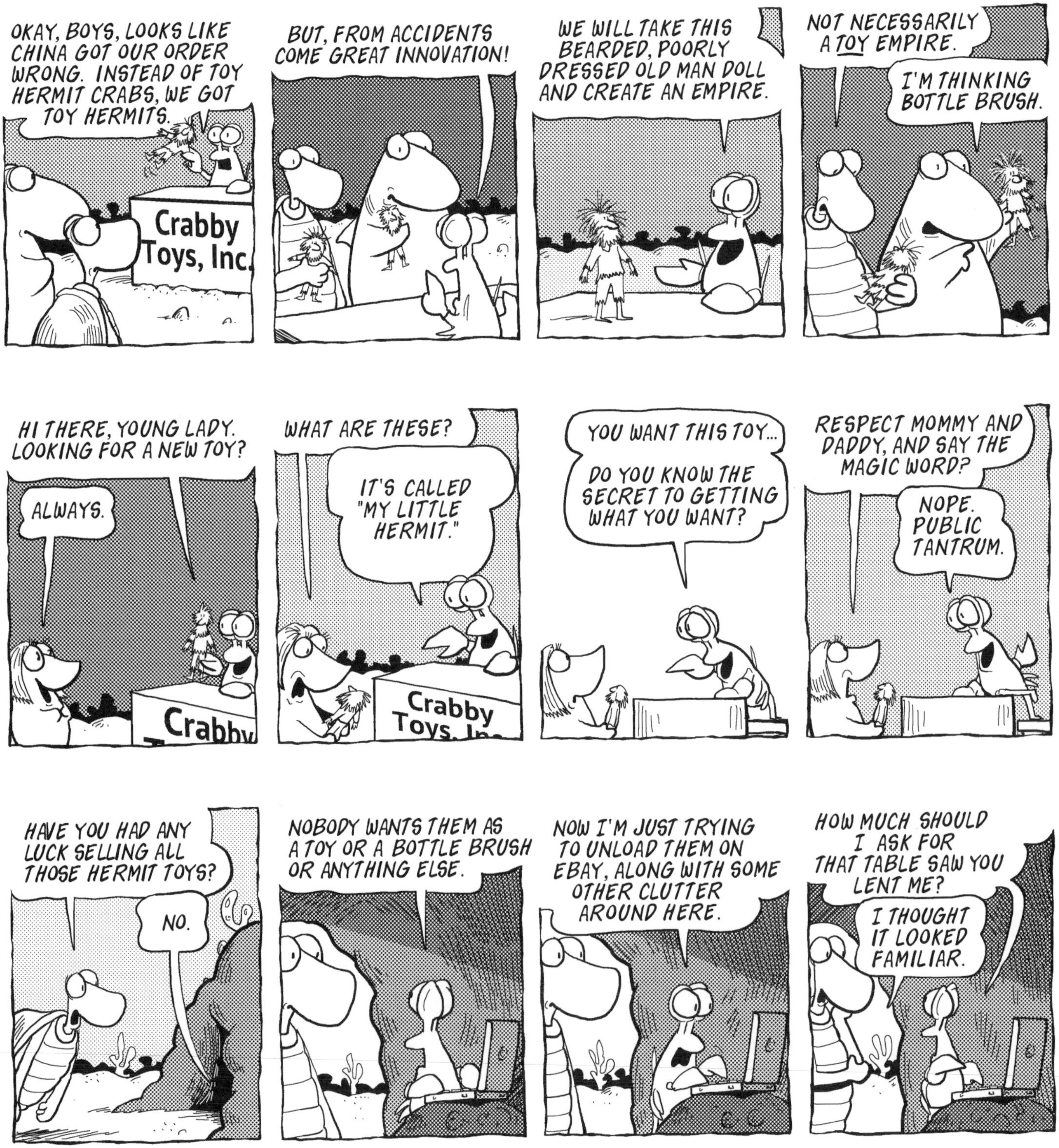
OKAY, BOYS, LOOKS LIKE CHINA GOT OUR ORDER WRONG. INSTEAD OF TOY HERMIT CRABS, WE GOT TOY HERMITS.
Crabby Toys, Inc.
BUT, FROM ACCIDENTS COME GREAT INNOVATION!
WE WILL TAKE THIS BEARDED, POORLY DRESSED OLD MAN DOLL AND CREATE AN EMPIRE.
NOT NECESSARILY A TOY EMPIRE.
I'M THINKING BOTTLE BRUSH.
HI THERE, YOUNG LADY. LOOKING FOR A NEW TOY?
ALWAYS.
WHAT ARE THESE?
IT'S CALLED "MY LITTLE HERMIT."
YOU WANT THIS TOY...
DO YOU KNOW THE SECRET TO GETTING WHAT YOU WANT?
RESPECT MOMMY AND DADDY, AND SAY THE MAGIC WORD?
NOPE. PUBLIC TANTRUM.
HAVE YOU HAD ANY LUCK SELLING ALL THOSE HERMIT TOYS?
NO.
NOBODY WANTS THEM AS A TOY OR A BOTTLE BRUSH OR ANYTHING ELSE.
NOW I'M JUST TRYING TO UNLOAD THEM ON EBAY, ALONG WITH SOME OTHER CLUTTER AROUND HERE.
HOW MUCH SHOULD I ASK FOR THAT TABLE SAW YOU LENT ME?
I THOUGHT IT LOOKED FAMILIAR.

Sherman's Lagoon is syndicated internationally by King Features Syndicate, Inc.
For information, write King Features Syndicate, Inc., 300 West Fifty-Seventh Street,
New York, NY 10019.

Andrews McMeel Publishing
a division of Andrews McMeel Universal
1130 Walnut Street, Kansas City, Missouri 64106

www.andrewsmcmeel.com

16 17 18 19 20 SDB 10 9 8 7 6 5 4 3 2

ISBN: 978-1-4494-6299-4

Library of Congress Control Number: 2015937252

Sherman's Lagoon may be viewed on the Internet at
www.shermanslagoon.com

—— **ATTENTION: SCHOOLS AND BUSINESSES** ——

Andrews McMeel books are available at quantity discounts with bulk purchase for
educational, business, or sales promotional use. For information, please e-mail the
Andrews McMeel Publishing Special Sales Department: specialsales@amuniversal.com.